VOLUME 1

GREEN LANTERN

INVICTUS

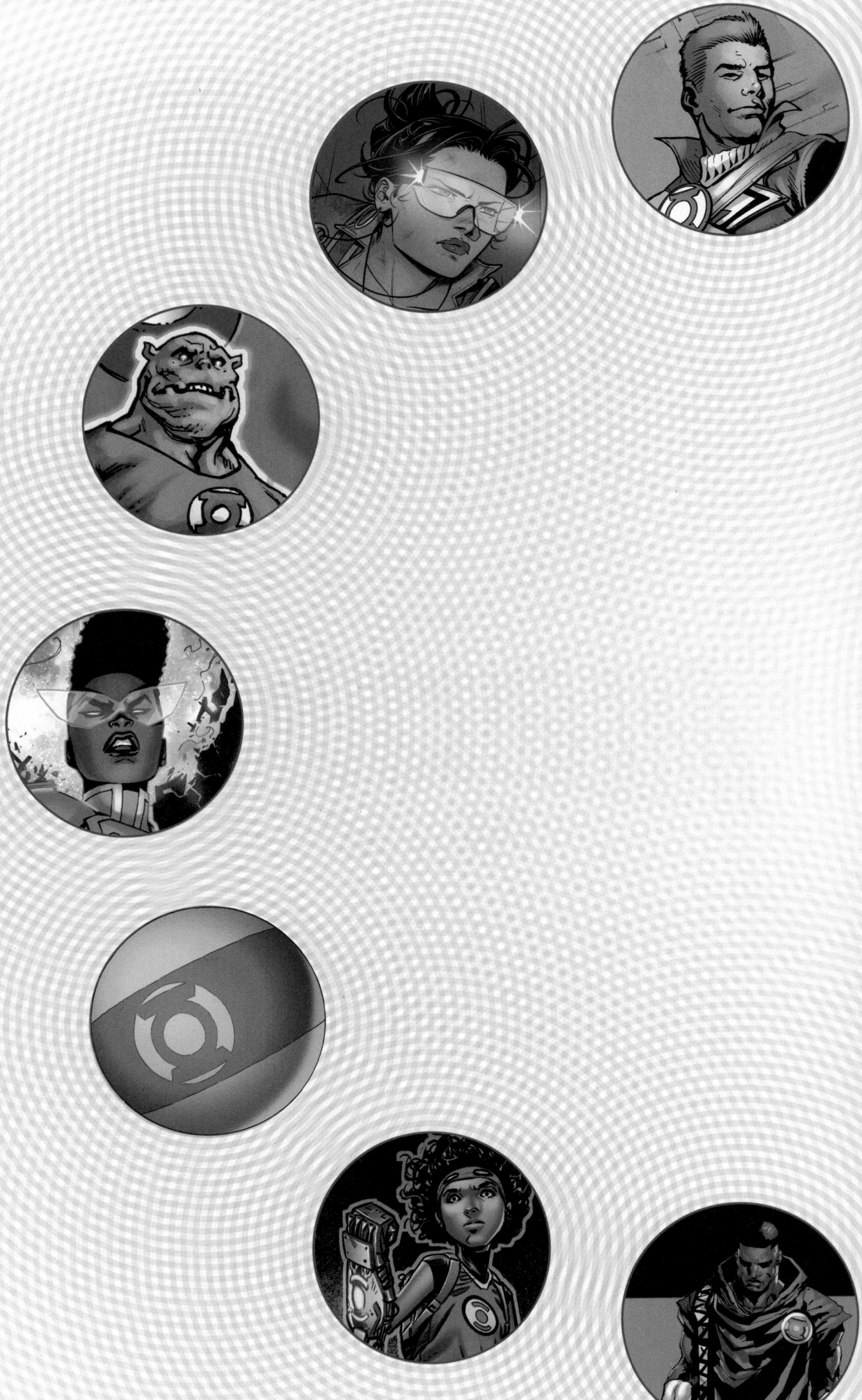

GEOFFREY THORNE
writer

TOM RANEY
MARCO SANTUCCI
DEXTER SOY
artists

MIKE ATIYEH
ALEX SINCLAIR
colorists

GREEN LANTERN
INVICTUS

ROB LEIGH
ANDWORLD DESIGN
letterers

BERNARD CHANG and **ALEX SINCLAIR**
collection cover artists

SUPERMAN created by **JERRY SIEGEL** and **JOE SHUSTER**
By special arrangement with the **Jerry Siegel** family

Mike Cotton Editor – Original Series & Collected Edition
Bixie Mathieu, Marquis Draper Assistant Editors – Original Series
Steve Cook Design Director – Books
Amie Brockway-Metcalf Publication Design
Christy Sawyer Publication Production

Marie Javins Editor-in-Chief, DC Comics

Daniel Cherry III Senior VP – General Manager
Jim Lee Publisher & Chief Creative Officer
Joen Choe VP – Global Brand & Creative Services
Don Falletti VP – Manufacturing Operations & Workflow Management
Lawrence Ganem VP – Talent Services
Alison Gill Senior VP – Manufacturing & Operations
Nick J. Napolitano VP – Manufacturing Administration & Design
Nancy Spears VP – Revenue

GREEN LANTERN VOL. 1: INVICTUS

Published by DC Comics. Compilation and all new material Copyright © 2021 DC Comics.
All Rights Reserved. Originally published in single magazine form in
Future State: Green Lantern 1-2, *Green Lantern* 1-4. Copyright © 2021 DC Comics.
All Rights Reserved. All characters, their distinctive likenesses, and related
elements featured in this publication are trademarks of DC Comics.
The stories, characters, and incidents featured in this publication are entirely fictional.
DC Comics does not read or accept unsolicited submissions of ideas, stories, or artwork.
DC – a WarnerMedia Company.

DC Comics, 2900 West Alameda Ave., Burbank, CA 91505
Printed by LSC Communications, Owensville, MO, USA. 11/12/21. First Printing.
ISBN: 978-1-77951-337-3

Library of Congress Cataloging-in-Publication Data is available.

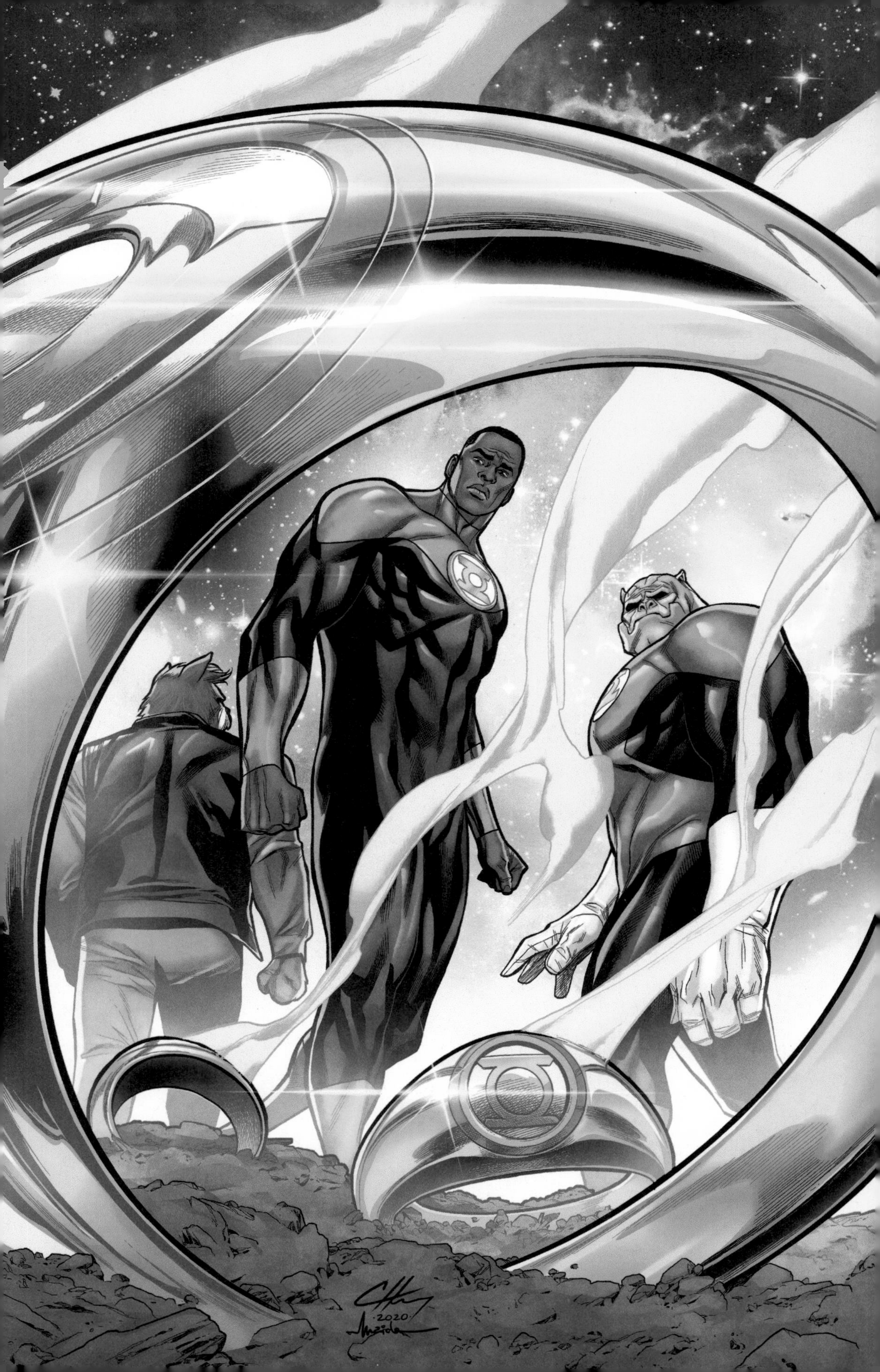

Future State: Green Lantern #1 main cover art
by Clayton Henry and Marcelo Maiolo

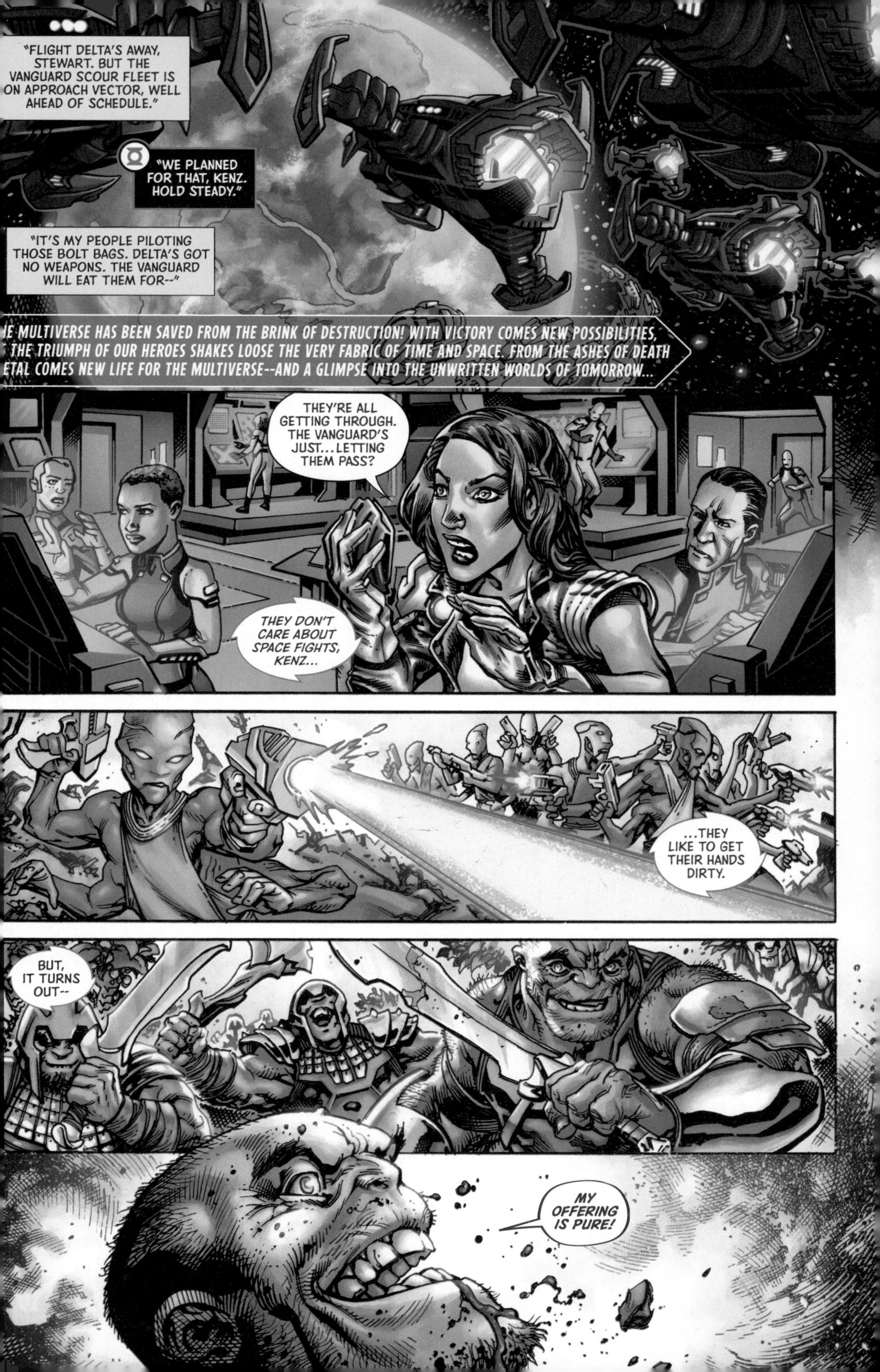
"FLIGHT DELTA'S AWAY, STEWART. BUT THE VANGUARD SCOUR FLEET IS ON APPROACH VECTOR, WELL AHEAD OF SCHEDULE."
"WE PLANNED FOR THAT, KENZ. HOLD STEADY."
"IT'S MY PEOPLE PILOTING THOSE BOLT BAGS. DELTA'S GOT NO WEAPONS. THE VANGUARD WILL EAT THEM FOR--"
E MULTIVERSE HAS BEEN SAVED FROM THE BRINK OF DESTRUCTION! WITH VICTORY COMES NEW POSSIBILITIES, THE TRIUMPH OF OUR HEROES SHAKES LOOSE THE VERY FABRIC OF TIME AND SPACE. FROM THE ASHES OF DEATH ETAL COMES NEW LIFE FOR THE MULTIVERSE--AND A GLIMPSE INTO THE UNWRITTEN WORLDS OF TOMORROW...
THEY'RE ALL GETTING THROUGH. THE VANGUARD'S JUST...LETTING THEM PASS?
THEY DON'T CARE ABOUT SPACE FIGHTS, KENZ...
...THEY LIKE TO GET THEIR HANDS DIRTY.
BUT, IT TURNS OUT--
MY OFFERING IS PURE!

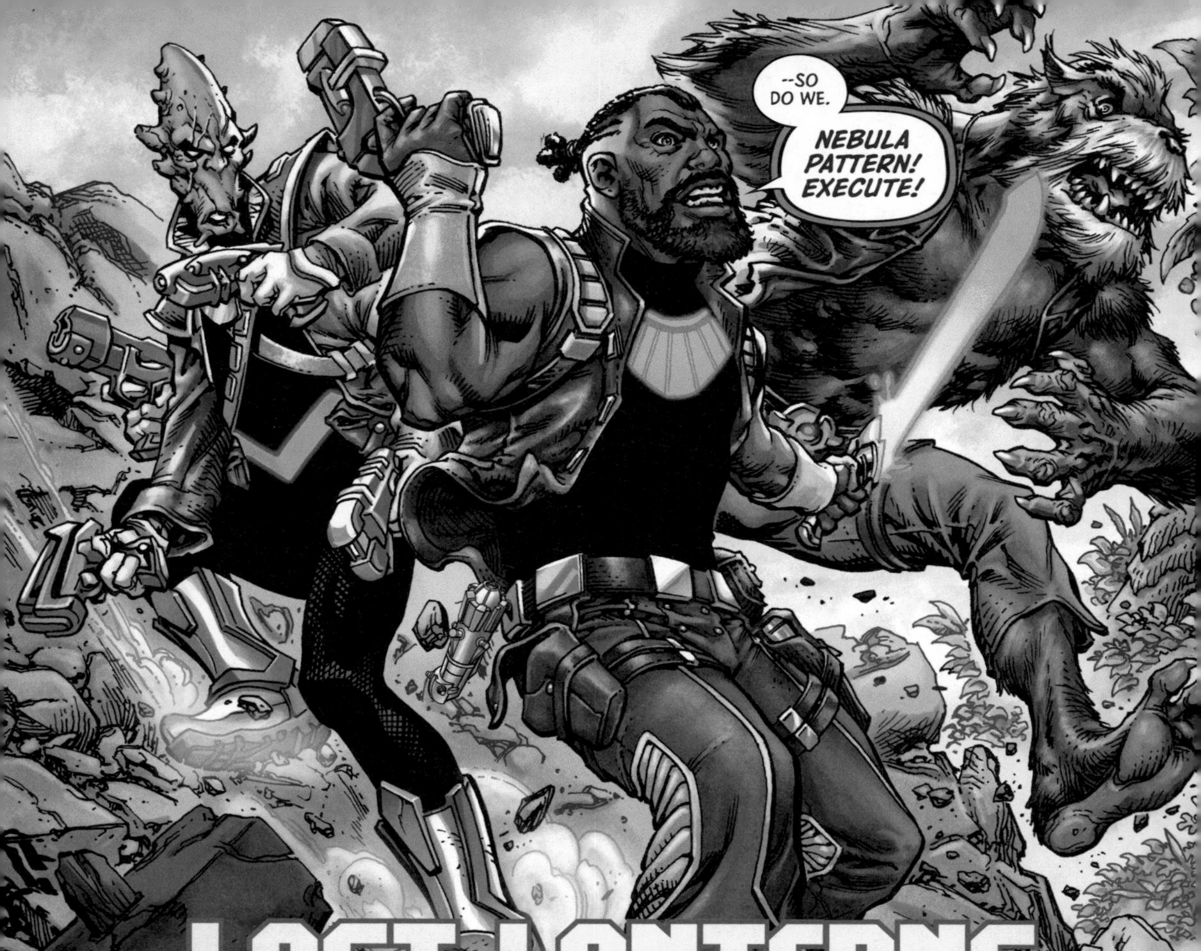
--SO DO WE.
NEBULA PATTERN! EXECUTE!

LAST LANTERNS

GEOFFREY THORNE Writer TOM RANEY Artist MIKE ATIYEH Colors ANDWORLD DESIGN Letters
CLAYTON HENRY & MARCELO MAIOLO Cover JAMAL CAMPBELL Variant cover
MARQUIS DRAPER Assistant Editor MIKE COTTON Editor ALEX R. CARR Group Editor

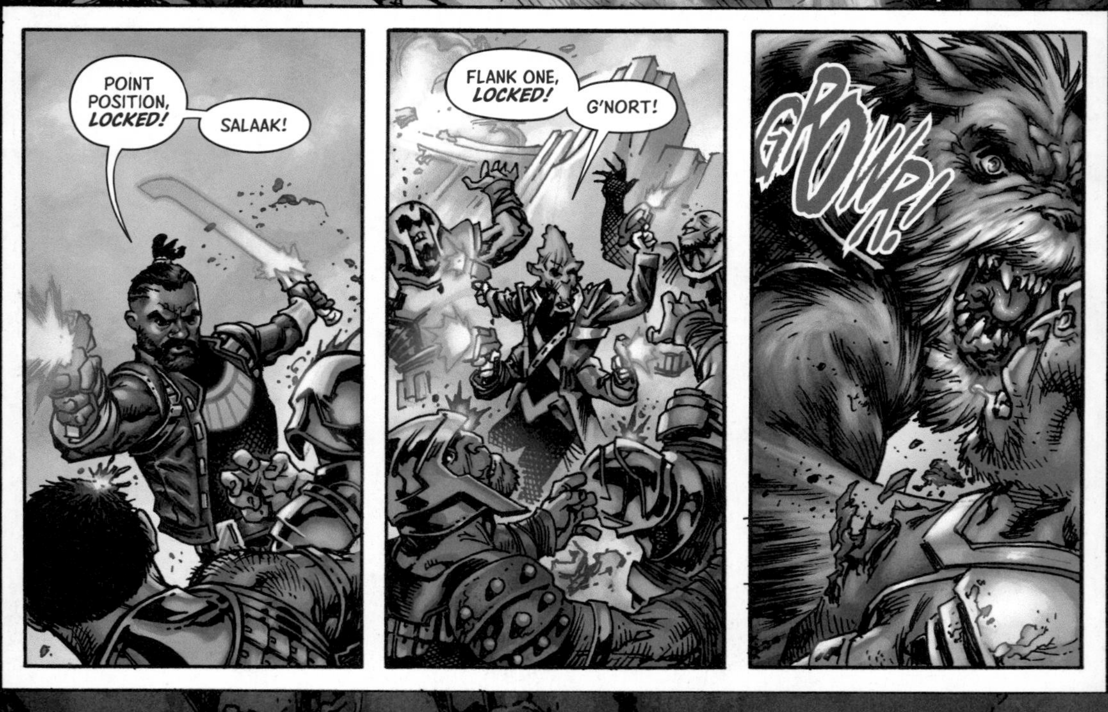
POINT POSITION, LOCKED!
SALAAK!
FLANK ONE, LOCKED!
G'NORT!
GROWR!

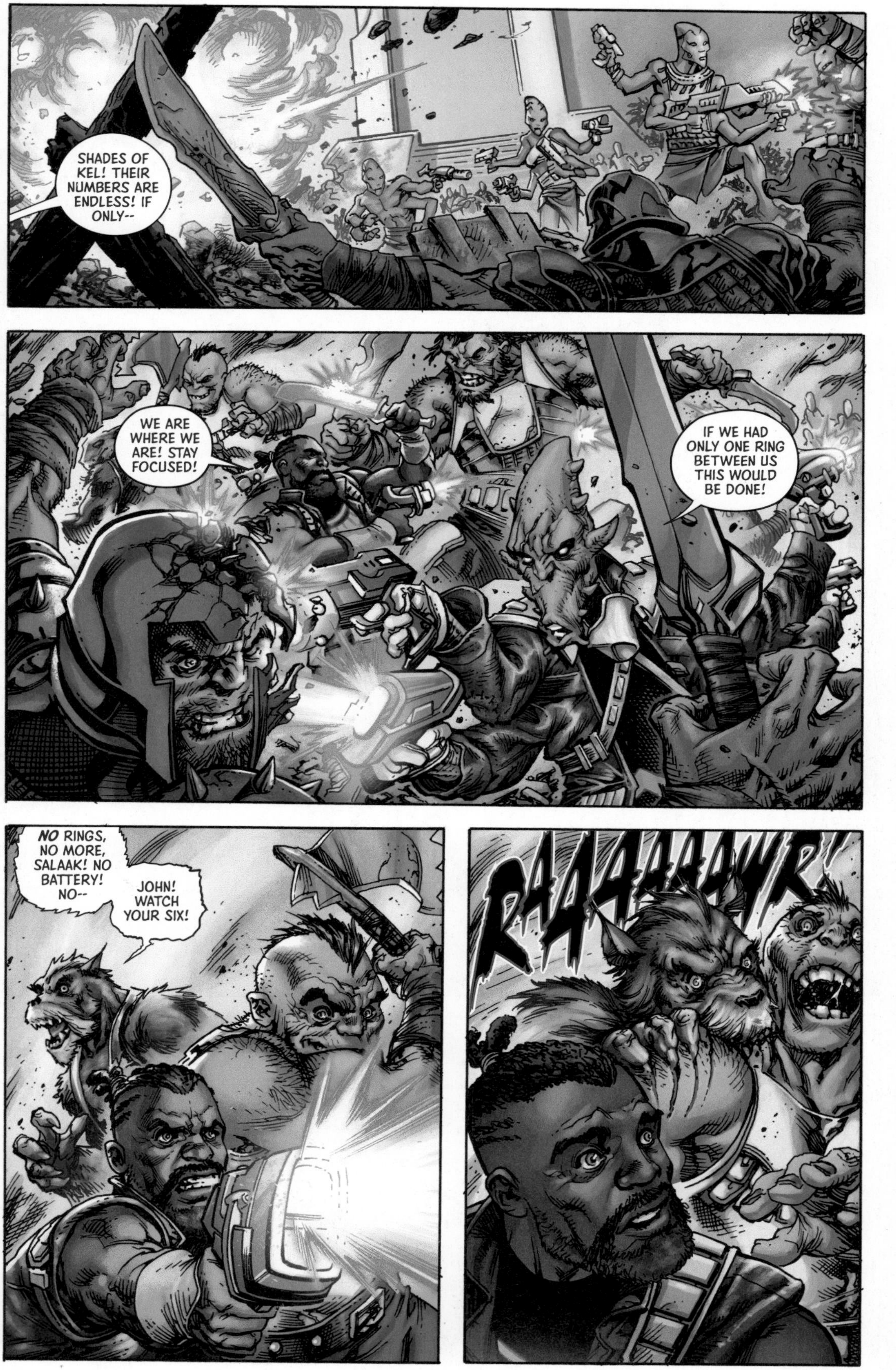

SHADES OF KEL! THEIR NUMBERS ARE ENDLESS! IF ONLY--
WE ARE WHERE WE ARE! STAY FOCUSED!
IF WE HAD ONLY ONE RING BETWEEN US THIS WOULD BE DONE!
NO RINGS, NO MORE, SALAAK! NO BATTERY! NO--
JOHN! WATCH YOUR SIX!
RAAAAAAAWR!

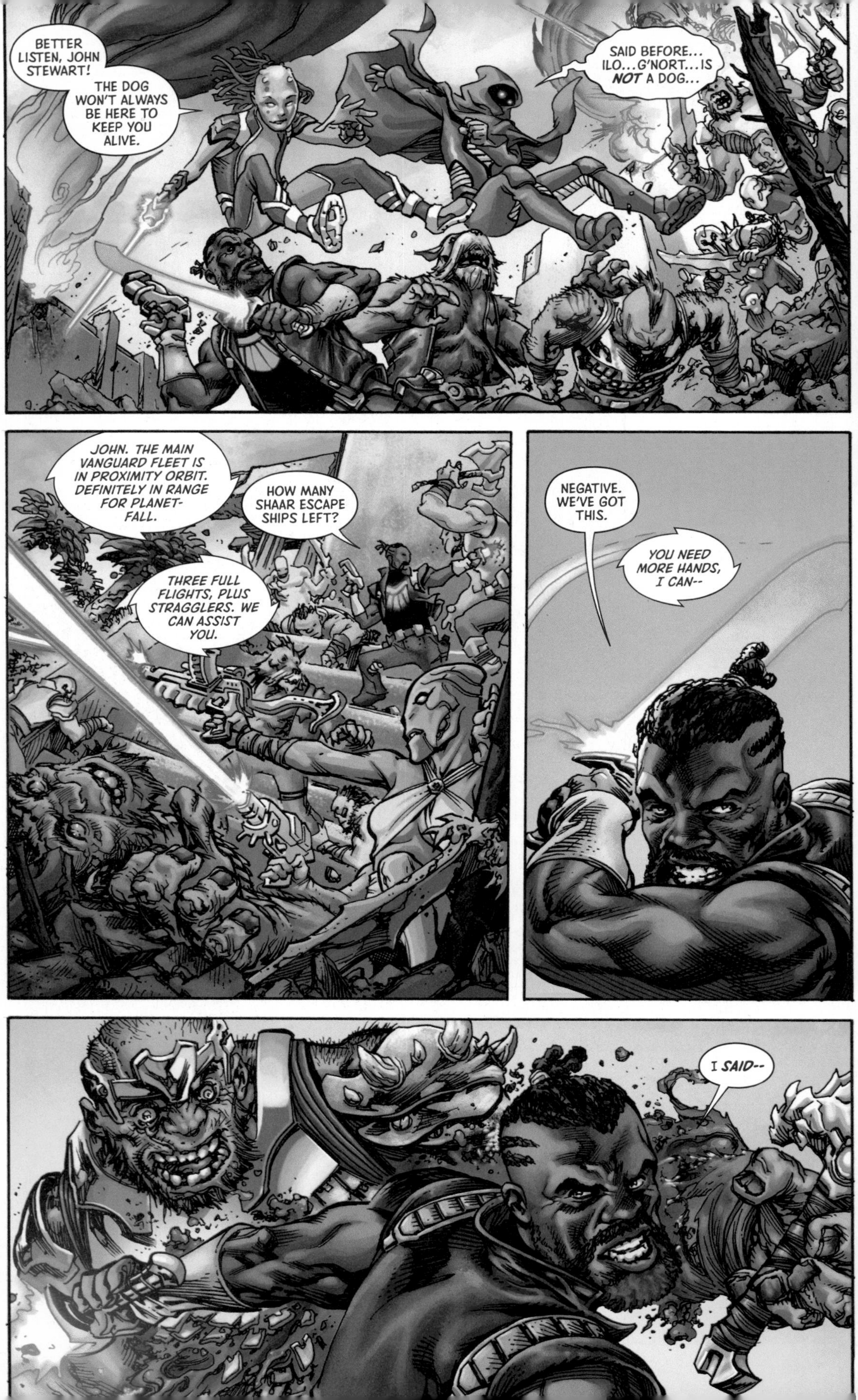
BETTER LISTEN, JOHN STEWART!
THE DOG WON'T ALWAYS BE HERE TO KEEP YOU ALIVE.
SAID BEFORE... ILO...G'NORT...IS *NOT* A DOG...
JOHN. THE MAIN VANGUARD FLEET IS IN PROXIMITY ORBIT. DEFINITELY IN RANGE FOR PLANET-FALL.
HOW MANY SHAAR ESCAPE SHIPS LEFT?
THREE FULL FLIGHTS, PLUS STRAGGLERS. WE CAN ASSIST YOU.
NEGATIVE. WE'VE GOT THIS.
YOU NEED MORE HANDS, I CAN--
I *SAID*--

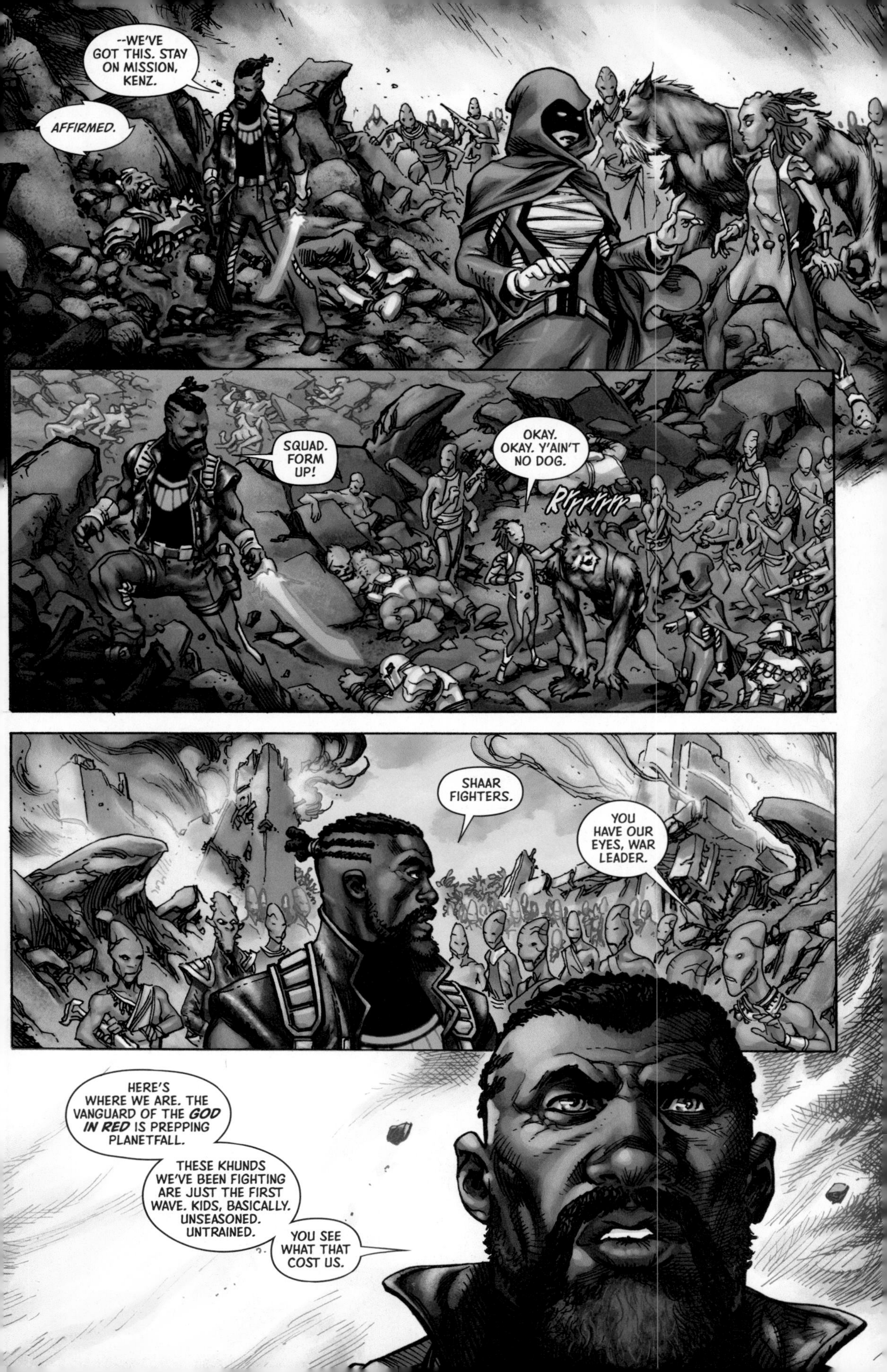
--WE'VE GOT THIS. STAY ON MISSION, KENZ.
AFFIRMED.
SQUAD. FORM UP!
OKAY. OKAY. Y'AIN'T NO DOG.
RRRRRRR
SHAAR FIGHTERS.
YOU HAVE OUR EYES, WAR LEADER.
HERE'S WHERE WE ARE. THE VANGUARD OF THE GOD IN RED IS PREPPING PLANETFALL.
THESE KHUNDS WE'VE BEEN FIGHTING ARE JUST THE FIRST WAVE. KIDS, BASICALLY. UNSEASONED. UNTRAINED.
YOU SEE WHAT THAT COST US.

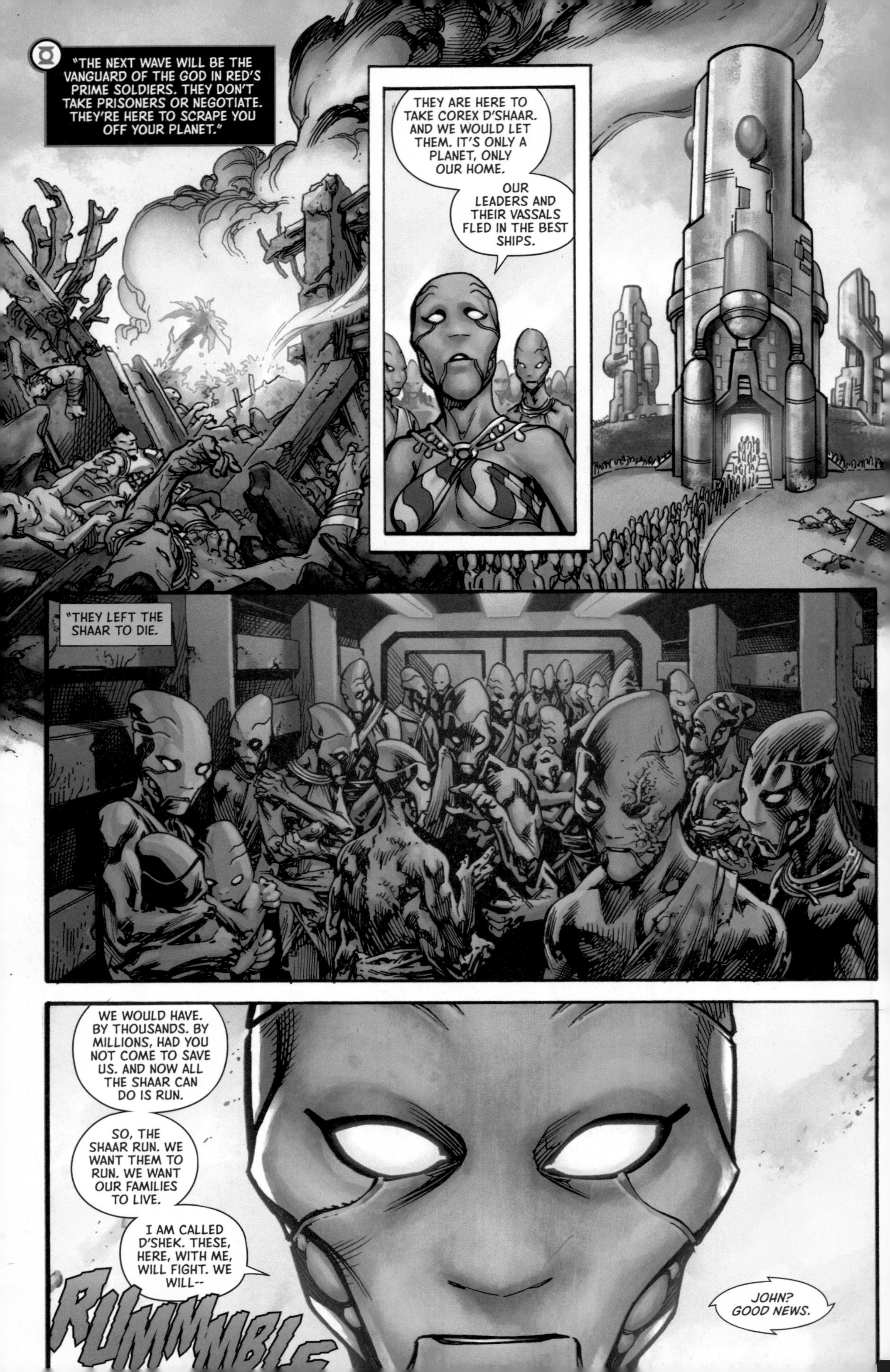
"THE NEXT WAVE WILL BE THE VANGUARD OF THE GOD IN RED'S PRIME SOLDIERS. THEY DON'T TAKE PRISONERS OR NEGOTIATE. THEY'RE HERE TO SCRAPE YOU OFF YOUR PLANET."
THEY ARE HERE TO TAKE COREX D'SHAAR. AND WE WOULD LET THEM. IT'S ONLY A PLANET, ONLY OUR HOME.
OUR LEADERS AND THEIR VASSALS FLED IN THE BEST SHIPS.
"THEY LEFT THE SHAAR TO DIE.
WE WOULD HAVE. BY THOUSANDS. BY MILLIONS, HAD YOU NOT COME TO SAVE US. AND NOW ALL THE SHAAR CAN DO IS RUN.
SO, THE SHAAR RUN. WE WANT THEM TO RUN. WE WANT OUR FAMILIES TO LIVE.
I AM CALLED D'SHEK. THESE, HERE, WITH ME, WILL FIGHT. WE WILL--
RUMMMBLE
JOHN? GOOD NEWS.

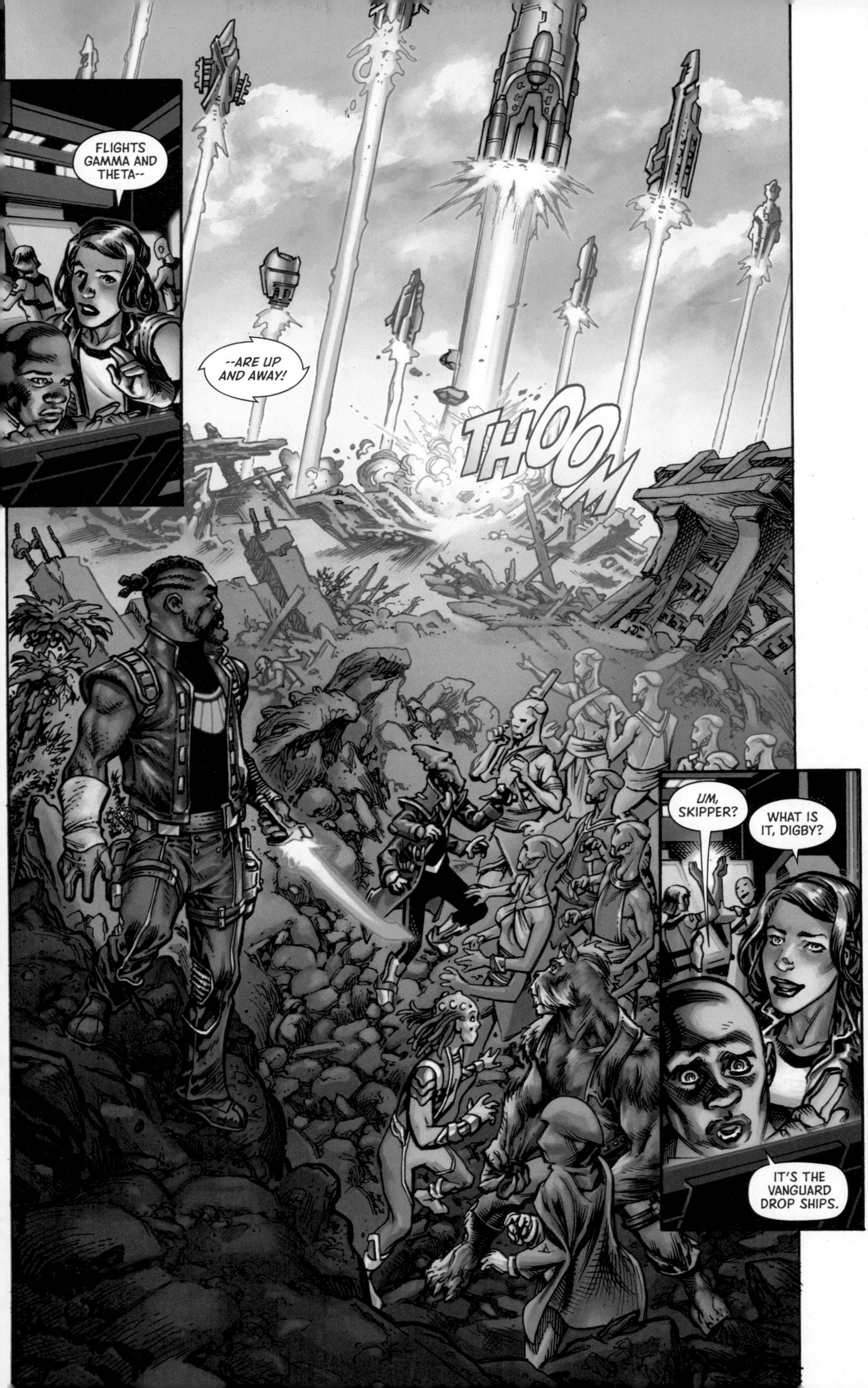
FLIGHTS GAMMA AND THETA--
--ARE UP AND AWAY!
THOOM
UM, SKIPPER?
WHAT IS IT, DIGBY?
IT'S THE VANGUARD DROP SHIPS.

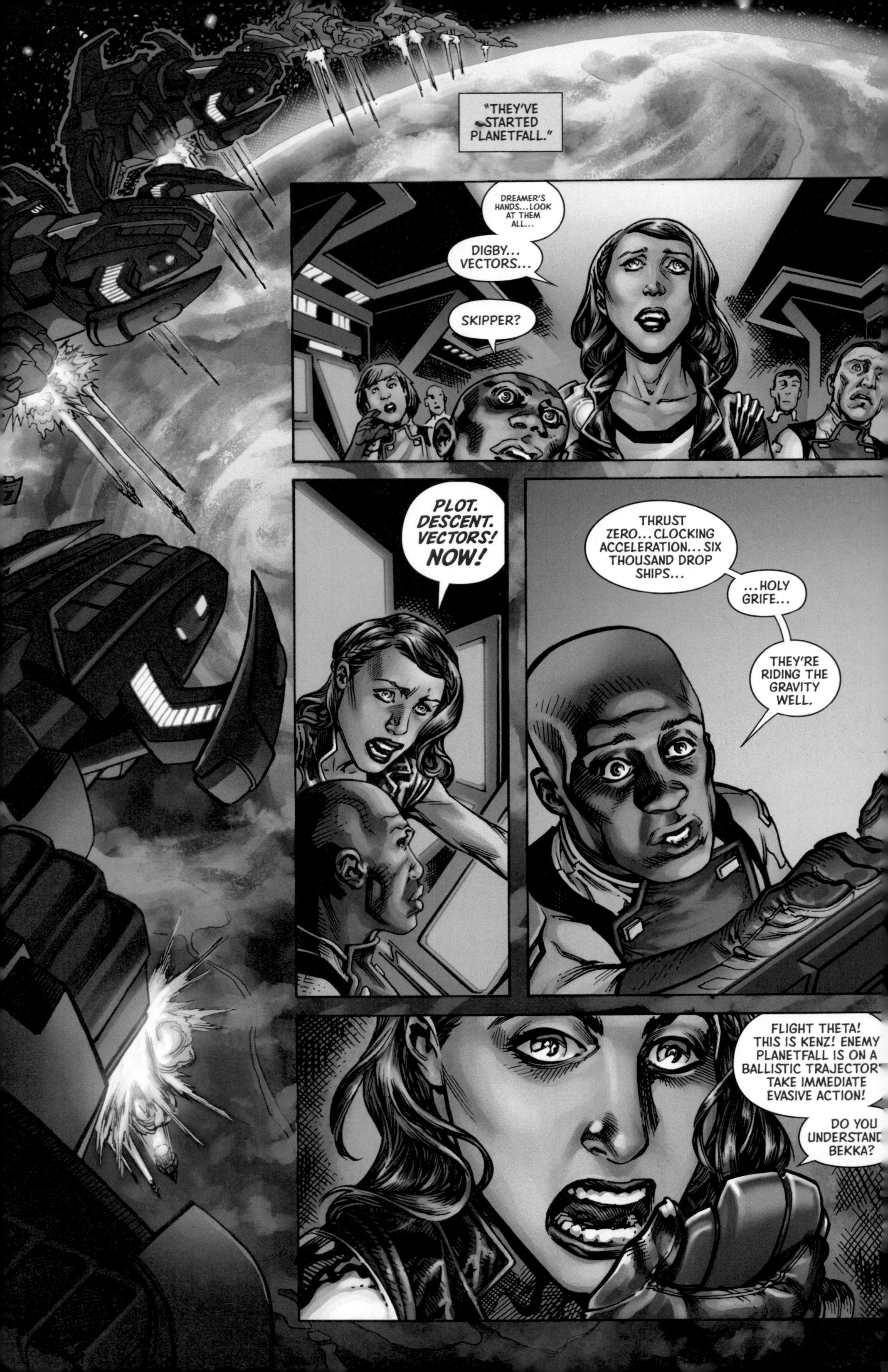
"THEY'VE STARTED PLANETFALL."
DREAMER'S HANDS...LOOK AT THEM ALL...
DIGBY... VECTORS...
SKIPPER?
PLOT. DESCENT. VECTORS! NOW!
THRUST ZERO...CLOCKING ACCELERATION...SIX THOUSAND DROP SHIPS...
...HOLY GRIFE...
THEY'RE RIDING THE GRAVITY WELL.
FLIGHT THETA! THIS IS KENZ! ENEMY PLANETFALL IS ON A BALLISTIC TRAJECTORY TAKE IMMEDIATE EVASIVE ACTION!
DO YOU UNDERSTAND BEKKA?

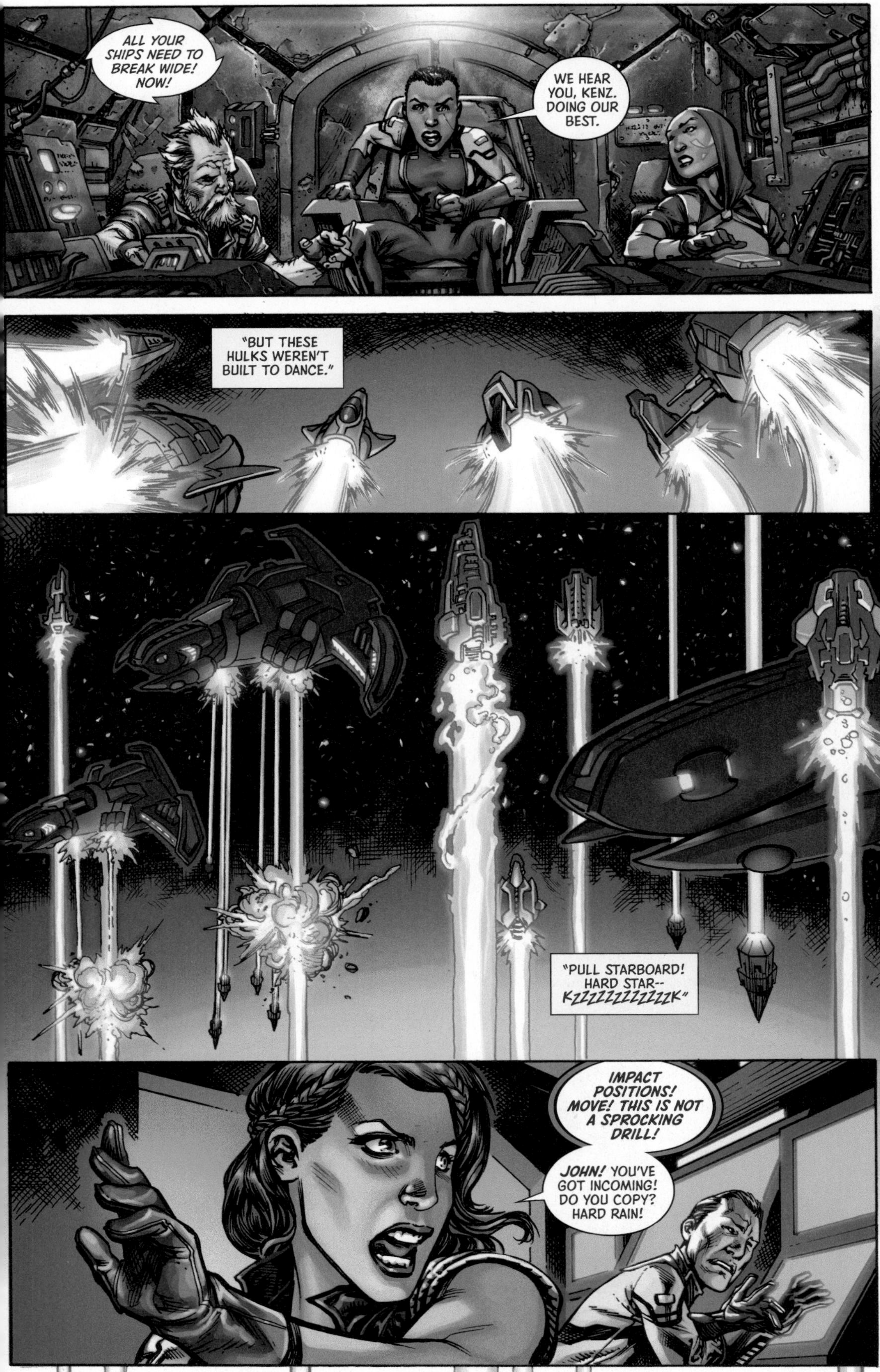
ALL YOUR SHIPS NEED TO BREAK WIDE! NOW!
WE HEAR YOU, KENZ. DOING OUR BEST.
"BUT THESE HULKS WEREN'T BUILT TO DANCE."
"PULL STARBOARD! HARD STAR-- KZZZZZZZZZZZZK"
IMPACT POSITIONS! MOVE! THIS IS NOT A SPROCKING DRILL!
JOHN! YOU'VE GOT INCOMING! DO YOU COPY? HARD RAIN!

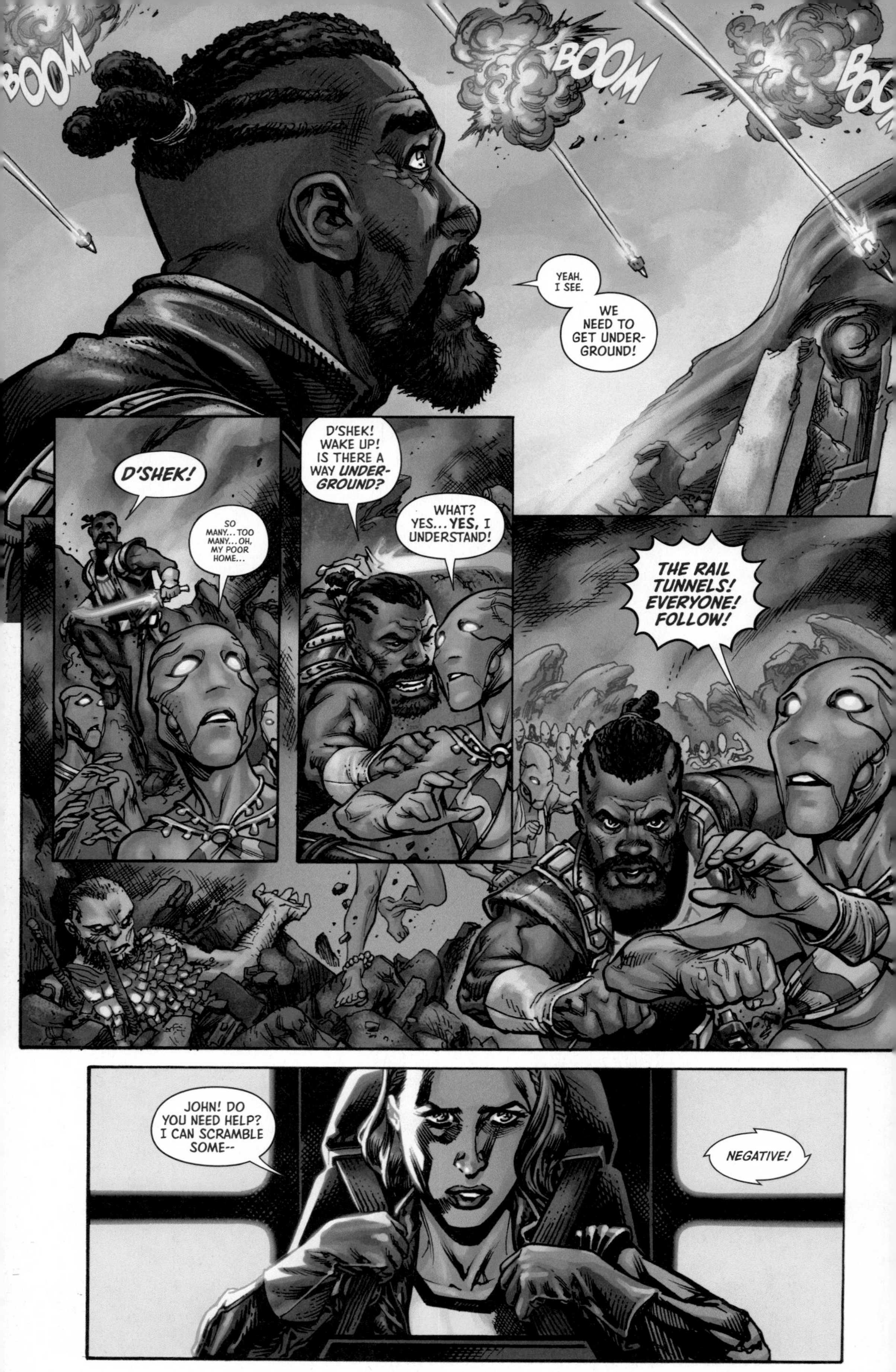
BOOM
BOOM
BOOM
YEAH. I SEE.
WE NEED TO GET UNDER-GROUND!
D'SHEK!
SO MANY...TOO MANY...OH, MY POOR HOME...
D'SHEK! WAKE UP! IS THERE A WAY UNDER-GROUND?
WHAT? YES...YES, I UNDERSTAND!
THE RAIL TUNNELS! EVERYONE! FOLLOW!
JOHN! DO YOU NEED HELP? I CAN SCRAMBLE SOME--
NEGATIVE!

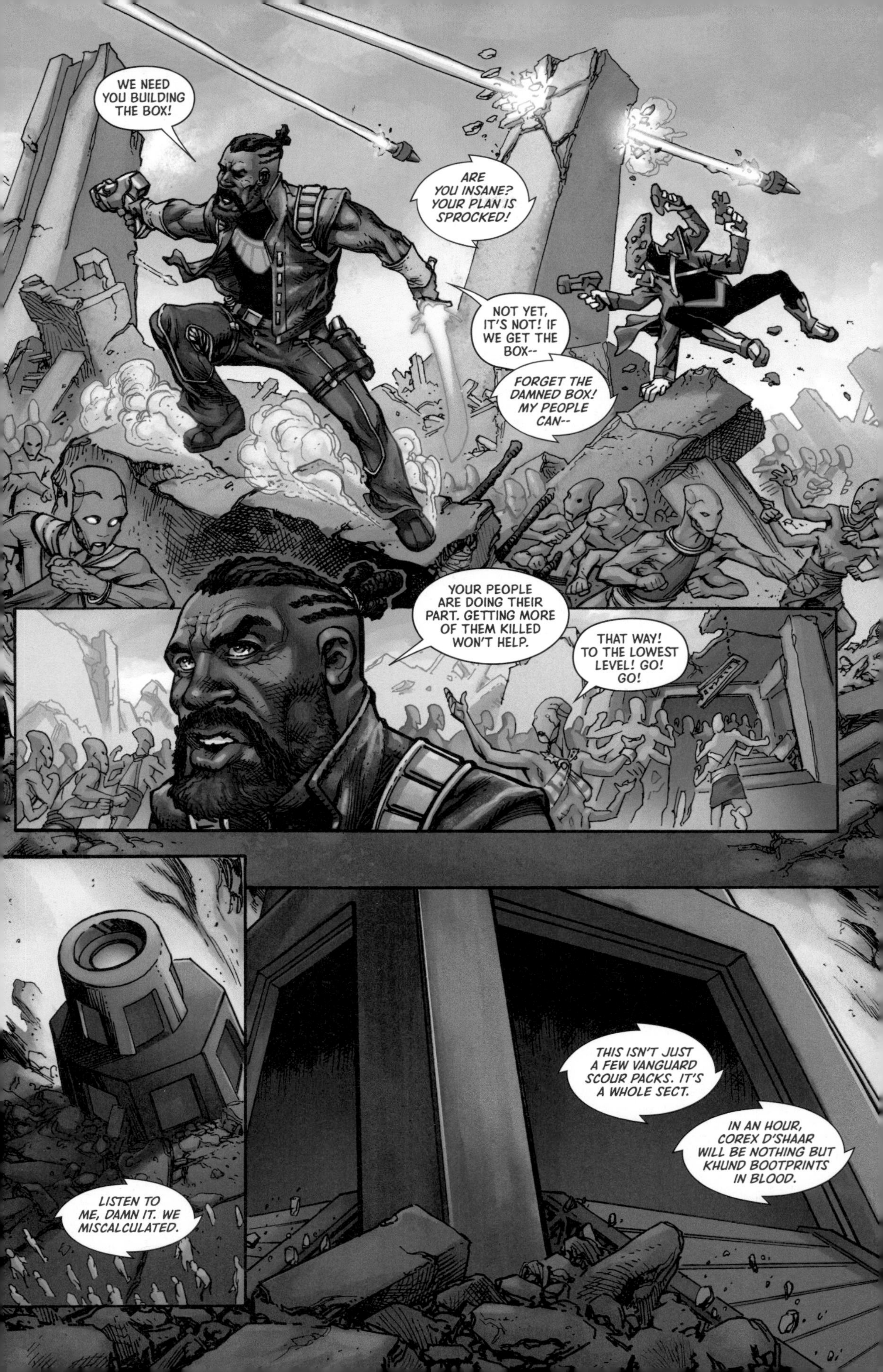
WE NEED YOU BUILDING THE BOX!
ARE YOU INSANE? YOUR PLAN IS SPROCKED!
NOT YET, IT'S NOT! IF WE GET THE BOX--
FORGET THE DAMNED BOX! MY PEOPLE CAN--
YOUR PEOPLE ARE DOING THEIR PART. GETTING MORE OF THEM KILLED WON'T HELP.
THAT WAY! TO THE LOWEST LEVEL! GO! GO!
LISTEN TO ME, DAMN IT. WE MISCALCULATED.
THIS ISN'T JUST A FEW VANGUARD SCOUR PACKS. IT'S A WHOLE SECT.
IN AN HOUR, COREX D'SHAAR WILL BE NOTHING BUT KHUND BOOTPRINTS IN BLOOD.

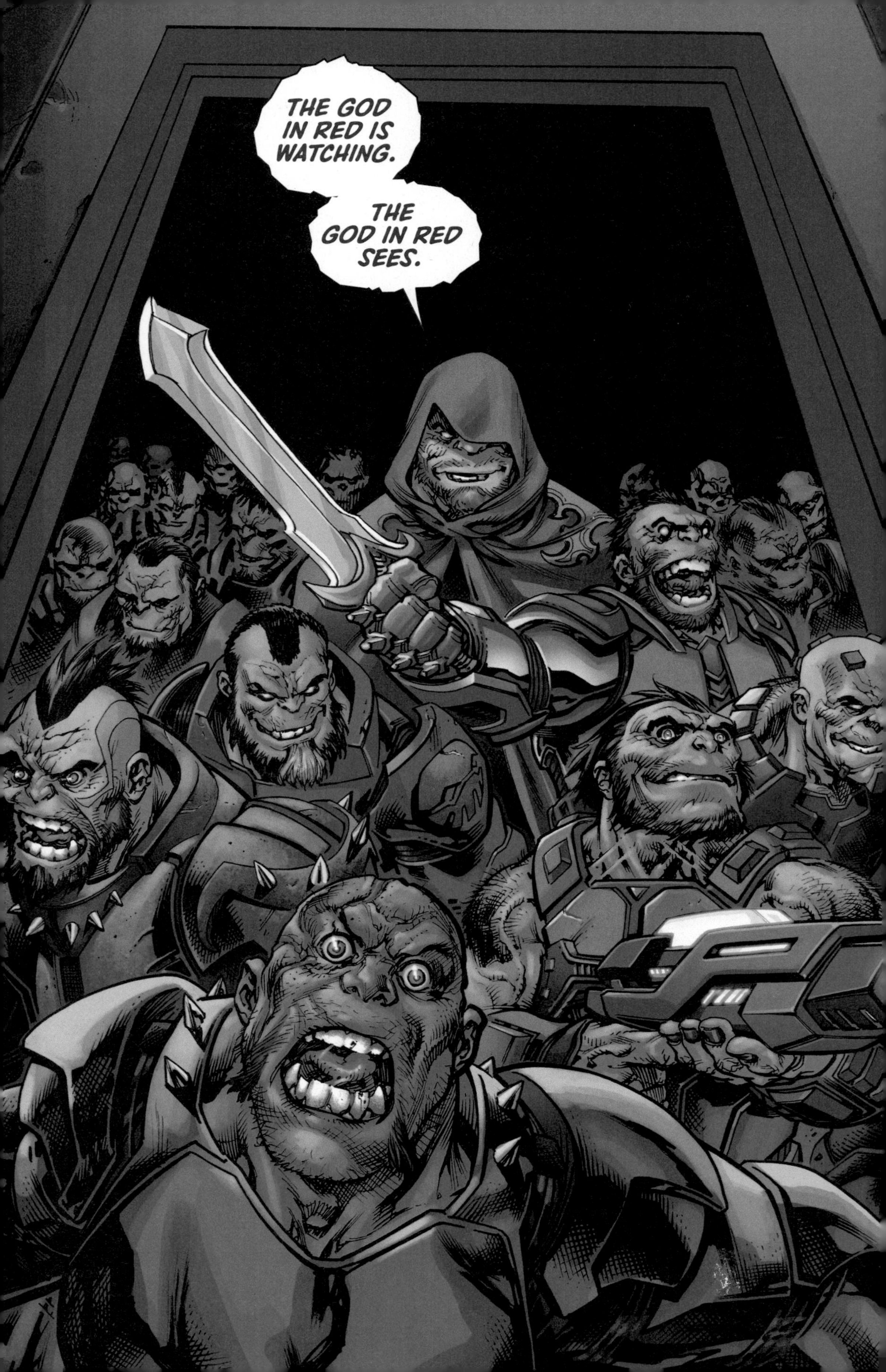
THE GOD IN RED IS WATCHING.
THE GOD IN RED SEES.

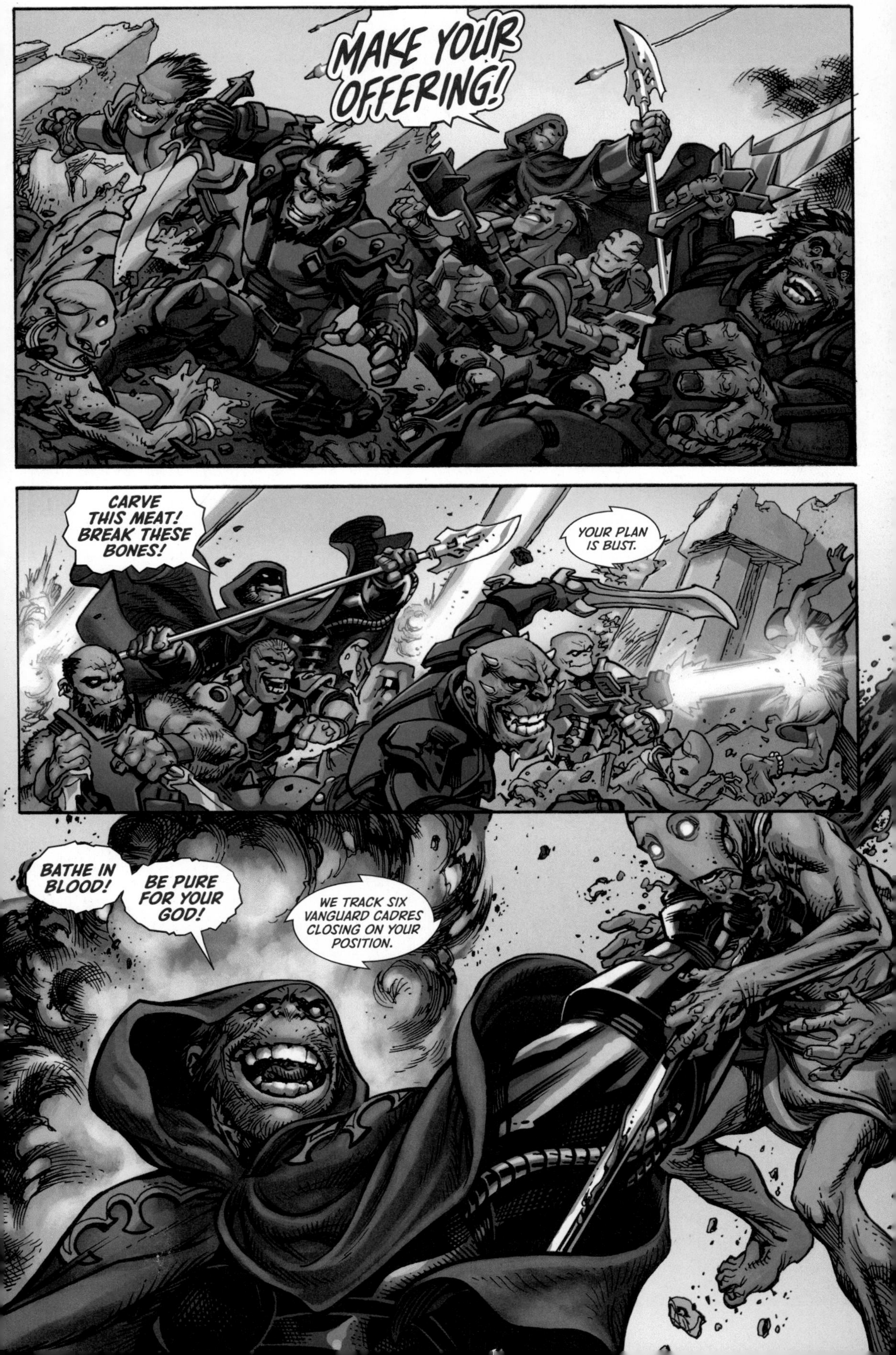
MAKE YOUR OFFERING!
CARVE THIS MEAT! BREAK THESE BONES!
YOUR PLAN IS BUST.
BATHE IN BLOOD!
BE PURE FOR YOUR GOD!
WE TRACK SIX VANGUARD CADRES CLOSING ON YOUR POSITION.

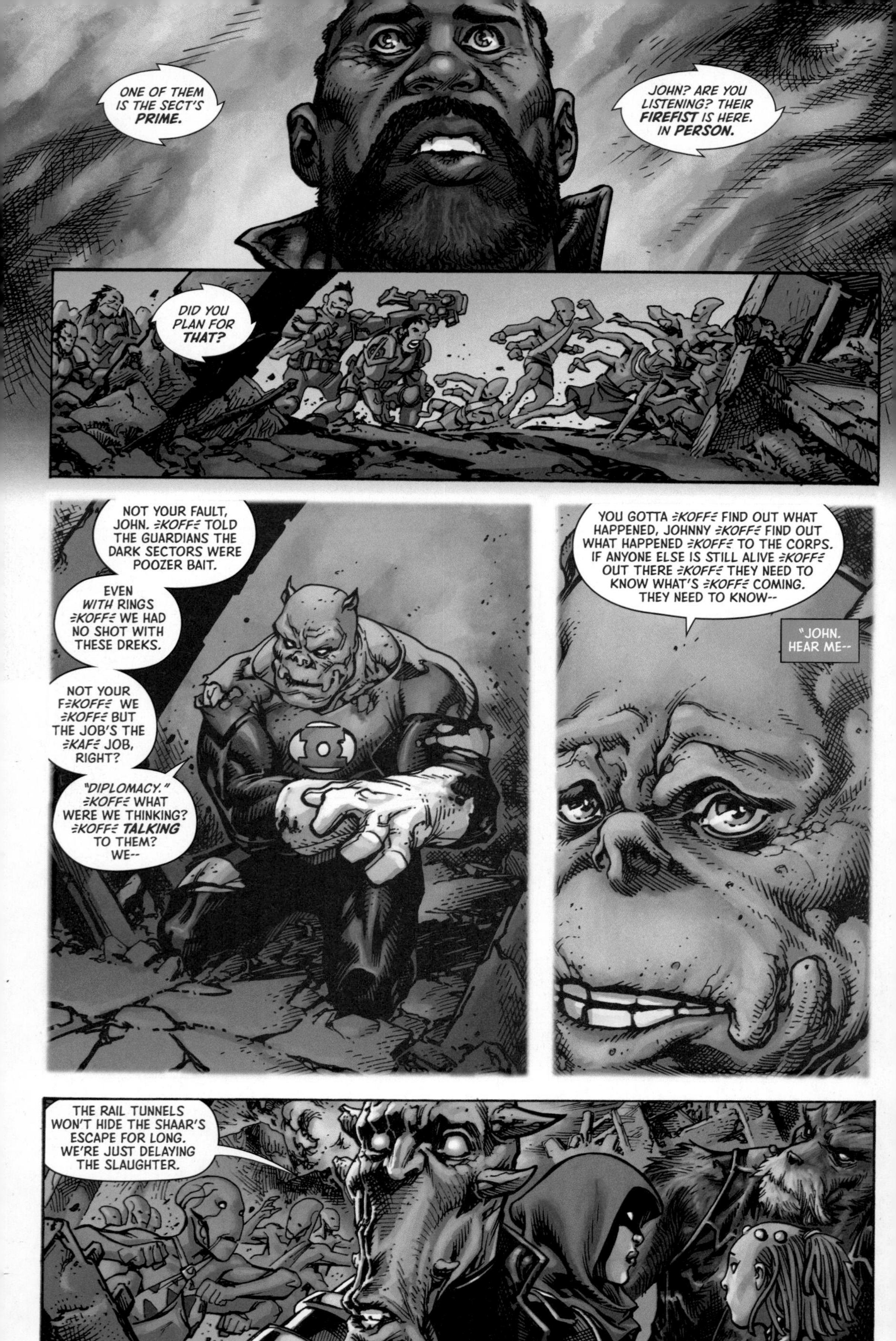
ONE OF THEM IS THE SECT'S **PRIME.**
JOHN? ARE YOU LISTENING? THEIR **FIREFIST** IS HERE. IN **PERSON.**
DID YOU PLAN FOR **THAT?**
NOT YOUR FAULT, JOHN. =KOFF= TOLD THE GUARDIANS THE DARK SECTORS WERE POOZER BAIT.
EVEN *WITH* RINGS =KOFF= WE HAD NO SHOT WITH THESE DREKS.
NOT YOUR F=KOFF= WE =KOFF= BUT THE JOB'S THE =KAF= JOB, RIGHT?
"DIPLOMACY." =KOFF= WHAT WERE WE THINKING? =KOFF= ***TALKING*** TO THEM? WE--
YOU GOTTA =KOFF= FIND OUT WHAT HAPPENED, JOHNNY =KOFF= FIND OUT WHAT HAPPENED =KOFF= TO THE CORPS. IF ANYONE ELSE IS STILL ALIVE =KOFF= OUT THERE =KOFF= THEY NEED TO KNOW WHAT'S =KOFF= COMING. THEY NEED TO KNOW--
"JOHN. HEAR ME--
THE RAIL TUNNELS WON'T HIDE THE SHAAR'S ESCAPE FOR LONG. WE'RE JUST DELAYING THE SLAUGHTER.

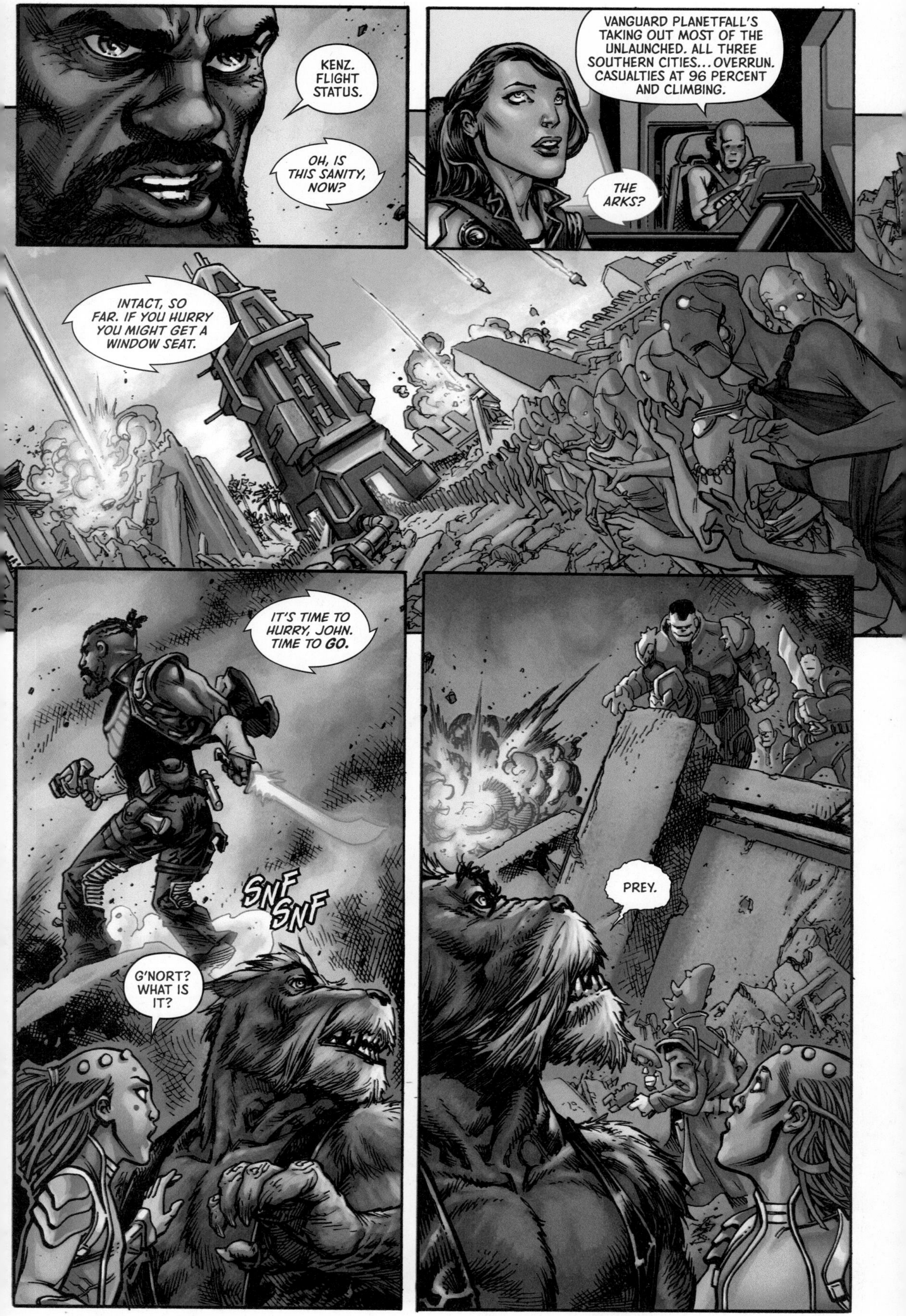
KENZ. FLIGHT STATUS.
OH, IS THIS SANITY, NOW?
VANGUARD PLANETFALL'S TAKING OUT MOST OF THE UNLAUNCHED. ALL THREE SOUTHERN CITIES... OVERRUN. CASUALTIES AT 96 PERCENT AND CLIMBING.
THE ARKS?
INTACT, SO FAR. IF YOU HURRY YOU MIGHT GET A WINDOW SEAT.
IT'S TIME TO HURRY, JOHN. TIME TO GO.
SNF SNF
G'NORT? WHAT IS IT?
PREY.

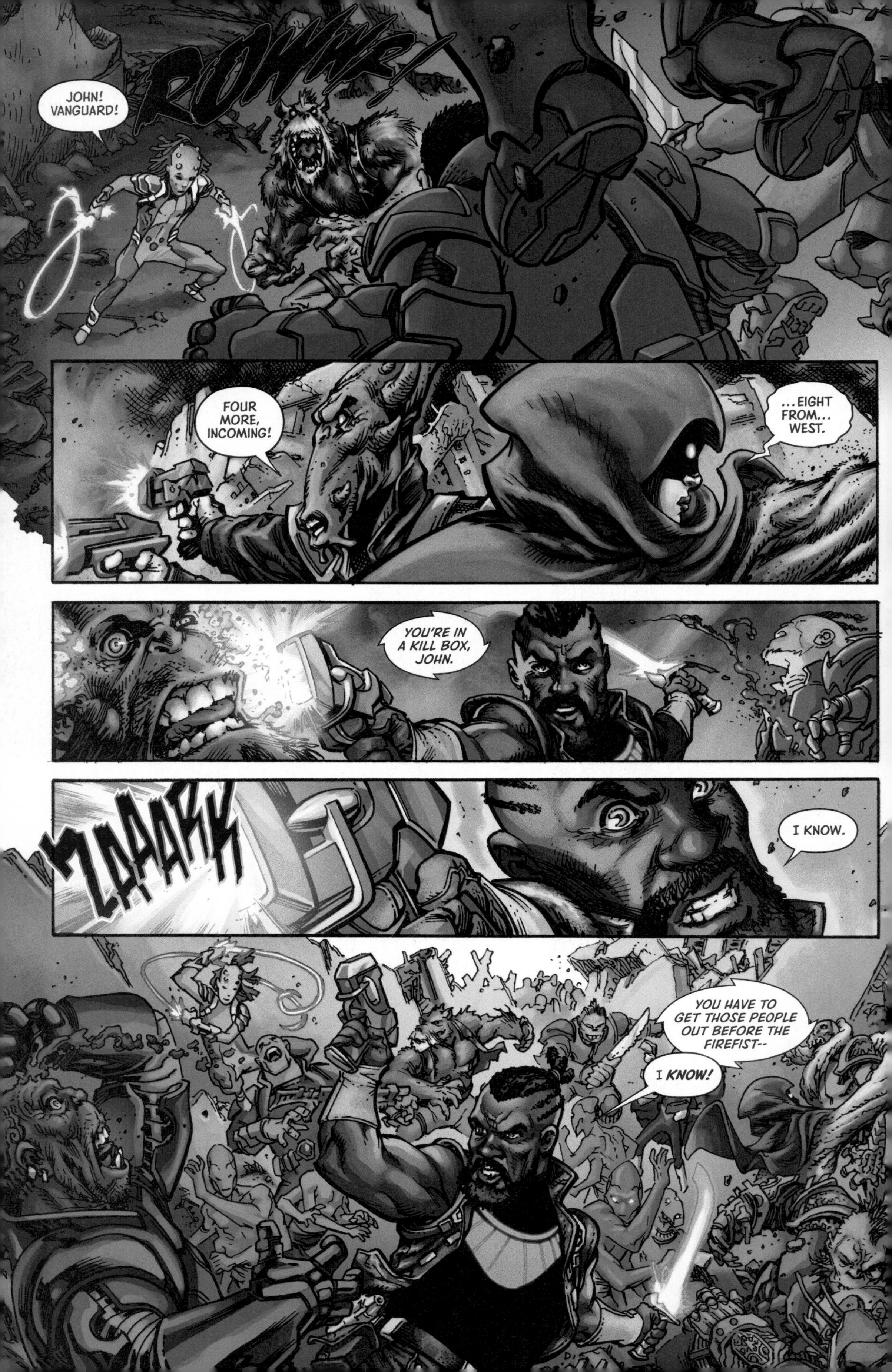
JOHN! VANGUARD!
ROWWR!
FOUR MORE, INCOMING!
...EIGHT FROM... WEST.
YOU'RE IN A KILL BOX, JOHN.
ZAARK
I KNOW.
YOU HAVE TO GET THOSE PEOPLE OUT BEFORE THE FIREFIST--
I KNOW!

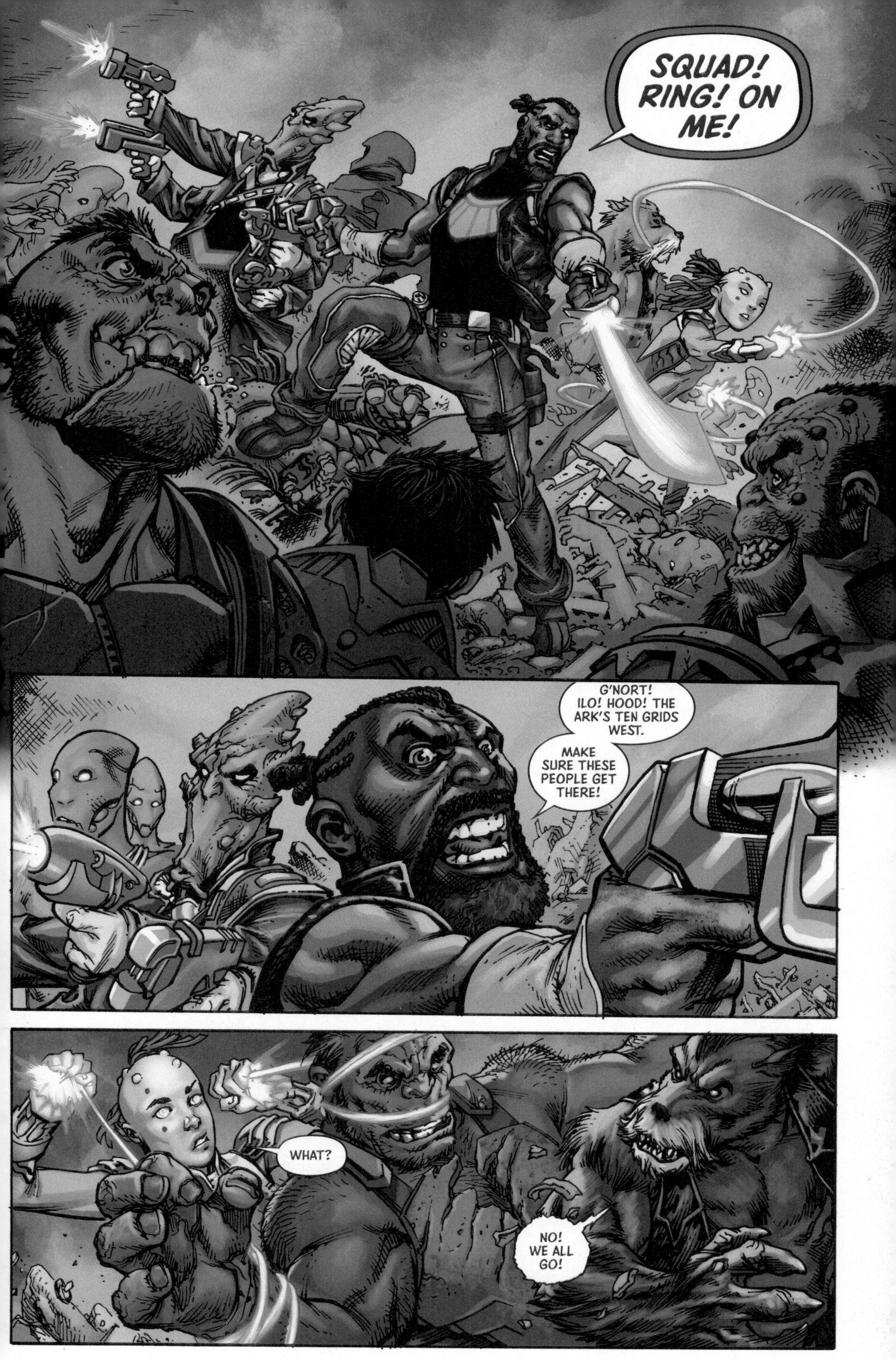
SQUAD! RING! ON ME!
G'NORT! ILO! HOOD! THE ARK'S TEN GRIDS WEST.
MAKE SURE THESE PEOPLE GET THERE!
WHAT?
NO! WE ALL GO!

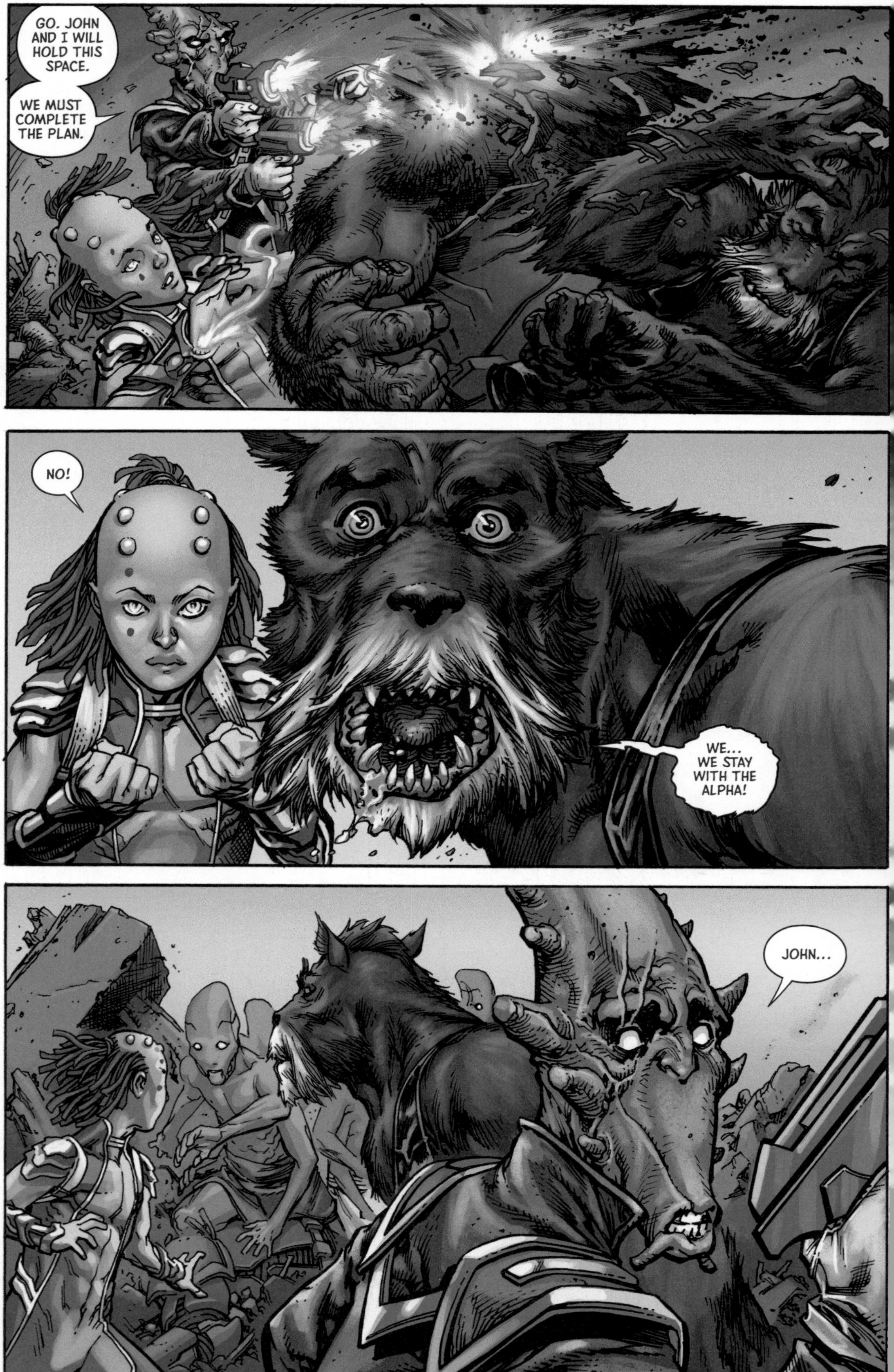
GO. JOHN AND I WILL HOLD THIS SPACE.
WE MUST COMPLETE THE PLAN.
NO!
WE... WE STAY WITH THE ALPHA!
JOHN...

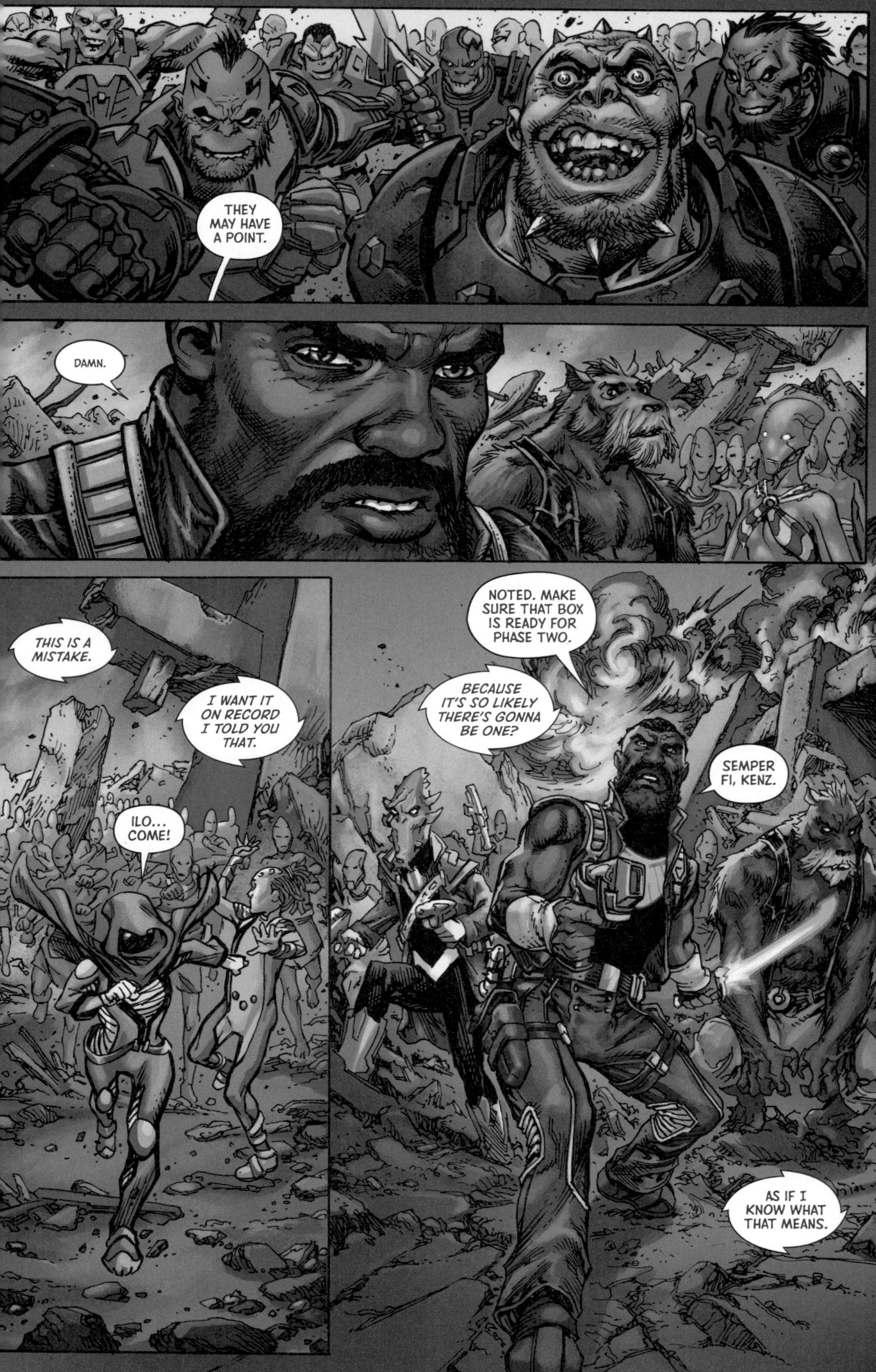
THEY MAY HAVE A POINT.
DAMN.
THIS IS A MISTAKE.
I WANT IT ON RECORD I TOLD YOU THAT.
ILO... COME!
NOTED. MAKE SURE THAT BOX IS READY FOR PHASE TWO.
BECAUSE IT'S SO LIKELY THERE'S GONNA BE ONE?
SEMPER FI, KENZ.
AS IF I KNOW WHAT THAT MEANS.

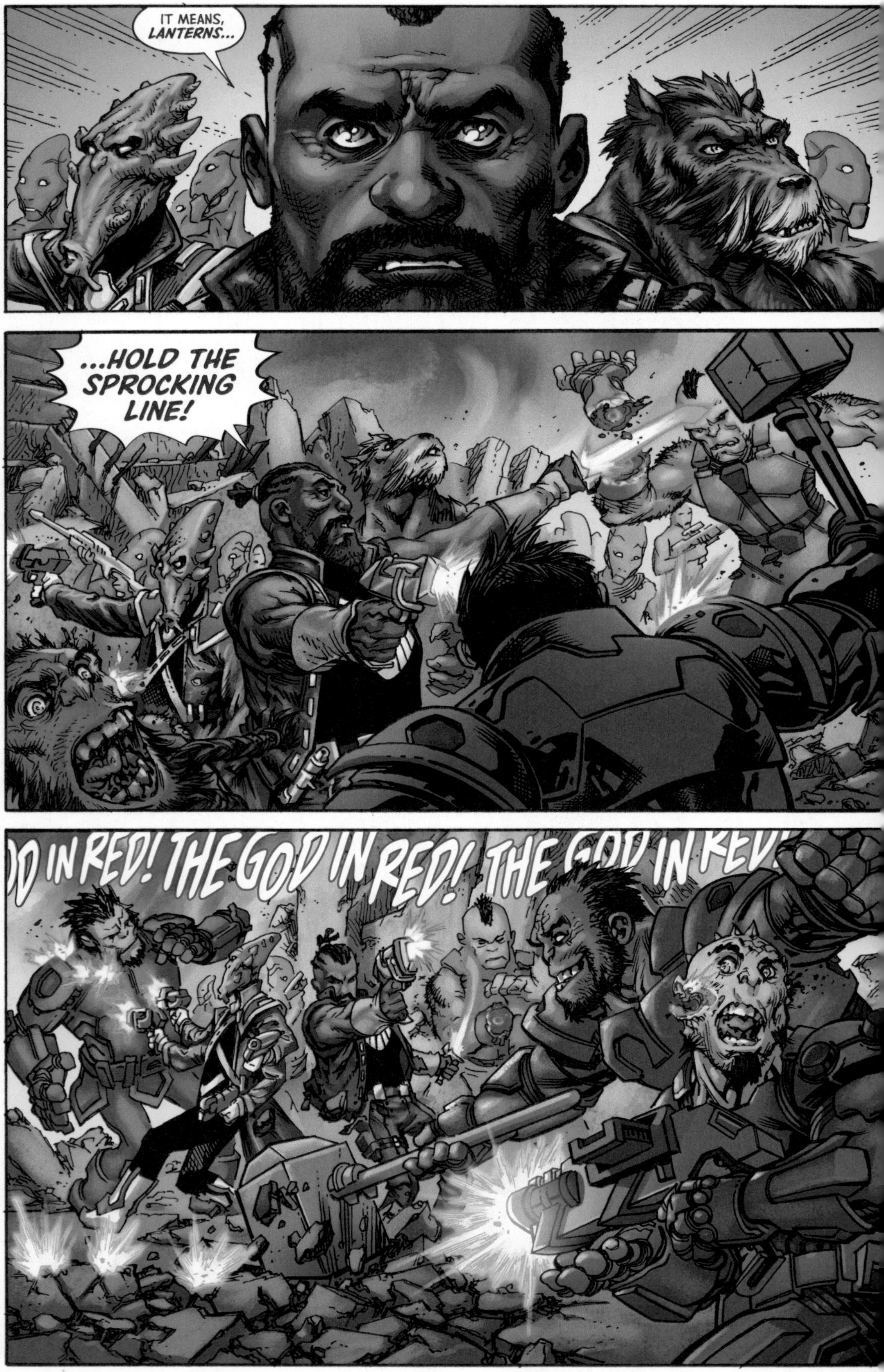
IT MEANS, LANTERNS...
...HOLD THE SPROCKING LINE!
OD IN RED! THE GOD IN RED! THE GOD IN RED!

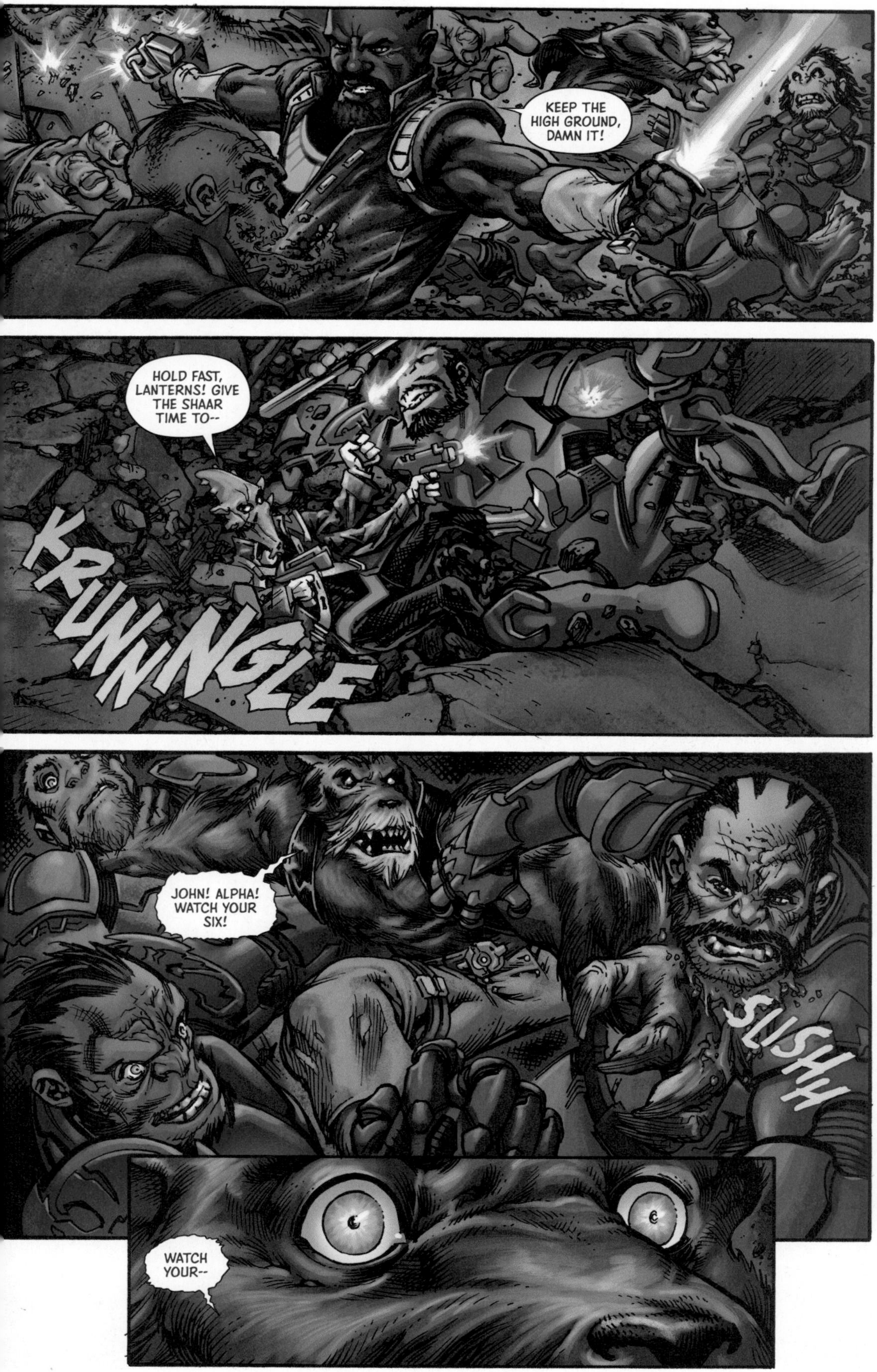
KEEP THE HIGH GROUND, DAMN IT!
HOLD FAST, LANTERNS! GIVE THE SHAAR TIME TO--
KRUNNNGLE
JOHN! ALPHA! WATCH YOUR SIX!
SLISHH
WATCH YOUR--

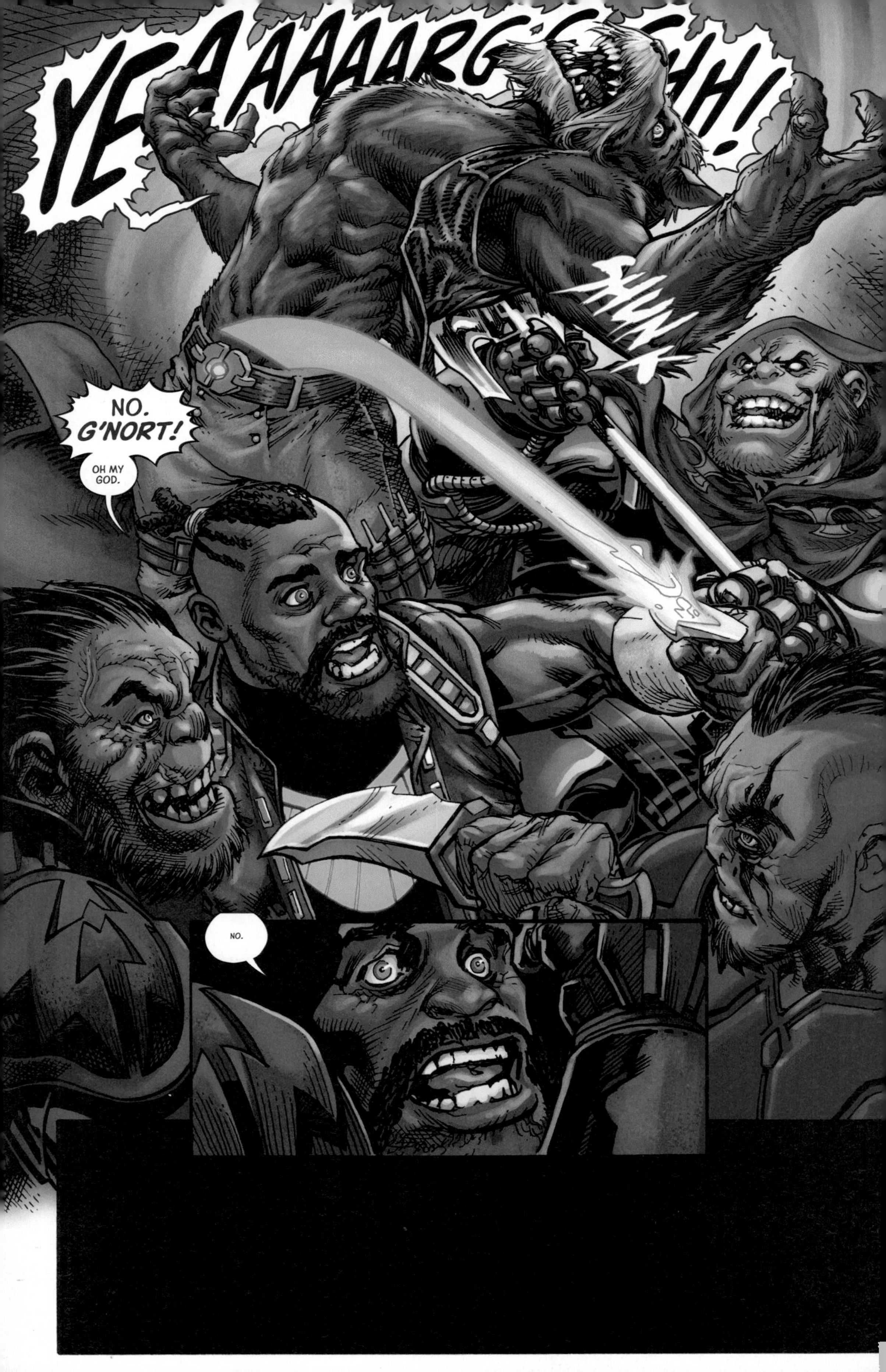
YEAAAAAARG-G-GHH!
NO. G'NORT!
OH MY GOD.
NO.

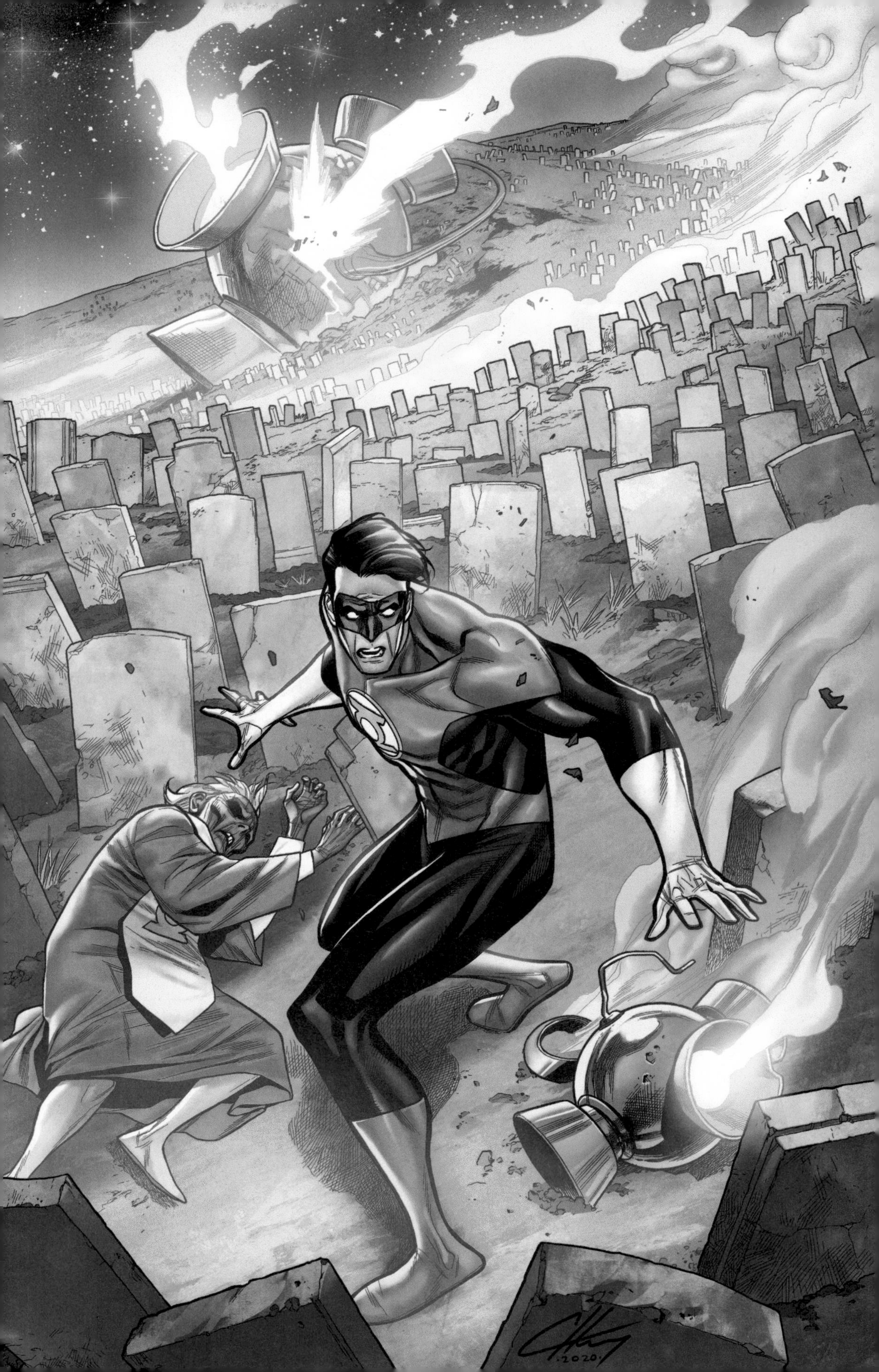

Future State: Green Lantern #2 main cover art
by Clayton Henry and Marcelo Maiolo

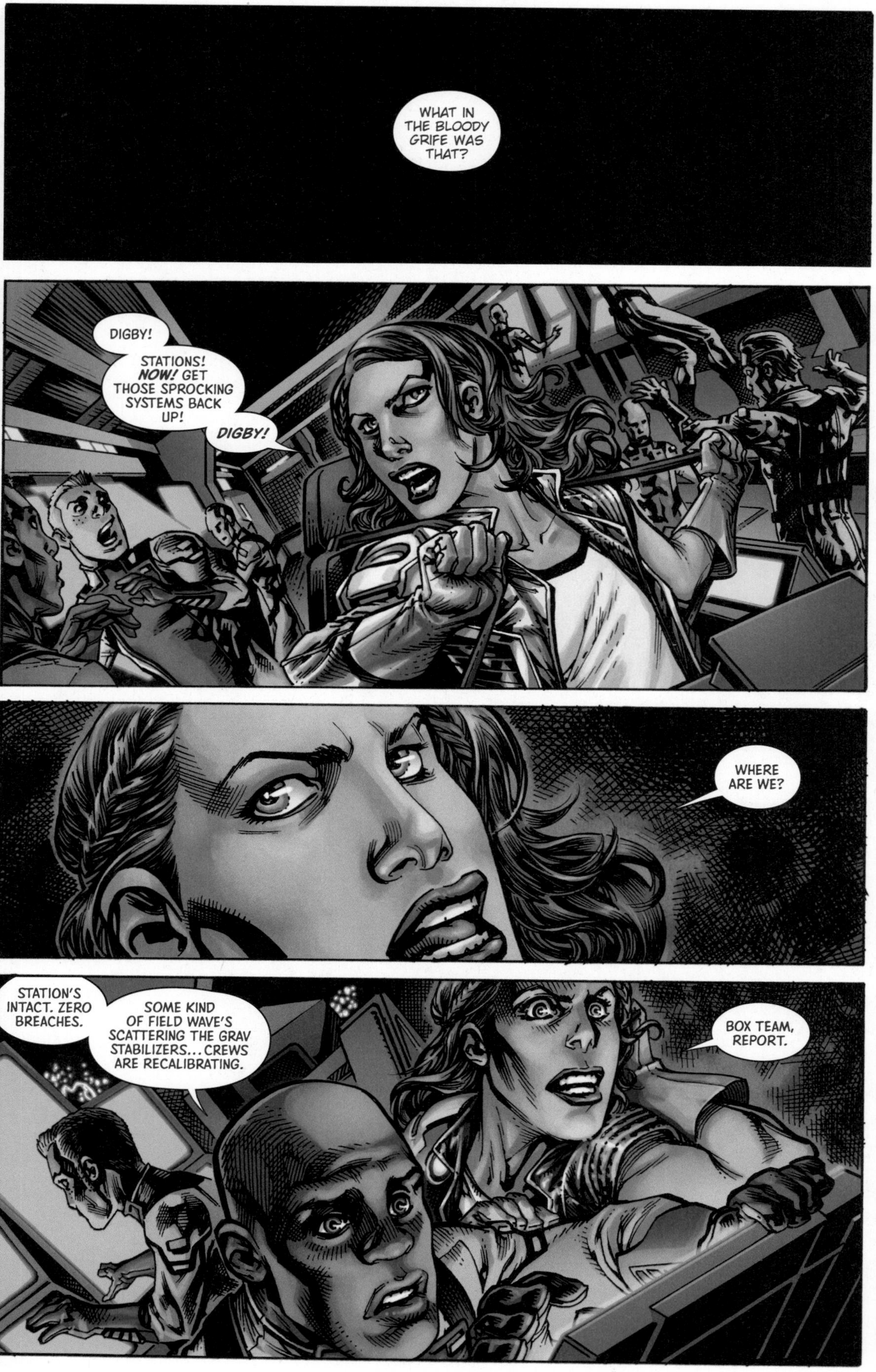
WHAT IN THE BLOODY GRIFE WAS THAT?
DIGBY!
STATIONS! *NOW!* GET THOSE SPROCKING SYSTEMS BACK UP!
DIGBY!
WHERE ARE WE?
STATION'S INTACT. ZERO BREACHES.
SOME KIND OF FIELD WAVE'S SCATTERING THE GRAV STABILIZERS... CREWS ARE RECALIBRATING.
BOX TEAM, REPORT.

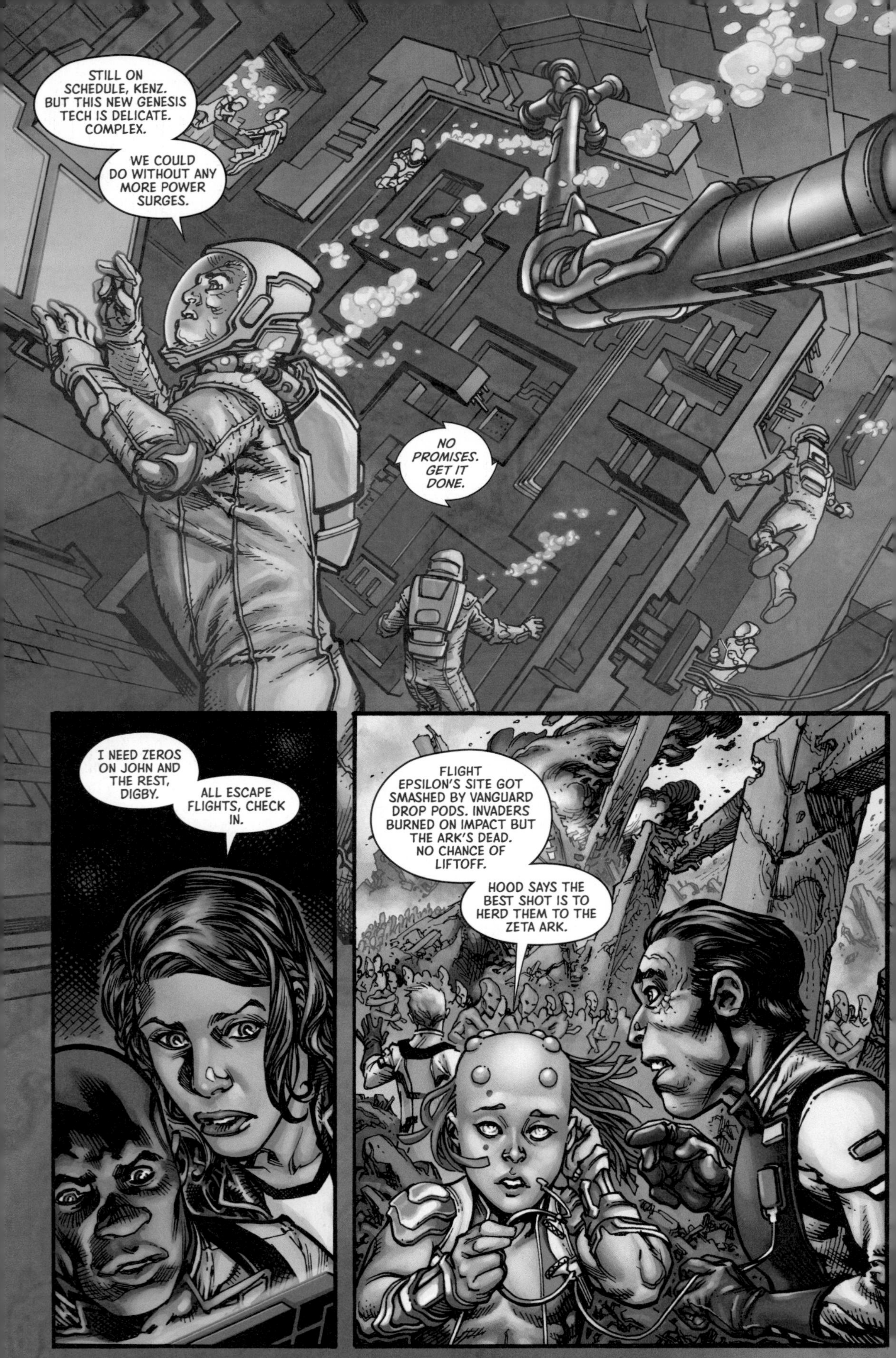
STILL ON SCHEDULE, KENZ. BUT THIS NEW GENESIS TECH IS DELICATE. COMPLEX.
WE COULD DO WITHOUT ANY MORE POWER SURGES.
NO PROMISES. GET IT DONE.
I NEED ZEROS ON JOHN AND THE REST, DIGBY.
ALL ESCAPE FLIGHTS, CHECK IN.
FLIGHT EPSILON'S SITE GOT SMASHED BY VANGUARD DROP PODS. INVADERS BURNED ON IMPACT BUT THE ARK'S DEAD. NO CHANCE OF LIFTOFF.
HOOD SAYS THE BEST SHOT IS TO HERD THEM TO THE ZETA ARK.

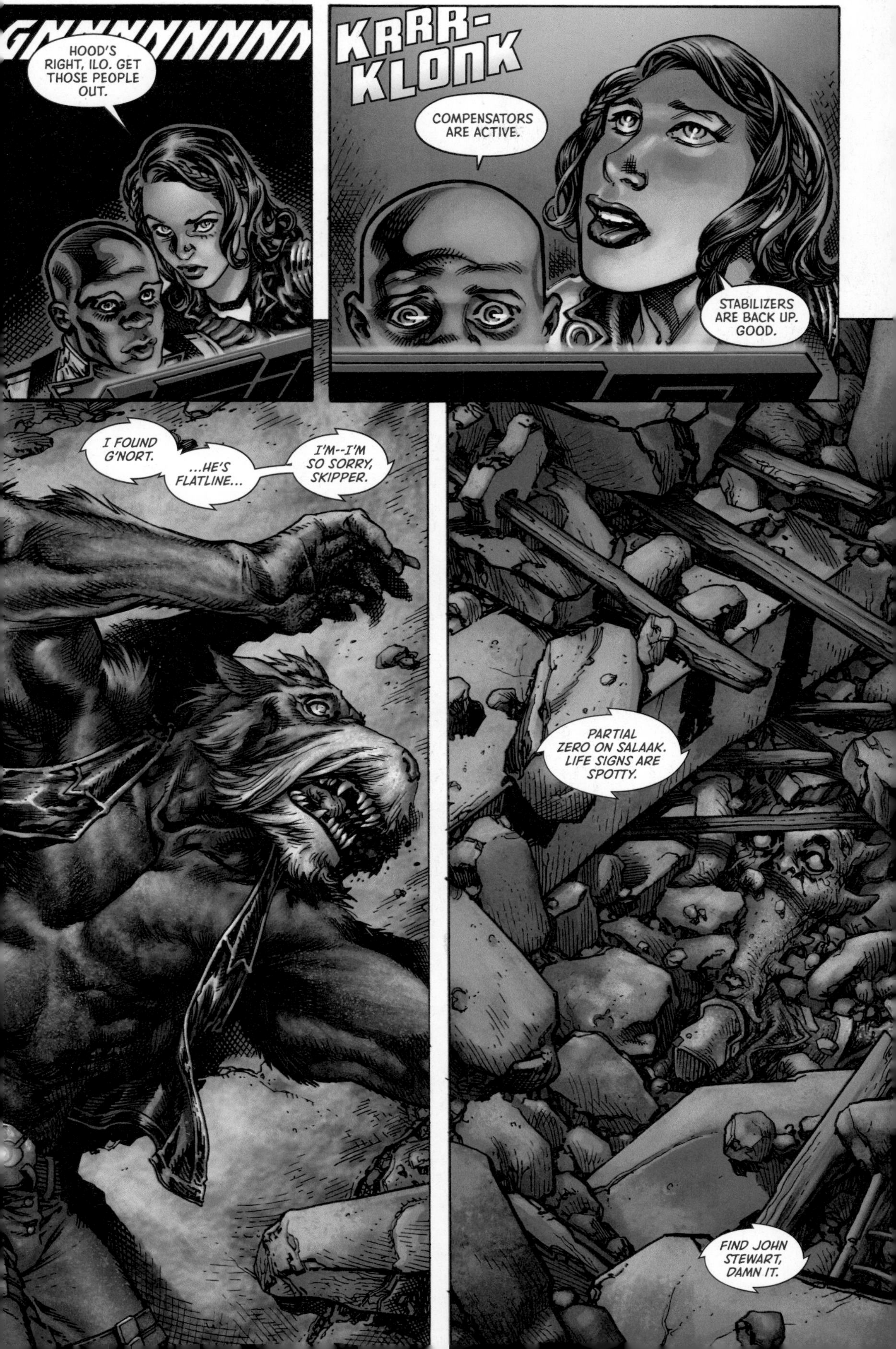
GNNNNNNNN
HOOD'S RIGHT, ILO. GET THOSE PEOPLE OUT.
KRRR-KLONK
COMPENSATORS ARE ACTIVE.
STABILIZERS ARE BACK UP. GOOD.
I FOUND G'NORT.
...HE'S FLATLINE...
I'M--I'M SO SORRY, SKIPPER.
PARTIAL ZERO ON SALAAK. LIFE SIGNS ARE SPOTTY.
FIND JOHN STEWART, DAMN IT.

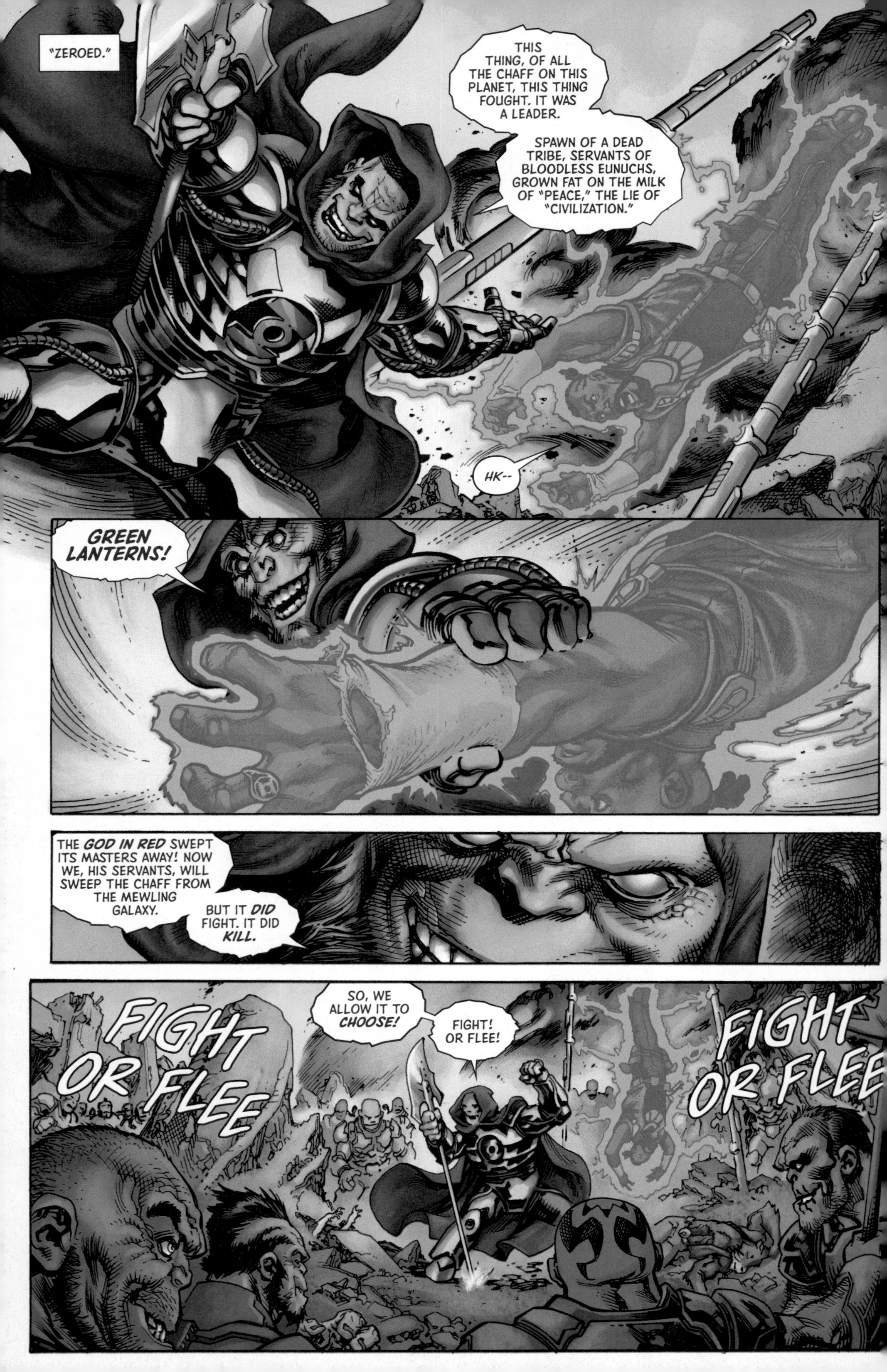
"ZEROED."
THIS THING, OF ALL THE CHAFF ON THIS PLANET, THIS THING FOUGHT. IT WAS A LEADER.
SPAWN OF A DEAD TRIBE, SERVANTS OF BLOODLESS EUNUCHS, GROWN FAT ON THE MILK OF "PEACE," THE LIE OF "CIVILIZATION."
HK--
GREEN LANTERNS!
THE GOD IN RED SWEPT ITS MASTERS AWAY! NOW WE, HIS SERVANTS, WILL SWEEP THE CHAFF FROM THE MEWLING GALAXY.
BUT IT DID FIGHT. IT DID KILL.
FIGHT OR FLEE
SO, WE ALLOW IT TO CHOOSE!
FIGHT! OR FLEE!
FIGHT OR FLEE

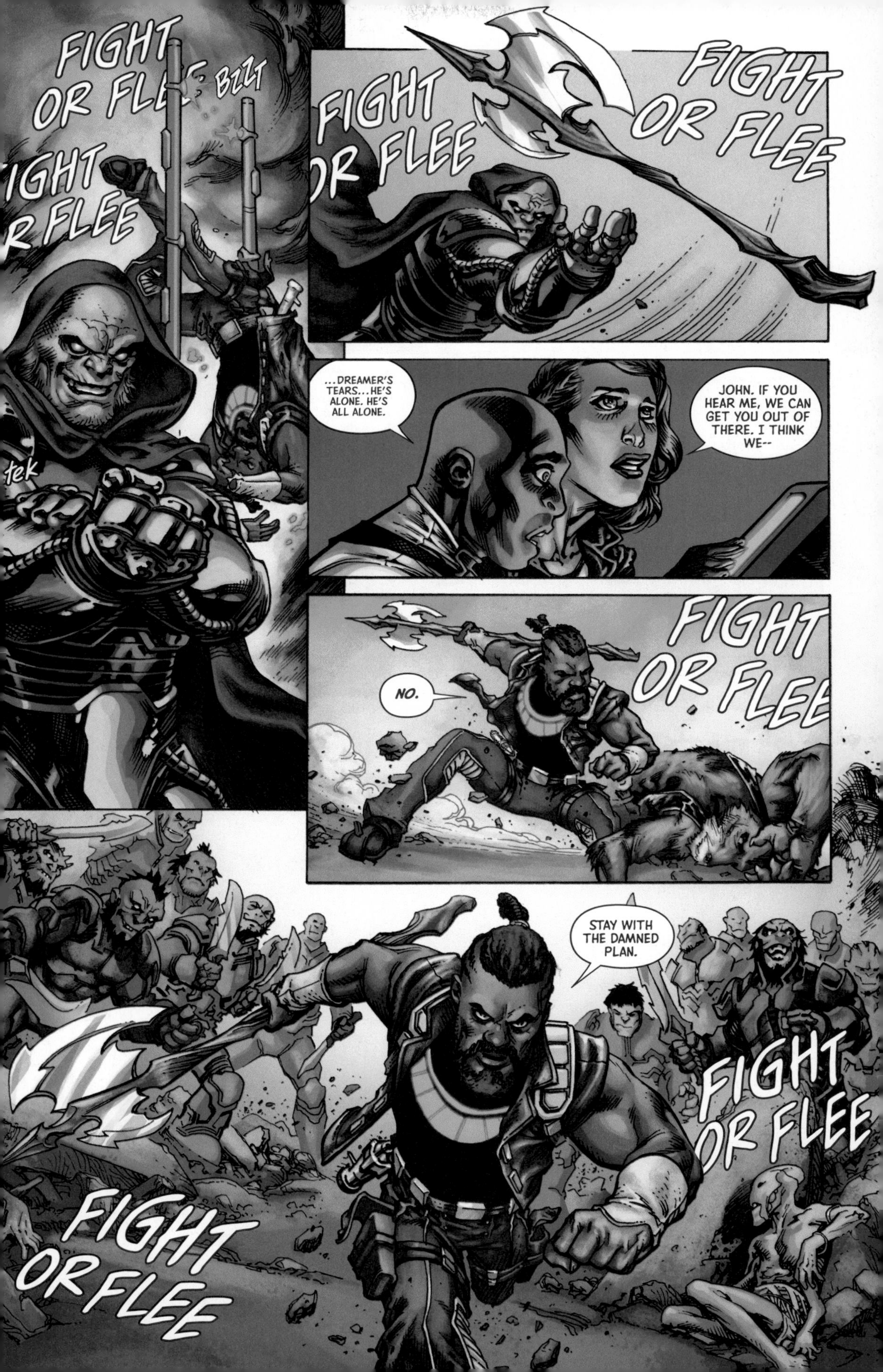

FIGHT OR FLEE
BZZT
FIGHT OR FLEE
tek
FIGHT OR FLEE
FIGHT OR FLEE
...DREAMER'S TEARS...HE'S ALONE. HE'S ALL ALONE.
JOHN. IF YOU HEAR ME, WE CAN GET YOU OUT OF THERE. I THINK WE--
FIGHT OR FLEE
NO.
STAY WITH THE DAMNED PLAN.
FIGHT OR FLEE
FIGHT OR FLEE

ACOLYTES! HUNT!

ILO. HOOD. STATUS.

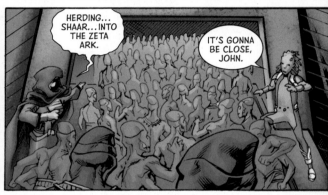

HERDING... SHAAR...INTO THE ZETA ARK.

IT'S GONNA BE CLOSE, JOHN.

STAND BY!

THERE IS...NO... TIME! SHOULD WE LET...ZETA FLIGHT GO...WITHOUT US?

JOHN, PLEASE RESPOND.

HE'S GOT FULL HANDS. I'M ON IT.

GET ALL THE SHAAR IN THE ARK!

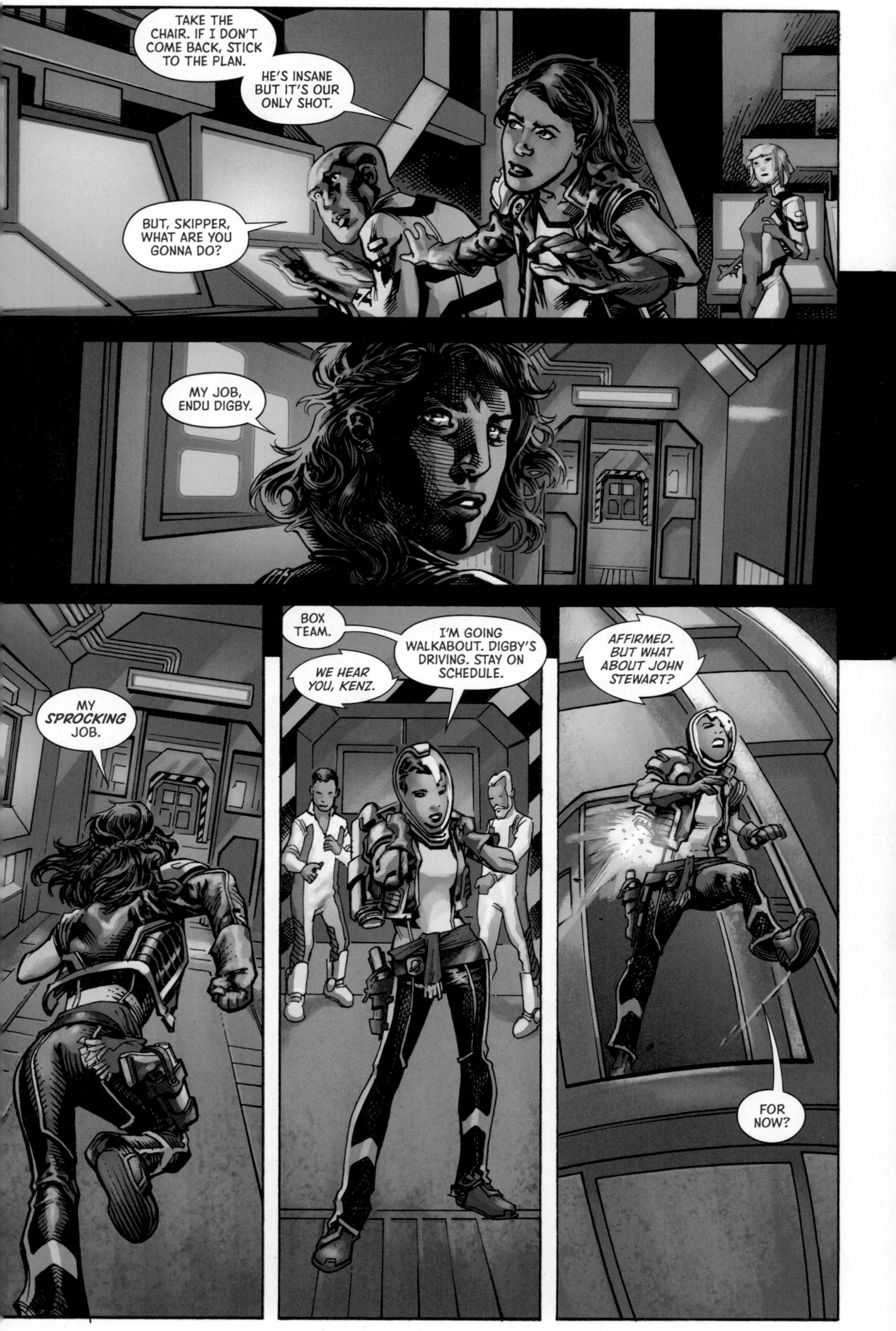
TAKE THE CHAIR. IF I DON'T COME BACK, STICK TO THE PLAN.
HE'S INSANE BUT IT'S OUR ONLY SHOT.
BUT, SKIPPER, WHAT ARE YOU GONNA DO?
MY JOB, ENDU DIGBY.
MY *SPROCKING* JOB.
BOX TEAM.
I'M GOING WALKABOUT. DIGBY'S DRIVING. STAY ON SCHEDULE.
WE HEAR YOU, KENZ.
AFFIRMED. BUT WHAT ABOUT JOHN STEWART?
FOR NOW?

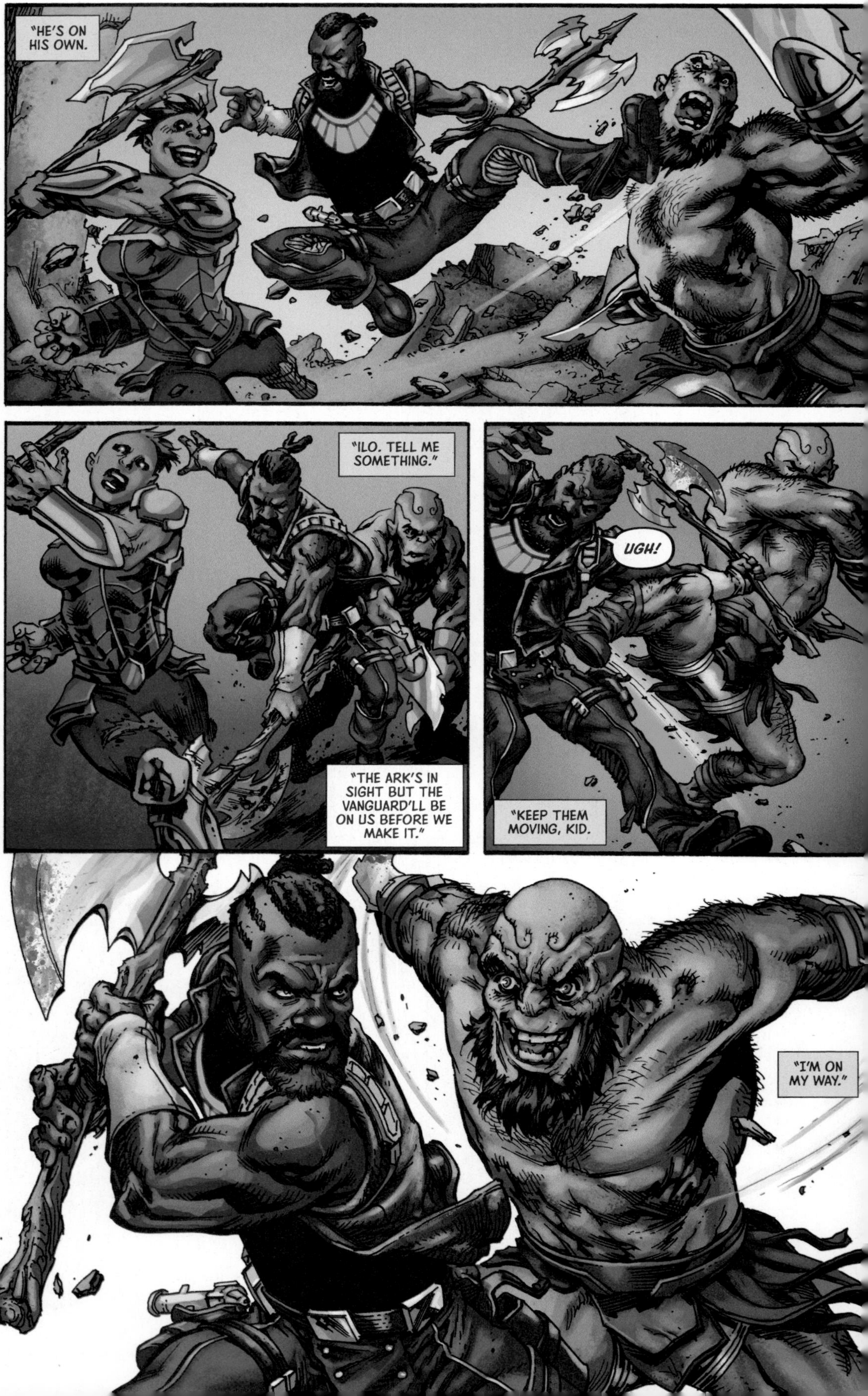
"HE'S ON HIS OWN.
"ILO. TELL ME SOMETHING."
"THE ARK'S IN SIGHT BUT THE VANGUARD'LL BE ON US BEFORE WE MAKE IT."
UGH!
"KEEP THEM MOVING, KID.
"I'M ON MY WAY."

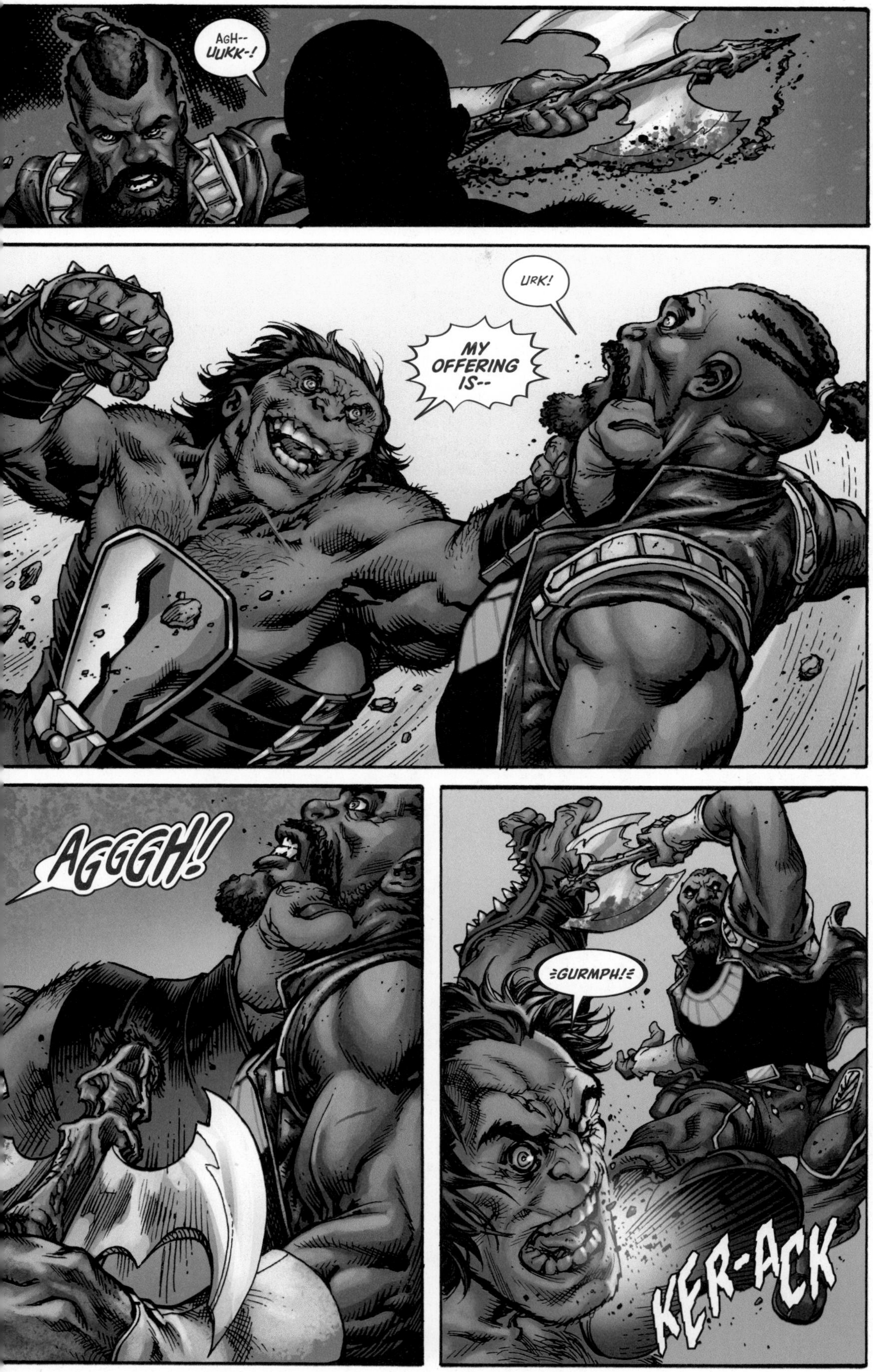
AGH--
UUKK-!
URK!
MY OFFERING IS--
AGGGH!
=GURMPH!=
KER-ACK

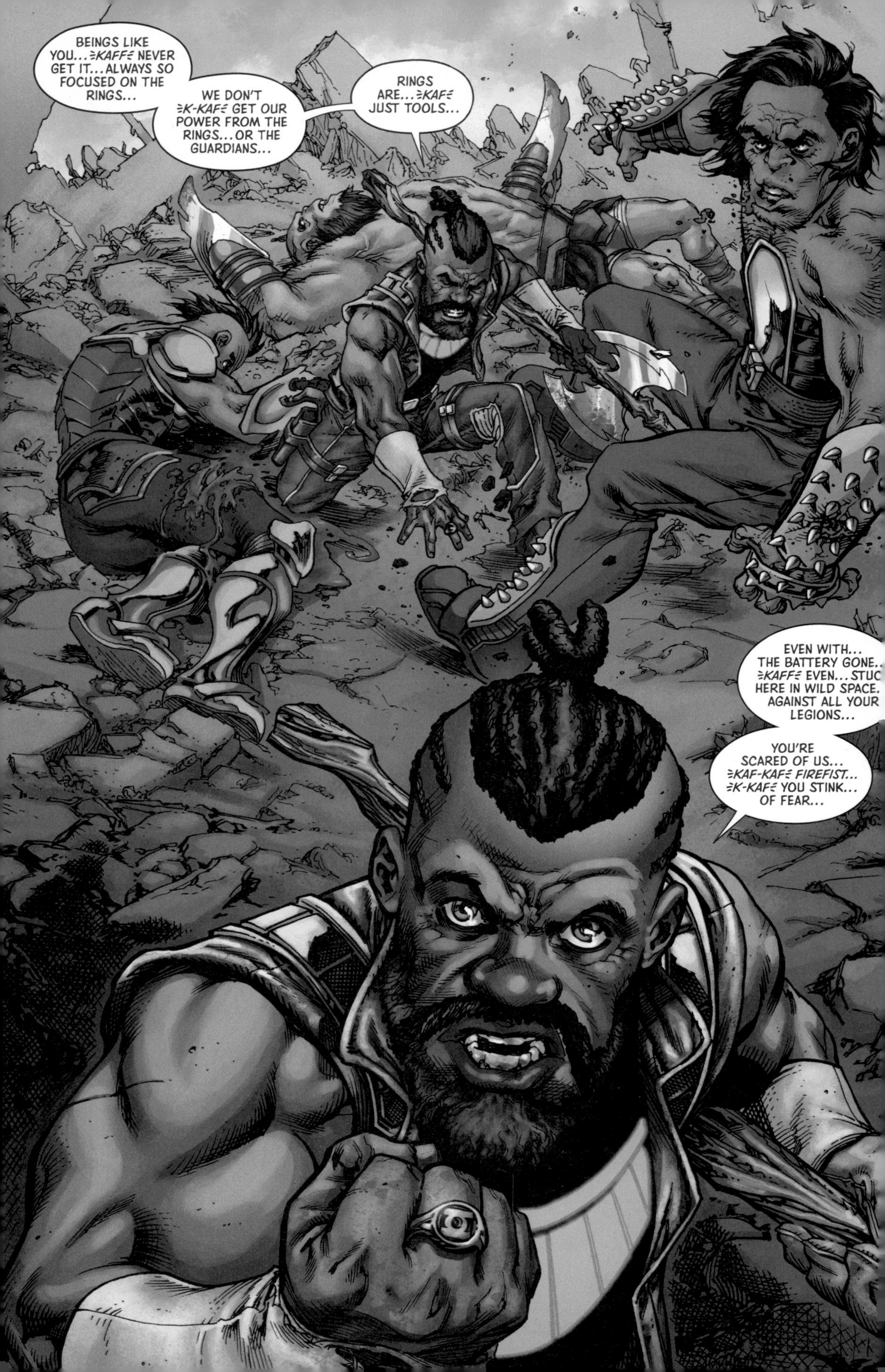
BEINGS LIKE YOU... ≡KAFF≡ NEVER GET IT... ALWAYS SO FOCUSED ON THE RINGS...
WE DON'T ≡K-KAF≡ GET OUR POWER FROM THE RINGS... OR THE GUARDIANS...
RINGS ARE... ≡KAF≡ JUST TOOLS...
EVEN WITH... THE BATTERY GONE... ≡KAFF≡ EVEN... STUC HERE IN WILD SPACE. AGAINST ALL YOUR LEGIONS...
YOU'RE SCARED OF US... ≡KAF-KAF≡ FIREFIST... ≡K-KAF≡ YOU STINK... OF FEAR...

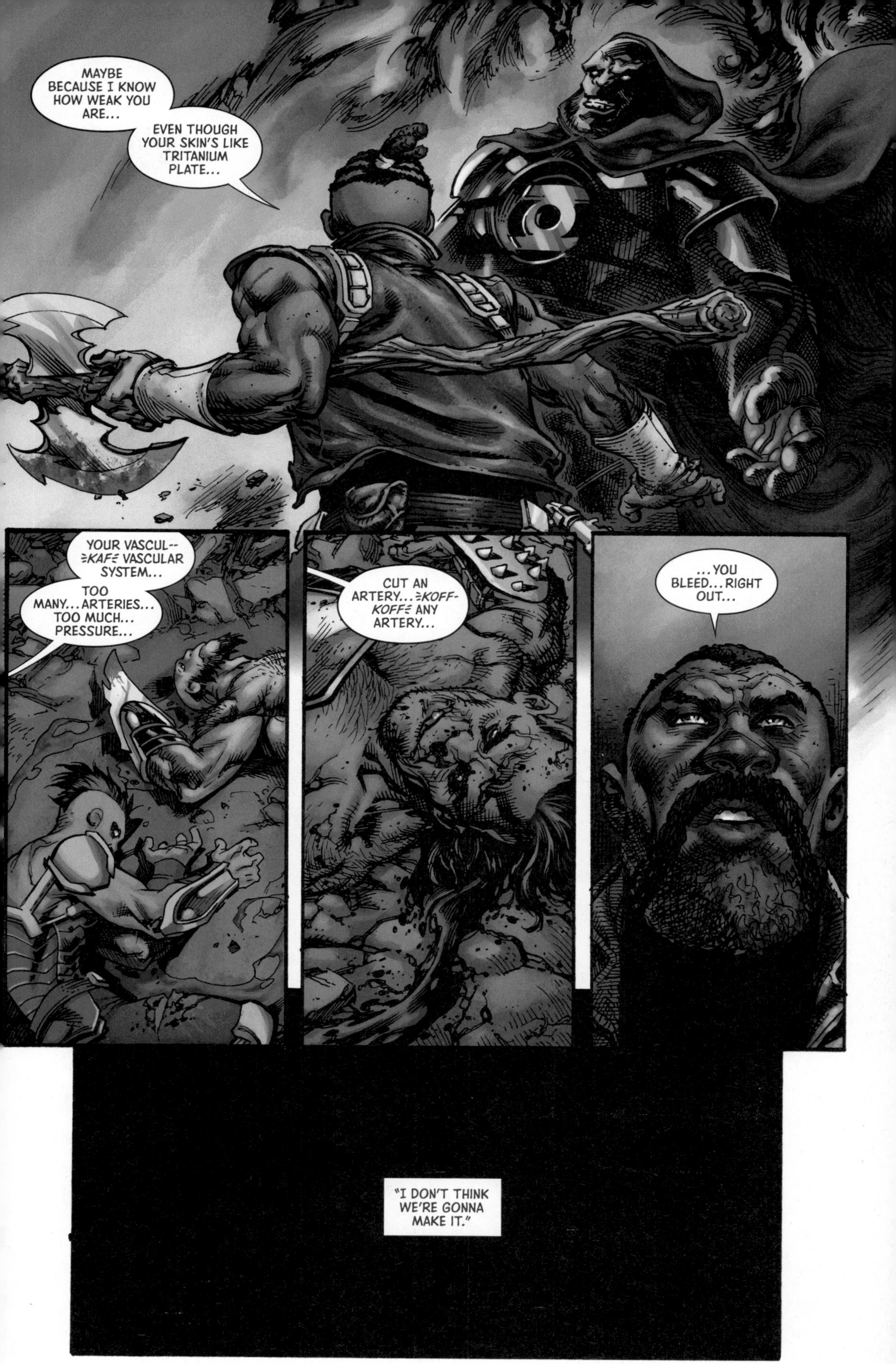
MAYBE BECAUSE I KNOW HOW WEAK YOU ARE...
EVEN THOUGH YOUR SKIN'S LIKE TRITANIUM PLATE...
YOUR VASCUL-- ≡KAF≡ VASCULAR SYSTEM...
TOO MANY...ARTERIES... TOO MUCH... PRESSURE...
CUT AN ARTERY...≡KOFF-KOFF≡ ANY ARTERY...
...YOU BLEED...RIGHT OUT...
"I DON'T THINK WE'RE GONNA MAKE IT."

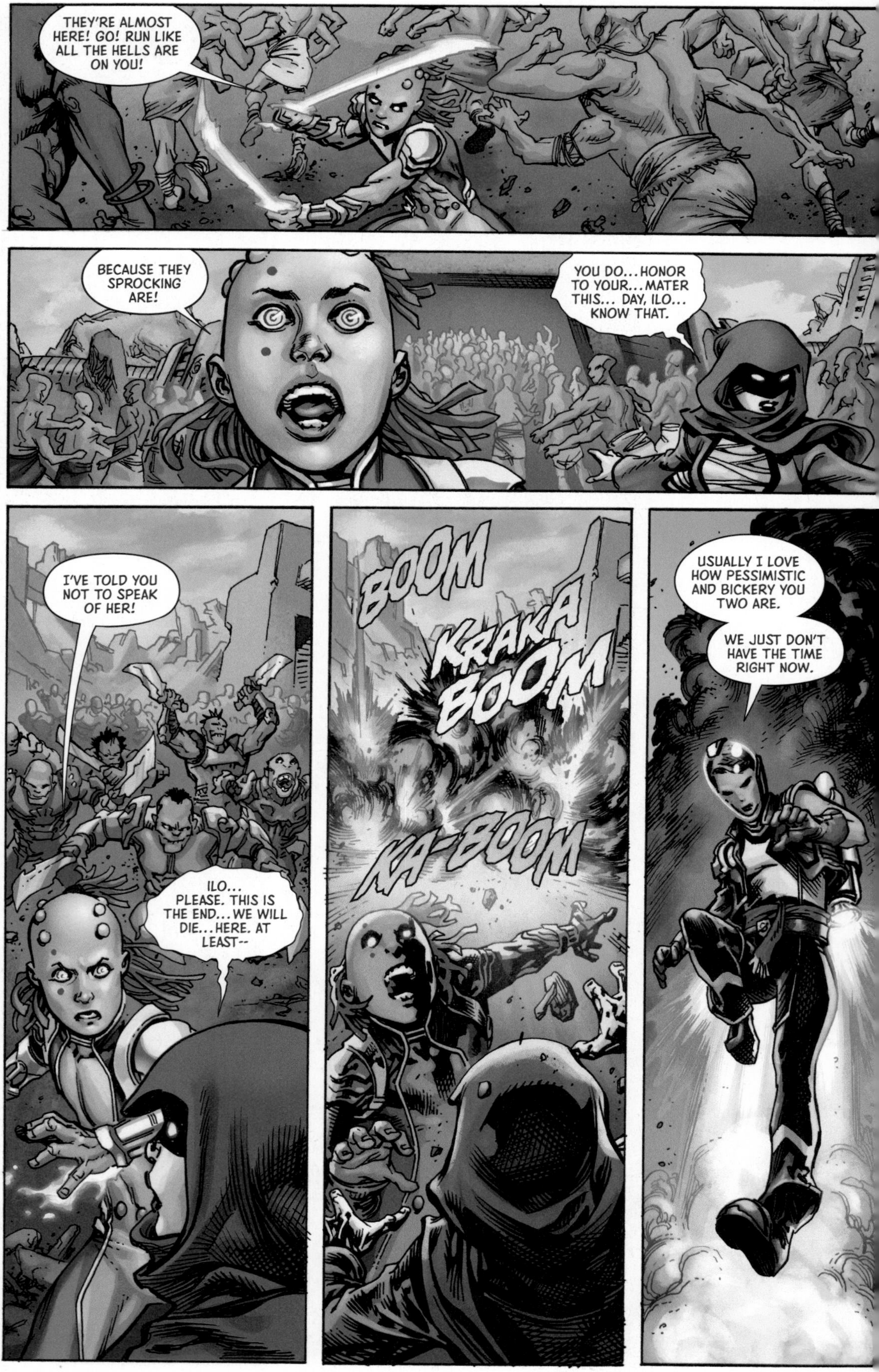
THEY'RE ALMOST HERE! GO! RUN LIKE ALL THE HELLS ARE ON YOU!
BECAUSE THEY SPROCKING ARE!
YOU DO... HONOR TO YOUR... MATER THIS... DAY, ILO... KNOW THAT.
I'VE TOLD YOU NOT TO SPEAK OF HER!
ILO... PLEASE. THIS IS THE END... WE WILL DIE... HERE. AT LEAST--
BOOM
KRAKA BOOM
KA-BOOM
USUALLY I LOVE HOW PESSIMISTIC AND BICKERY YOU TWO ARE.
WE JUST DON'T HAVE THE TIME RIGHT NOW.

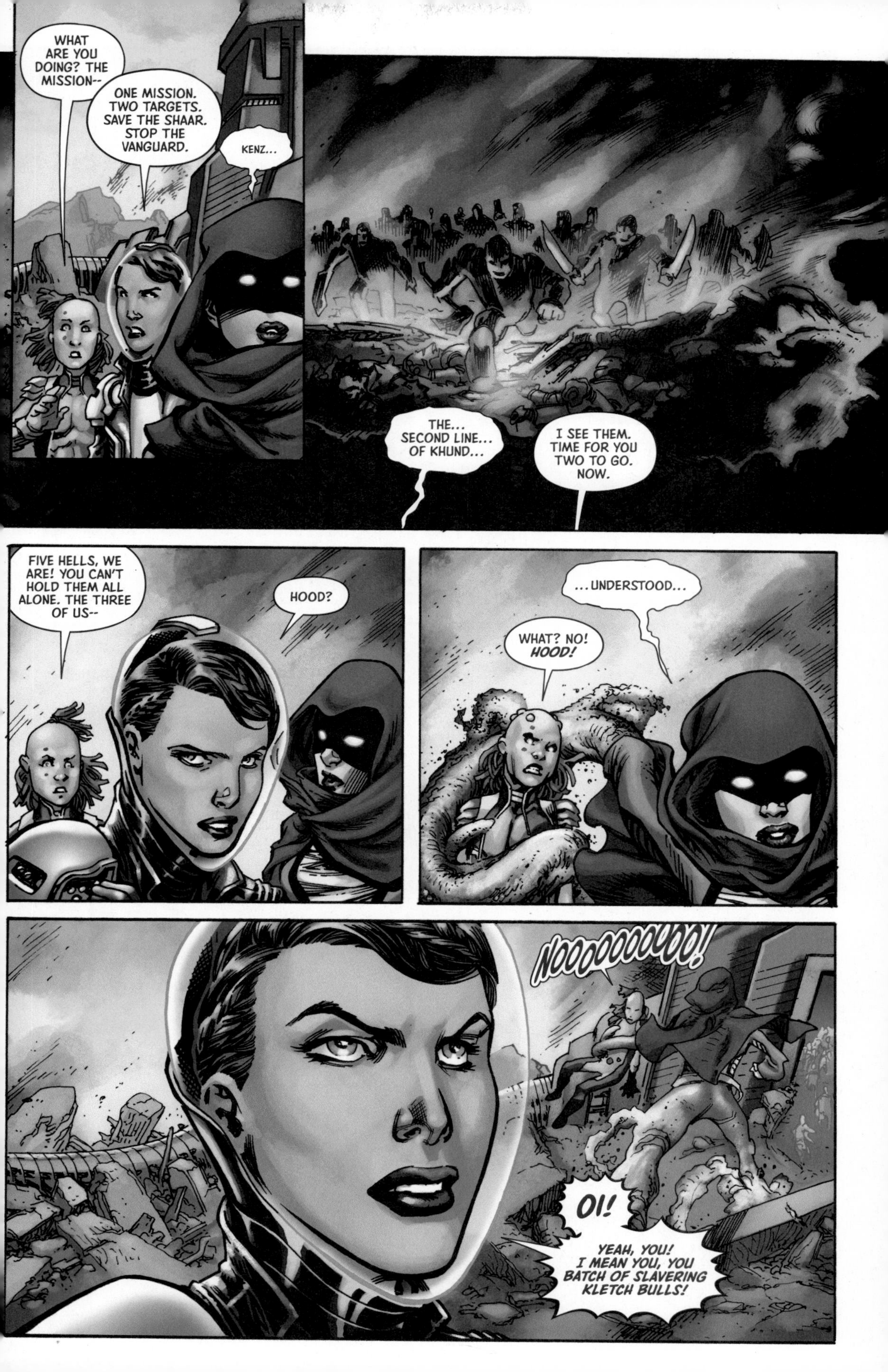
WHAT ARE YOU DOING? THE MISSION--
ONE MISSION. TWO TARGETS. SAVE THE SHAAR. STOP THE VANGUARD.
KENZ...
THE... SECOND LINE... OF KHUND...
I SEE THEM. TIME FOR YOU TWO TO GO. NOW.
FIVE HELLS, WE ARE! YOU CAN'T HOLD THEM ALL ALONE. THE THREE OF US--
HOOD?
...UNDERSTOOD...
WHAT? NO! *HOOD!*
NOOOOOOOOOO!
OI!
YEAH, YOU! I MEAN YOU, YOU BATCH OF SLAVERING KLETCH BULLS!

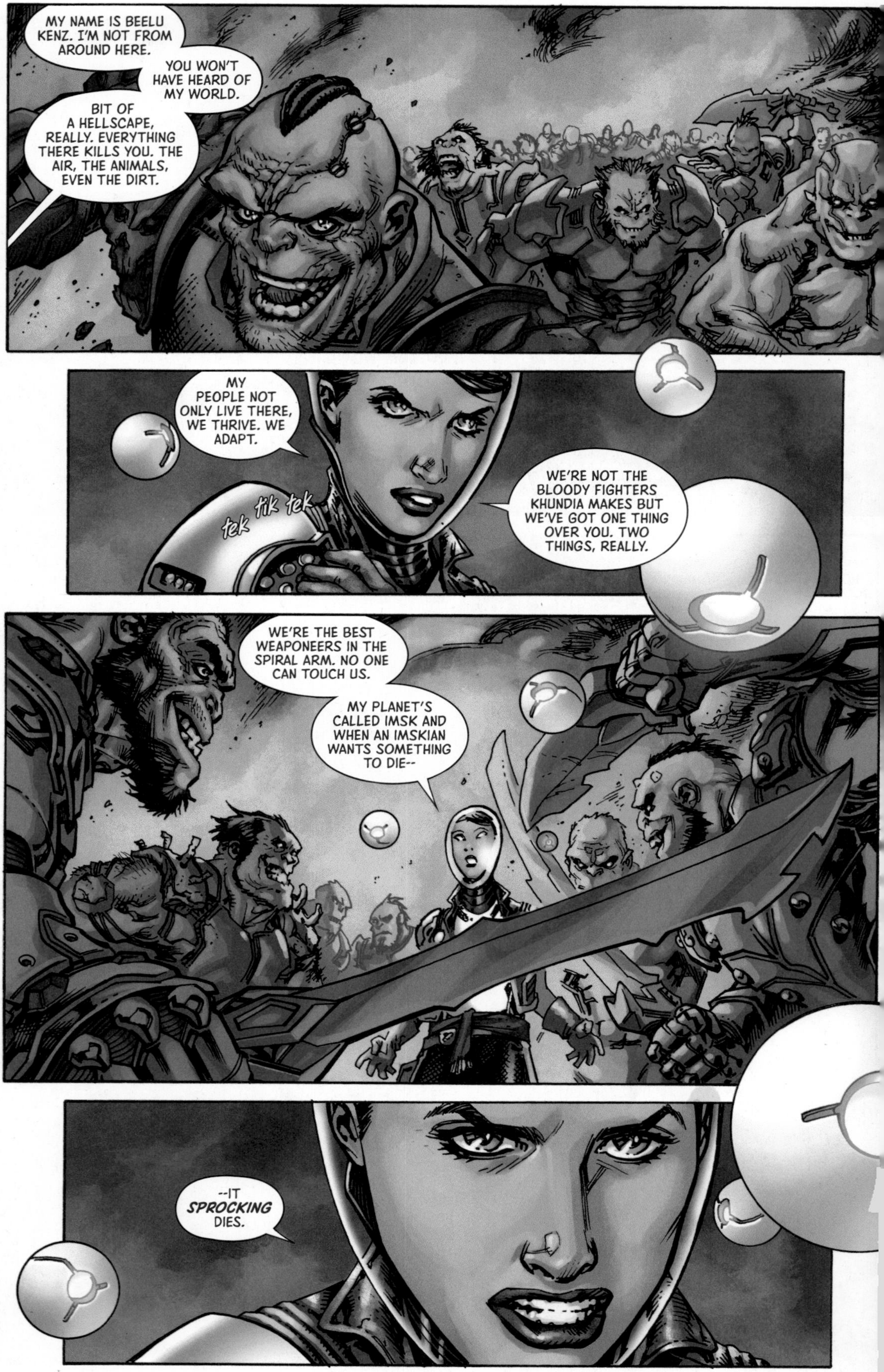
MY NAME IS BEELU KENZ. I'M NOT FROM AROUND HERE.
YOU WON'T HAVE HEARD OF MY WORLD.
BIT OF A HELLSCAPE, REALLY. EVERYTHING THERE KILLS YOU. THE AIR, THE ANIMALS, EVEN THE DIRT.
MY PEOPLE NOT ONLY LIVE THERE, WE THRIVE. WE ADAPT.
tek tik tek
WE'RE NOT THE BLOODY FIGHTERS KHUNDIA MAKES BUT WE'VE GOT ONE THING OVER YOU. TWO THINGS, REALLY.
WE'RE THE BEST WEAPONEERS IN THE SPIRAL ARM. NO ONE CAN TOUCH US.
MY PLANET'S CALLED IMSK AND WHEN AN IMSKIAN WANTS SOMETHING TO DIE--
--IT SPROCKING DIES.

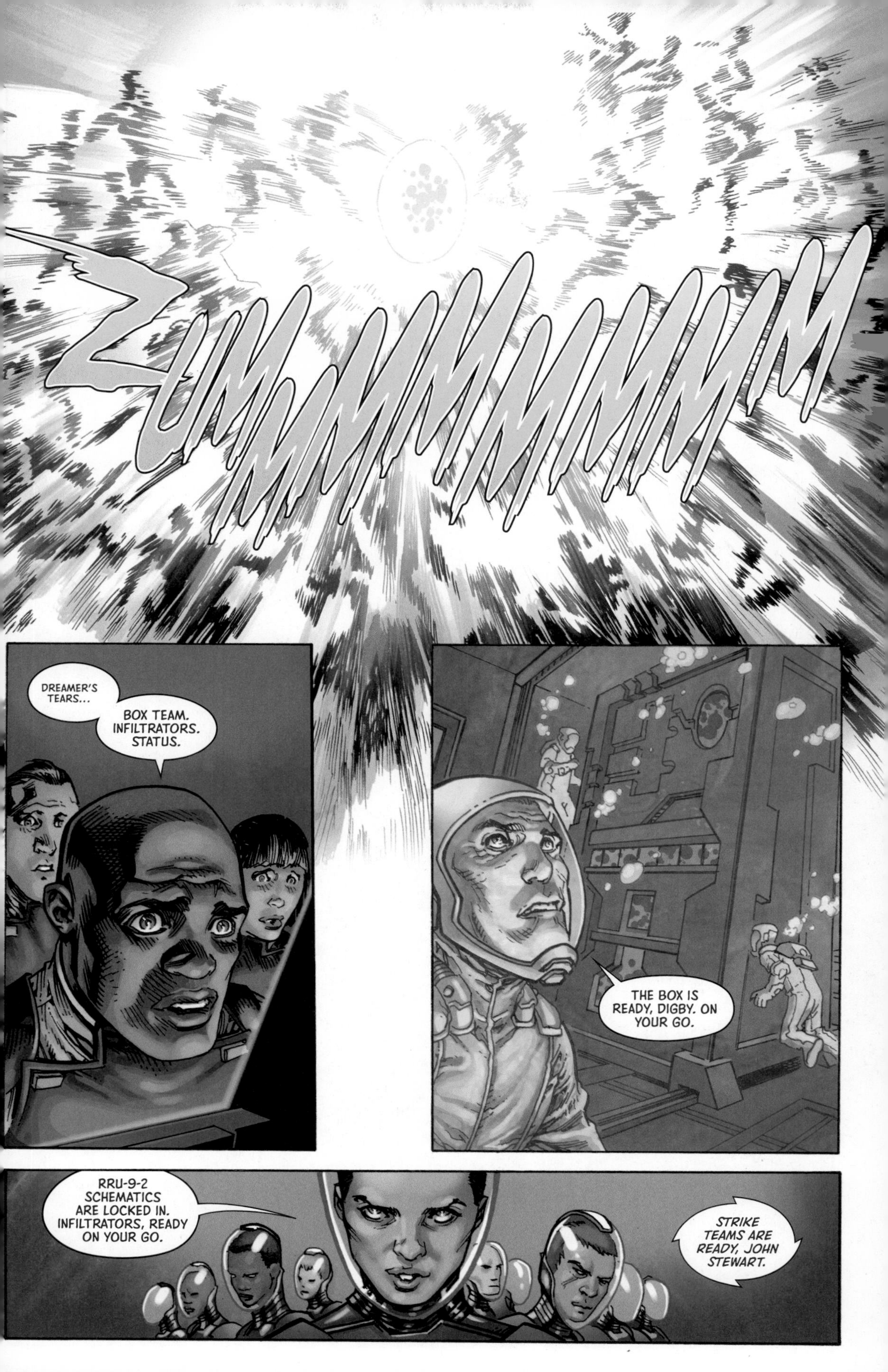
ZUMMMMMMMMMMMM
DREAMER'S TEARS...
BOX TEAM. INFILTRATORS. STATUS.
THE BOX IS READY, DIGBY. ON YOUR GO.
RRU-9-2 SCHEMATICS ARE LOCKED IN. INFILTRATORS, READY ON YOUR GO.
STRIKE TEAMS ARE READY, JOHN STEWART.

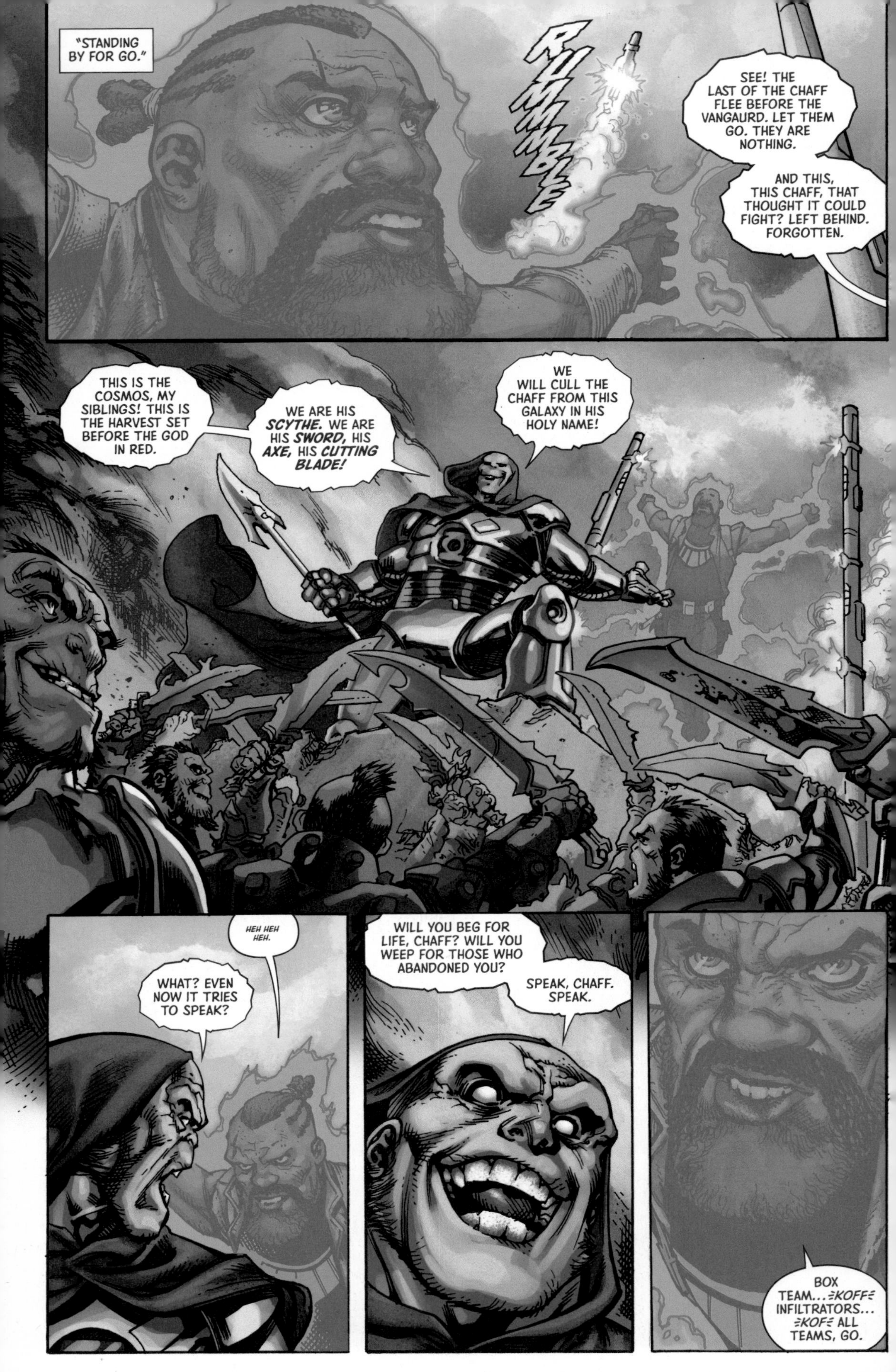
"STANDING BY FOR GO."
RUMMMBLE
SEE! THE LAST OF THE CHAFF FLEE BEFORE THE VANGAURD. LET THEM GO. THEY ARE NOTHING.
AND THIS, THIS CHAFF, THAT THOUGHT IT COULD FIGHT? LEFT BEHIND. FORGOTTEN.
THIS IS THE COSMOS, MY SIBLINGS! THIS IS THE HARVEST SET BEFORE THE GOD IN RED.
WE ARE HIS *SCYTHE.* WE ARE HIS *SWORD,* HIS *AXE,* HIS *CUTTING BLADE!*
WE WILL CULL THE CHAFF FROM THIS GALAXY IN HIS HOLY NAME!
HEH HEH HEH.
WHAT? EVEN NOW IT TRIES TO SPEAK?
WILL YOU BEG FOR LIFE, CHAFF? WILL YOU WEEP FOR THOSE WHO ABANDONED YOU?
SPEAK, CHAFF. SPEAK.
BOX TEAM... *KOFF* INFILTRATORS... *KOFF* ALL TEAMS, GO.

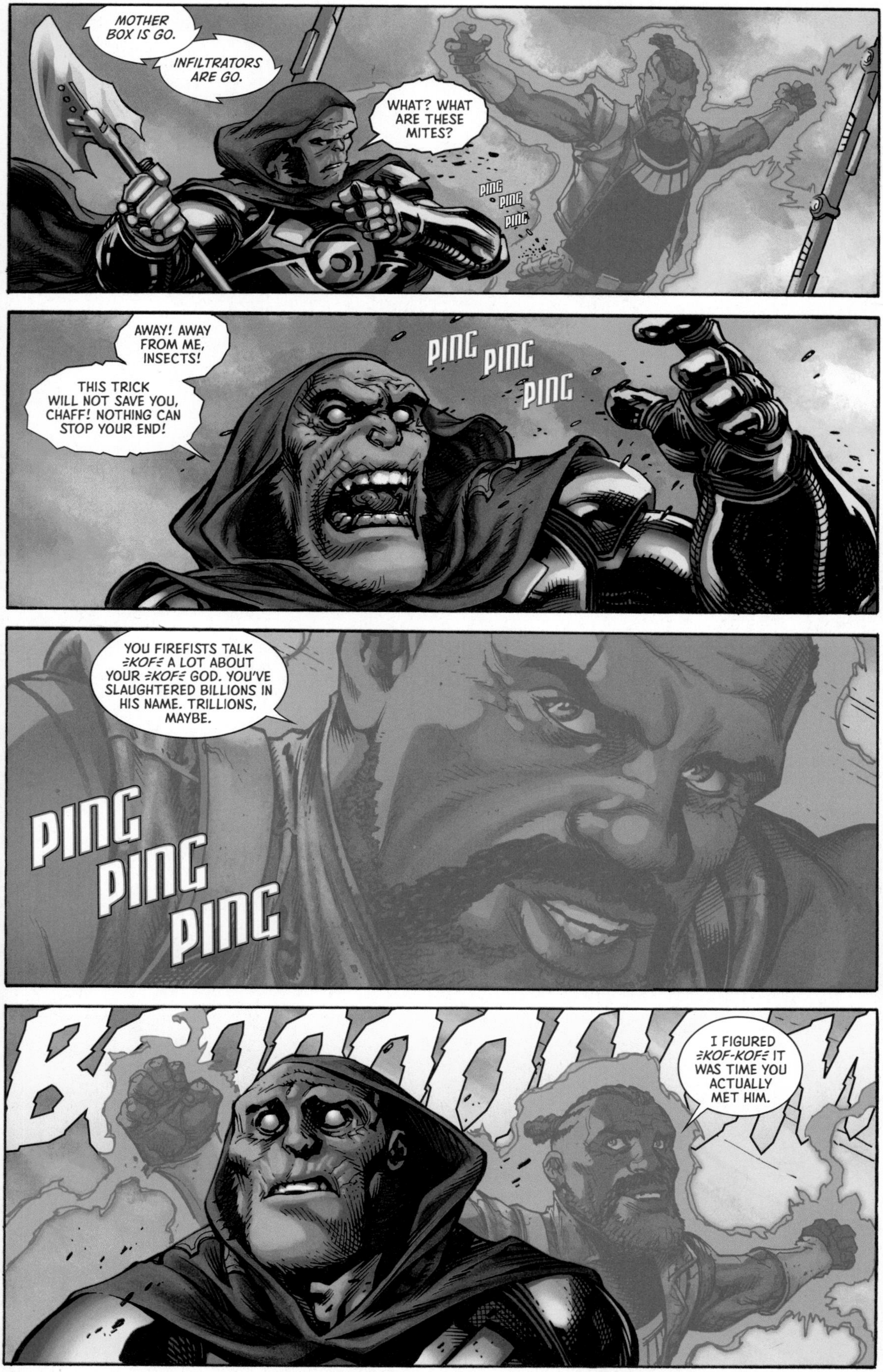

MOTHER BOX IS GO.
INFILTRATORS ARE GO.
WHAT? WHAT ARE THESE MITES?
PING PING PING
AWAY! AWAY FROM ME, INSECTS!
THIS TRICK WILL NOT SAVE YOU, CHAFF! NOTHING CAN STOP YOUR END!
PING PING PING
YOU FIREFISTS TALK =KOF= A LOT ABOUT YOUR =KOF= GOD. YOU'VE SLAUGHTERED BILLIONS IN HIS NAME. TRILLIONS, MAYBE.
PING PING PING
I FIGURED =KOF-KOF= IT WAS TIME YOU ACTUALLY MET HIM.

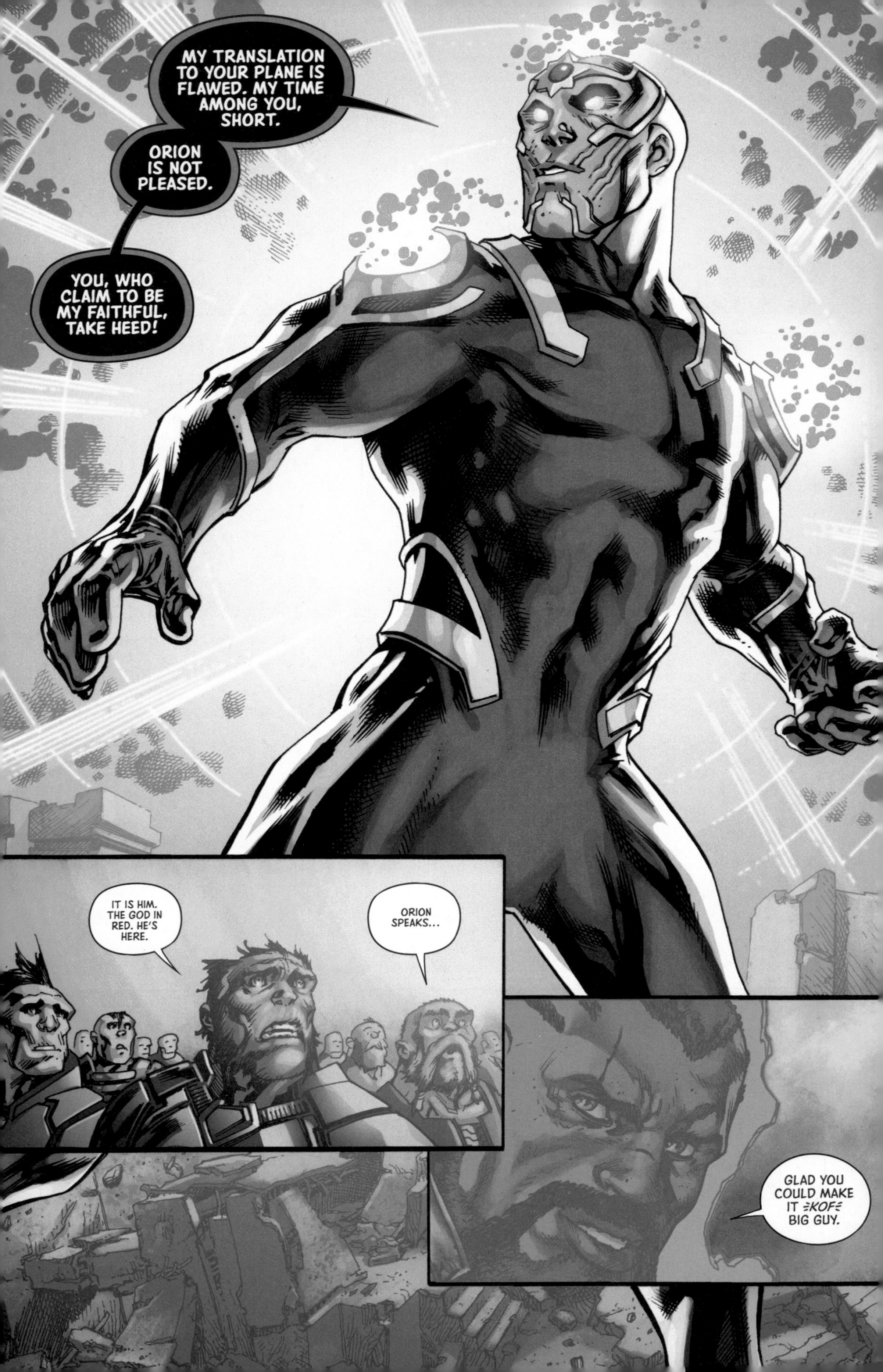
MY TRANSLATION TO YOUR PLANE IS FLAWED. MY TIME AMONG YOU, SHORT.
ORION IS NOT PLEASED.
YOU, WHO CLAIM TO BE MY FAITHFUL, TAKE HEED!
IT IS HIM. THE GOD IN RED. HE'S HERE.
ORION SPEAKS...
GLAD YOU COULD MAKE IT *KOF* BIG GUY.

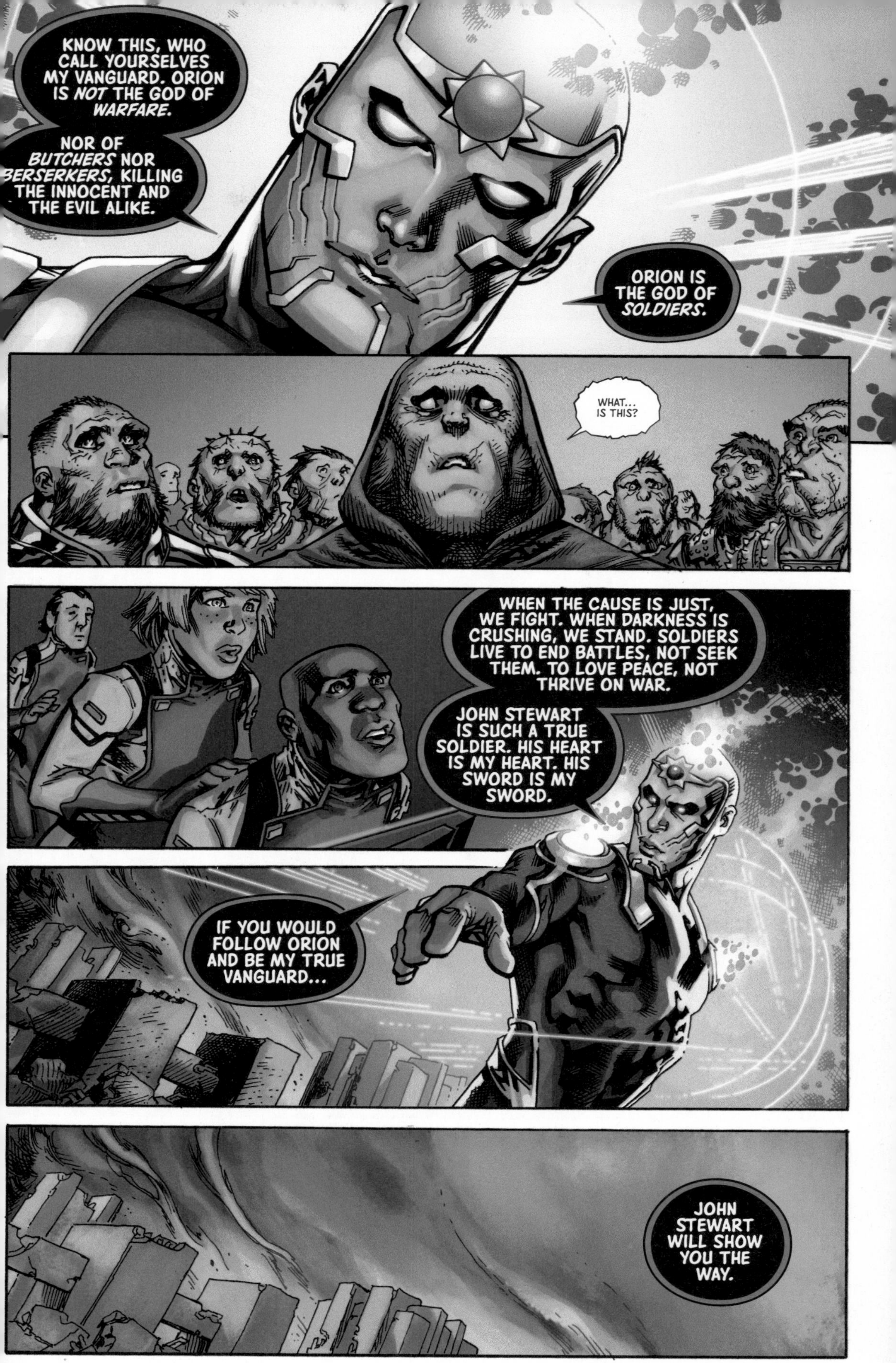
KNOW THIS, WHO CALL YOURSELVES MY VANGUARD. ORION IS *NOT* THE GOD OF *WARFARE.*
NOR OF *BUTCHERS* NOR *BERSERKERS,* KILLING THE INNOCENT AND THE EVIL ALIKE.
ORION IS THE GOD OF *SOLDIERS.*
WHAT... IS THIS?
WHEN THE CAUSE IS JUST, WE FIGHT. WHEN DARKNESS IS CRUSHING, WE STAND. SOLDIERS LIVE TO END BATTLES, NOT SEEK THEM. TO LOVE PEACE, NOT THRIVE ON WAR.
JOHN STEWART IS SUCH A TRUE SOLDIER. HIS HEART IS MY HEART. HIS SWORD IS MY SWORD.
IF YOU WOULD FOLLOW ORION AND BE MY TRUE VANGUARD...
JOHN STEWART WILL SHOW YOU THE WAY.

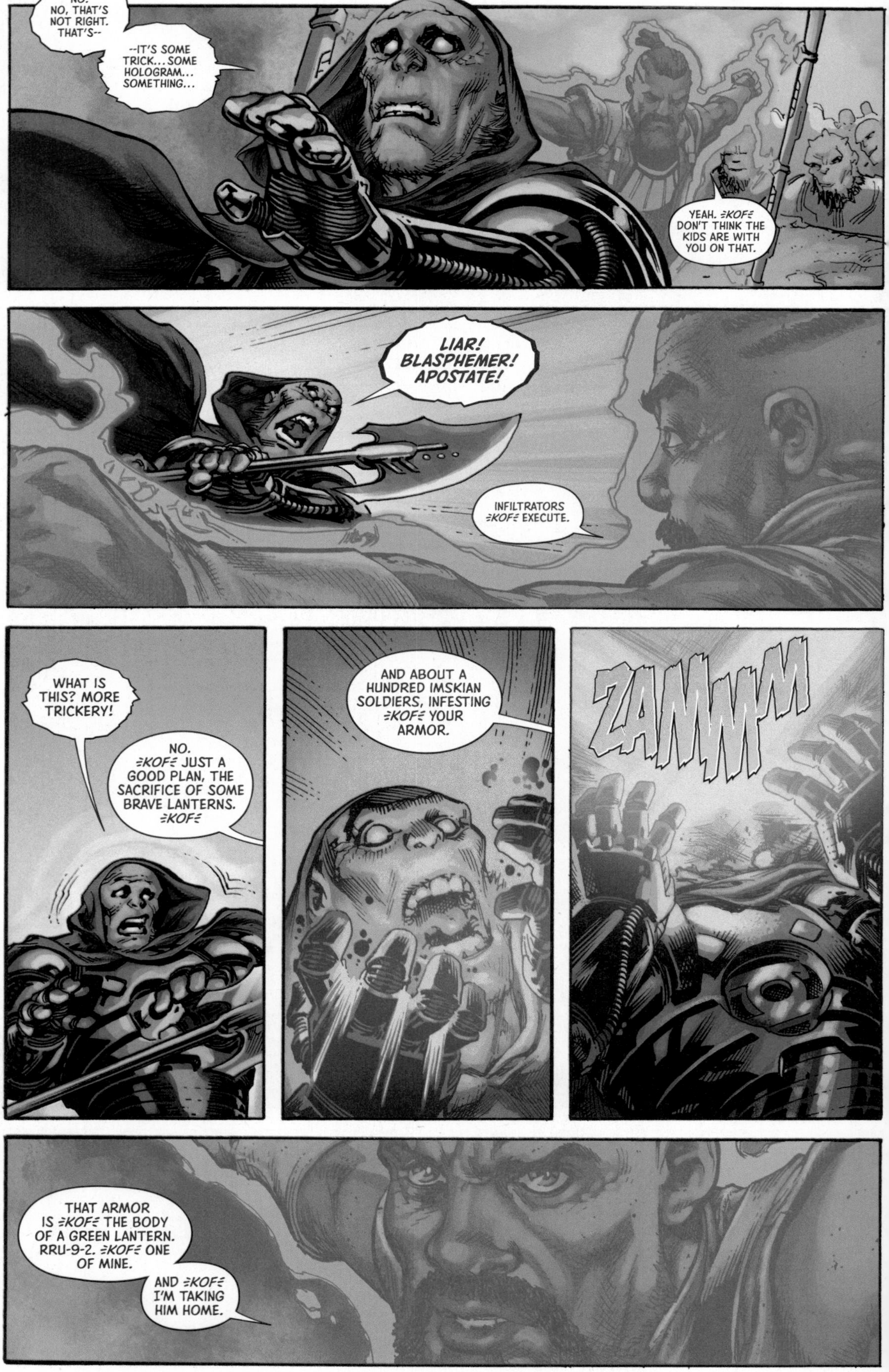
NO. NO, THAT'S NOT RIGHT. THAT'S--
--IT'S SOME TRICK... SOME HOLOGRAM... SOMETHING...
YEAH. =KOF= DON'T THINK THE KIDS ARE WITH YOU ON THAT.
LIAR! BLASPHEMER! APOSTATE!
INFILTRATORS =KOF= EXECUTE.
WHAT IS THIS? MORE TRICKERY!
NO. =KOF= JUST A GOOD PLAN, THE SACRIFICE OF SOME BRAVE LANTERNS. =KOF=
AND ABOUT A HUNDRED IMSKIAN SOLDIERS, INFESTING =KOF= YOUR ARMOR.
ZAMMM
THAT ARMOR IS =KOF= THE BODY OF A GREEN LANTERN. RRU-9-2. =KOF= ONE OF MINE.
AND =KOF= I'M TAKING HIM HOME.

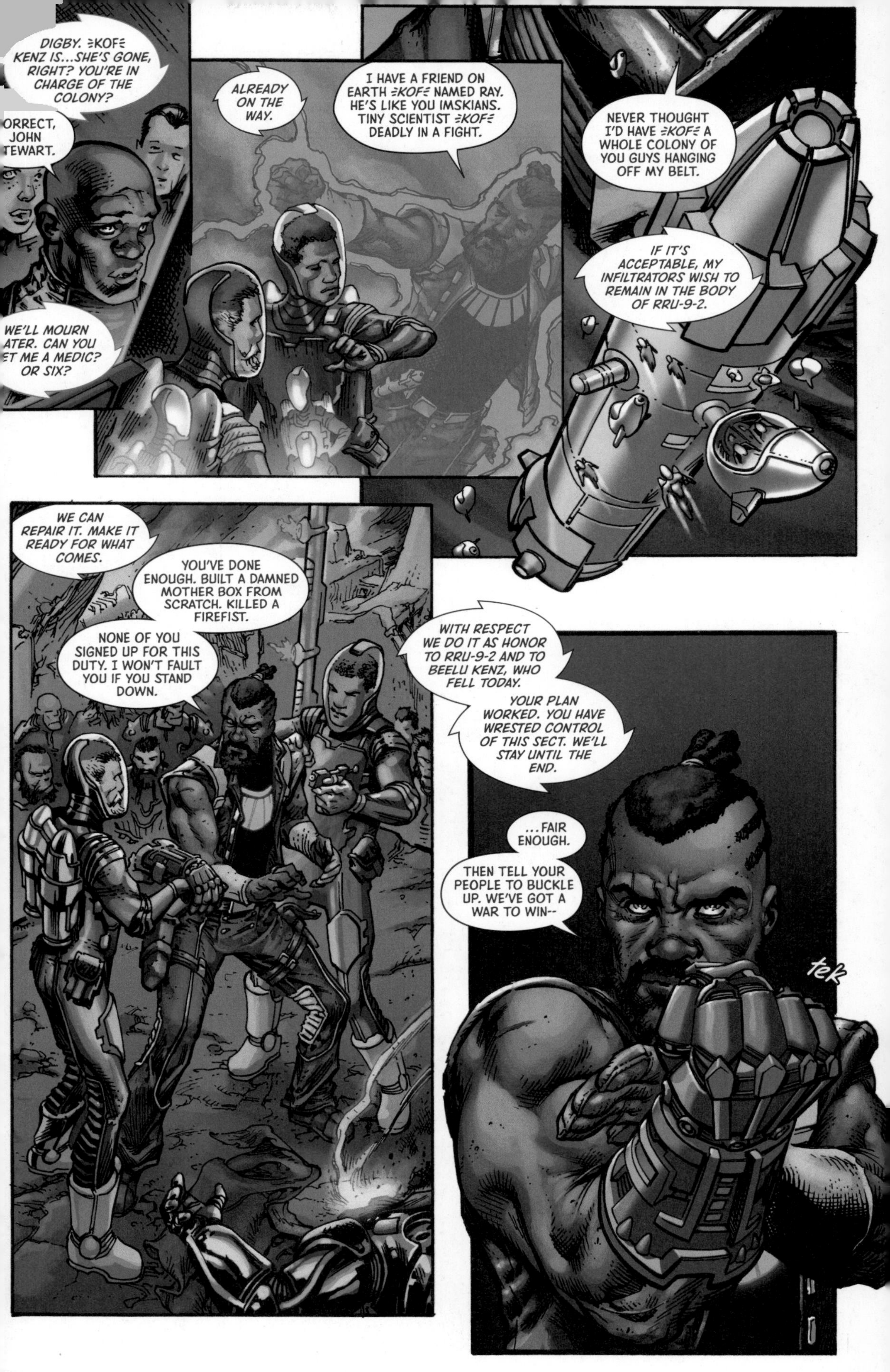
DIGBY. ≡KOF≡ KENZ IS...SHE'S GONE, RIGHT? YOU'RE IN CHARGE OF THE COLONY?
ORRECT, JOHN TEWART.
WE'LL MOURN ATER. CAN YOU T ME A MEDIC? OR SIX?
ALREADY ON THE WAY.
I HAVE A FRIEND ON EARTH ≡KOF≡ NAMED RAY. HE'S LIKE YOU IMSKIANS. TINY SCIENTIST ≡KOF≡ DEADLY IN A FIGHT.
NEVER THOUGHT I'D HAVE ≡KOF≡ A WHOLE COLONY OF YOU GUYS HANGING OFF MY BELT.
IF IT'S ACCEPTABLE, MY INFILTRATORS WISH TO REMAIN IN THE BODY OF RRU-9-2.
WE CAN REPAIR IT. MAKE IT READY FOR WHAT COMES.
YOU'VE DONE ENOUGH. BUILT A DAMNED MOTHER BOX FROM SCRATCH. KILLED A FIREFIST.
NONE OF YOU SIGNED UP FOR THIS DUTY. I WON'T FAULT YOU IF YOU STAND DOWN.
WITH RESPECT WE DO IT AS HONOR TO RRU-9-2 AND TO BEELU KENZ, WHO FELL TODAY.
YOUR PLAN WORKED. YOU HAVE WRESTED CONTROL OF THIS SECT. WE'LL STAY UNTIL THE END.
...FAIR ENOUGH.
THEN TELL YOUR PEOPLE TO BUCKLE UP. WE'VE GOT A WAR TO WIN--
tek

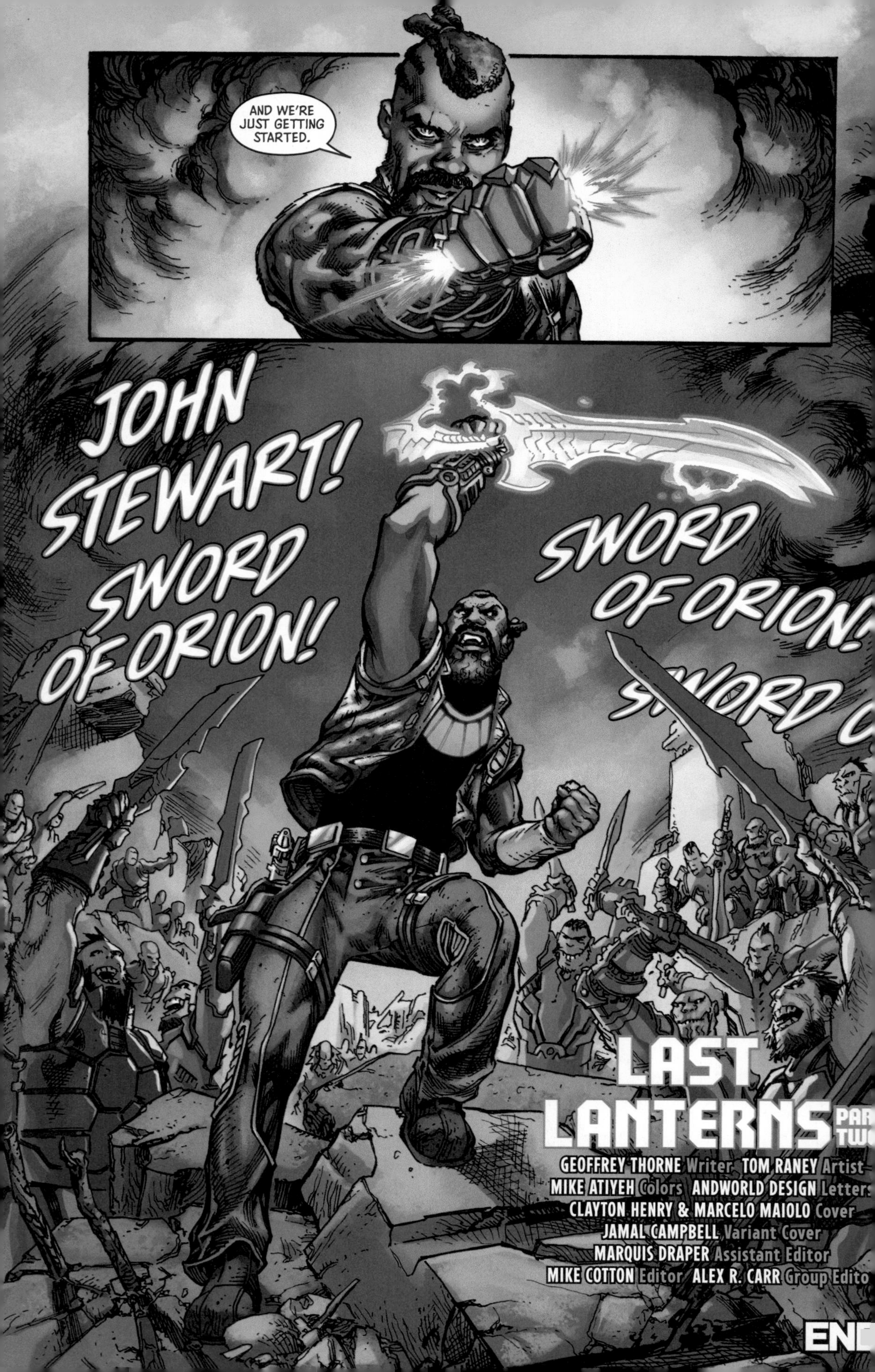

AND WE'RE JUST GETTING STARTED.
JOHN STEWART! SWORD OF ORION!
SWORD OF ORION!
SWORD O
LAST LANTERNS PART TWO
GEOFFREY THORNE Writer TOM RANEY Artist
MIKE ATIYEH Colors ANDWORLD DESIGN Letters
CLAYTON HENRY & MARCELO MAIOLO Cover
JAMAL CAMPBELL Variant Cover
MARQUIS DRAPER Assistant Editor
MIKE COTTON Editor ALEX R. CARR Group Editor
END

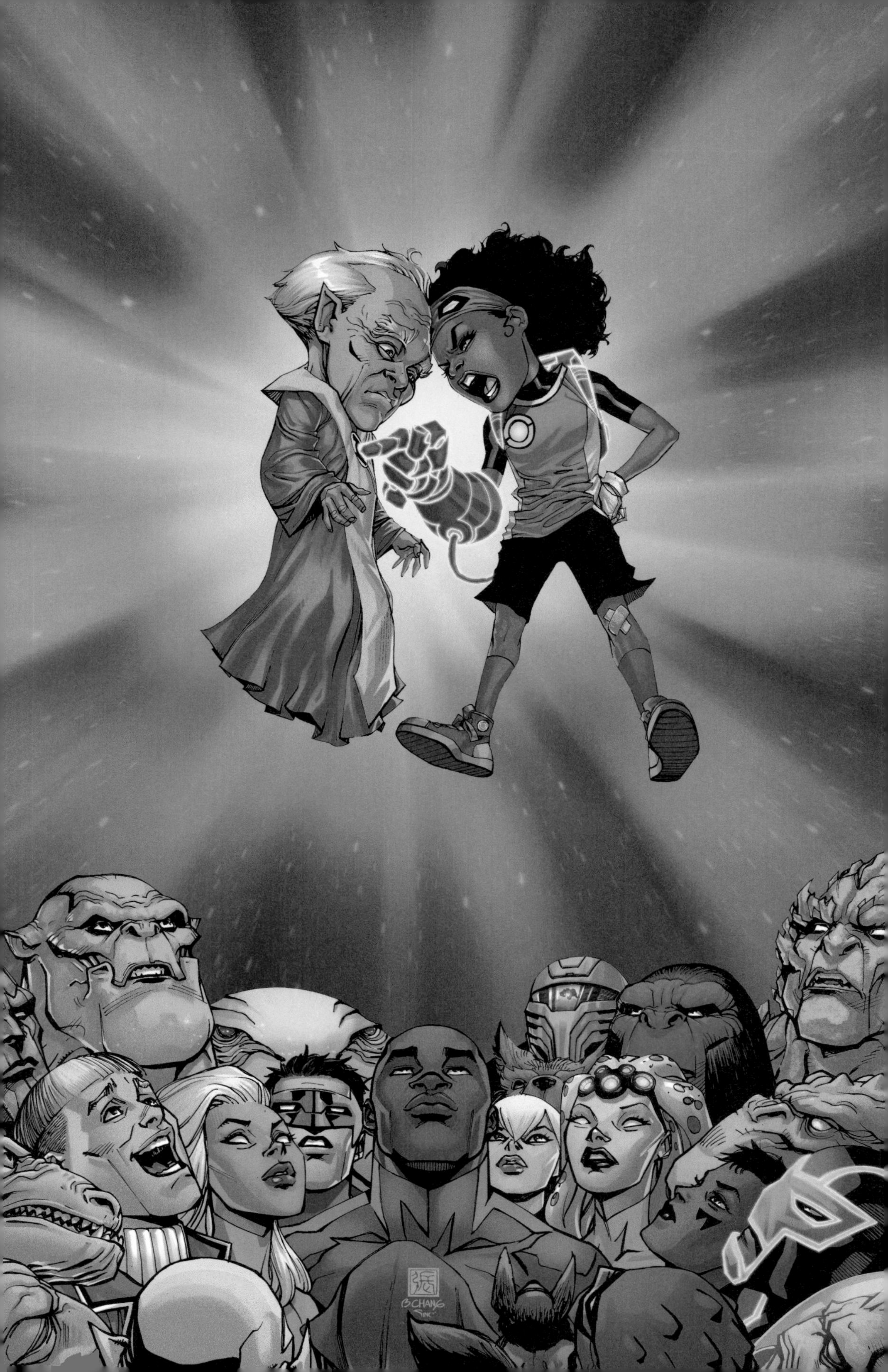

Green Lantern #1 main cover art
by Bernard Chang and Alex Sinclair

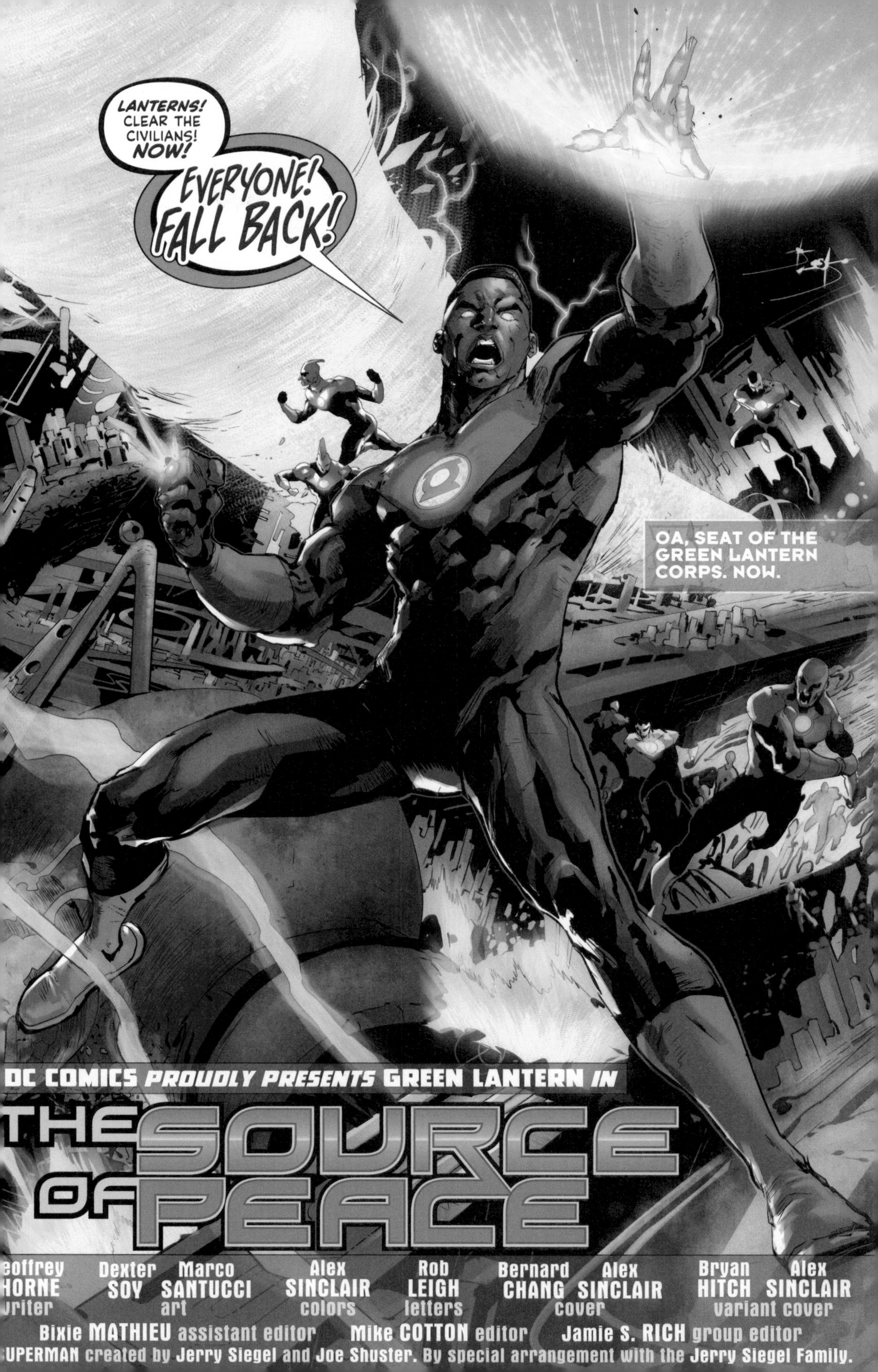
LANTERNS! CLEAR THE CIVILIANS! NOW!
EVERYONE! FALL BACK!
OA, SEAT OF THE GREEN LANTERN CORPS. NOW.
DC COMICS PROUDLY PRESENTS GREEN LANTERN IN
THE SOURCE OF PEACE
eoffrey HORNE uriter
Dexter SOY
Marco SANTUCCI art
Alex SINCLAIR colors
Rob LEIGH letters
Bernard CHANG Alex SINCLAIR cover
Bryan HITCH Alex SINCLAIR variant cover
Bixie MATHIEU assistant editor
Mike COTTON editor
Jamie S. RICH group editor
UPERMAN created by Jerry Siegel and Joe Shuster. By special arrangement with the Jerry Siegel Family.

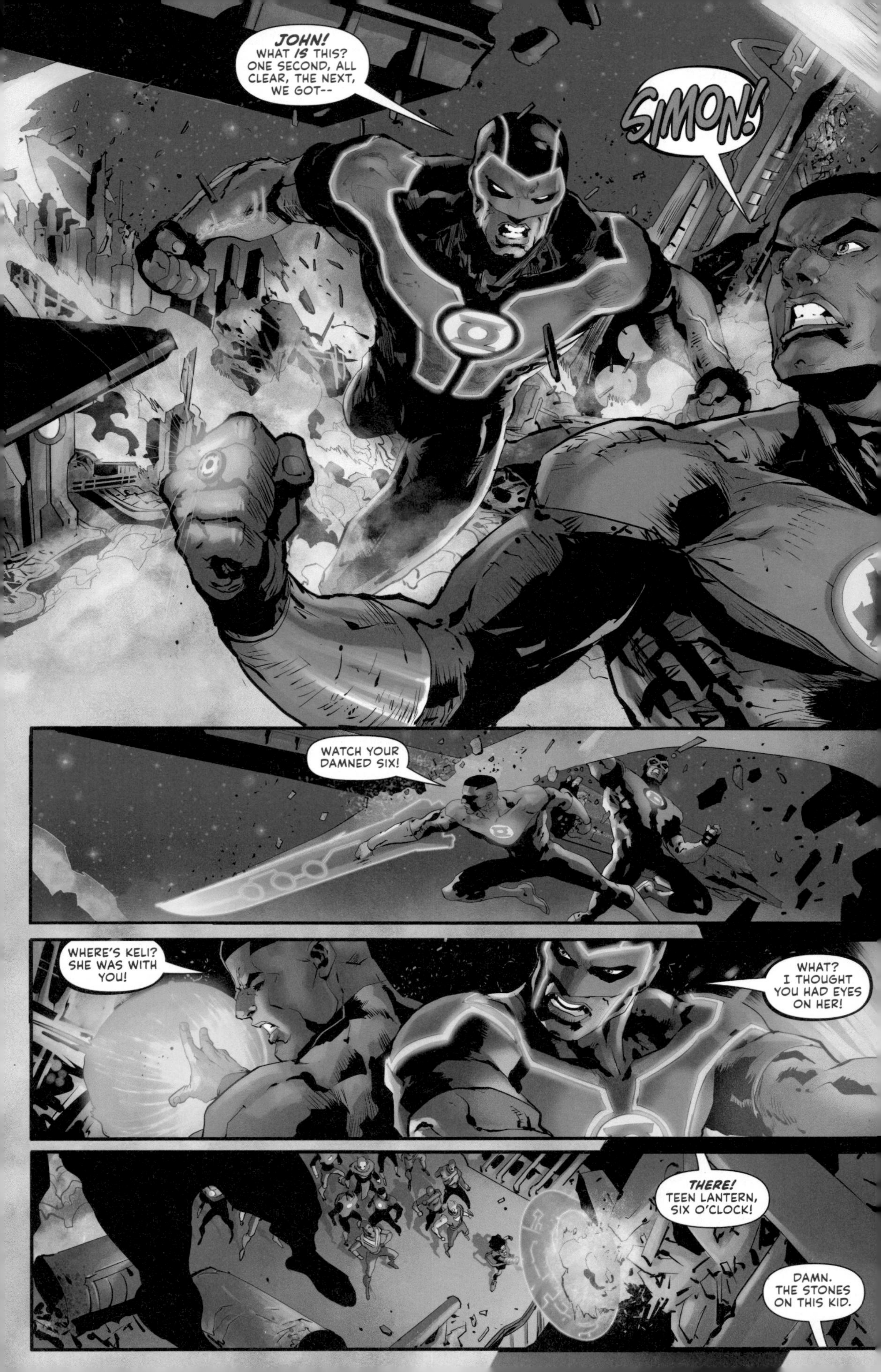
JOHN! WHAT IS THIS? ONE SECOND, ALL CLEAR, THE NEXT, WE GOT--
SIMON!
WATCH YOUR DAMNED SIX!
WHERE'S KELI? SHE WAS WITH YOU!
WHAT? I THOUGHT YOU HAD EYES ON HER!
THERE! TEEN LANTERN, SIX O'CLOCK!
DAMN. THE STONES ON THIS KID.

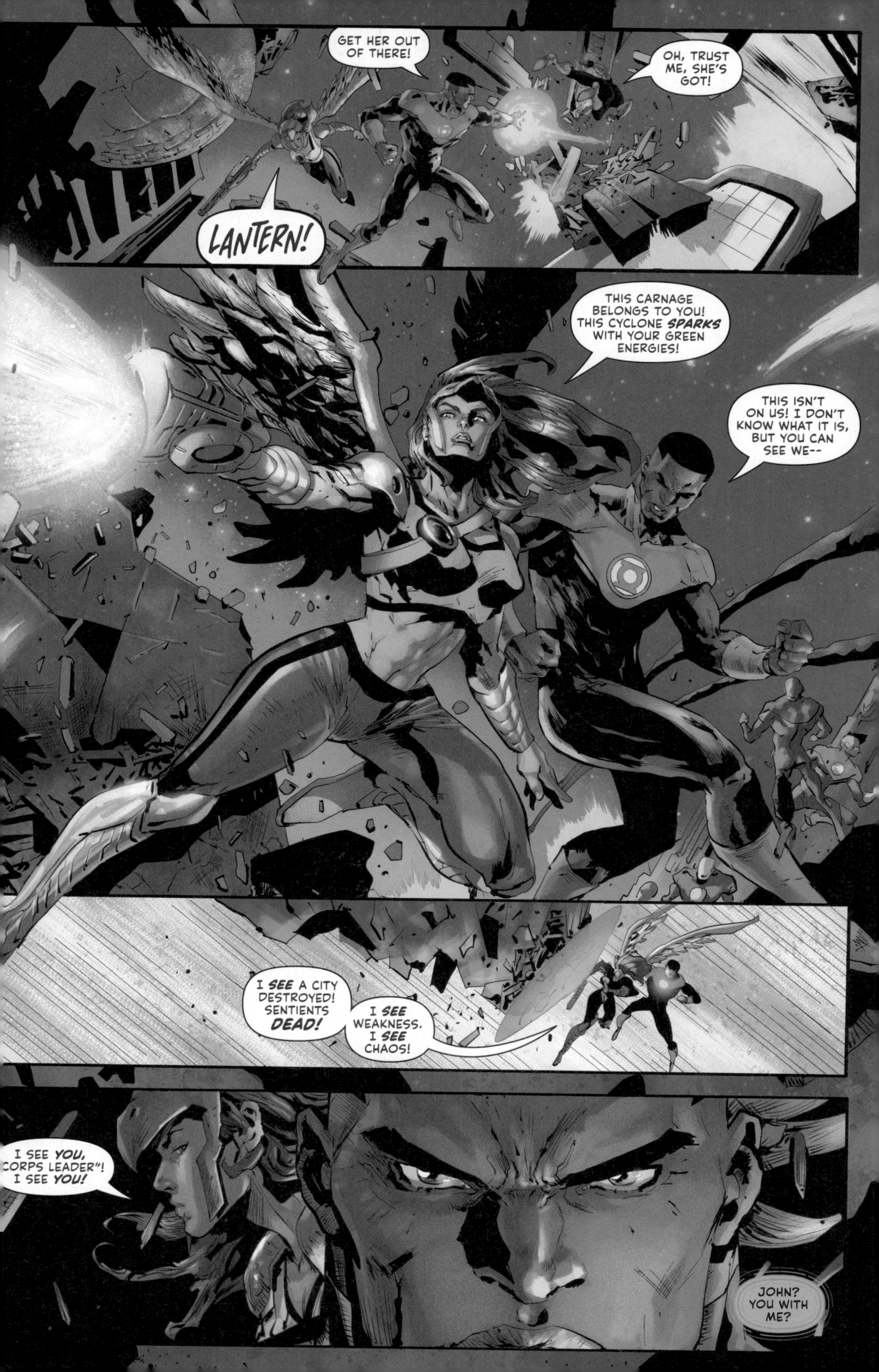
GET HER OUT OF THERE!
OH, TRUST ME, SHE'S GOT!
LANTERN!
THIS CARNAGE BELONGS TO YOU! THIS CYCLONE SPARKS WITH YOUR GREEN ENERGIES!
THIS ISN'T ON US! I DON'T KNOW WHAT IT IS, BUT YOU CAN SEE WE--
I SEE A CITY DESTROYED! SENTIENTS DEAD!
I SEE WEAKNESS. I SEE CHAOS!
I SEE YOU, "CORPS LEADER"! I SEE YOU!
JOHN? YOU WITH ME?

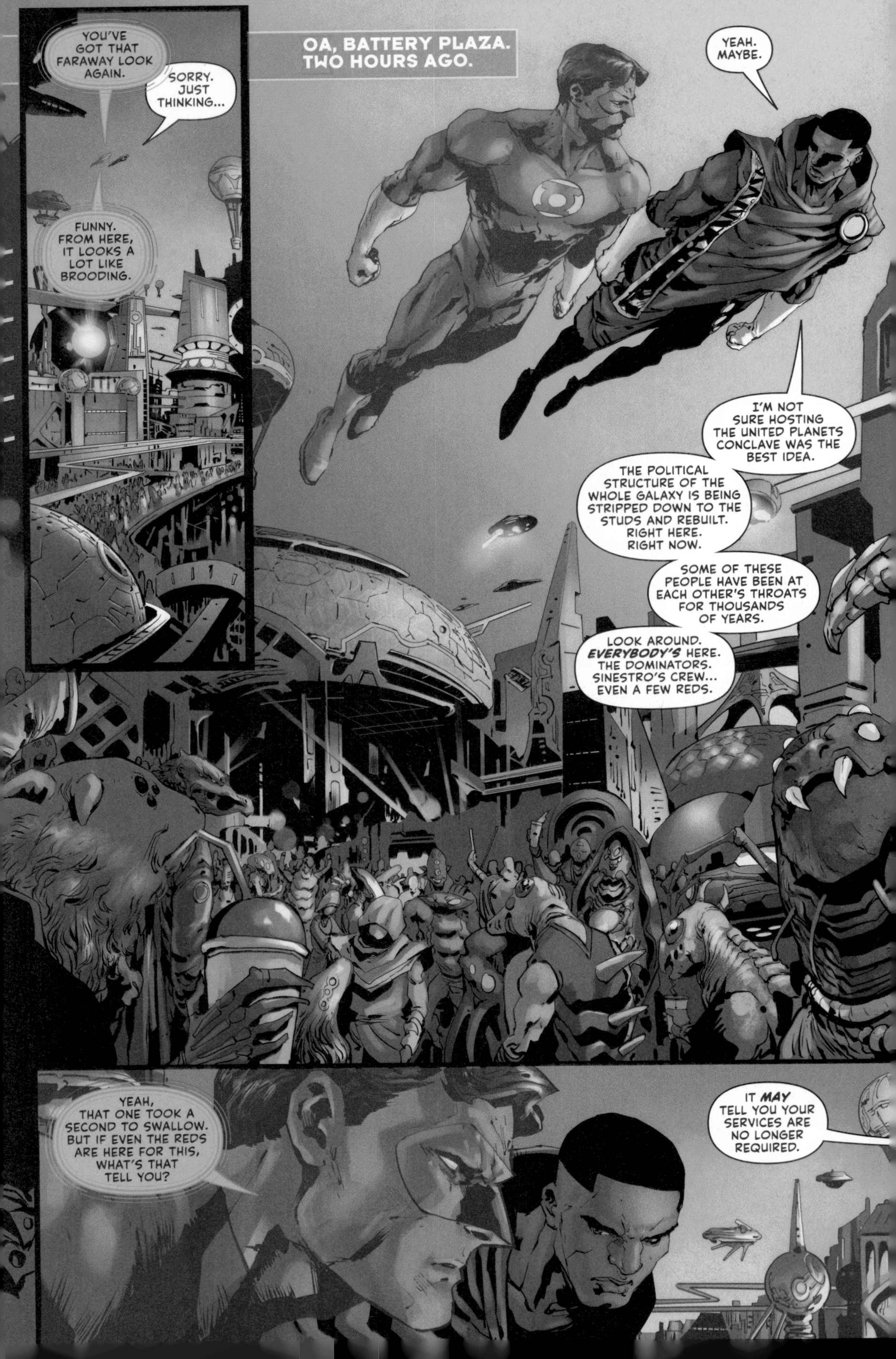

YOU'VE GOT THAT FARAWAY LOOK AGAIN.
SORRY. JUST THINKING...
FUNNY. FROM HERE, IT LOOKS A LOT LIKE BROODING.
OA, BATTERY PLAZA. TWO HOURS AGO.
YEAH. MAYBE.
I'M NOT SURE HOSTING THE UNITED PLANETS CONCLAVE WAS THE BEST IDEA.
THE POLITICAL STRUCTURE OF THE WHOLE GALAXY IS BEING STRIPPED DOWN TO THE STUDS AND REBUILT. RIGHT HERE. RIGHT NOW.
SOME OF THESE PEOPLE HAVE BEEN AT EACH OTHER'S THROATS FOR THOUSANDS OF YEARS.
LOOK AROUND. EVERYBODY'S HERE. THE DOMINATORS. SINESTRO'S CREW... EVEN A FEW REDS.
YEAH, THAT ONE TOOK A SECOND TO SWALLOW. BUT IF EVEN THE REDS ARE HERE FOR THIS, WHAT'S THAT TELL YOU?
IT MAY TELL YOU YOUR SERVICES ARE NO LONGER REQUIRED.

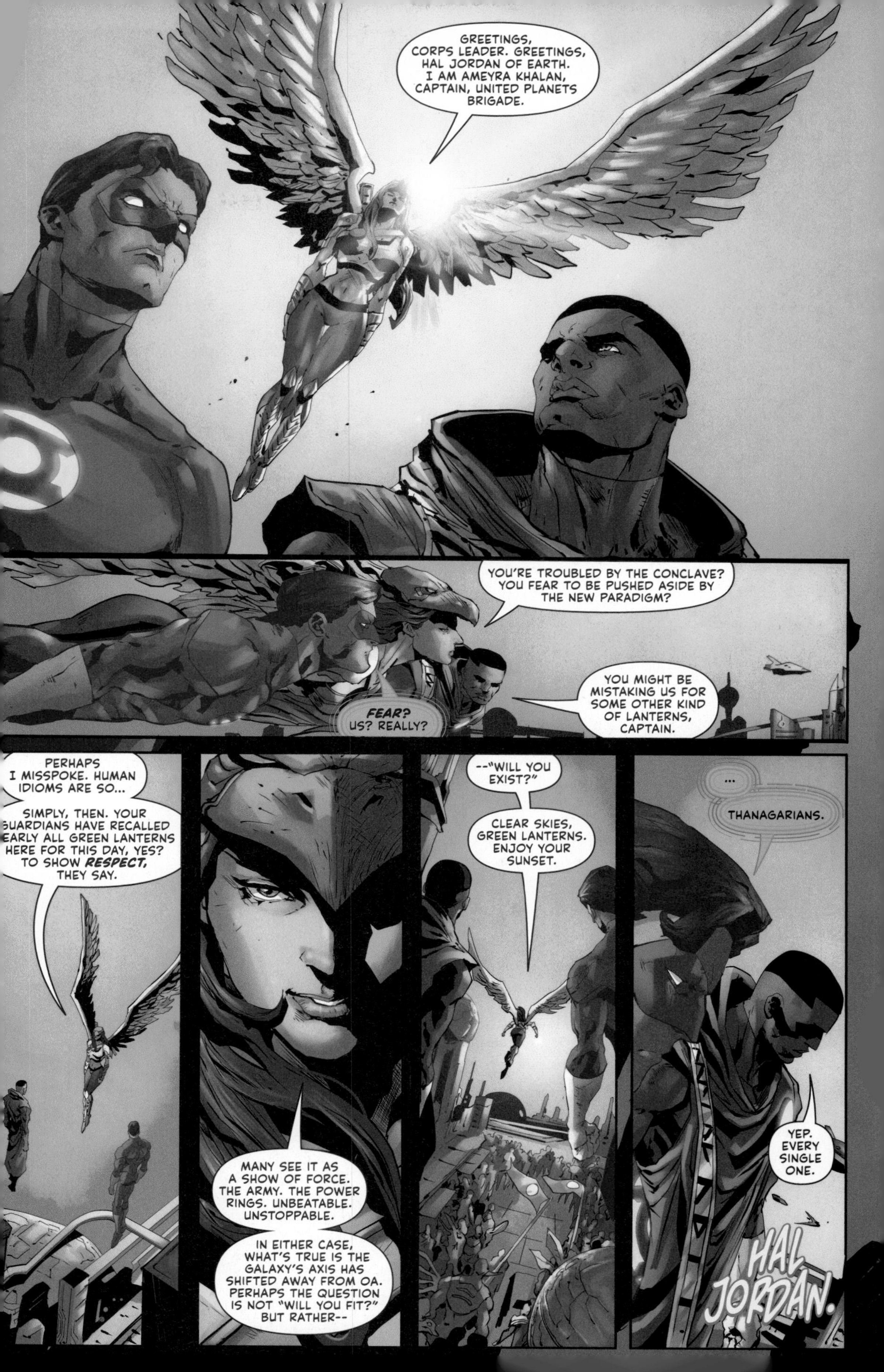

GREETINGS, CORPS LEADER. GREETINGS, HAL JORDAN OF EARTH. I AM AMEYRA KHALAN, CAPTAIN, UNITED PLANETS BRIGADE.
YOU'RE TROUBLED BY THE CONCLAVE? YOU FEAR TO BE PUSHED ASIDE BY THE NEW PARADIGM?
FEAR? US? REALLY?
YOU MIGHT BE MISTAKING US FOR SOME OTHER KIND OF LANTERNS, CAPTAIN.
PERHAPS I MISSPOKE. HUMAN IDIOMS ARE SO...
SIMPLY, THEN. YOUR GUARDIANS HAVE RECALLED NEARLY ALL GREEN LANTERNS HERE FOR THIS DAY, YES? TO SHOW RESPECT, THEY SAY.
MANY SEE IT AS A SHOW OF FORCE. THE ARMY. THE POWER RINGS. UNBEATABLE. UNSTOPPABLE.
IN EITHER CASE, WHAT'S TRUE IS THE GALAXY'S AXIS HAS SHIFTED AWAY FROM OA. PERHAPS THE QUESTION IS NOT "WILL YOU FIT?" BUT RATHER--
--"WILL YOU EXIST?"
CLEAR SKIES, GREEN LANTERNS. ENJOY YOUR SUNSET.
...
THANAGARIANS.
YEP. EVERY SINGLE ONE.
HAL JORDAN.

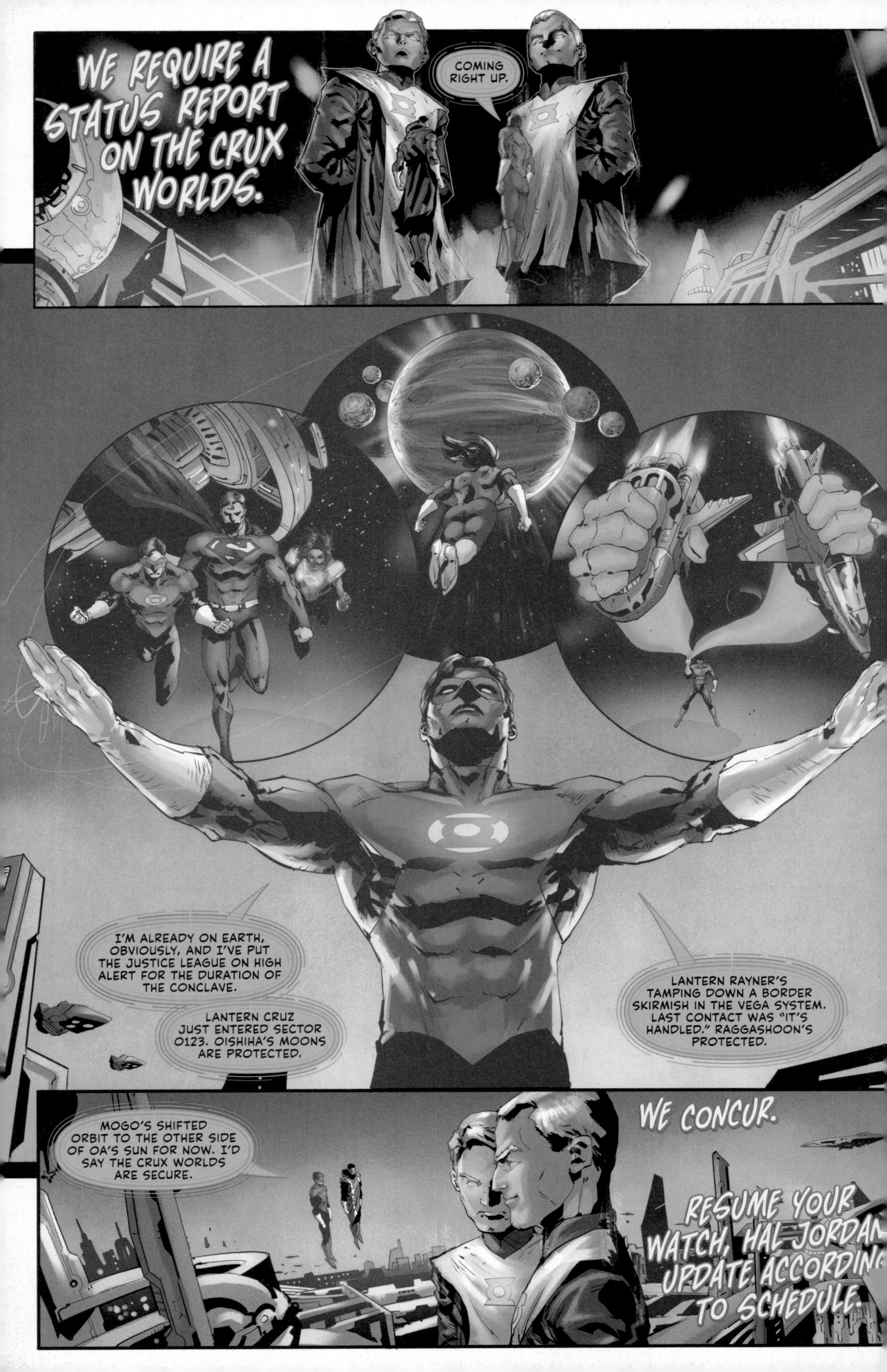
WE REQUIRE A STATUS REPORT ON THE CRUX WORLDS.
COMING RIGHT UP.
I'M ALREADY ON EARTH, OBVIOUSLY, AND I'VE PUT THE JUSTICE LEAGUE ON HIGH ALERT FOR THE DURATION OF THE CONCLAVE.
LANTERN CRUZ JUST ENTERED SECTOR 0123. OISHIHA'S MOONS ARE PROTECTED.
LANTERN RAYNER'S TAMPING DOWN A BORDER SKIRMISH IN THE VEGA SYSTEM. LAST CONTACT WAS "IT'S HANDLED." RAGGASHOON'S PROTECTED.
MOGO'S SHIFTED ORBIT TO THE OTHER SIDE OF OA'S SUN FOR NOW. I'D SAY THE CRUX WORLDS ARE SECURE.
WE CONCUR.
RESUME YOUR WATCH, HAL JORDAN. UPDATE ACCORDING TO SCHEDULE.

THAT'S MY CUE.

JOHN, IF YOU NEED ME, I'M A HYPER-JUMP AWAY. OR A BOOM TUBE. OR WHATEVER IT TAKES.

SAME TO YOU, BROTHER.

THROTTLE BACK ON THE BROODING. THE CONCLAVE'S A GOOD THING.

PEOPLE ARE FINALLY TALKING INSTEAD OF TRYING TO MURDER EACH OTHER WHOLESALE. REMEMBER WHAT THE BLUES SAY...

..."ALL WILL BE WELL."

JOHN STEWART. PLEASE JOIN US IN THE EVALUATION CRÈCHE.

ON MY WAY.

HOW'S KELI'S EXAM GOING?

WE DEEM THE SELF-DESCRIBED TEEN LANTERN TO BE A QUANTUM CONUNDRUM.

MEANING?

MEANING THE ANSWER TO YOUR QUERY REMAINS YES AND--

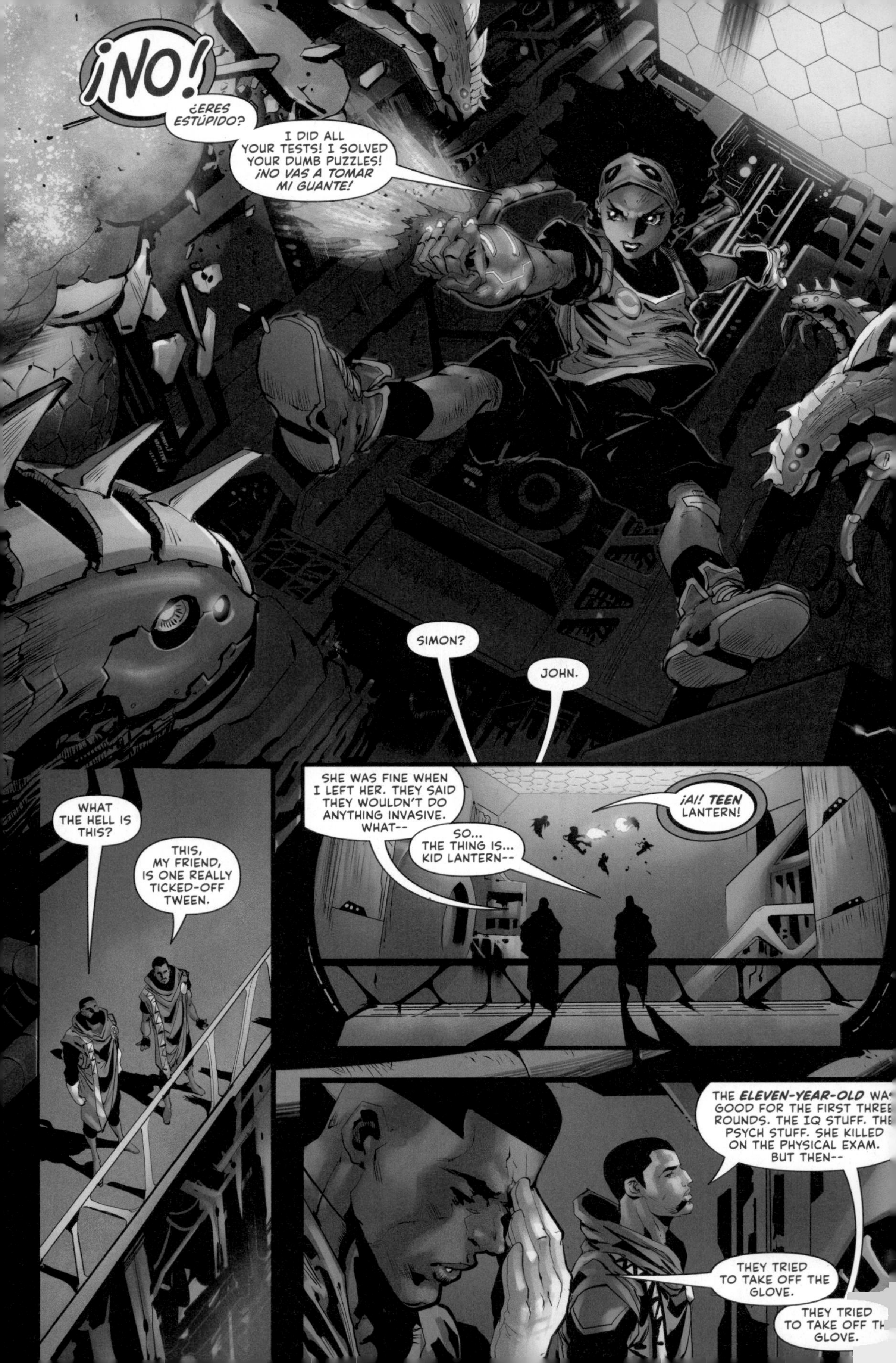
¡NO!
¿ERES ESTÚPIDO?
I DID ALL YOUR TESTS! I SOLVED YOUR DUMB PUZZLES! ¡NO VAS A TOMAR MI GUANTE!
SIMON?
JOHN.
WHAT THE HELL IS THIS?
THIS, MY FRIEND, IS ONE REALLY TICKED-OFF TWEEN.
SHE WAS FINE WHEN I LEFT HER. THEY SAID THEY WOULDN'T DO ANYTHING INVASIVE. WHAT--
SO... THE THING IS... KID LANTERN--
¡AI! TEEN LANTERN!
THE ELEVEN-YEAR-OLD WAS GOOD FOR THE FIRST THREE ROUNDS. THE IQ STUFF. THE PSYCH STUFF. SHE KILLED ON THE PHYSICAL EXAM. BUT THEN--
THEY TRIED TO TAKE OFF THE GLOVE.
THEY TRIED TO TAKE OFF THE GLOVE.

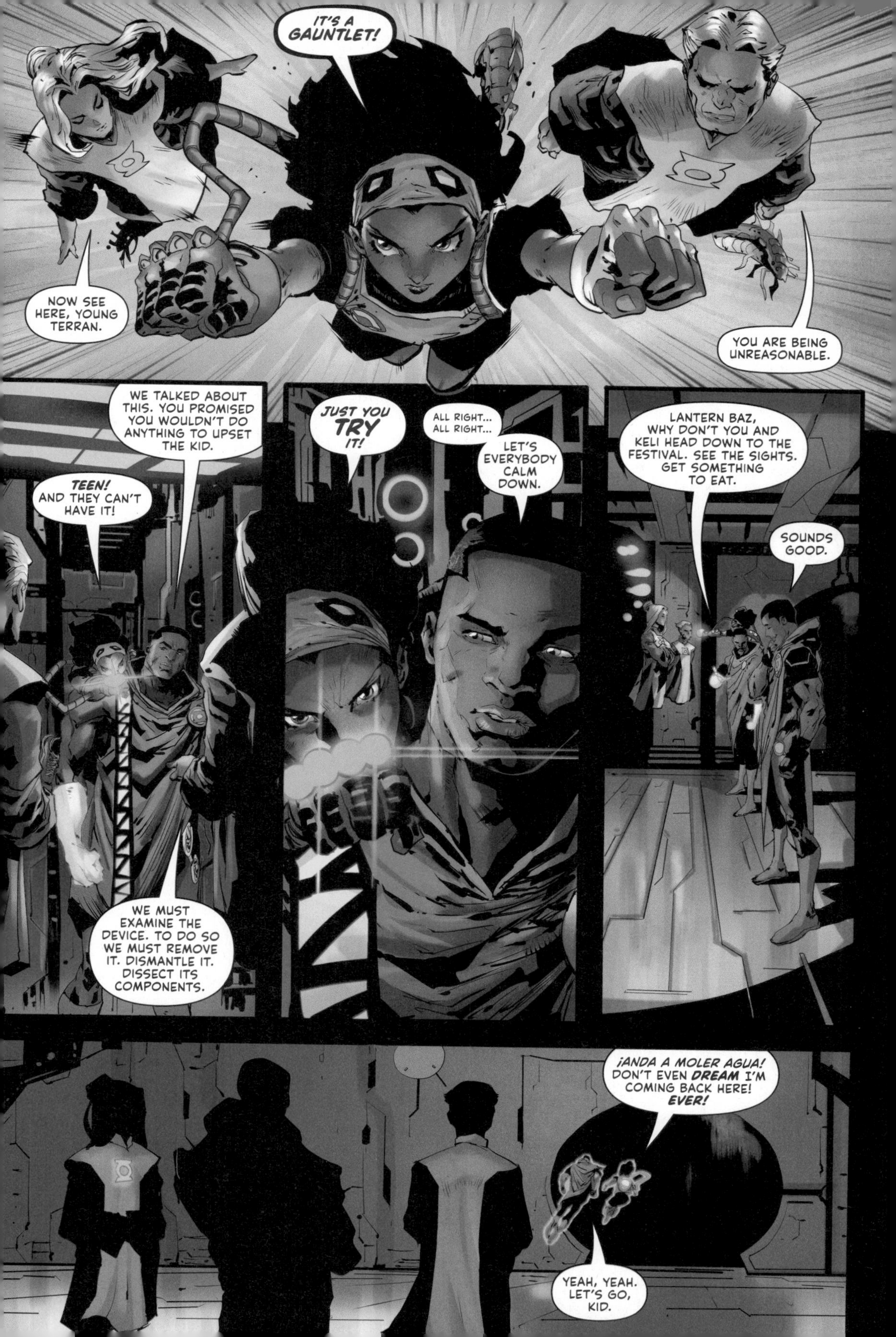
IT'S A GAUNTLET!
NOW SEE HERE, YOUNG TERRAN.
YOU ARE BEING UNREASONABLE.
WE TALKED ABOUT THIS. YOU PROMISED YOU WOULDN'T DO ANYTHING TO UPSET THE KID.
TEEN! AND THEY CAN'T HAVE IT!
WE MUST EXAMINE THE DEVICE. TO DO SO WE MUST REMOVE IT. DISMANTLE IT. DISSECT ITS COMPONENTS.
JUST YOU TRY IT!
ALL RIGHT... ALL RIGHT...
LET'S EVERYBODY CALM DOWN.
LANTERN BAZ, WHY DON'T YOU AND KELI HEAD DOWN TO THE FESTIVAL. SEE THE SIGHTS. GET SOMETHING TO EAT.
SOUNDS GOOD.
¡ANDA A MOLER AGUA! DON'T EVEN DREAM I'M COMING BACK HERE! EVER!
YEAH, YEAH. LET'S GO, KID.

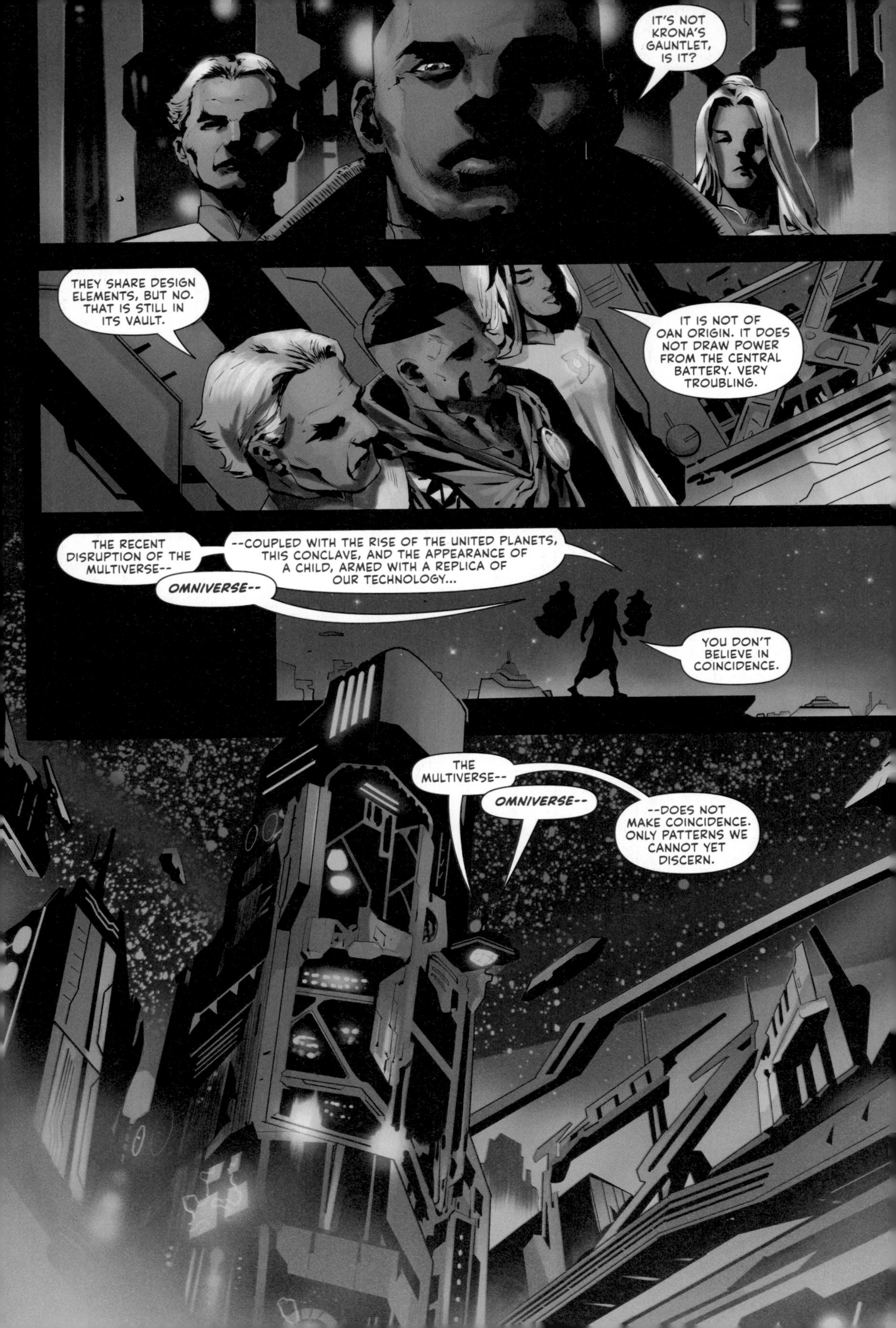
IT'S NOT KRONA'S GAUNTLET, IS IT?
THEY SHARE DESIGN ELEMENTS, BUT NO. THAT IS STILL IN ITS VAULT.
IT IS NOT OF OAN ORIGIN. IT DOES NOT DRAW POWER FROM THE CENTRAL BATTERY. VERY TROUBLING.
THE RECENT DISRUPTION OF THE MULTIVERSE--
OMNIVERSE--
--COUPLED WITH THE RISE OF THE UNITED PLANETS, THIS CONCLAVE, AND THE APPEARANCE OF A CHILD, ARMED WITH A REPLICA OF OUR TECHNOLOGY...
YOU DON'T BELIEVE IN COINCIDENCE.
THE MULTIVERSE--
OMNIVERSE--
--DOES NOT MAKE COINCIDENCE. ONLY PATTERNS WE CANNOT YET DISCERN.

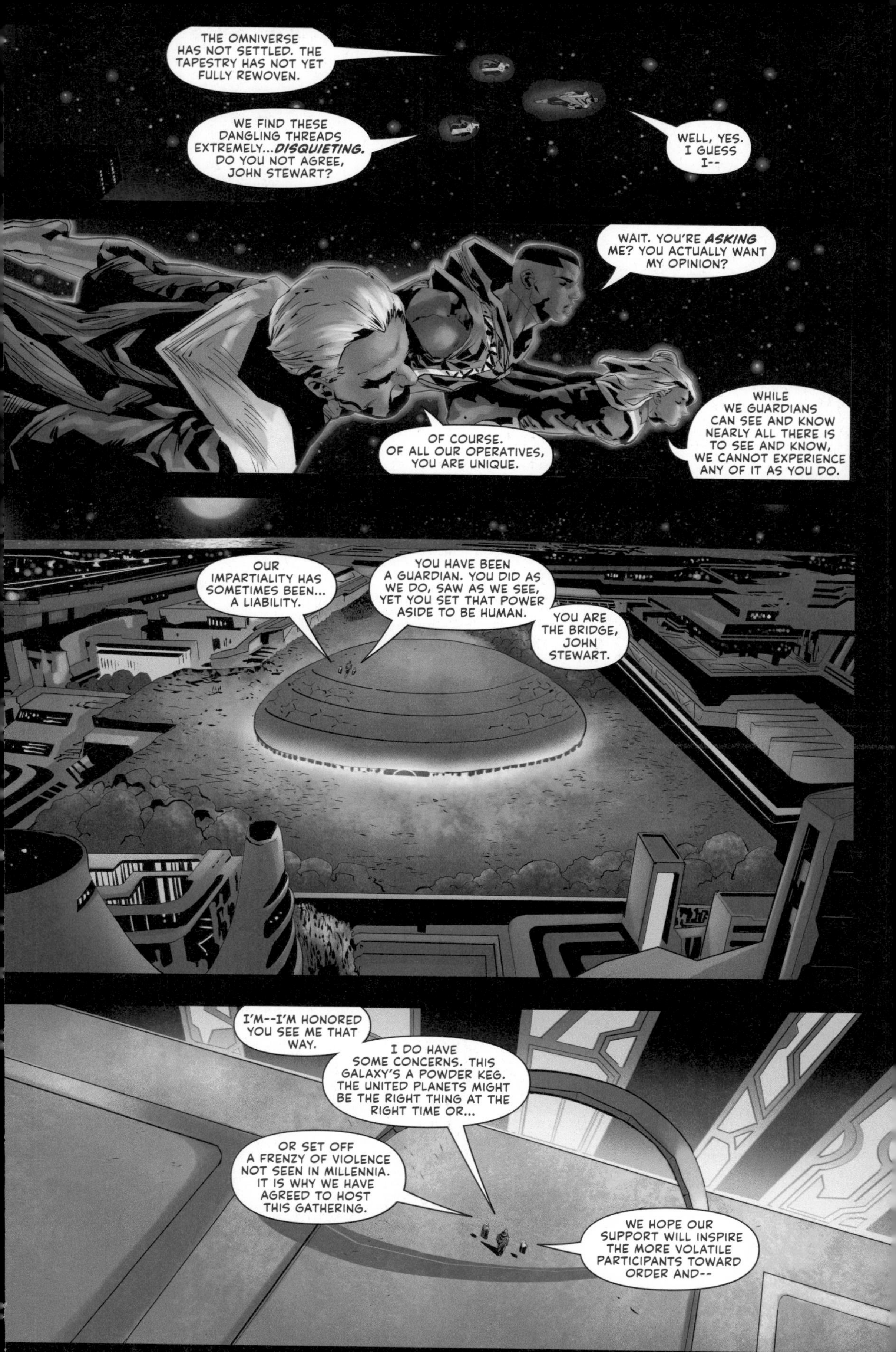
THE OMNIVERSE HAS NOT SETTLED. THE TAPESTRY HAS NOT YET FULLY REWOVEN.
WE FIND THESE DANGLING THREADS EXTREMELY...*DISQUIETING.* DO YOU NOT AGREE, JOHN STEWART?
WELL, YES. I GUESS I--
WAIT. YOU'RE *ASKING* ME? YOU ACTUALLY WANT MY OPINION?
OF COURSE. OF ALL OUR OPERATIVES, YOU ARE UNIQUE.
WHILE WE GUARDIANS CAN SEE AND KNOW NEARLY ALL THERE IS TO SEE AND KNOW, WE CANNOT EXPERIENCE ANY OF IT AS YOU DO.
OUR IMPARTIALITY HAS SOMETIMES BEEN... A LIABILITY.
YOU HAVE BEEN A GUARDIAN. YOU DID AS WE DO, SAW AS WE SEE, YET YOU SET THAT POWER ASIDE TO BE HUMAN.
YOU ARE THE BRIDGE, JOHN STEWART.
I'M--I'M HONORED YOU SEE ME THAT WAY.
I DO HAVE SOME CONCERNS. THIS GALAXY'S A POWDER KEG. THE UNITED PLANETS MIGHT BE THE RIGHT THING AT THE RIGHT TIME OR...
OR SET OFF A FRENZY OF VIOLENCE NOT SEEN IN MILLENNIA. IT IS WHY WE HAVE AGREED TO HOST THIS GATHERING.
WE HOPE OUR SUPPORT WILL INSPIRE THE MORE VOLATILE PARTICIPANTS TOWARD ORDER AND--

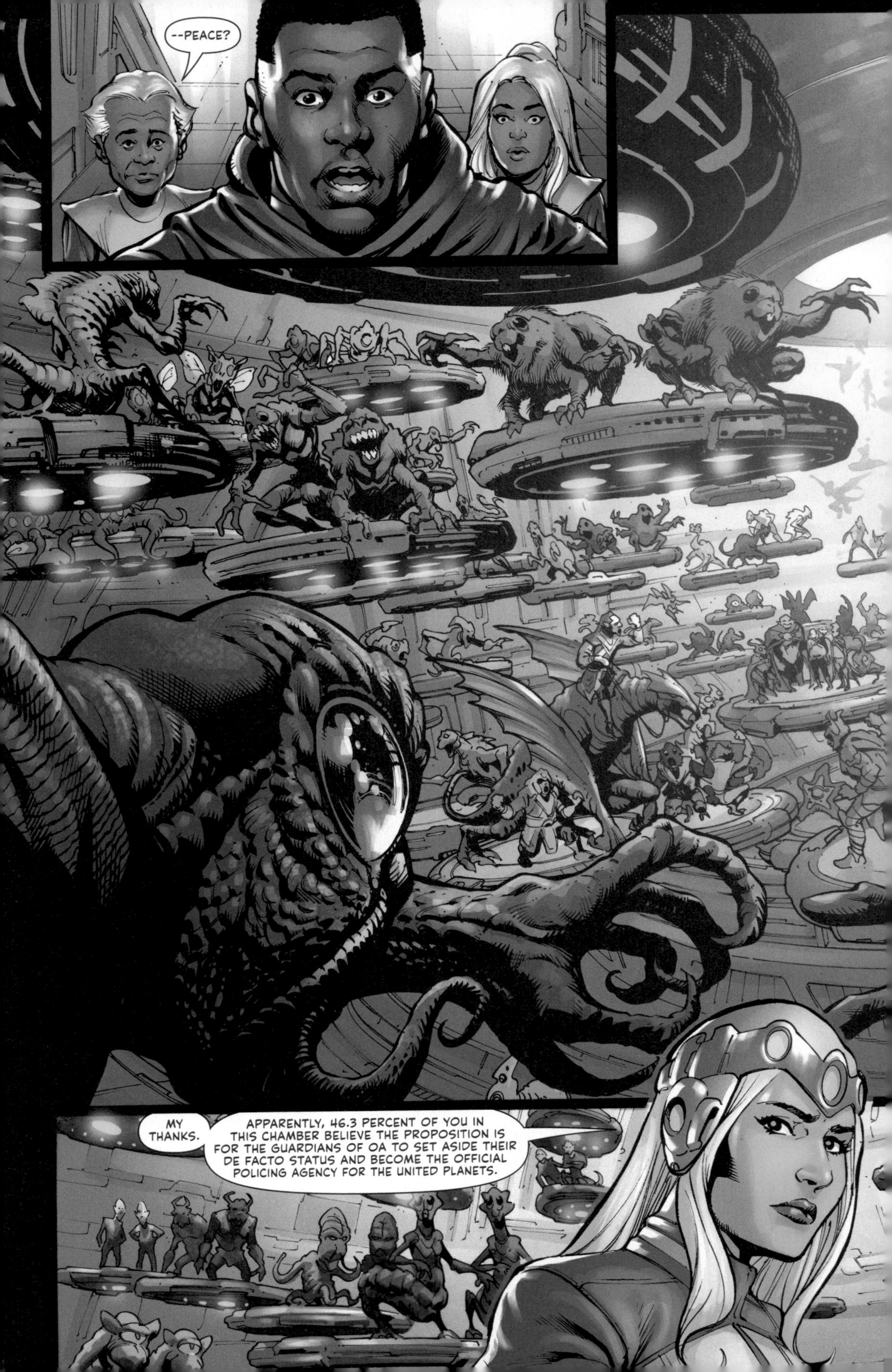
--PEACE?
MY THANKS.
APPARENTLY, 46.3 PERCENT OF YOU IN THIS CHAMBER BELIEVE THE PROPOSITION IS FOR THE GUARDIANS OF OA TO SET ASIDE THEIR DE FACTO STATUS AND BECOME THE OFFICIAL POLICING AGENCY FOR THE UNITED PLANETS.

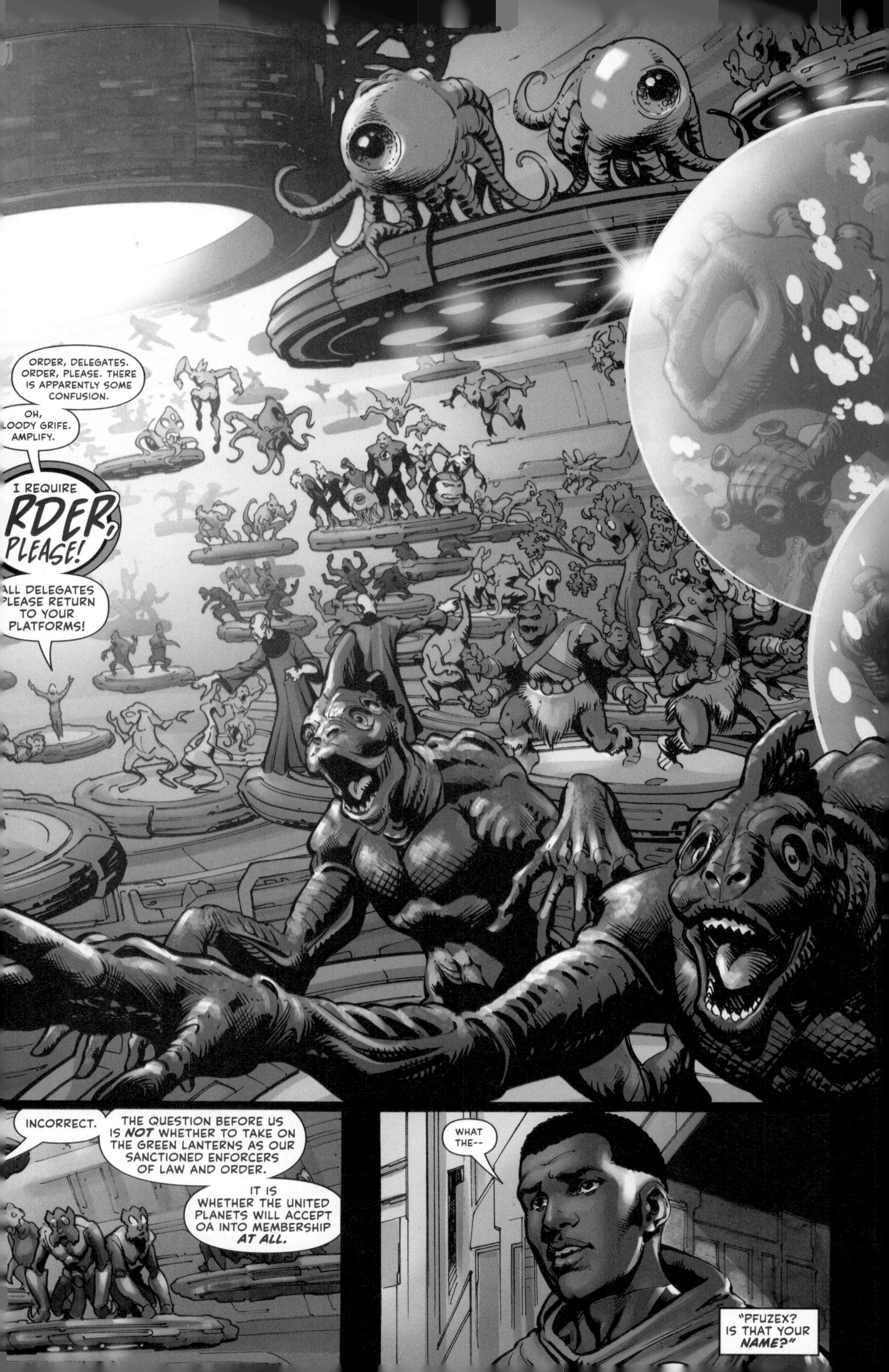
ORDER, DELEGATES. ORDER, PLEASE. THERE IS APPARENTLY SOME CONFUSION.
OH, LOODY GRIFE. AMPLIFY.
I REQUIRE RDER, PLEASE!
ALL DELEGATES PLEASE RETURN TO YOUR PLATFORMS!
INCORRECT.
THE QUESTION BEFORE US IS NOT WHETHER TO TAKE ON THE GREEN LANTERNS AS OUR SANCTIONED ENFORCERS OF LAW AND ORDER.
IT IS WHETHER THE UNITED PLANETS WILL ACCEPT OA INTO MEMBERSHIP AT ALL.
WHAT THE--
"PFUZEX? IS THAT YOUR NAME?"

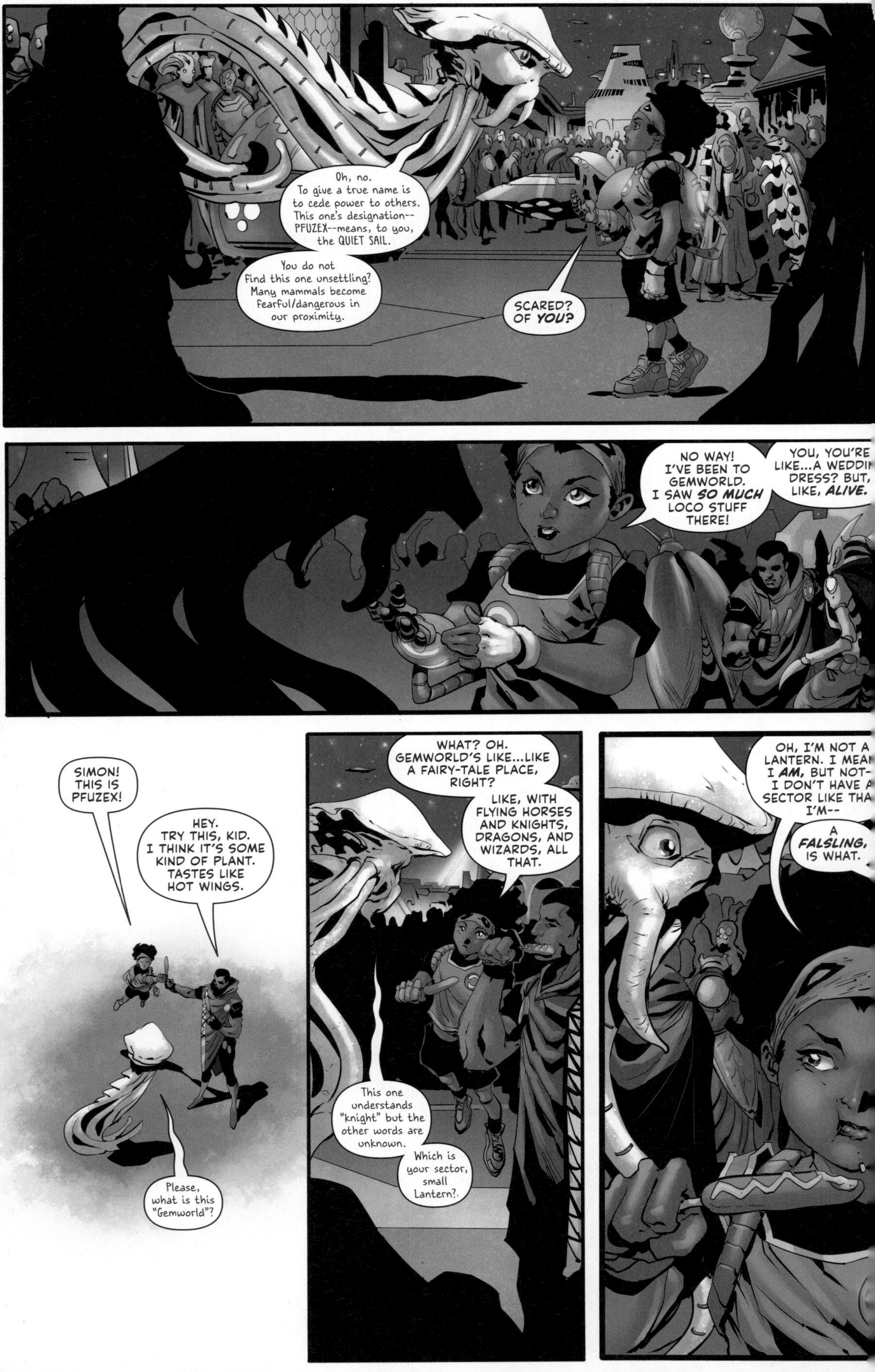
Oh, no. To give a true name is to cede power to others. This one's designation--PFUZEX--means, to you, the QUIET SAIL.
You do not find this one unsettling? Many mammals become fearful/dangerous in our proximity.
SCARED? OF YOU?
NO WAY! I'VE BEEN TO GEMWORLD. I SAW SO MUCH LOCO STUFF THERE!
YOU, YOU'RE LIKE...A WEDDI DRESS? BUT, LIKE, ALIVE.
SIMON! THIS IS PFUZEX!
HEY. TRY THIS, KID. I THINK IT'S SOME KIND OF PLANT. TASTES LIKE HOT WINGS.
Please, what is this "Gemworld"?
WHAT? OH. GEMWORLD'S LIKE...LIKE A FAIRY-TALE PLACE, RIGHT?
LIKE, WITH FLYING HORSES AND KNIGHTS, DRAGONS, AND WIZARDS, ALL THAT.
This one understands "knight" but the other words are unknown.
Which is your sector, small Lantern?
OH, I'M NOT A LANTERN. I MEA I AM, BUT NOT- I DON'T HAVE A SECTOR LIKE THA I'M--
A FALSLING, IS WHAT.

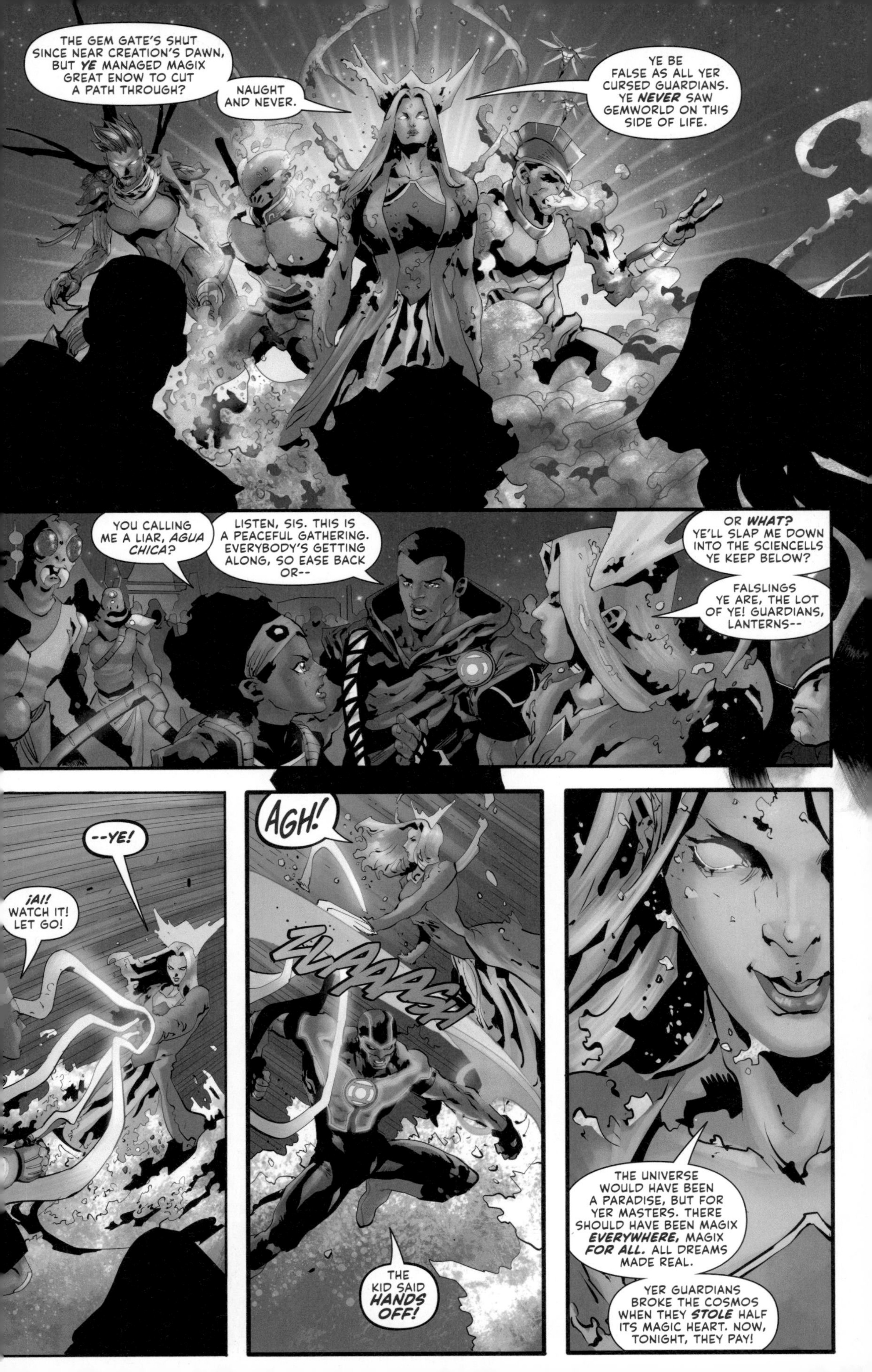
THE GEM GATE'S SHUT SINCE NEAR CREATION'S DAWN, BUT YE MANAGED MAGIX GREAT ENOW TO CUT A PATH THROUGH?
NAUGHT AND NEVER.
YE BE FALSE AS ALL YER CURSED GUARDIANS. YE NEVER SAW GEMWORLD ON THIS SIDE OF LIFE.
YOU CALLING ME A LIAR, AGUA CHICA?
LISTEN, SIS. THIS IS A PEACEFUL GATHERING. EVERYBODY'S GETTING ALONG, SO EASE BACK OR--
OR WHAT? YE'LL SLAP ME DOWN INTO THE SCIENCELLS YE KEEP BELOW?
FALSLINGS YE ARE, THE LOT OF YE! GUARDIANS, LANTERNS--
--YE!
¡AI! WATCH IT! LET GO!
AGH!
ZLAAAASH
THE KID SAID HANDS OFF!
THE UNIVERSE WOULD HAVE BEEN A PARADISE, BUT FOR YER MASTERS. THERE SHOULD HAVE BEEN MAGIX EVERYWHERE, MAGIX FOR ALL. ALL DREAMS MADE REAL.
YER GUARDIANS BROKE THE COSMOS WHEN THEY STOLE HALF ITS MAGIC HEART. NOW, TONIGHT, THEY PAY!

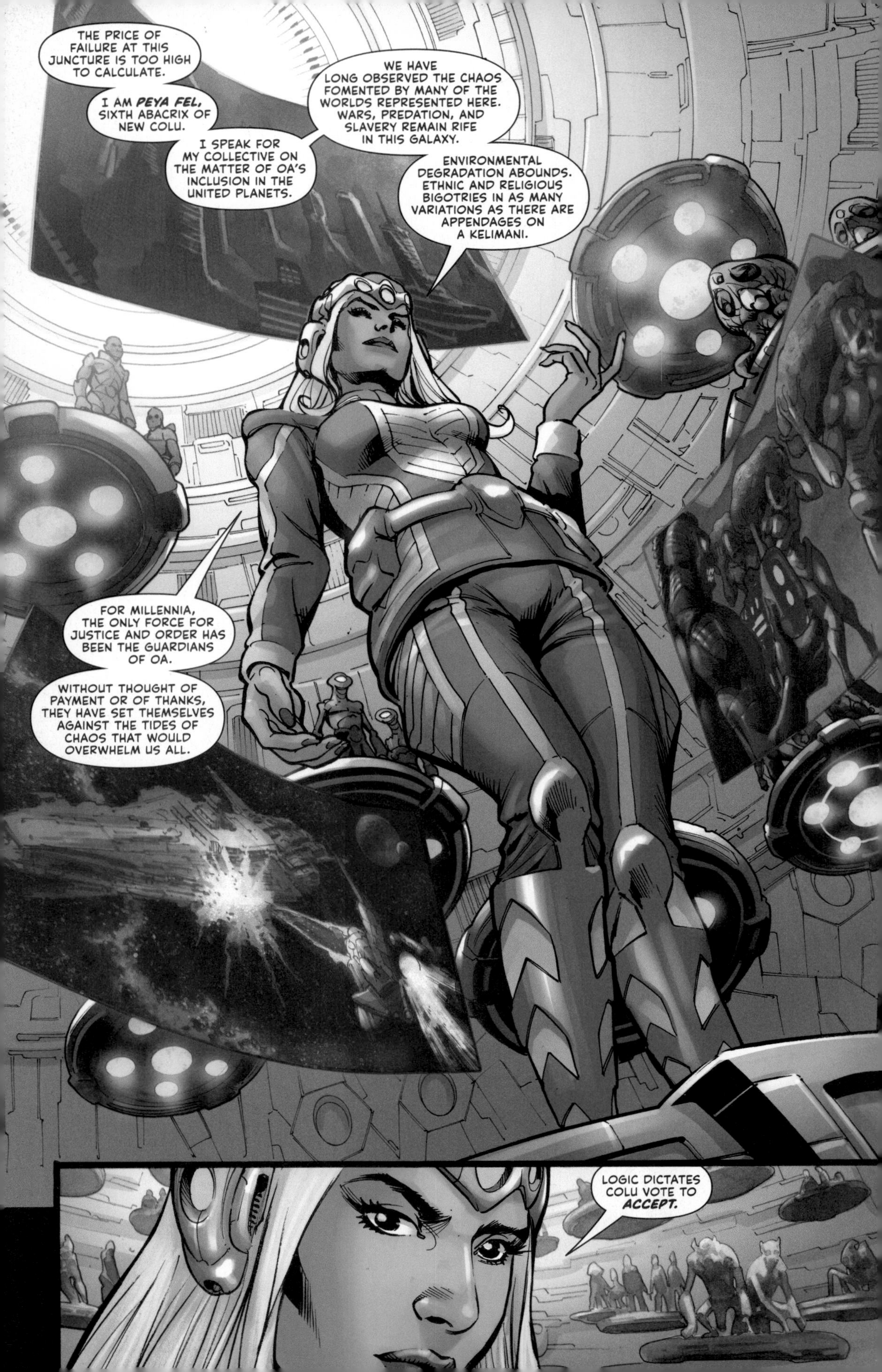
THE PRICE OF FAILURE AT THIS JUNCTURE IS TOO HIGH TO CALCULATE.
I AM PEYA FEL, SIXTH ABACRIX OF NEW COLU.
I SPEAK FOR MY COLLECTIVE ON THE MATTER OF OA'S INCLUSION IN THE UNITED PLANETS.
WE HAVE LONG OBSERVED THE CHAOS FOMENTED BY MANY OF THE WORLDS REPRESENTED HERE. WARS, PREDATION, AND SLAVERY REMAIN RIFE IN THIS GALAXY.
ENVIRONMENTAL DEGRADATION ABOUNDS. ETHNIC AND RELIGIOUS BIGOTRIES IN AS MANY VARIATIONS AS THERE ARE APPENDAGES ON A KELIMANI.
FOR MILLENNIA, THE ONLY FORCE FOR JUSTICE AND ORDER HAS BEEN THE GUARDIANS OF OA.
WITHOUT THOUGHT OF PAYMENT OR OF THANKS, THEY HAVE SET THEMSELVES AGAINST THE TIDES OF CHAOS THAT WOULD OVERWHELM US ALL.
LOGIC DICTATES COLU VOTE TO ACCEPT.

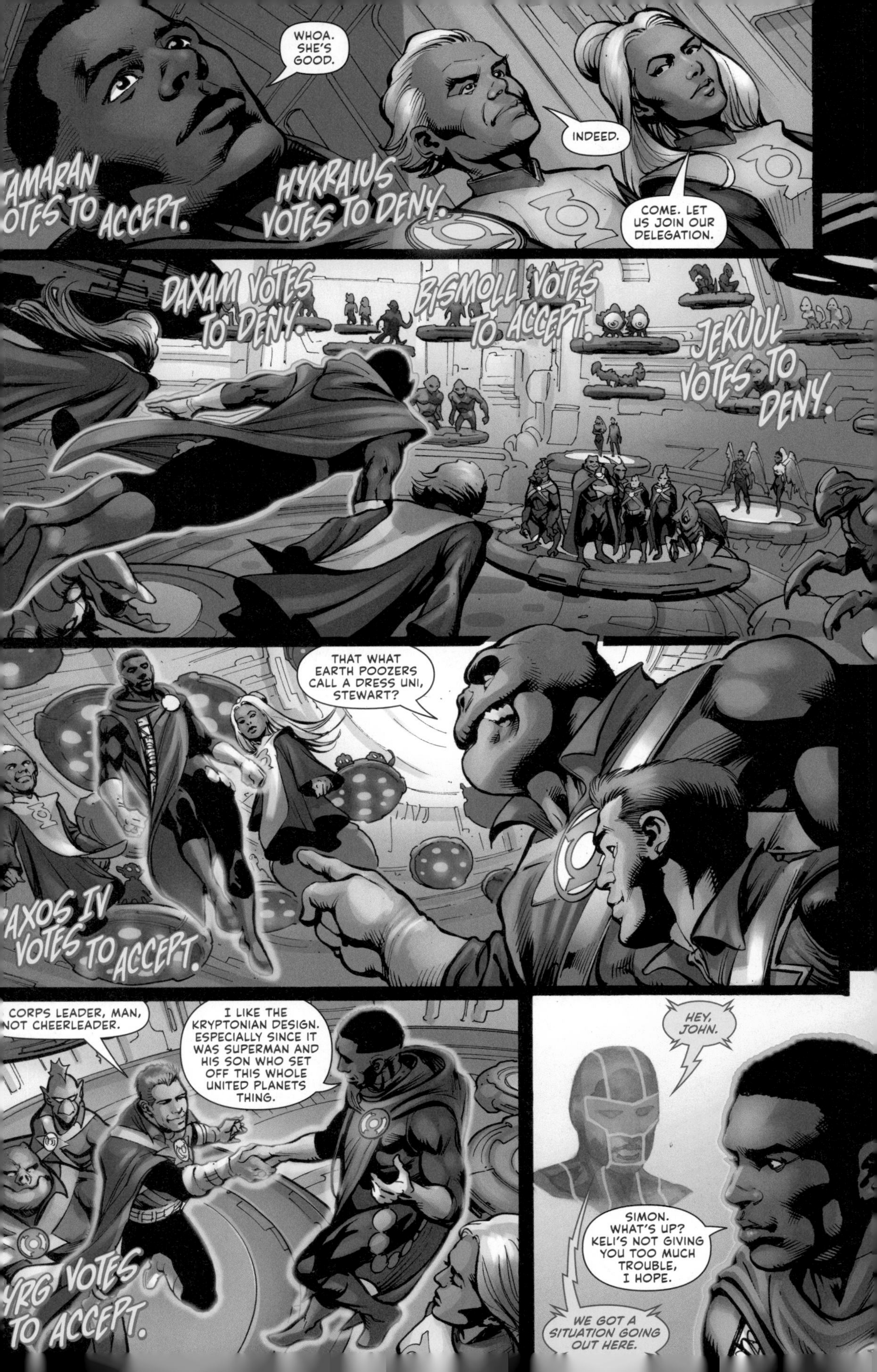
WHOA. SHE'S GOOD.
AMARAN OTES TO ACCEPT.
HYKRAIUS VOTES TO DENY.
INDEED.
COME. LET US JOIN OUR DELEGATION.
DAXAM VOTES TO DENY.
BISMOLL VOTES TO ACCEPT.
JEKUUL VOTES TO DENY.
THAT WHAT EARTH POOZERS CALL A DRESS UNI, STEWART?
AXOS IV VOTES TO ACCEPT.
CORPS LEADER, MAN, NOT CHEERLEADER.
I LIKE THE KRYPTONIAN DESIGN. ESPECIALLY SINCE IT WAS SUPERMAN AND HIS SON WHO SET OFF THIS WHOLE UNITED PLANETS THING.
YRG VOTES TO ACCEPT.
HEY, JOHN.
SIMON. WHAT'S UP? KELI'S NOT GIVING YOU TOO MUCH TROUBLE, I HOPE.
WE GOT A SITUATION GOING OUT HERE.

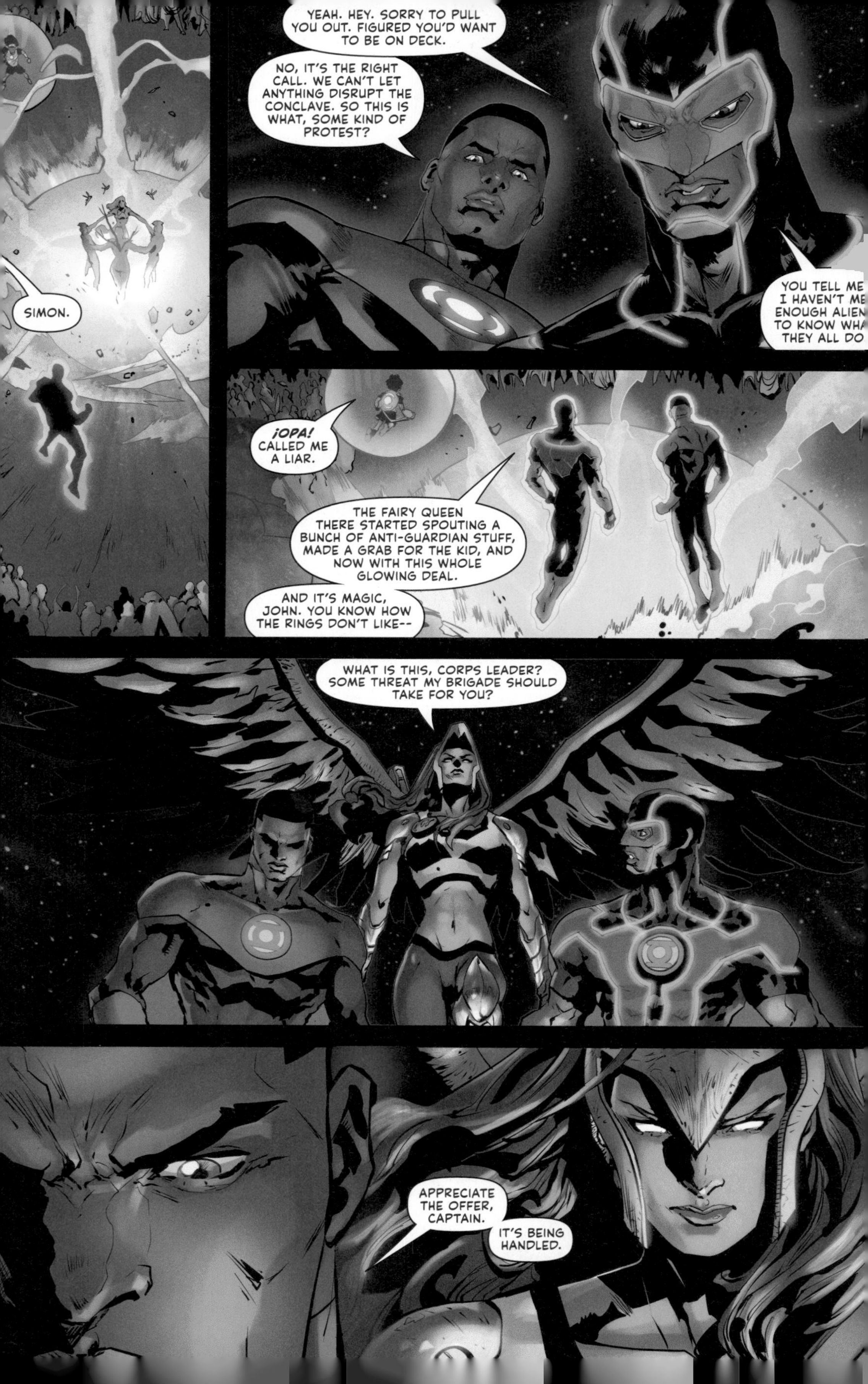
YEAH. HEY. SORRY TO PULL YOU OUT. FIGURED YOU'D WANT TO BE ON DECK.
NO, IT'S THE RIGHT CALL. WE CAN'T LET ANYTHING DISRUPT THE CONCLAVE. SO THIS IS WHAT, SOME KIND OF PROTEST?
SIMON.
YOU TELL ME I HAVEN'T ME ENOUGH ALIEN TO KNOW WHA THEY ALL DO
¡OPA! CALLED ME A LIAR.
THE FAIRY QUEEN THERE STARTED SPOUTING A BUNCH OF ANTI-GUARDIAN STUFF, MADE A GRAB FOR THE KID, AND NOW WITH THIS WHOLE GLOWING DEAL.
AND IT'S MAGIC, JOHN. YOU KNOW HOW THE RINGS DON'T LIKE--
WHAT IS THIS, CORPS LEADER? SOME THREAT MY BRIGADE SHOULD TAKE FOR YOU?
APPRECIATE THE OFFER, CAPTAIN.
IT'S BEING HANDLED.

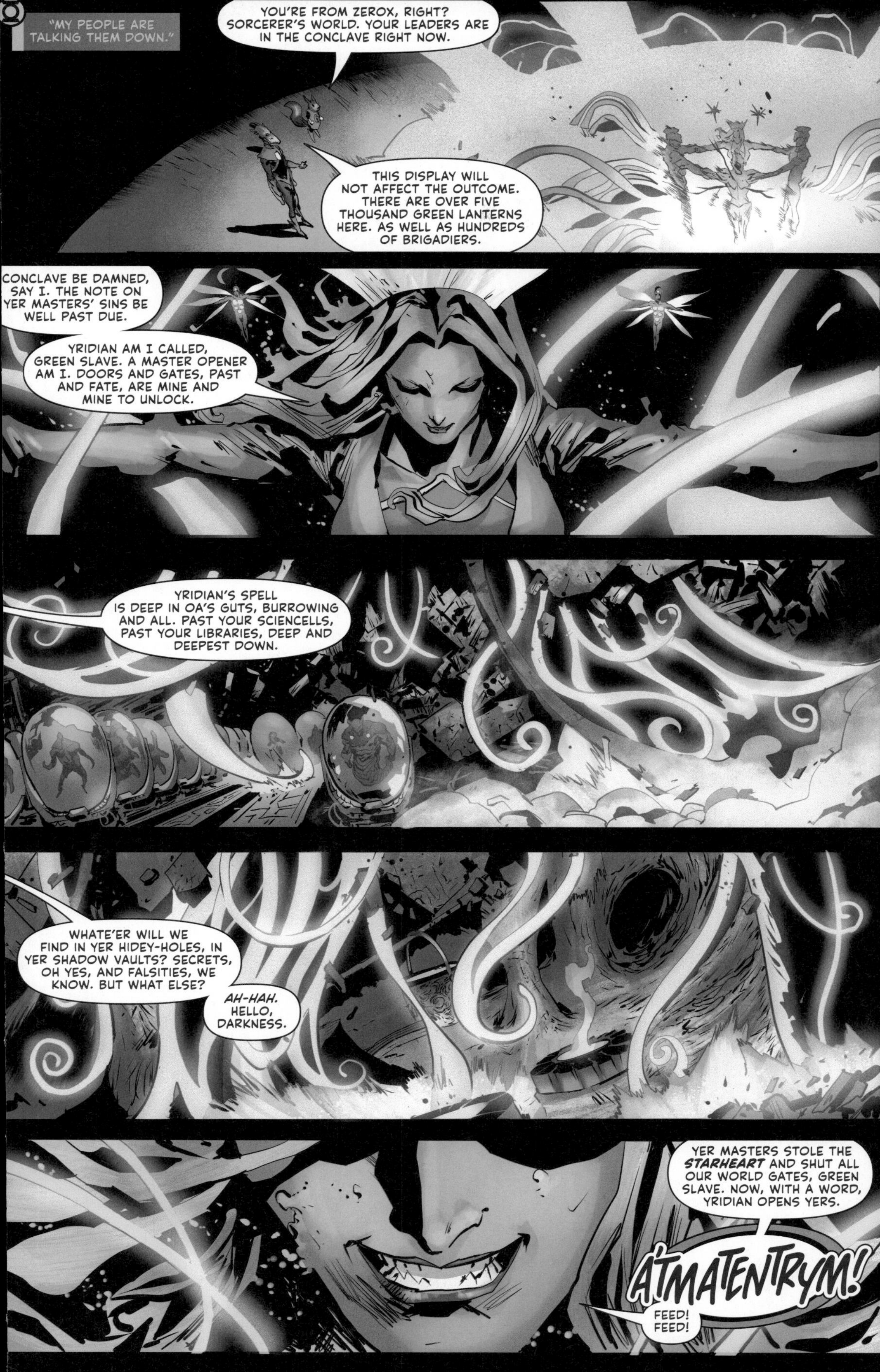
"MY PEOPLE ARE TALKING THEM DOWN."
YOU'RE FROM ZEROX, RIGHT? SORCERER'S WORLD. YOUR LEADERS ARE IN THE CONCLAVE RIGHT NOW.
THIS DISPLAY WILL NOT AFFECT THE OUTCOME. THERE ARE OVER FIVE THOUSAND GREEN LANTERNS HERE. AS WELL AS HUNDREDS OF BRIGADIERS.
CONCLAVE BE DAMNED, SAY I. THE NOTE ON YER MASTERS' SINS BE WELL PAST DUE.
YRIDIAN AM I CALLED, GREEN SLAVE. A MASTER OPENER AM I. DOORS AND GATES, PAST AND FATE, ARE MINE AND MINE TO UNLOCK.
YRIDIAN'S SPELL IS DEEP IN OA'S GUTS, BURROWING AND ALL. PAST YOUR SCIENCELLS, PAST YOUR LIBRARIES, DEEP AND DEEPEST DOWN.
WHATE'ER WILL WE FIND IN YER HIDEY-HOLES, IN YER SHADOW VAULTS? SECRETS, OH YES, AND FALSITIES, WE KNOW. BUT WHAT ELSE?
AH-HAH. HELLO, DARKNESS.
YER MASTERS STOLE THE ***STARHEART*** AND SHUT ALL OUR WORLD GATES, GREEN SLAVE. NOW, WITH A WORD, YRIDIAN OPENS YERS.
A'TMATENTRYM!
FEED! FEED!

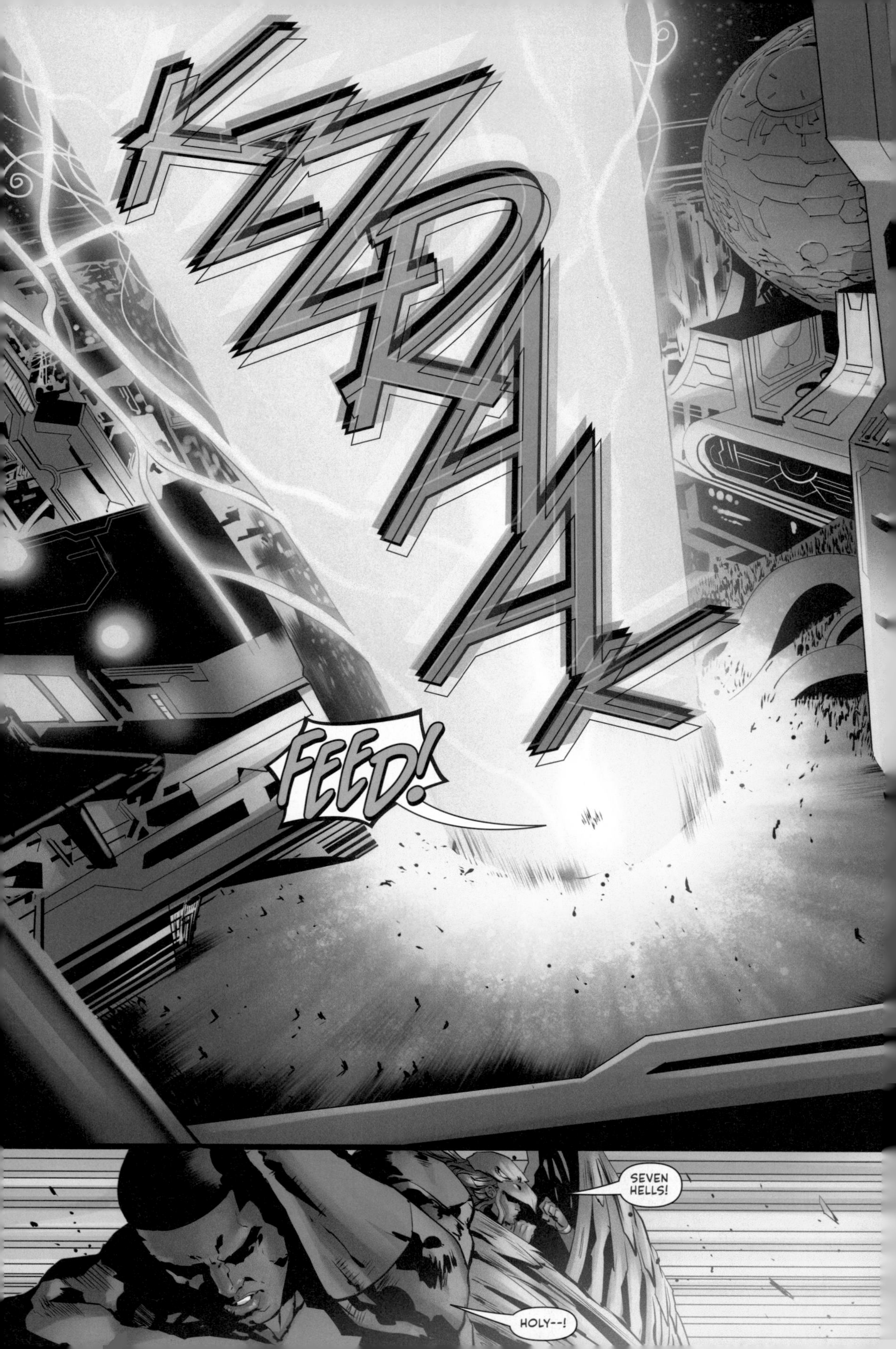
KZZAAAK
FEED!
SEVEN HELLS!
HOLY--!

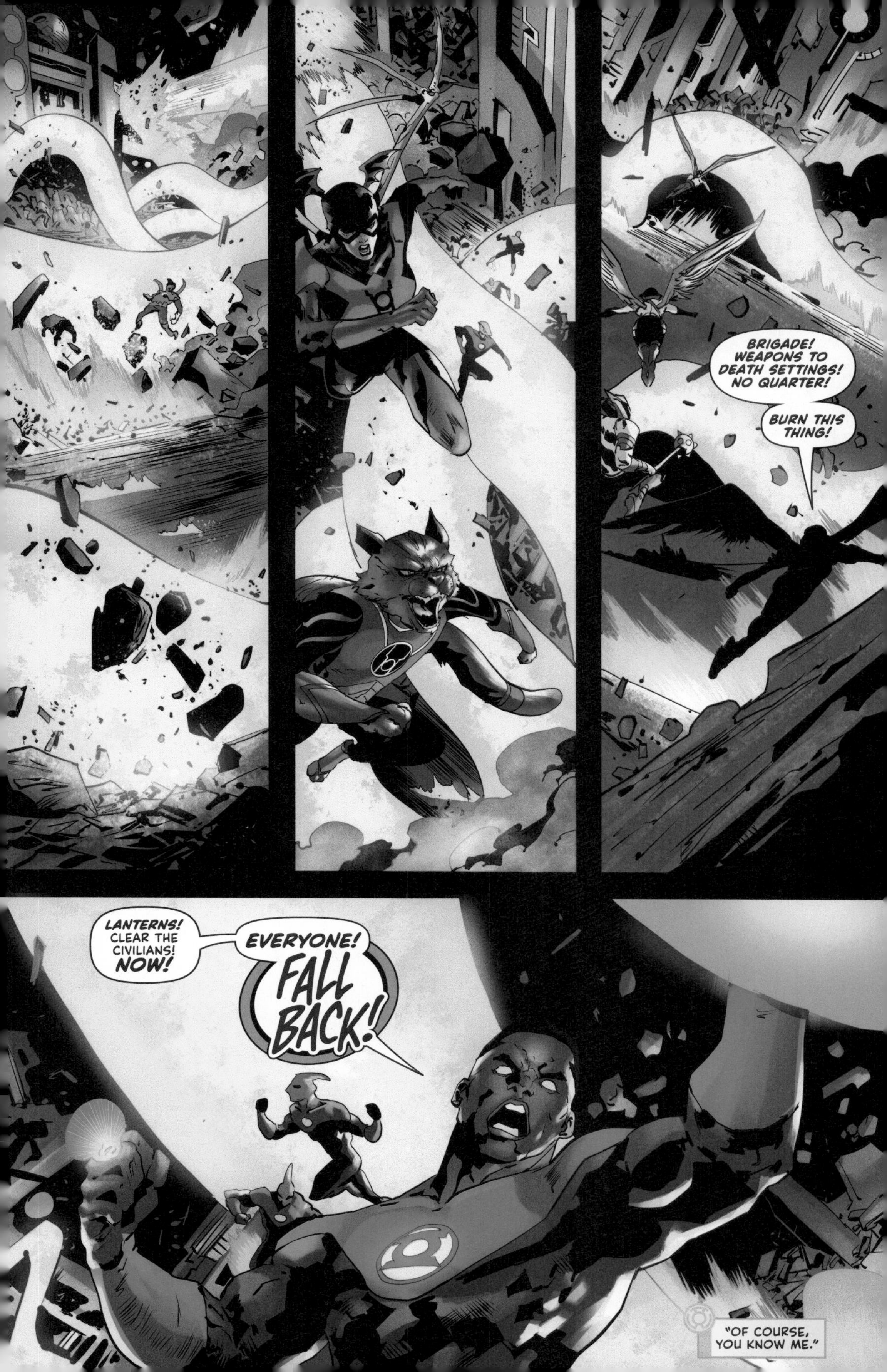
BRIGADE! WEAPONS TO DEATH SETTINGS! NO QUARTER!
BURN THIS THING!
LANTERNS! CLEAR THE CIVILIANS! NOW!
EVERYONE! FALL BACK!
"OF COURSE, YOU KNOW ME."

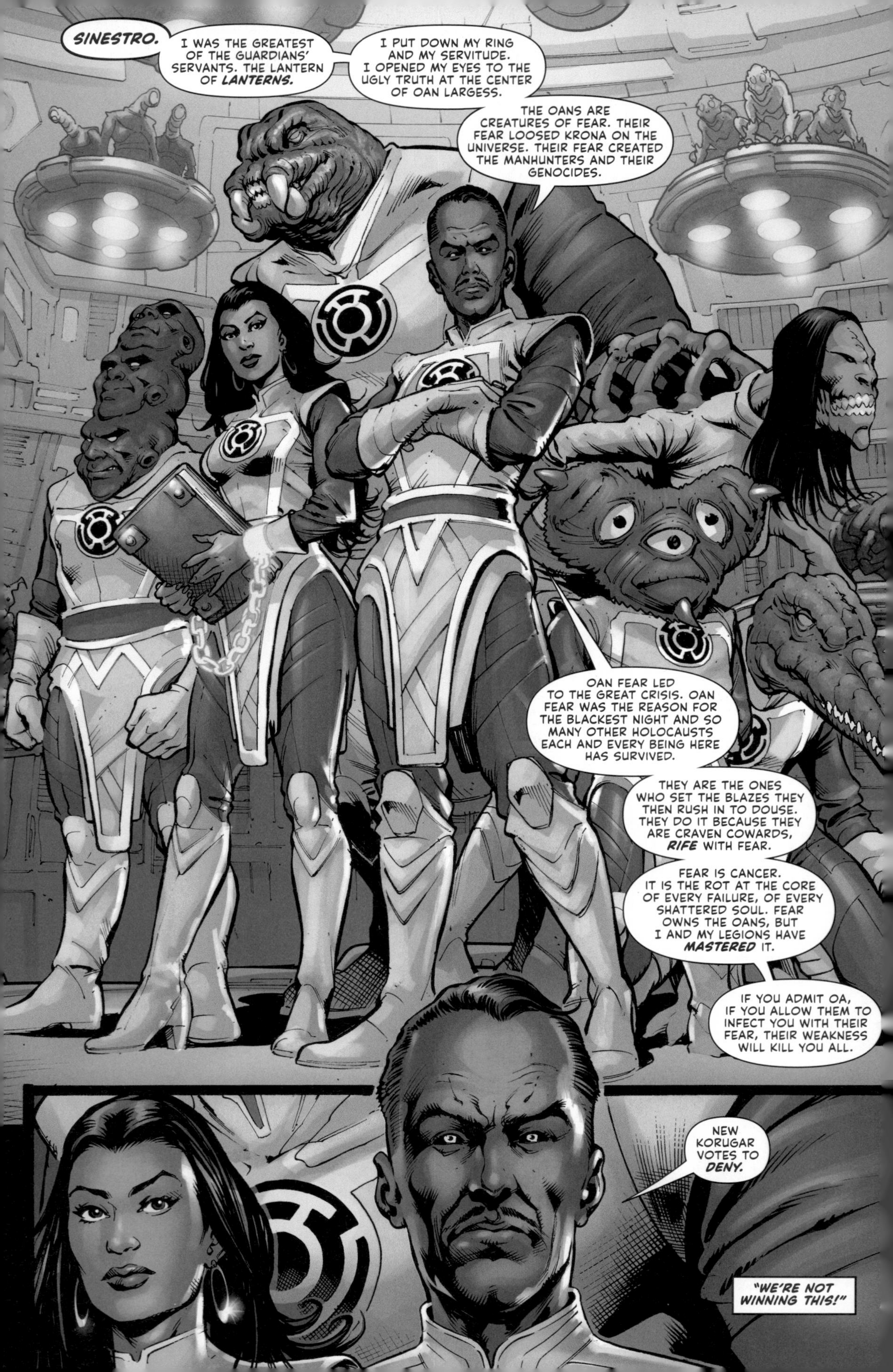
SINESTRO.
I WAS THE GREATEST OF THE GUARDIANS' SERVANTS. THE LANTERN OF LANTERNS.
I PUT DOWN MY RING AND MY SERVITUDE. I OPENED MY EYES TO THE UGLY TRUTH AT THE CENTER OF OAN LARGESS.
THE OANS ARE CREATURES OF FEAR. THEIR FEAR LOOSED KRONA ON THE UNIVERSE. THEIR FEAR CREATED THE MANHUNTERS AND THEIR GENOCIDES.
OAN FEAR LED TO THE GREAT CRISIS. OAN FEAR WAS THE REASON FOR THE BLACKEST NIGHT AND SO MANY OTHER HOLOCAUSTS EACH AND EVERY BEING HERE HAS SURVIVED.
THEY ARE THE ONES WHO SET THE BLAZES THEY THEN RUSH IN TO DOUSE. THEY DO IT BECAUSE THEY ARE CRAVEN COWARDS, RIFE WITH FEAR.
FEAR IS CANCER. IT IS THE ROT AT THE CORE OF EVERY FAILURE, OF EVERY SHATTERED SOUL. FEAR OWNS THE OANS, BUT I AND MY LEGIONS HAVE MASTERED IT.
IF YOU ADMIT OA, IF YOU ALLOW THEM TO INFECT YOU WITH THEIR FEAR, THEIR WEAKNESS WILL KILL YOU ALL.
NEW KORUGAR VOTES TO DENY.
"WE'RE NOT WINNING THIS!"

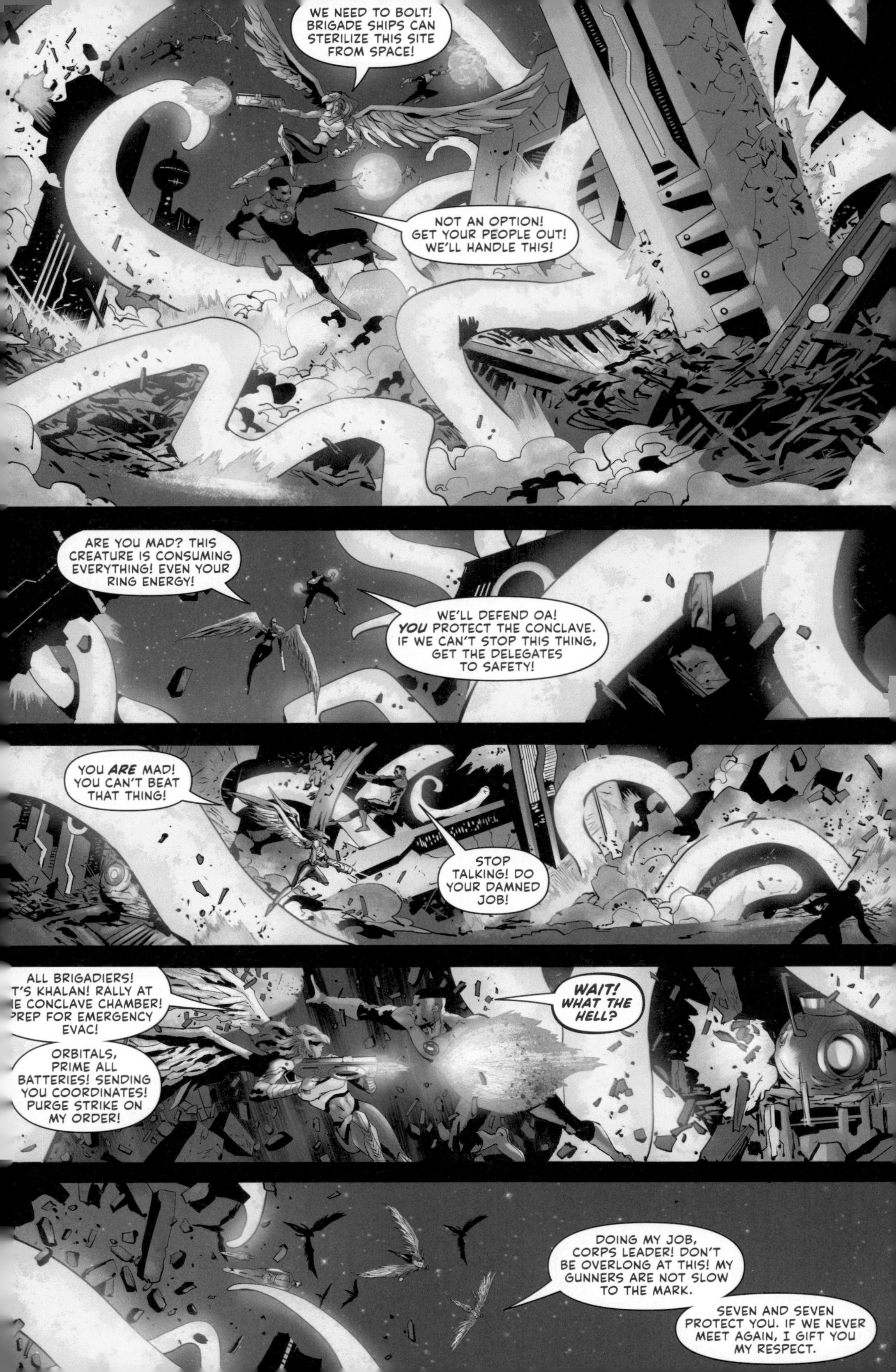

WE NEED TO BOLT! BRIGADE SHIPS CAN STERILIZE THIS SITE FROM SPACE!
NOT AN OPTION! GET YOUR PEOPLE OUT! WE'LL HANDLE THIS!
ARE YOU MAD? THIS CREATURE IS CONSUMING EVERYTHING! EVEN YOUR RING ENERGY!
WE'LL DEFEND OA! ***YOU*** PROTECT THE CONCLAVE. IF WE CAN'T STOP THIS THING, GET THE DELEGATES TO SAFETY!
YOU ***ARE*** MAD! YOU CAN'T BEAT THAT THING!
STOP TALKING! DO YOUR DAMNED JOB!
ALL BRIGADIERS! 'T'S KHALAN! RALLY AT E CONCLAVE CHAMBER! PREP FOR EMERGENCY EVAC!
WAIT! WHAT THE HELL?
ORBITALS, PRIME ALL BATTERIES! SENDING YOU COORDINATES! PURGE STRIKE ON MY ORDER!
DOING MY JOB, CORPS LEADER! DON'T BE OVERLONG AT THIS! MY GUNNERS ARE NOT SLOW TO THE MARK.
SEVEN AND SEVEN PROTECT YOU. IF WE NEVER MEET AGAIN, I GIFT YOU MY RESPECT.

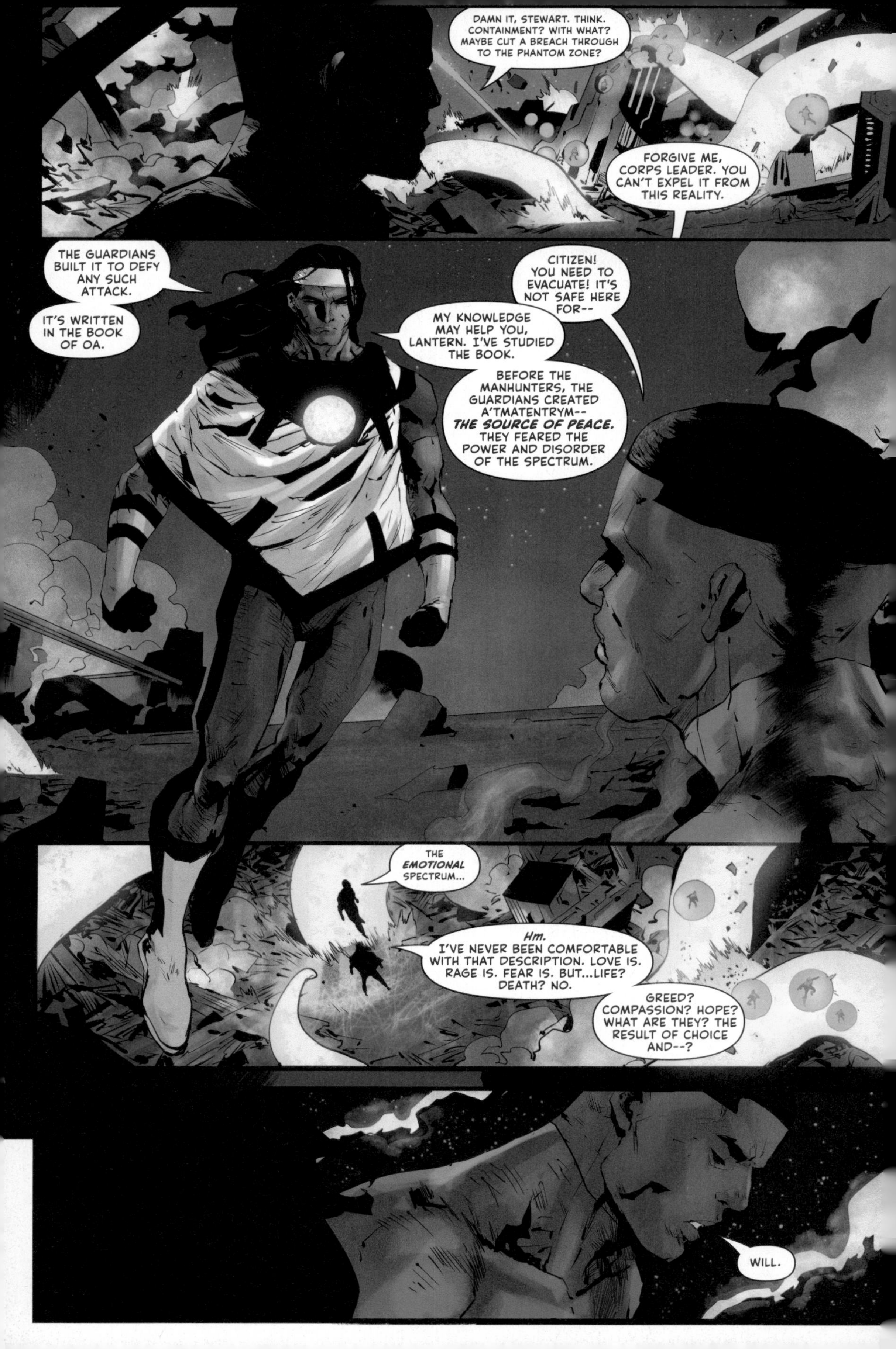
DAMN IT, STEWART. THINK. CONTAINMENT? WITH WHAT? MAYBE CUT A BREACH THROUGH TO THE PHANTOM ZONE?
FORGIVE ME, CORPS LEADER. YOU CAN'T EXPEL IT FROM THIS REALITY.
THE GUARDIANS BUILT IT TO DEFY ANY SUCH ATTACK.
IT'S WRITTEN IN THE BOOK OF OA.
CITIZEN! YOU NEED TO EVACUATE! IT'S NOT SAFE HERE FOR--
MY KNOWLEDGE MAY HELP YOU, LANTERN. I'VE STUDIED THE BOOK.
BEFORE THE MANHUNTERS, THE GUARDIANS CREATED A'TMATENTRYM-- ***THE SOURCE OF PEACE.*** THEY FEARED THE POWER AND DISORDER OF THE SPECTRUM.
THE ***EMOTIONAL*** SPECTRUM...
Hm. I'VE NEVER BEEN COMFORTABLE WITH THAT DESCRIPTION. LOVE IS. RAGE IS. FEAR IS. BUT...LIFE? DEATH? NO.
GREED? COMPASSION? HOPE? WHAT ARE THEY? THE RESULT OF CHOICE AND--?
WILL.

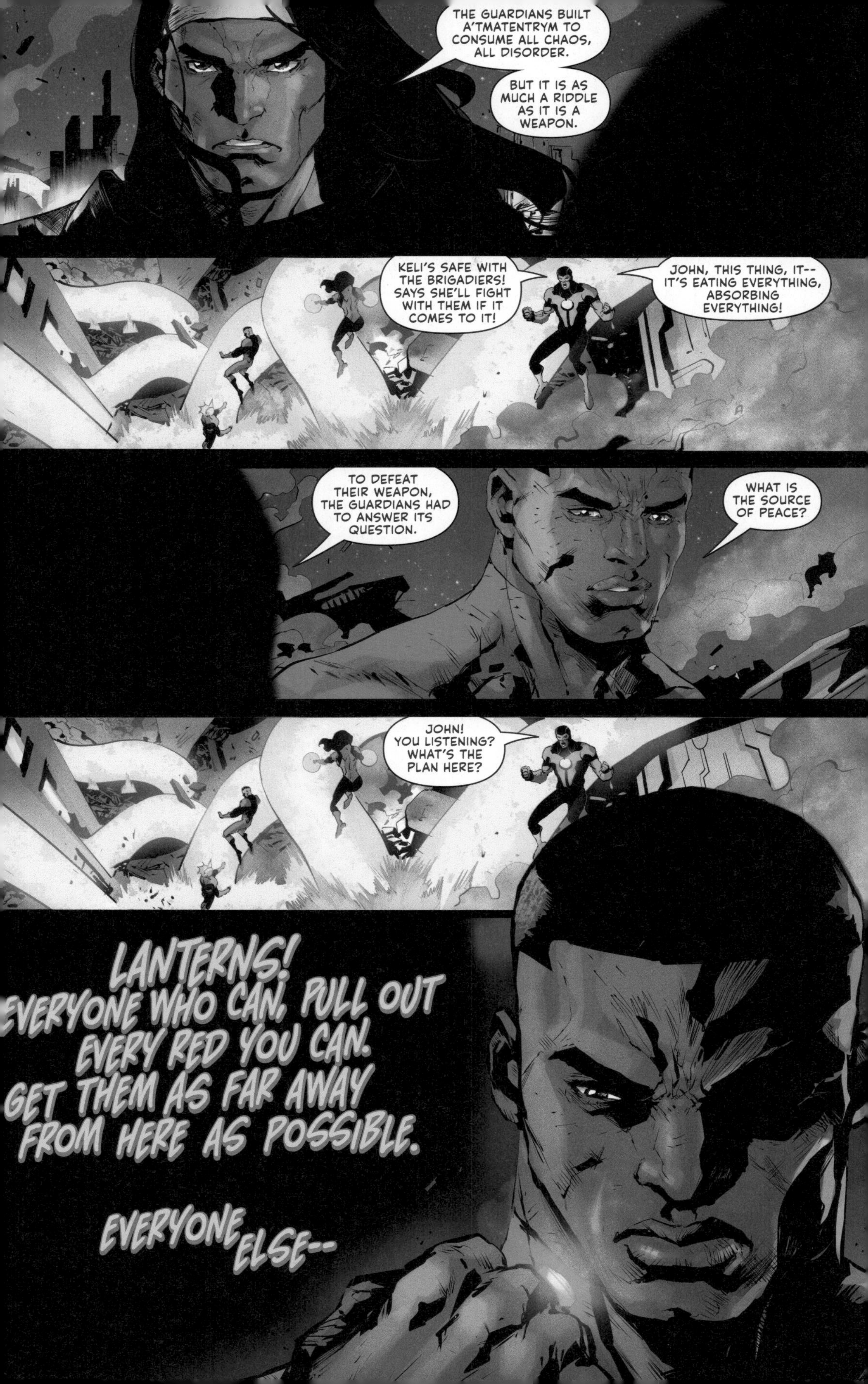
THE GUARDIANS BUILT A'TMATENTRYM TO CONSUME ALL CHAOS, ALL DISORDER.
BUT IT IS AS MUCH A RIDDLE AS IT IS A WEAPON.
KELI'S SAFE WITH THE BRIGADIERS! SAYS SHE'LL FIGHT WITH THEM IF IT COMES TO IT!
JOHN, THIS THING, IT-- IT'S EATING EVERYTHING, ABSORBING EVERYTHING!
TO DEFEAT THEIR WEAPON, THE GUARDIANS HAD TO ANSWER ITS QUESTION.
WHAT IS THE SOURCE OF PEACE?
JOHN! YOU LISTENING? WHAT'S THE PLAN HERE?
LANTERNS! EVERYONE WHO CAN, PULL OUT EVERY RED YOU CAN. GET THEM AS FAR AWAY FROM HERE AS POSSIBLE.
EVERYONE ELSE--

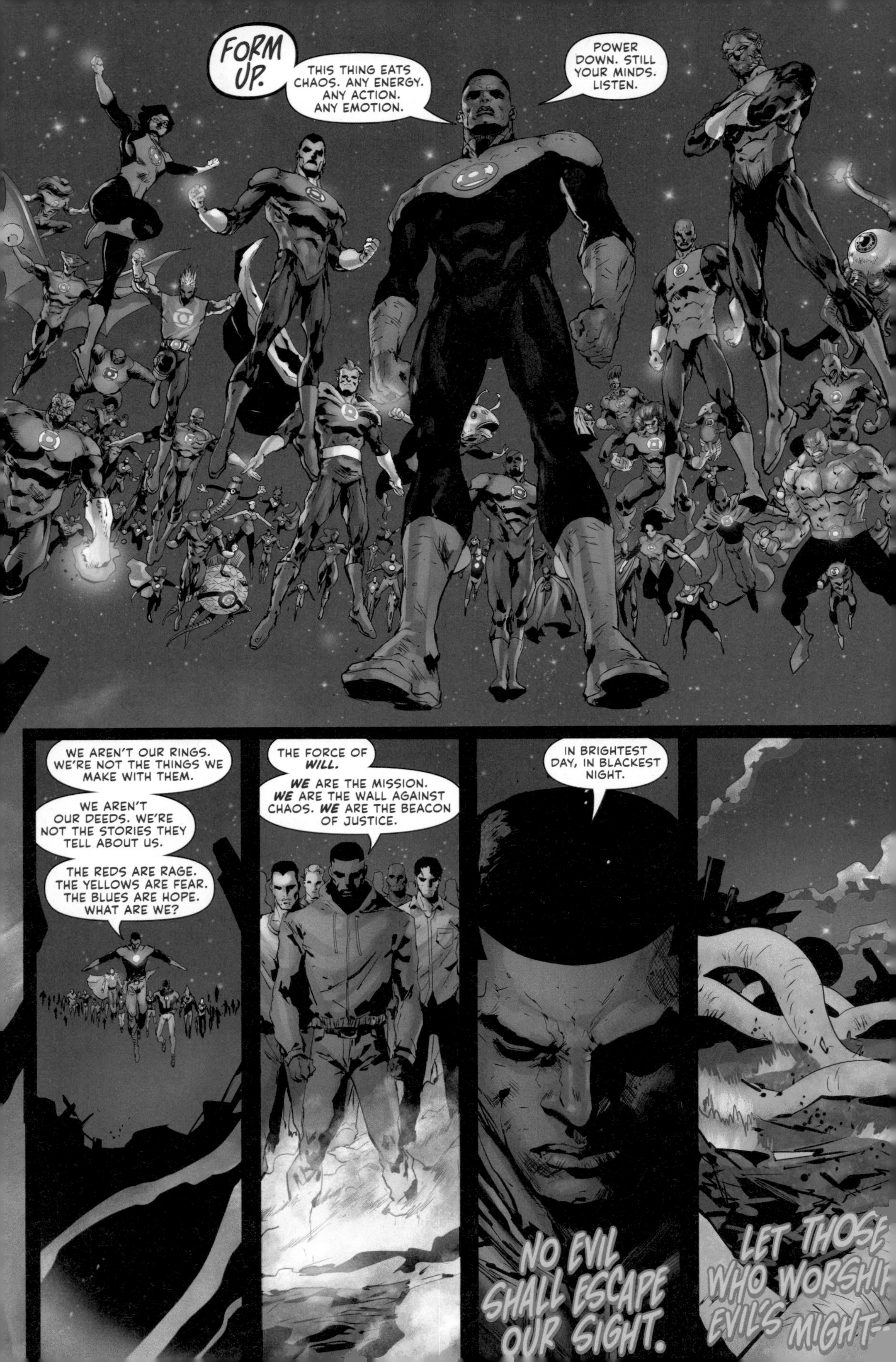
FORM UP.
THIS THING EATS CHAOS. ANY ENERGY. ANY ACTION. ANY EMOTION.
POWER DOWN. STILL YOUR MINDS. LISTEN.
WE AREN'T OUR RINGS. WE'RE NOT THE THINGS WE MAKE WITH THEM.
WE AREN'T OUR DEEDS. WE'RE NOT THE STORIES THEY TELL ABOUT US.
THE REDS ARE RAGE. THE YELLOWS ARE FEAR. THE BLUES ARE HOPE. WHAT ARE WE?
THE FORCE OF WILL.
WE ARE THE MISSION. WE ARE THE WALL AGAINST CHAOS. WE ARE THE BEACON OF JUSTICE.
IN BRIGHTEST DAY, IN BLACKEST NIGHT.
NO EVIL SHALL ESCAPE OUR SIGHT.
LET THOSE WHO WORSHIP EVIL'S MIGHT--

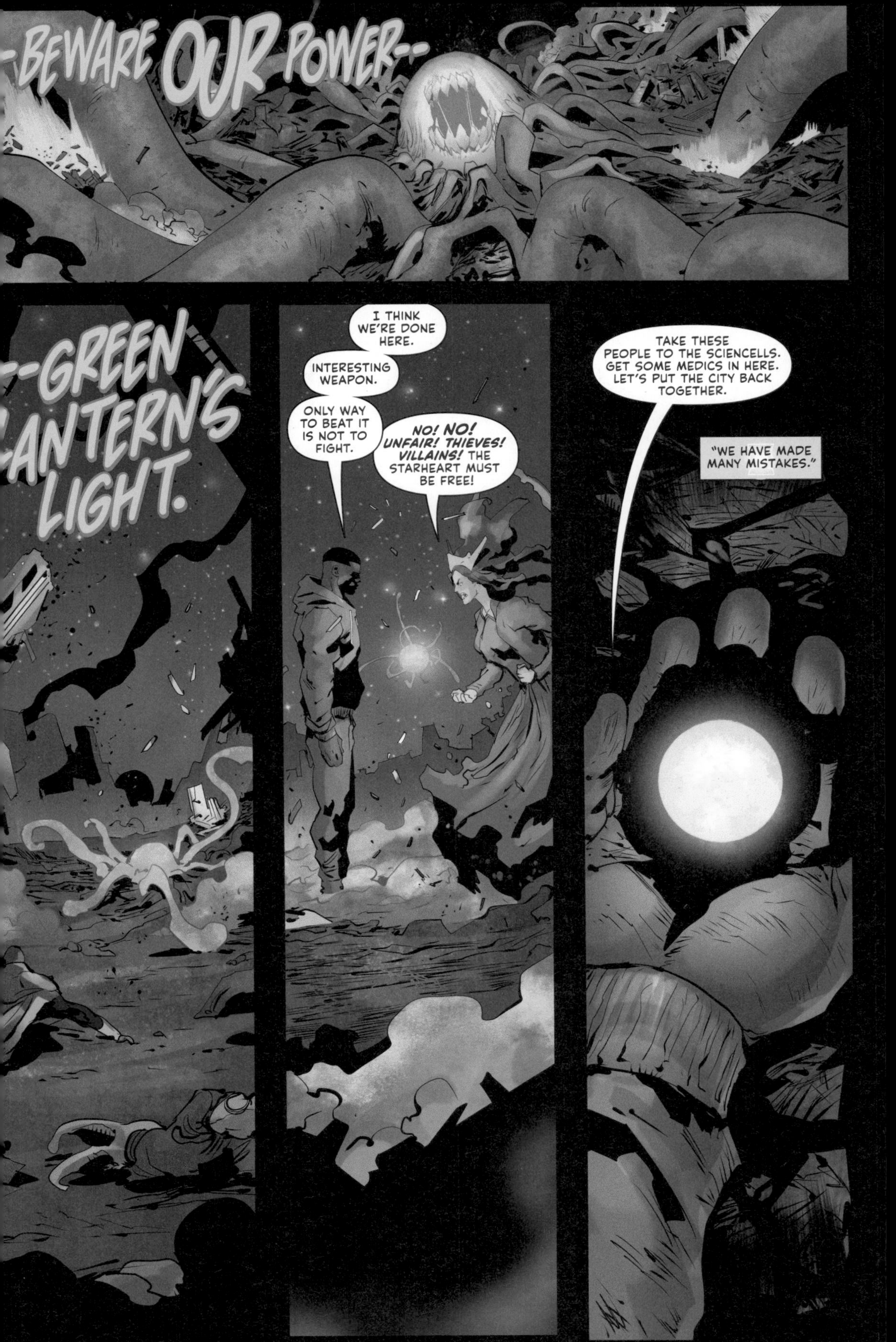
--BEWARE OUR POWER--
--GREEN LANTERN'S LIGHT.
I THINK WE'RE DONE HERE.
INTERESTING WEAPON.
ONLY WAY TO BEAT IT IS NOT TO FIGHT.
NO! NO! UNFAIR! THIEVES! VILLAINS! THE STARHEART MUST BE FREE!
TAKE THESE PEOPLE TO THE SCIENCELLS. GET SOME MEDICS IN HERE. LET'S PUT THE CITY BACK TOGETHER.
"WE HAVE MADE MANY MISTAKES."

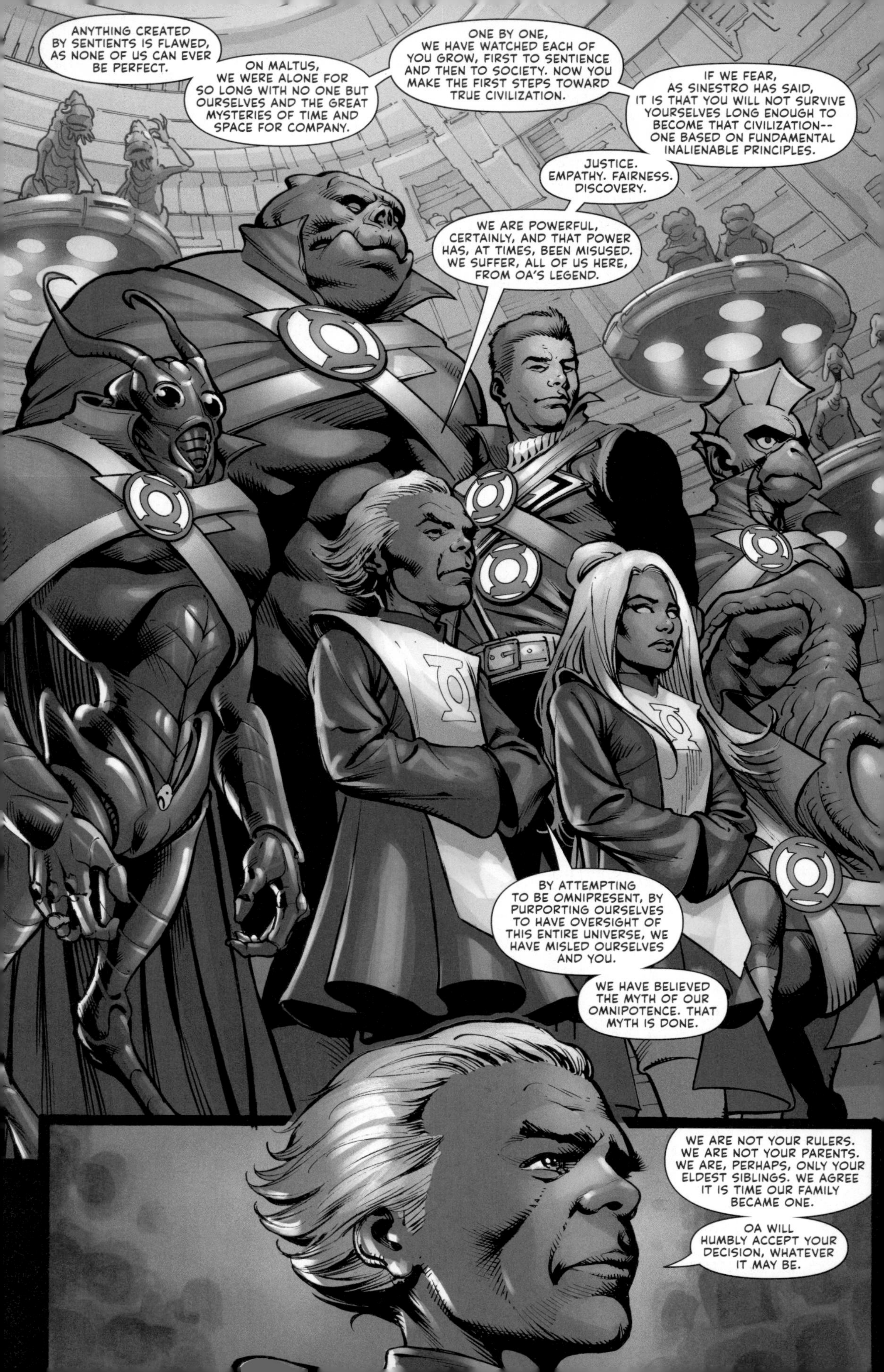
ANYTHING CREATED BY SENTIENTS IS FLAWED, AS NONE OF US CAN EVER BE PERFECT.
ON MALTUS, WE WERE ALONE FOR SO LONG WITH NO ONE BUT OURSELVES AND THE GREAT MYSTERIES OF TIME AND SPACE FOR COMPANY.
ONE BY ONE, WE HAVE WATCHED EACH OF YOU GROW, FIRST TO SENTIENCE AND THEN TO SOCIETY. NOW YOU MAKE THE FIRST STEPS TOWARD TRUE CIVILIZATION.
IF WE FEAR, AS SINESTRO HAS SAID, IT IS THAT YOU WILL NOT SURVIVE YOURSELVES LONG ENOUGH TO BECOME THAT CIVILIZATION-- ONE BASED ON FUNDAMENTAL INALIENABLE PRINCIPLES.
JUSTICE. EMPATHY. FAIRNESS. DISCOVERY.
WE ARE POWERFUL, CERTAINLY, AND THAT POWER HAS, AT TIMES, BEEN MISUSED. WE SUFFER, ALL OF US HERE, FROM OA'S LEGEND.
BY ATTEMPTING TO BE OMNIPRESENT, BY PURPORTING OURSELVES TO HAVE OVERSIGHT OF THIS ENTIRE UNIVERSE, WE HAVE MISLED OURSELVES AND YOU.
WE HAVE BELIEVED THE MYTH OF OUR OMNIPOTENCE. THAT MYTH IS DONE.
WE ARE NOT YOUR RULERS. WE ARE NOT YOUR PARENTS. WE ARE, PERHAPS, ONLY YOUR ELDEST SIBLINGS. WE AGREE IT IS TIME OUR FAMILY BECAME ONE.
OA WILL HUMBLY ACCEPT YOUR DECISION, WHATEVER IT MAY BE.

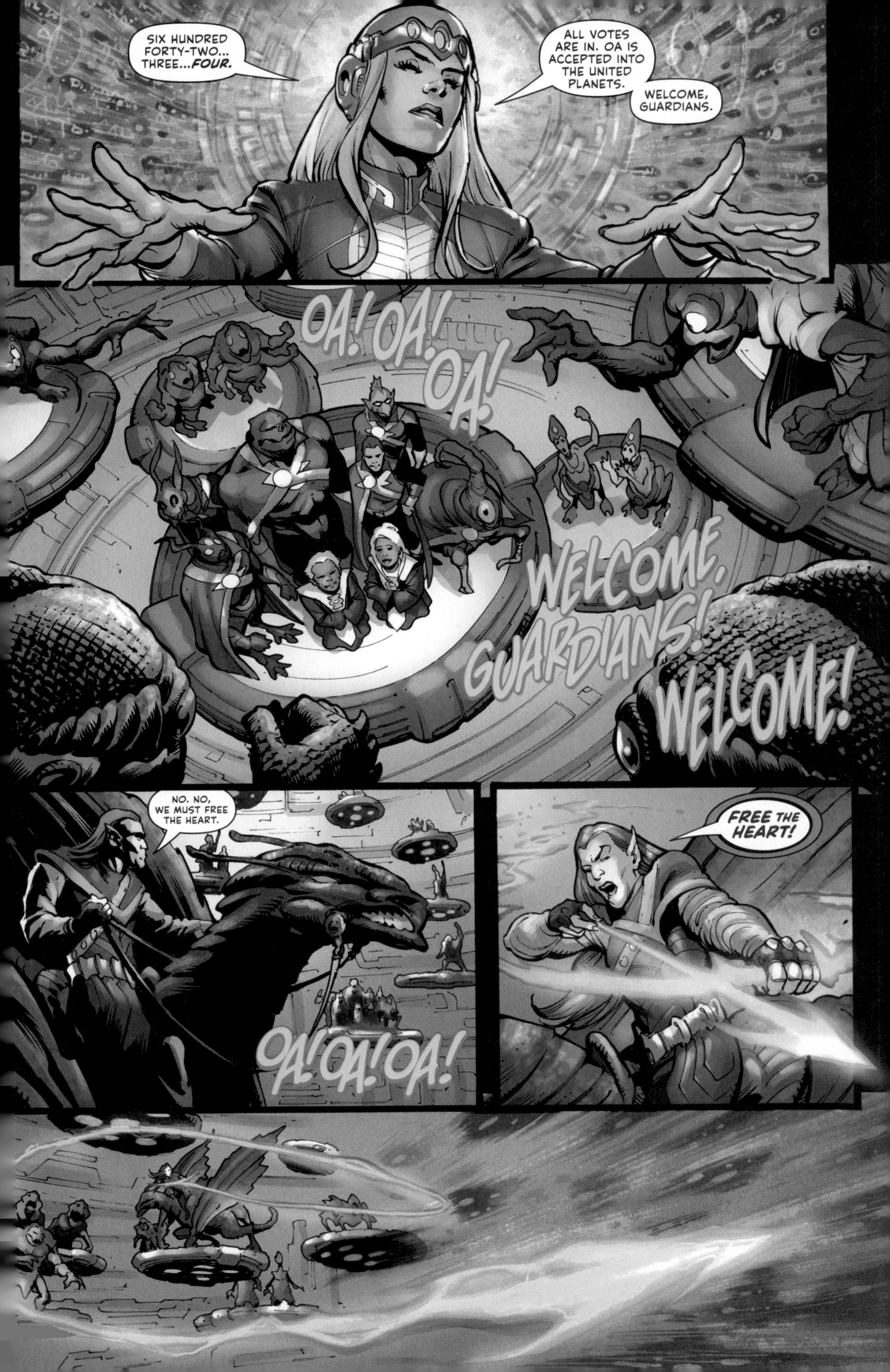
SIX HUNDRED FORTY-TWO... THREE...*FOUR.*
ALL VOTES ARE IN. OA IS ACCEPTED INTO THE UNITED PLANETS.
WELCOME, GUARDIANS.
OA! OA! OA!
WELCOME, GUARDIANS!
WELCOME!
NO. NO, WE MUST FREE THE HEART.
OA! OA! OA!
FREE THE HEART!

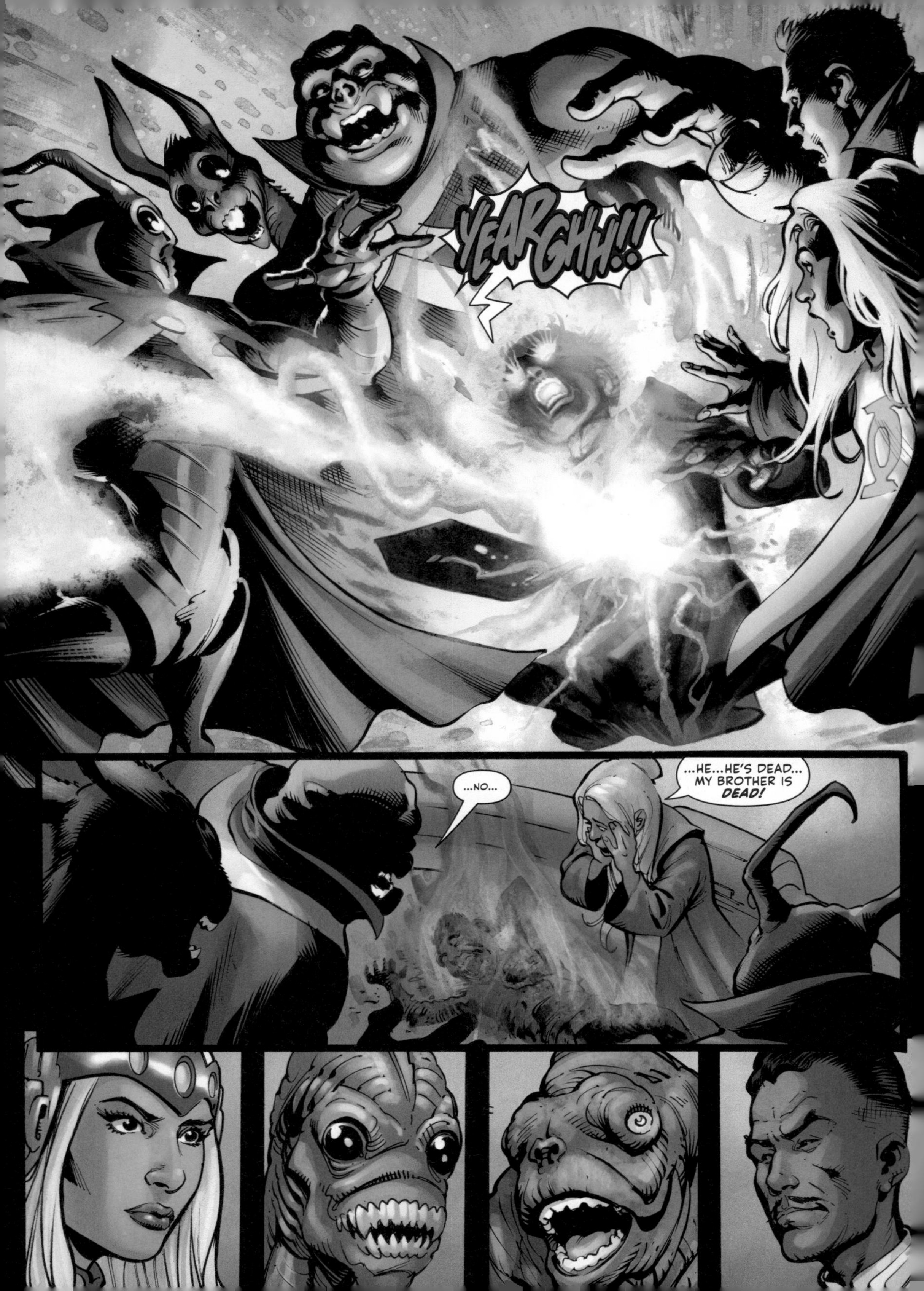
YEARGHH!!
...NO...
...HE...HE'S DEAD... MY BROTHER IS DEAD!

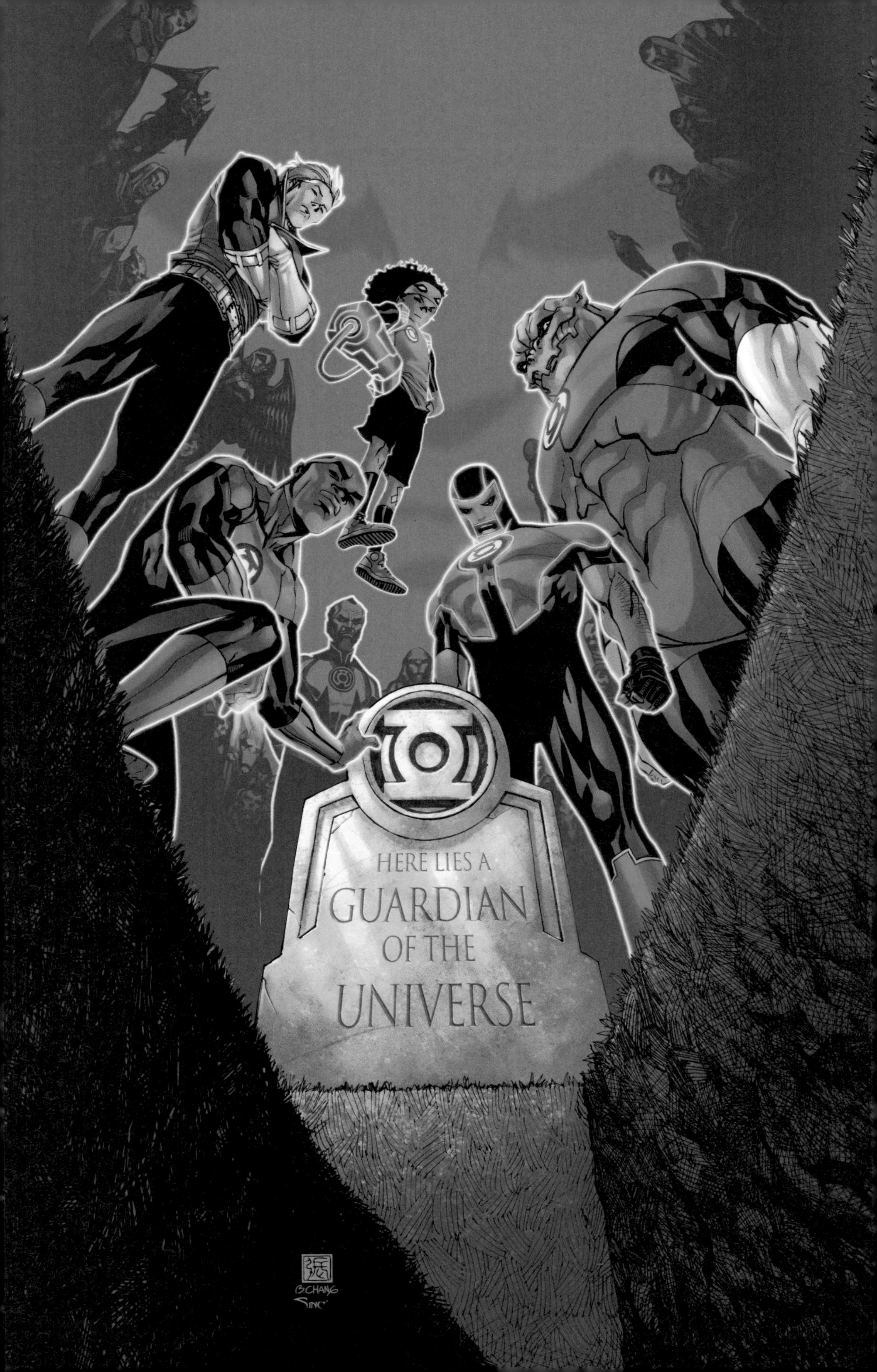
HERE LIES A
GUARDIAN
OF THE
UNIVERSE

Green Lantern #2 main cover art
by Bernard Chang and Alex Sinclair

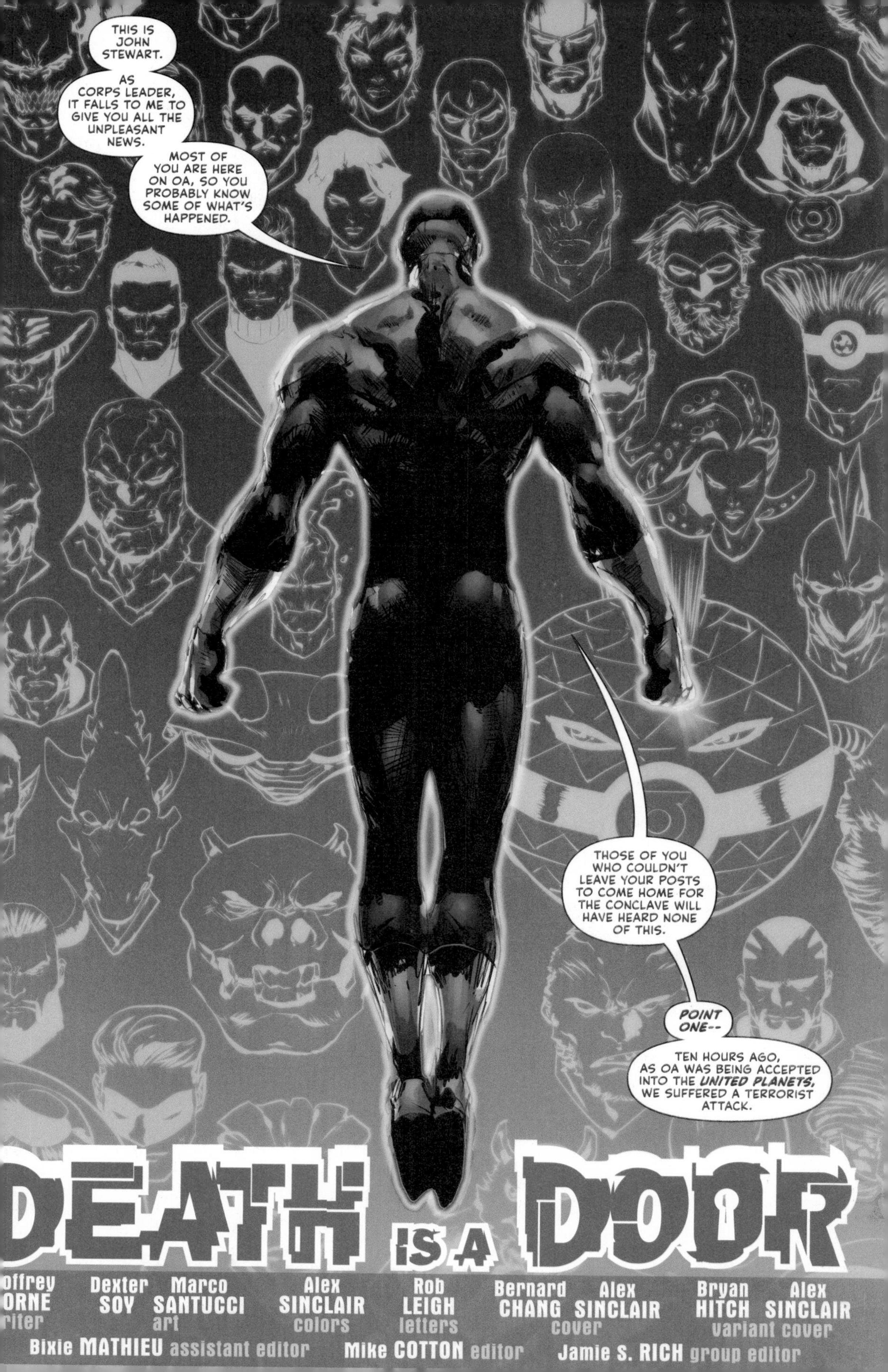

THIS IS JOHN STEWART.
AS CORPS LEADER, IT FALLS TO ME TO GIVE YOU ALL THE UNPLEASANT NEWS.
MOST OF YOU ARE HERE ON OA, SO YOU PROBABLY KNOW SOME OF WHAT'S HAPPENED.
THOSE OF YOU WHO COULDN'T LEAVE YOUR POSTS TO COME HOME FOR THE CONCLAVE WILL HAVE HEARD NONE OF THIS.
POINT ONE--
TEN HOURS AGO, AS OA WAS BEING ACCEPTED INTO THE *UNITED PLANETS,* WE SUFFERED A TERRORIST ATTACK.
DEATH IS A DOOR
offrey ORNE riter
Dexter SOY
Marco SANTUCCI art
Alex SINCLAIR colors
Rob LEIGH letters
Bernard CHANG Alex SINCLAIR cover
Bryan HITCH Alex SINCLAIR variant cover
Bixie MATHIEU assistant editor
Mike COTTON editor
Jamie S. RICH group editor

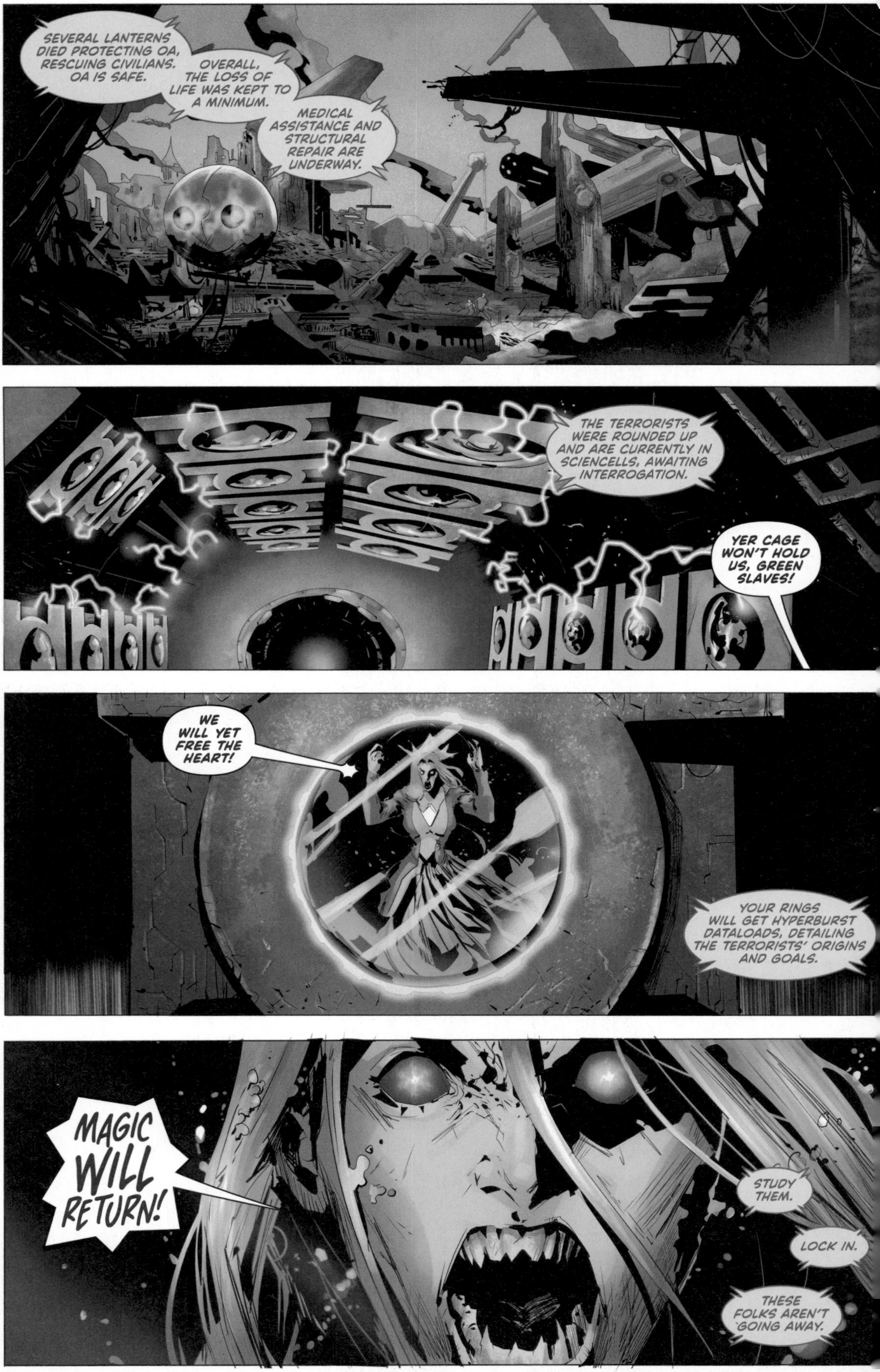
SEVERAL LANTERNS DIED PROTECTING OA, RESCUING CIVILIANS. OA IS SAFE.
OVERALL, THE LOSS OF LIFE WAS KEPT TO A MINIMUM.
MEDICAL ASSISTANCE AND STRUCTURAL REPAIR ARE UNDERWAY.
THE TERRORISTS WERE ROUNDED UP AND ARE CURRENTLY IN SCIENCELLS, AWAITING INTERROGATION.
YER CAGE WON'T HOLD US, GREEN SLAVES!
WE WILL YET FREE THE HEART!
YOUR RINGS WILL GET HYPERBURST DATALOADS, DETAILING THE TERRORISTS' ORIGINS AND GOALS.
MAGIC WILL RETURN!
STUDY THEM.
LOCK IN.
THESE FOLKS AREN'T GOING AWAY.

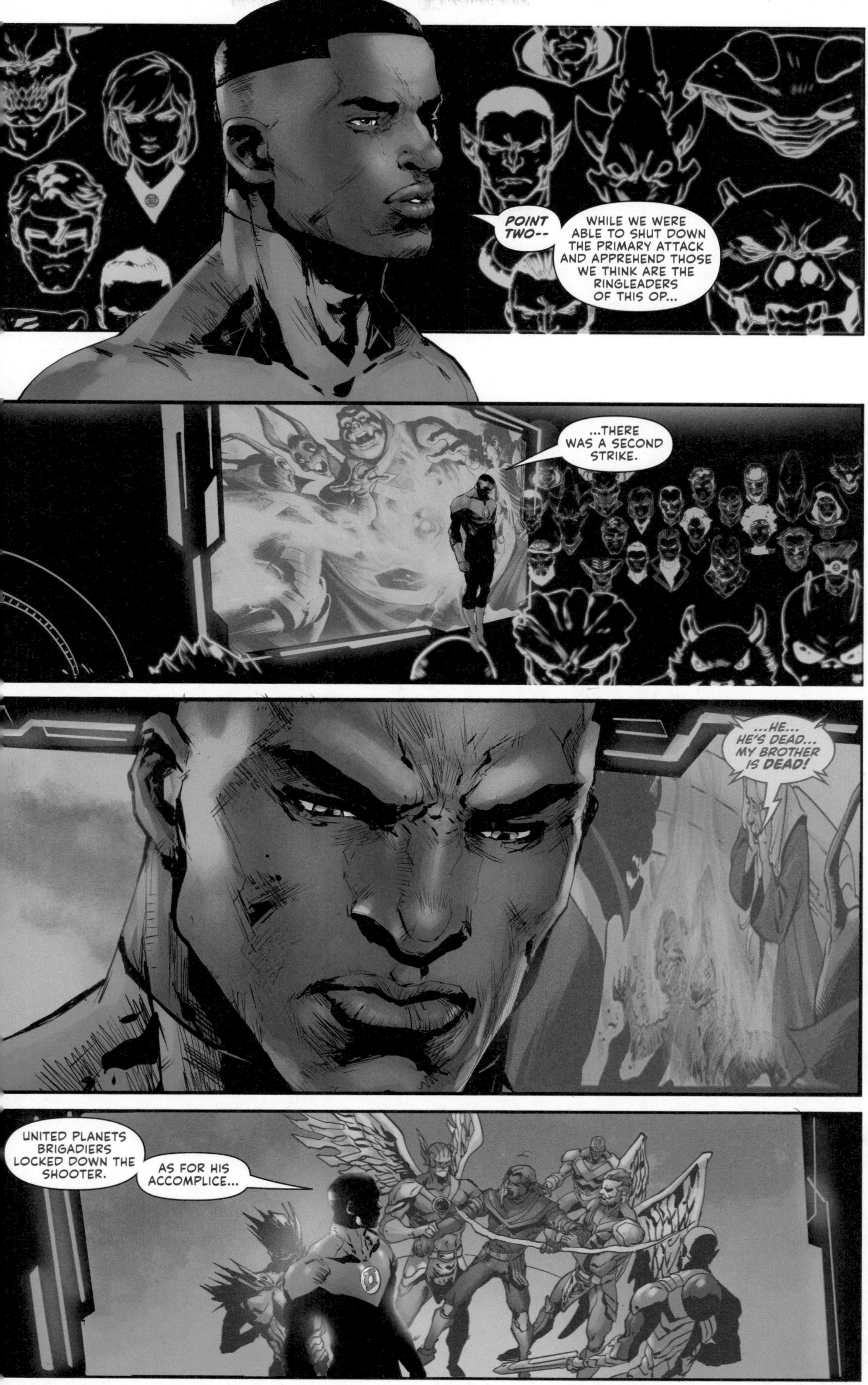
POINT TWO--
WHILE WE WERE ABLE TO SHUT DOWN THE PRIMARY ATTACK AND APPREHEND THOSE WE THINK ARE THE RINGLEADERS OF THIS OP...
...THERE WAS A SECOND STRIKE.
...HE... HE'S DEAD... MY BROTHER IS DEAD!
UNITED PLANETS BRIGADIERS LOCKED DOWN THE SHOOTER.
AS FOR HIS ACCOMPLICE...

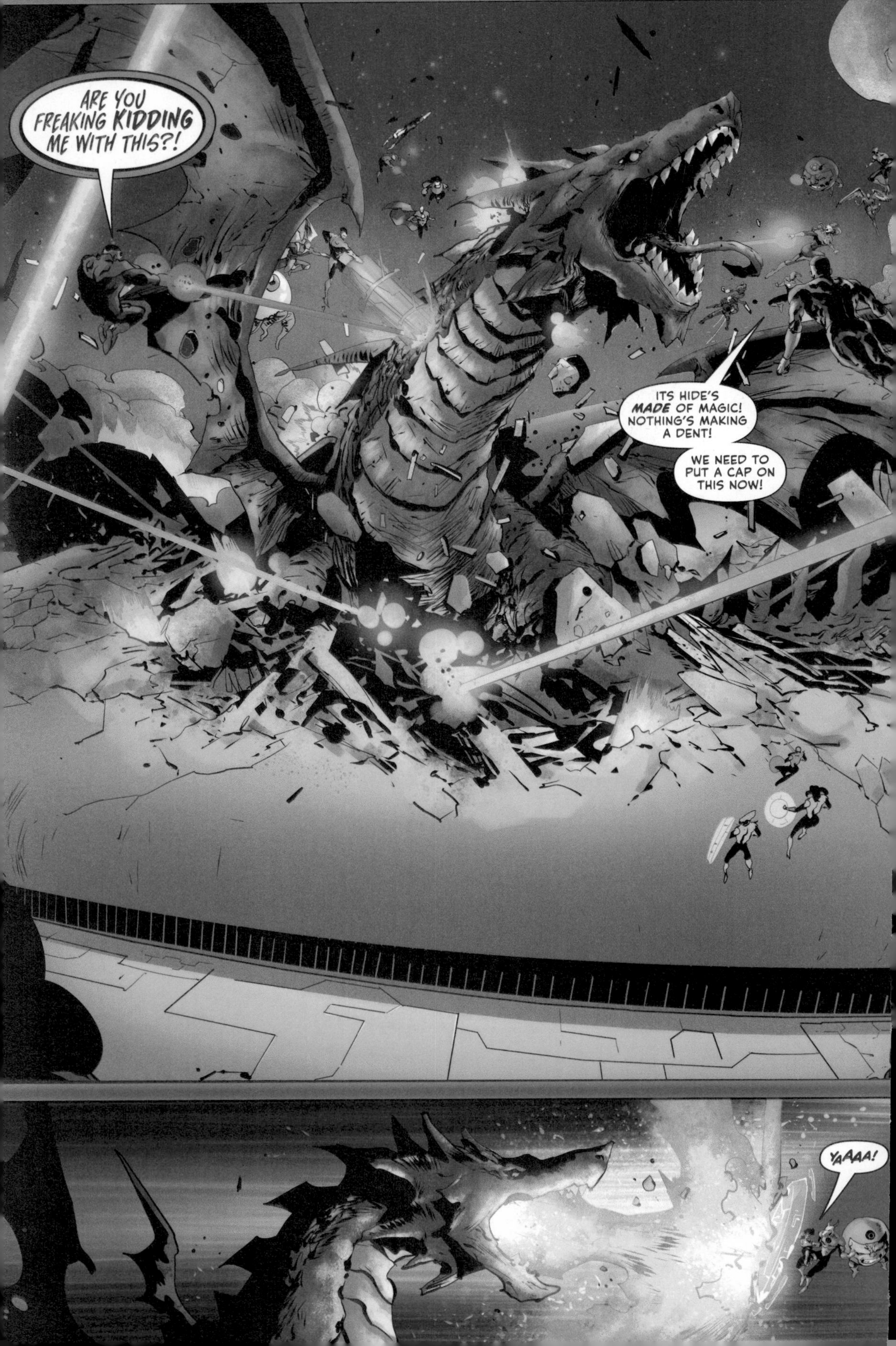
ARE YOU FREAKING KIDDING ME WITH THIS?!
ITS HIDE'S MADE OF MAGIC! NOTHING'S MAKING A DENT!
WE NEED TO PUT A CAP ON THIS NOW!
YAAAA!

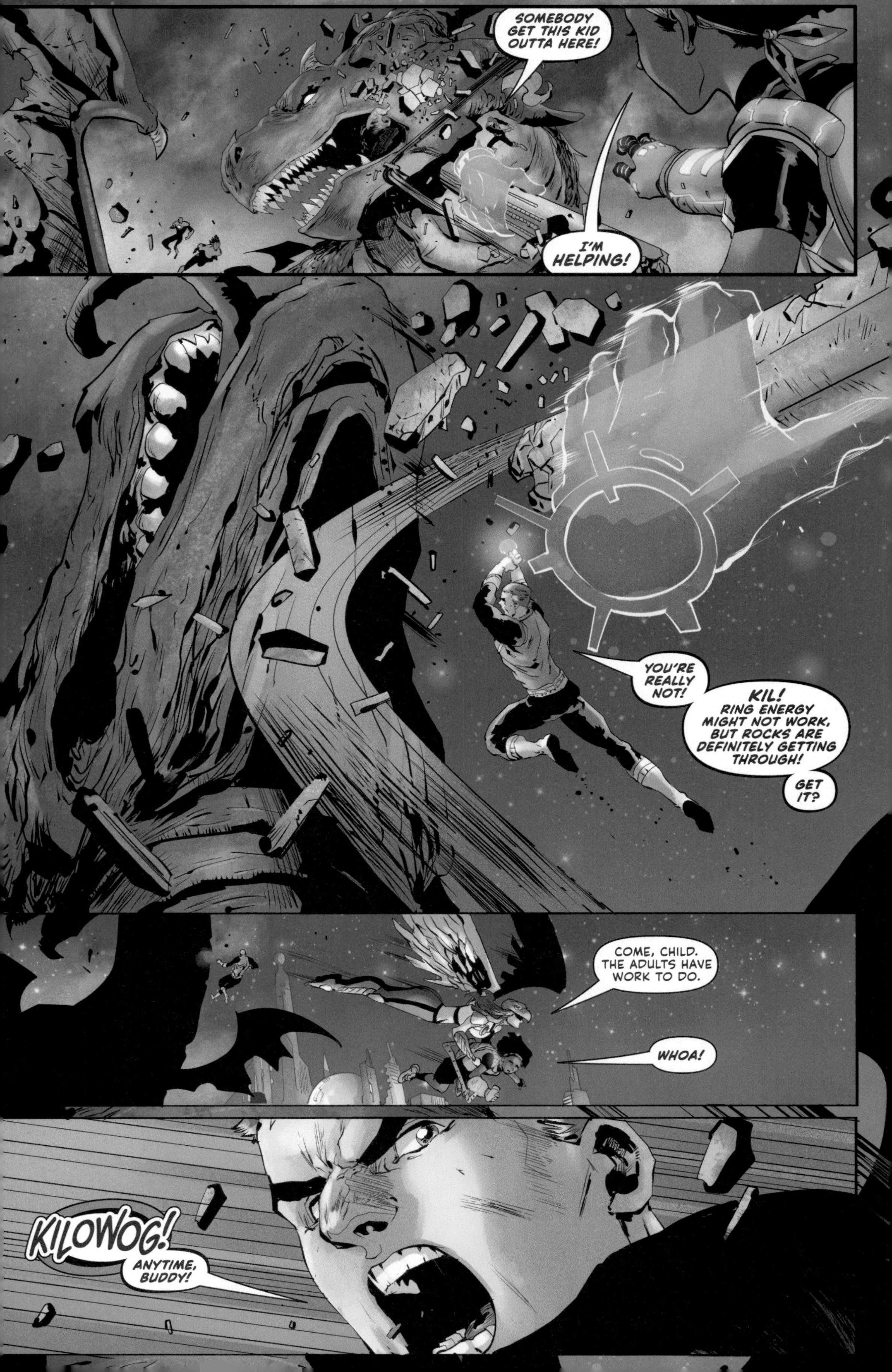
SOMEBODY GET THIS KID OUTTA HERE!
I'M HELPING!
YOU'RE REALLY NOT!
KIL! RING ENERGY MIGHT NOT WORK, BUT ROCKS ARE DEFINITELY GETTING THROUGH!
GET IT?
COME, CHILD. THE ADULTS HAVE WORK TO DO.
WHOA!
KILOWOG!
ANYTIME, BUDDY!

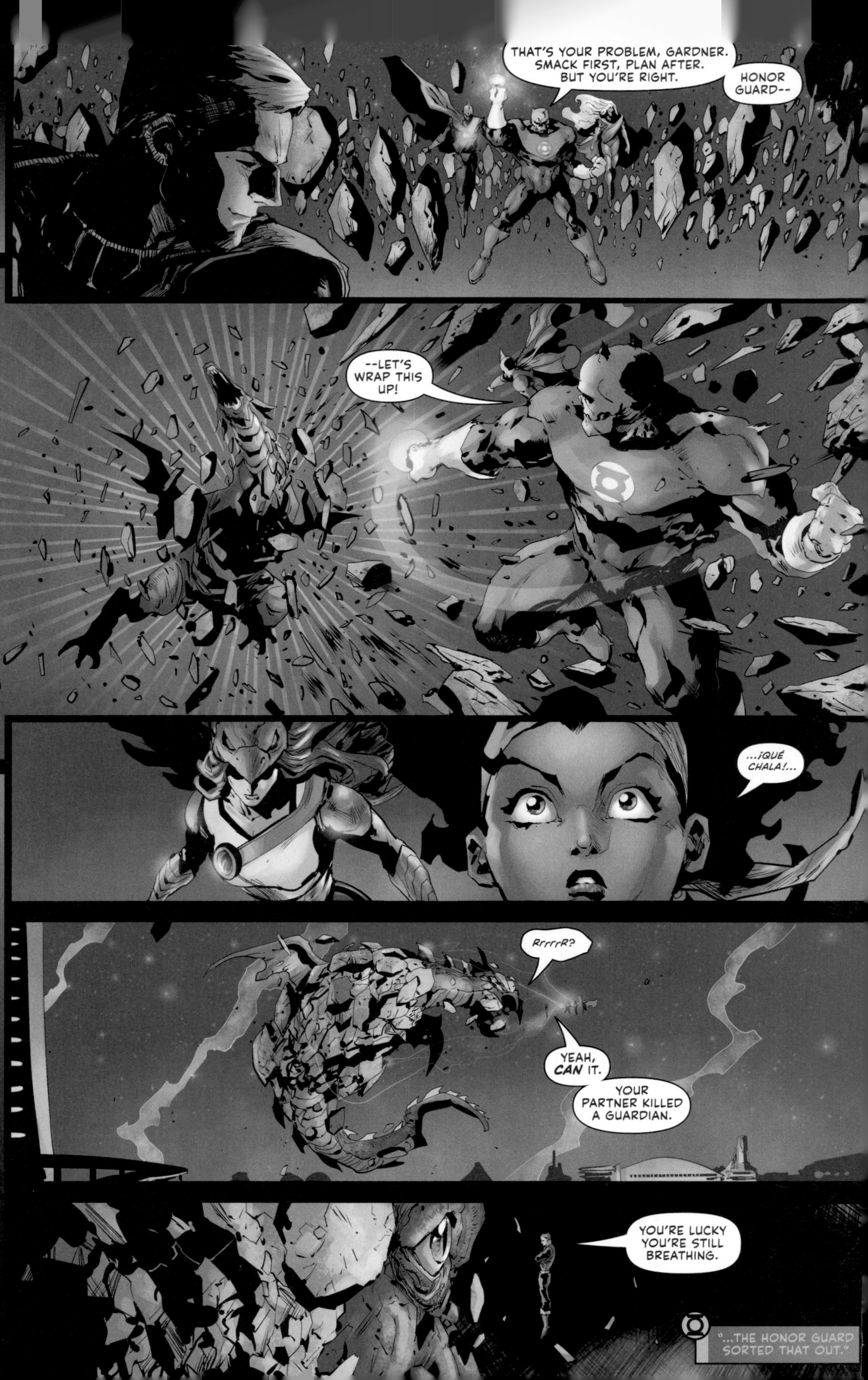
THAT'S YOUR PROBLEM, GARDNER. SMACK FIRST, PLAN AFTER. BUT YOU'RE RIGHT.
HONOR GUARD--
--LET'S WRAP THIS UP!
...¡QUÉ CHALA!...
RrrrrR?
YEAH, CAN IT.
YOUR PARTNER KILLED A GUARDIAN.
YOU'RE LUCKY YOU'RE STILL BREATHING.
"...THE HONOR GUARD SORTED THAT OUT."

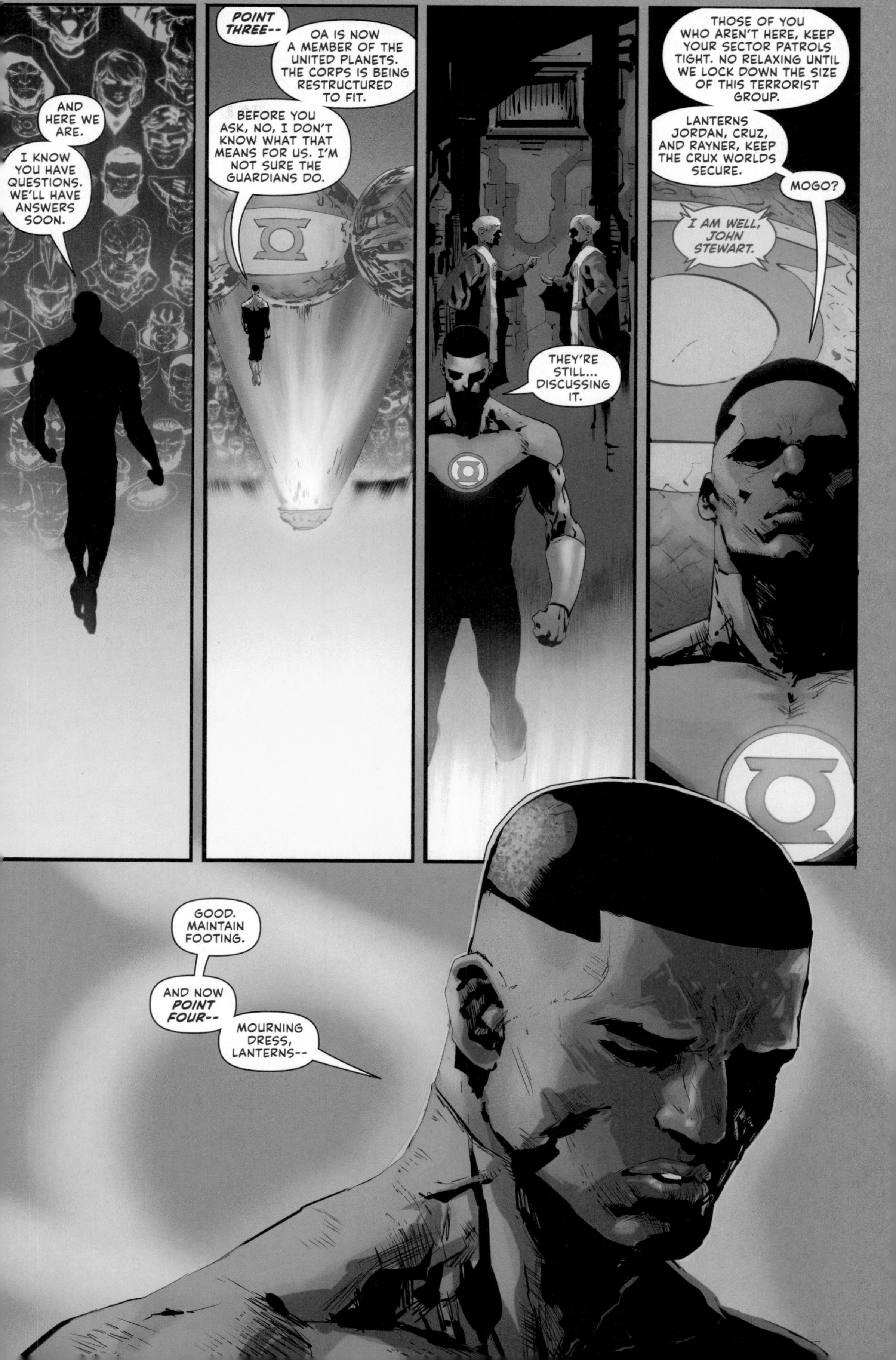
AND HERE WE ARE.
I KNOW YOU HAVE QUESTIONS. WE'LL HAVE ANSWERS SOON.
POINT THREE--
OA IS NOW A MEMBER OF THE UNITED PLANETS. THE CORPS IS BEING RESTRUCTURED TO FIT.
BEFORE YOU ASK, NO, I DON'T KNOW WHAT THAT MEANS FOR US. I'M NOT SURE THE GUARDIANS DO.
THEY'RE STILL... DISCUSSING IT.
THOSE OF YOU WHO AREN'T HERE, KEEP YOUR SECTOR PATROLS TIGHT. NO RELAXING UNTIL WE LOCK DOWN THE SIZE OF THIS TERRORIST GROUP.
LANTERNS JORDAN, CRUZ, AND RAYNER, KEEP THE CRUX WORLDS SECURE.
MOGO?
I AM WELL, JOHN STEWART.
GOOD. MAINTAIN FOOTING.
AND NOW POINT FOUR--
MOURNING DRESS, LANTERNS--

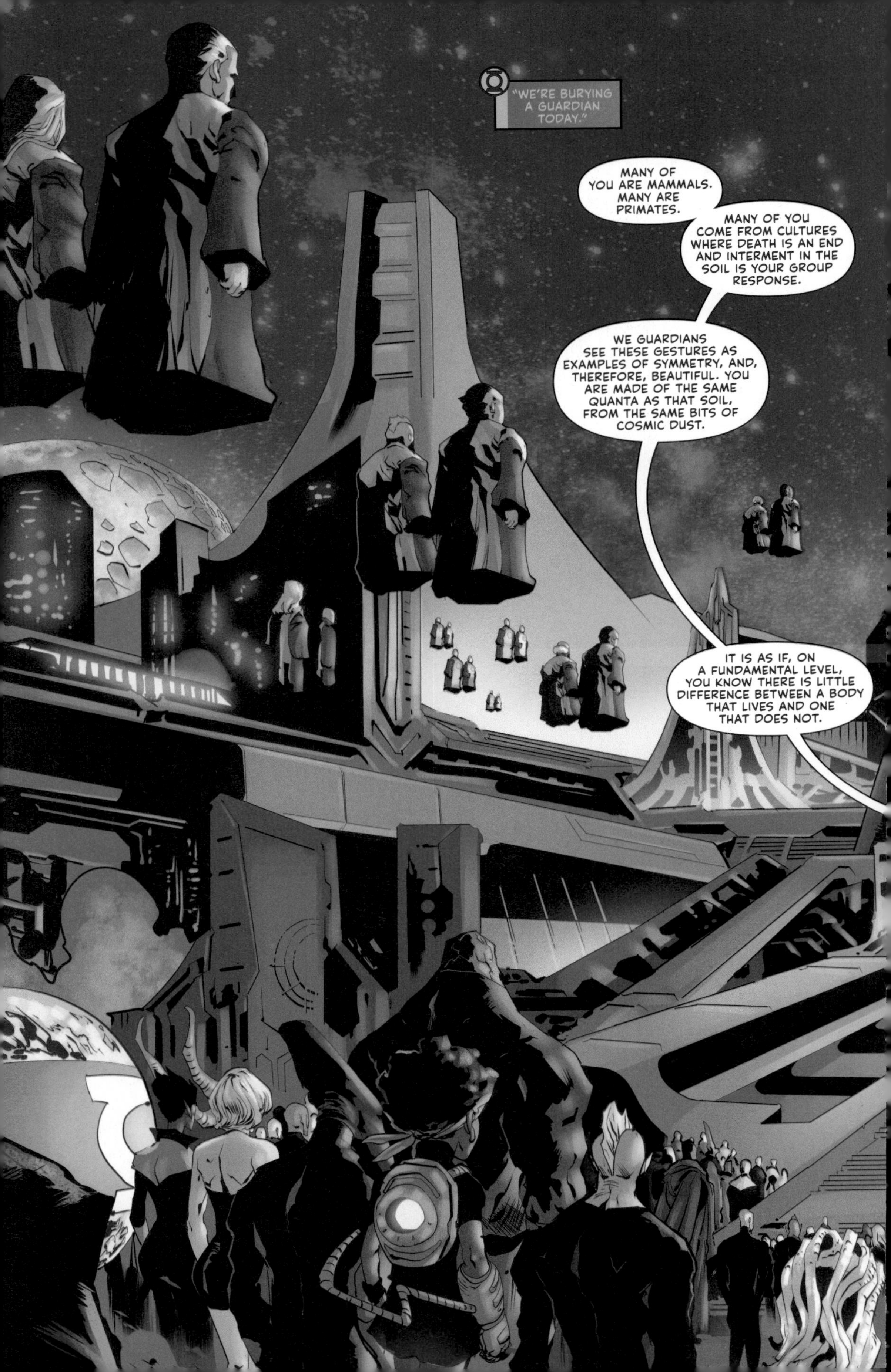
"WE'RE BURYING A GUARDIAN TODAY."
MANY OF YOU ARE MAMMALS. MANY ARE PRIMATES.
MANY OF YOU COME FROM CULTURES WHERE DEATH IS AN END AND INTERMENT IN THE SOIL IS YOUR GROUP RESPONSE.
WE GUARDIANS SEE THESE GESTURES AS EXAMPLES OF SYMMETRY, AND, THEREFORE, BEAUTIFUL. YOU ARE MADE OF THE SAME QUANTA AS THAT SOIL, FROM THE SAME BITS OF COSMIC DUST.
IT IS AS IF, ON A FUNDAMENTAL LEVEL, YOU KNOW THERE IS LITTLE DIFFERENCE BETWEEN A BODY THAT LIVES AND ONE THAT DOES NOT.

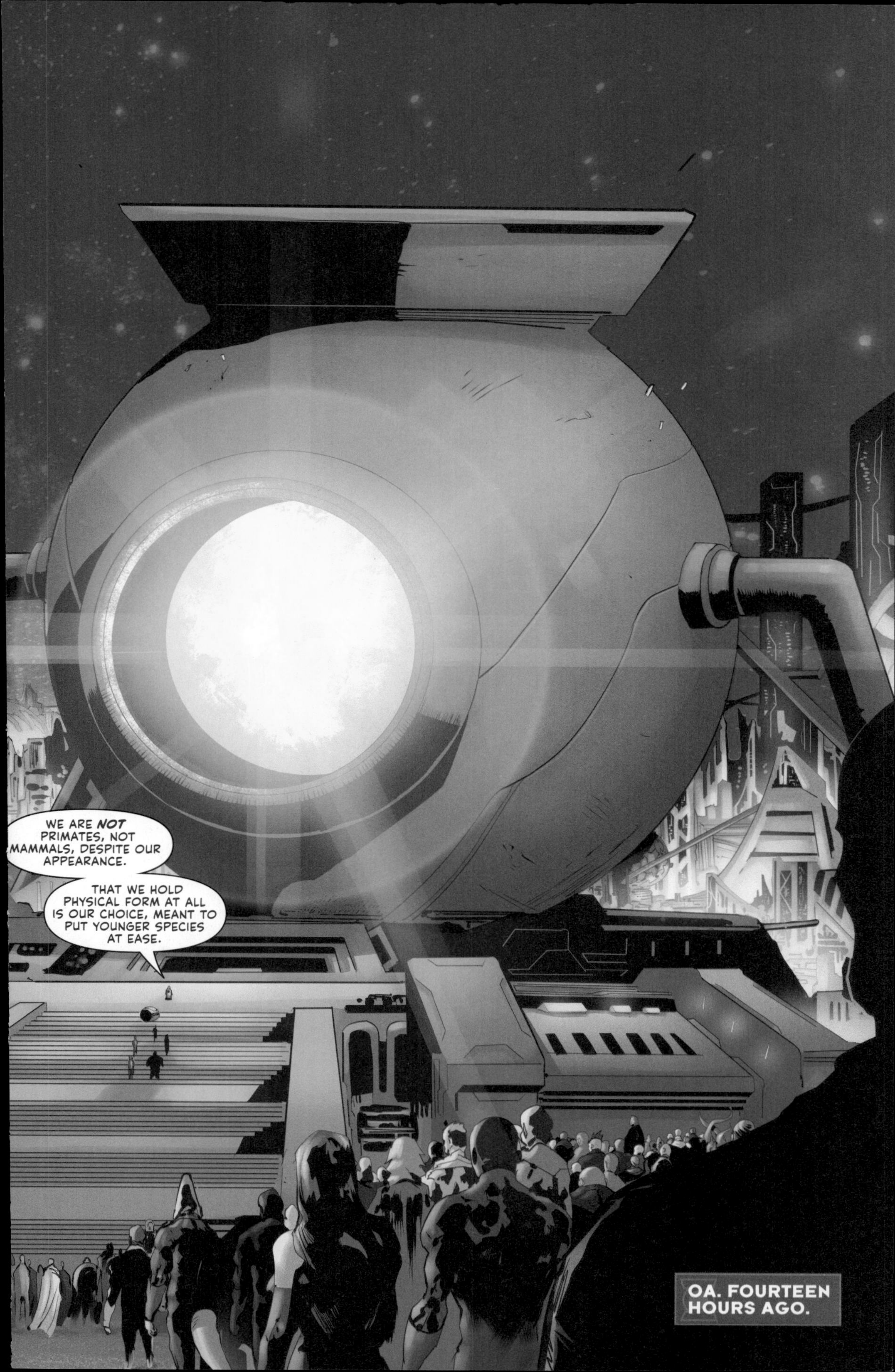
WE ARE NOT PRIMATES, NOT MAMMALS, DESPITE OUR APPEARANCE.
THAT WE HOLD PHYSICAL FORM AT ALL IS OUR CHOICE, MEANT TO PUT YOUNGER SPECIES AT EASE.
OA. FOURTEEN HOURS AGO.

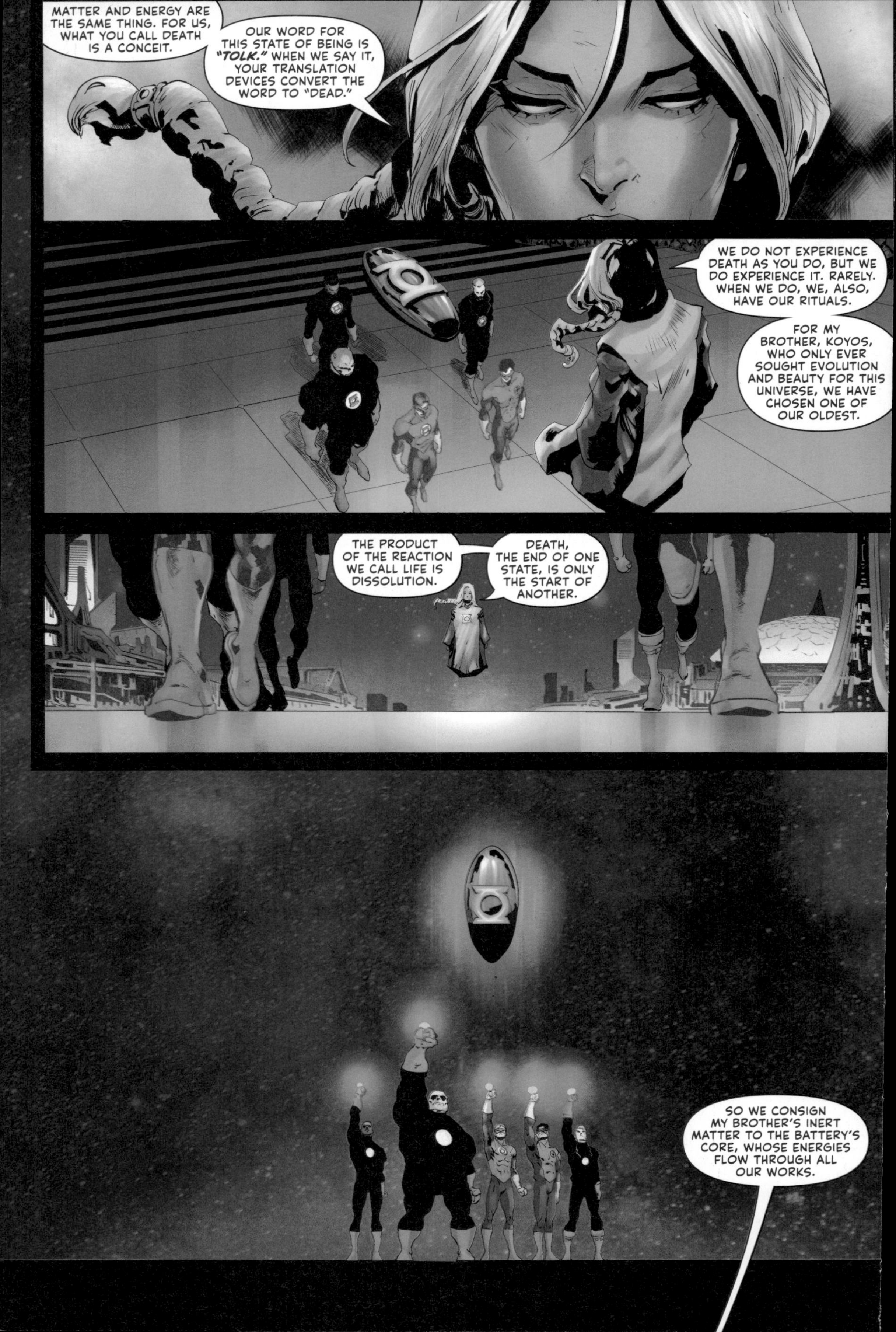
MATTER AND ENERGY ARE THE SAME THING. FOR US, WHAT YOU CALL DEATH IS A CONCEIT.
OUR WORD FOR THIS STATE OF BEING IS "TOLK." WHEN WE SAY IT, YOUR TRANSLATION DEVICES CONVERT THE WORD TO "DEAD."
WE DO NOT EXPERIENCE DEATH AS YOU DO, BUT WE DO EXPERIENCE IT. RARELY. WHEN WE DO, WE, ALSO, HAVE OUR RITUALS.
FOR MY BROTHER, KOYOS, WHO ONLY EVER SOUGHT EVOLUTION AND BEAUTY FOR THIS UNIVERSE, WE HAVE CHOSEN ONE OF OUR OLDEST.
THE PRODUCT OF THE REACTION WE CALL LIFE IS DISSOLUTION.
DEATH, THE END OF ONE STATE, IS ONLY THE START OF ANOTHER.
SO WE CONSIGN MY BROTHER'S INERT MATTER TO THE BATTERY'S CORE, WHOSE ENERGIES FLOW THROUGH ALL OUR WORKS.

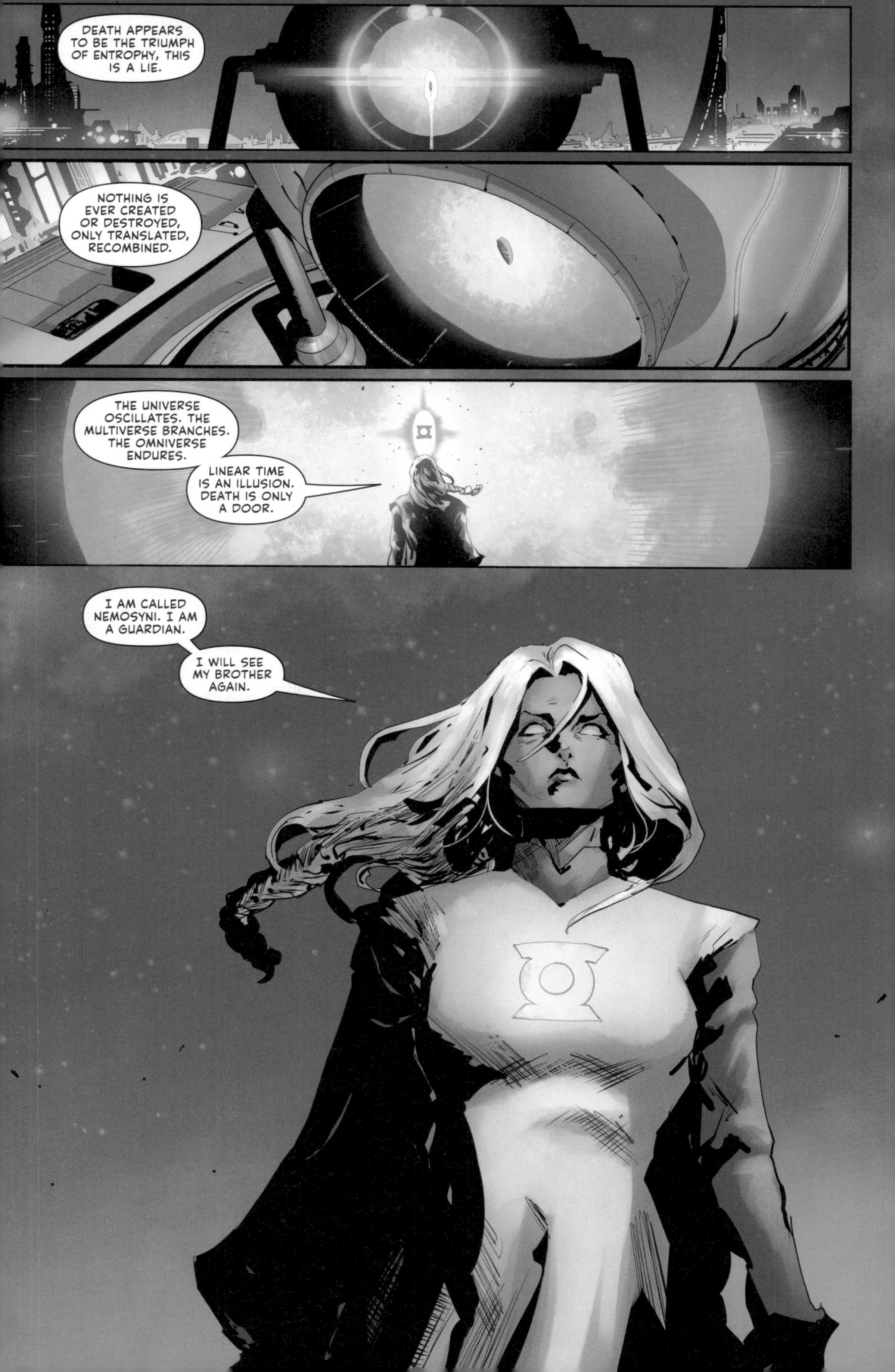
DEATH APPEARS TO BE THE TRIUMPH OF ENTROPHY, THIS IS A LIE.
NOTHING IS EVER CREATED OR DESTROYED, ONLY TRANSLATED, RECOMBINED.
THE UNIVERSE OSCILLATES. THE MULTIVERSE BRANCHES. THE OMNIVERSE ENDURES.
LINEAR TIME IS AN ILLUSION. DEATH IS ONLY A DOOR.
I AM CALLED NEMOSYNI. I AM A GUARDIAN.
I WILL SEE MY BROTHER AGAIN.

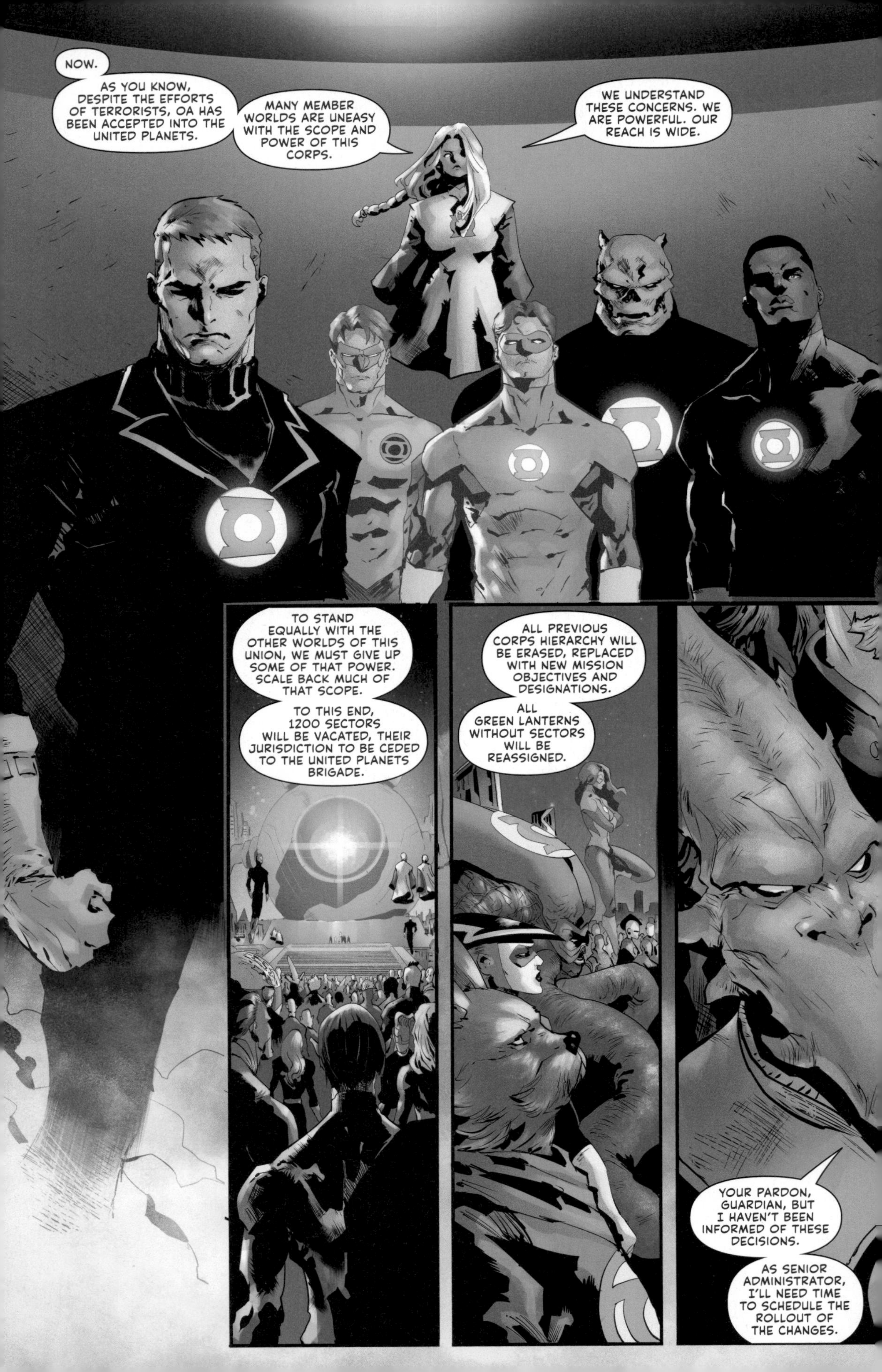
NOW.
AS YOU KNOW, DESPITE THE EFFORTS OF TERRORISTS, OA HAS BEEN ACCEPTED INTO THE UNITED PLANETS.
MANY MEMBER WORLDS ARE UNEASY WITH THE SCOPE AND POWER OF THIS CORPS.
WE UNDERSTAND THESE CONCERNS. WE ARE POWERFUL. OUR REACH IS WIDE.
TO STAND EQUALLY WITH THE OTHER WORLDS OF THIS UNION, WE MUST GIVE UP SOME OF THAT POWER. SCALE BACK MUCH OF THAT SCOPE.
TO THIS END, 1200 SECTORS WILL BE VACATED, THEIR JURISDICTION TO BE CEDED TO THE UNITED PLANETS BRIGADE.
ALL PREVIOUS CORPS HIERARCHY WILL BE ERASED, REPLACED WITH NEW MISSION OBJECTIVES AND DESIGNATIONS.
ALL GREEN LANTERNS WITHOUT SECTORS WILL BE REASSIGNED.
YOUR PARDON, GUARDIAN, BUT I HAVEN'T BEEN INFORMED OF THESE DECISIONS.
AS SENIOR ADMINISTRATOR, I'LL NEED TIME TO SCHEDULE THE ROLLOUT OF THE CHANGES.

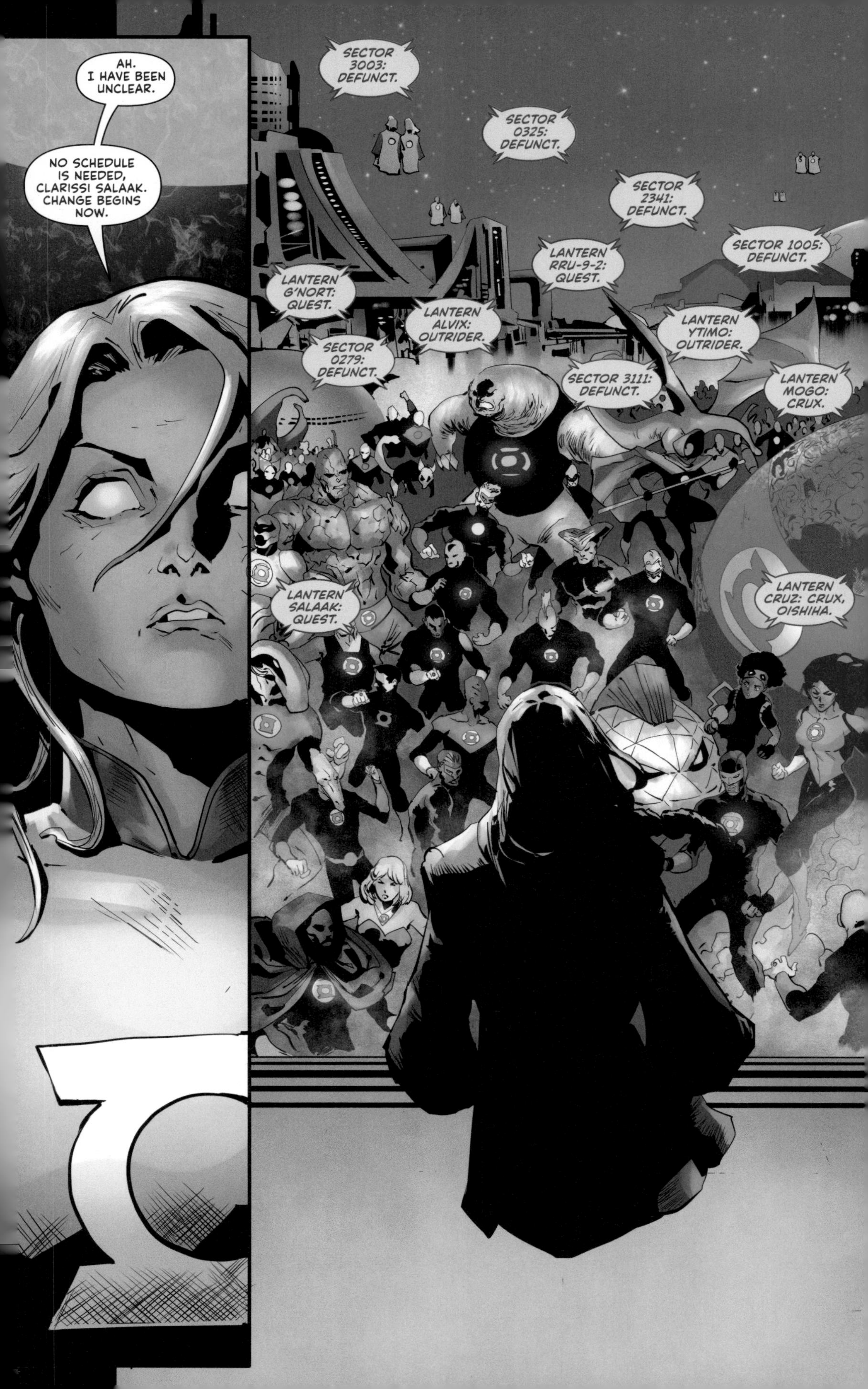
AH. I HAVE BEEN UNCLEAR.
NO SCHEDULE IS NEEDED, CLARISSI SALAAK. CHANGE BEGINS NOW.
SECTOR 3003: DEFUNCT.
SECTOR 0325: DEFUNCT.
SECTOR 2341: DEFUNCT.
SECTOR 1005: DEFUNCT.
LANTERN RRU-9-2: QUEST.
LANTERN G'NORT: QUEST.
LANTERN ALVIX: OUTRIDER.
LANTERN YTIMO: OUTRIDER.
SECTOR 0279: DEFUNCT.
SECTOR 3111: DEFUNCT.
LANTERN MOGO: CRUX.
LANTERN SALAAK: QUEST.
LANTERN CRUZ: CRUX, OISHIHA.

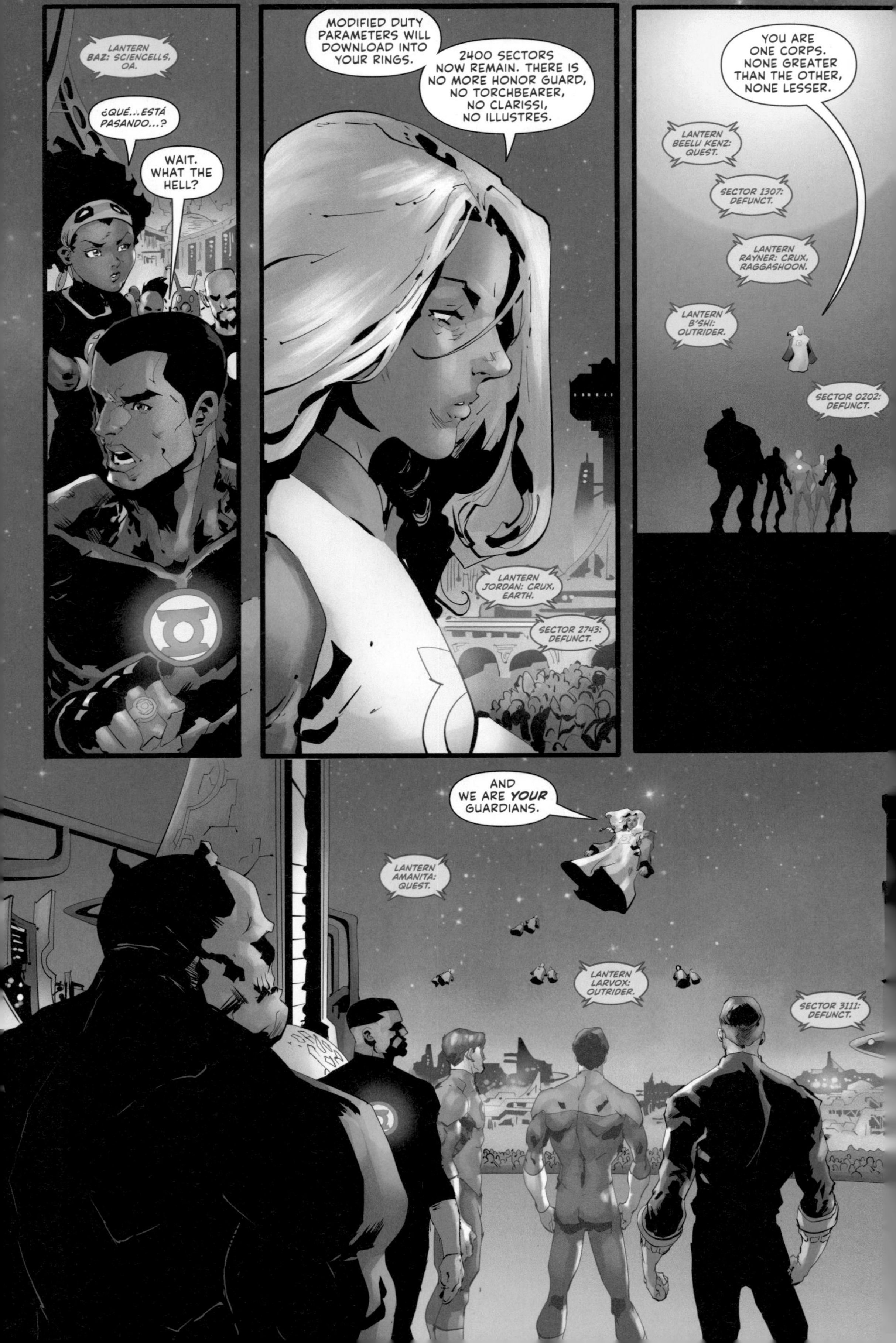
LANTERN BAZ: SCIENCELLS, OA.
¿QUÉ...ESTÁ PASANDO...?
WAIT. WHAT THE HELL?
MODIFIED DUTY PARAMETERS WILL DOWNLOAD INTO YOUR RINGS.
2400 SECTORS NOW REMAIN. THERE IS NO MORE HONOR GUARD, NO TORCHBEARER, NO CLARISSI, NO ILLUSTRES.
LANTERN JORDAN: CRUX, EARTH.
SECTOR 2743: DEFUNCT.
YOU ARE ONE CORPS. NONE GREATER THAN THE OTHER, NONE LESSER.
LANTERN BEELU KENZ: QUEST.
SECTOR 1307: DEFUNCT.
LANTERN RAYNER: CRUX, RAGGASHOON.
LANTERN B'SHI: OUTRIDER.
SECTOR 0202: DEFUNCT.
AND WE ARE YOUR GUARDIANS.
LANTERN AMANITA: QUEST.
LANTERN LARVOX: OUTRIDER.
SECTOR 3111: DEFUNCT.

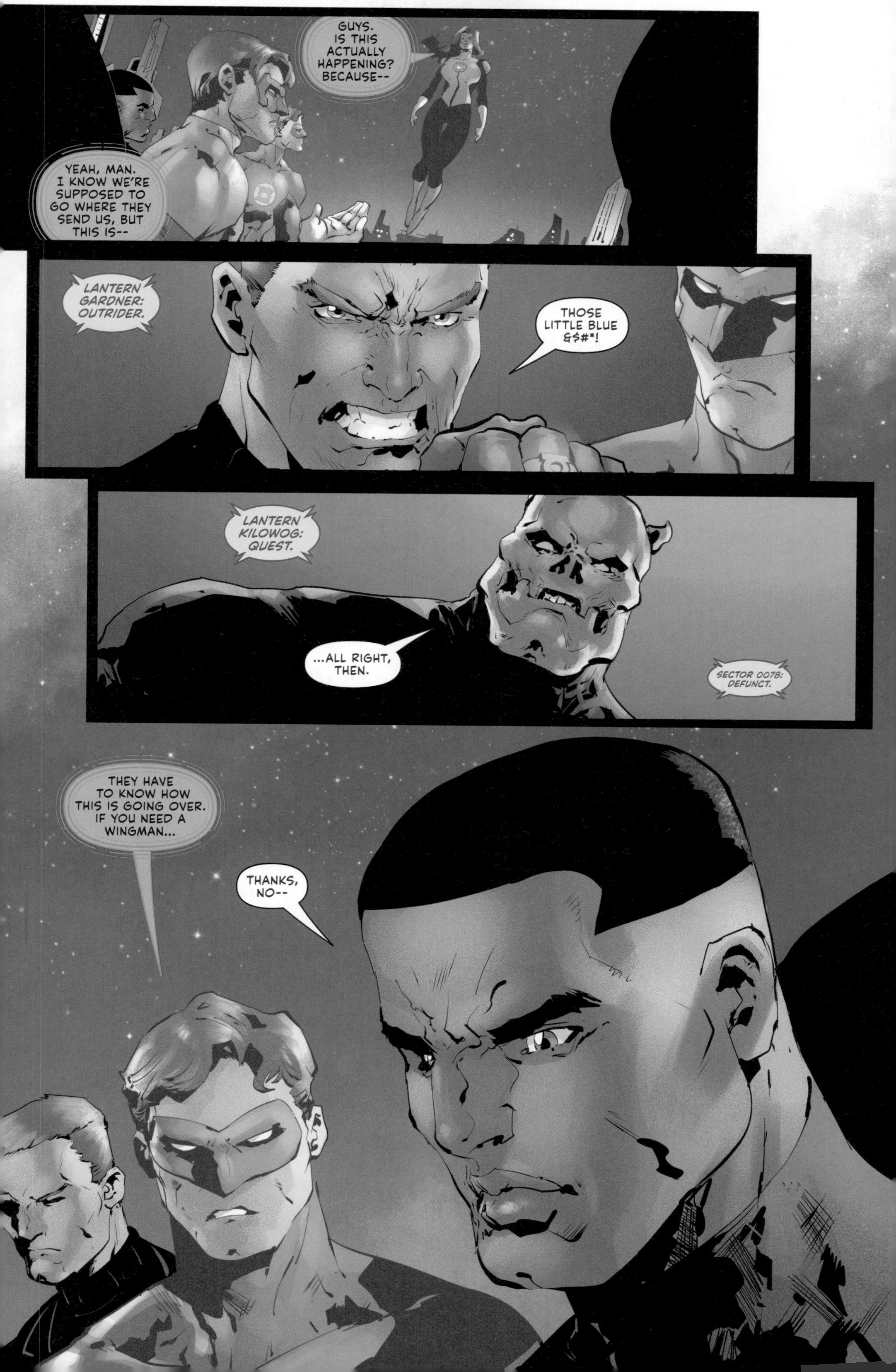

YEAH, MAN. I KNOW WE'RE SUPPOSED TO GO WHERE THEY SEND US, BUT THIS IS--
GUYS. IS THIS ACTUALLY HAPPENING? BECAUSE--
LANTERN GARDNER: OUTRIDER.
THOSE LITTLE BLUE &$#*!
LANTERN KILOWOG: QUEST.
...ALL RIGHT, THEN.
SECTOR 0078: DEFUNCT.
THEY HAVE TO KNOW HOW THIS IS GOING OVER. IF YOU NEED A WINGMAN...
THANKS, NO--

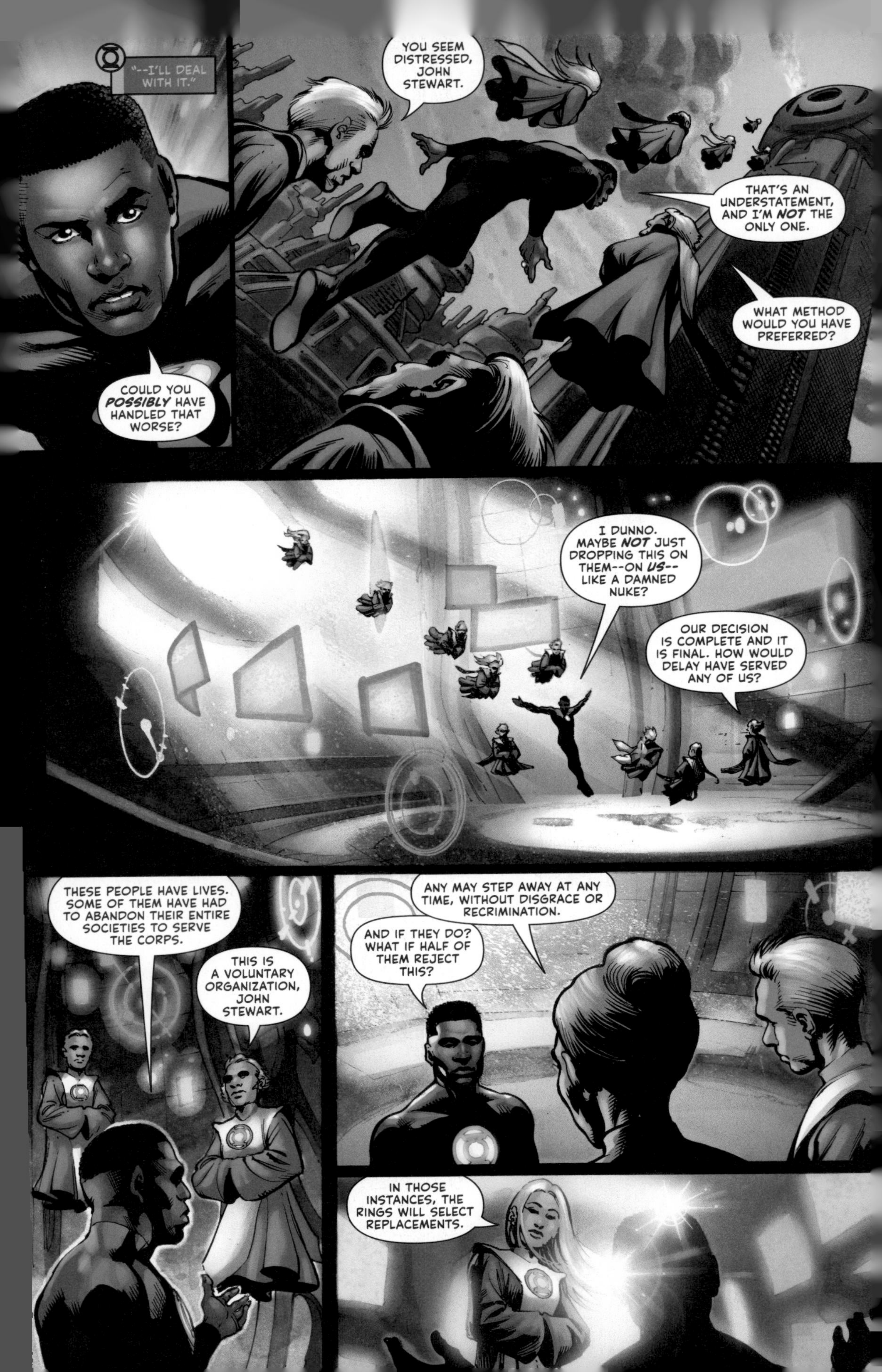
"--I'LL DEAL WITH IT."
COULD YOU *POSSIBLY* HAVE HANDLED THAT WORSE?
YOU SEEM DISTRESSED, JOHN STEWART.
THAT'S AN UNDERSTATEMENT, AND I'M *NOT* THE ONLY ONE.
WHAT METHOD WOULD YOU HAVE PREFERRED?
I DUNNO. MAYBE *NOT* JUST DROPPING THIS ON THEM--ON *US*--LIKE A DAMNED NUKE?
OUR DECISION IS COMPLETE AND IT IS FINAL. HOW WOULD DELAY HAVE SERVED ANY OF US?
THESE PEOPLE HAVE LIVES. SOME OF THEM HAVE HAD TO ABANDON THEIR ENTIRE SOCIETIES TO SERVE THE CORPS.
THIS IS A VOLUNTARY ORGANIZATION, JOHN STEWART.
ANY MAY STEP AWAY AT ANY TIME, WITHOUT DISGRACE OR RECRIMINATION.
AND IF THEY DO? WHAT IF HALF OF THEM REJECT THIS?
IN THOSE INSTANCES, THE RINGS WILL SELECT REPLACEMENTS.

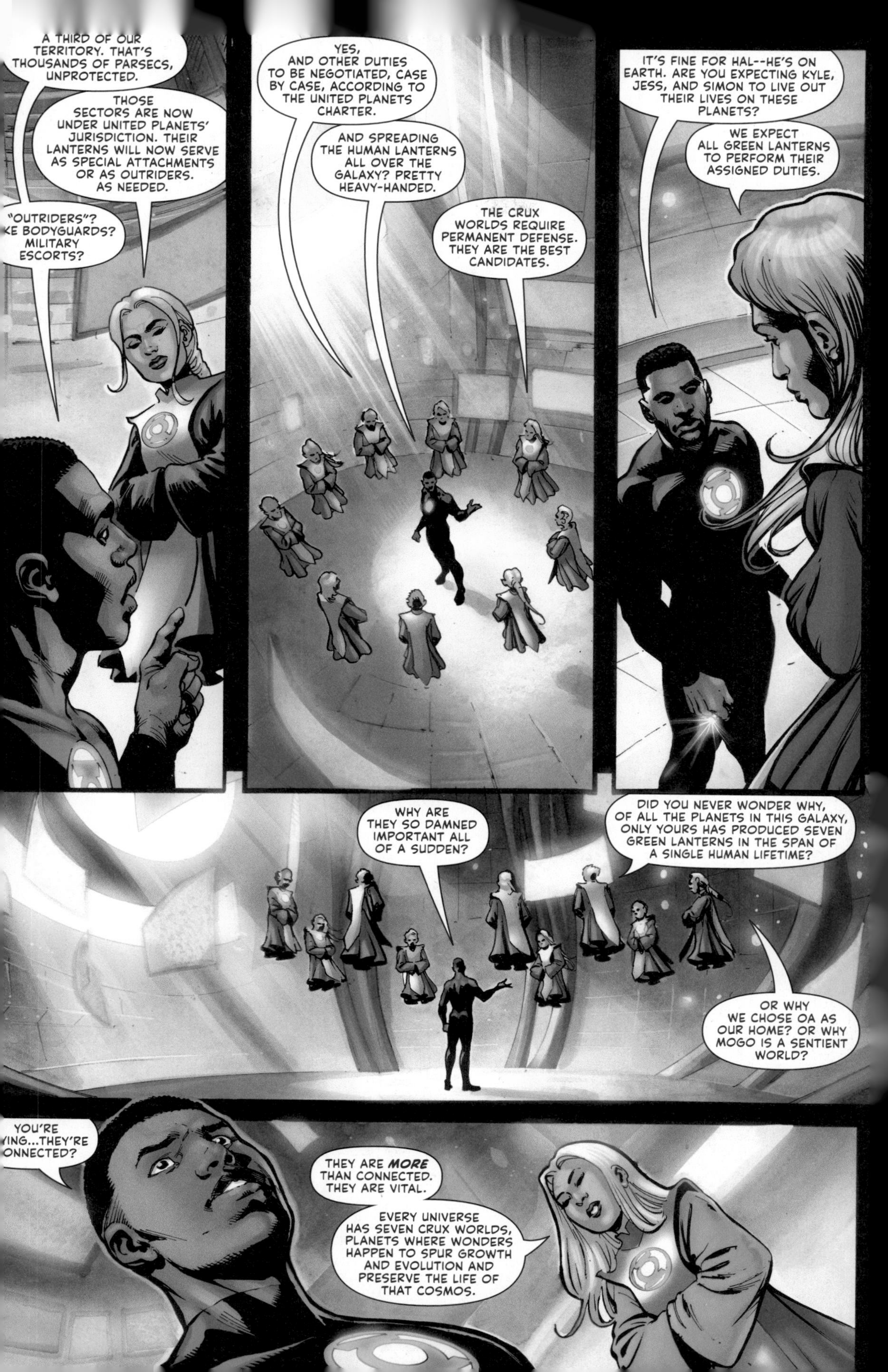
A THIRD OF OUR TERRITORY. THAT'S THOUSANDS OF PARSECS, UNPROTECTED.
THOSE SECTORS ARE NOW UNDER UNITED PLANETS' JURISDICTION. THEIR LANTERNS WILL NOW SERVE AS SPECIAL ATTACHMENTS OR AS OUTRIDERS. AS NEEDED.
"OUTRIDERS"? KE BODYGUARDS? MILITARY ESCORTS?
YES, AND OTHER DUTIES TO BE NEGOTIATED, CASE BY CASE, ACCORDING TO THE UNITED PLANETS CHARTER.
AND SPREADING THE HUMAN LANTERNS ALL OVER THE GALAXY? PRETTY HEAVY-HANDED.
THE CRUX WORLDS REQUIRE PERMANENT DEFENSE. THEY ARE THE BEST CANDIDATES.
IT'S FINE FOR HAL--HE'S ON EARTH. ARE YOU EXPECTING KYLE, JESS, AND SIMON TO LIVE OUT THEIR LIVES ON THESE PLANETS?
WE EXPECT ALL GREEN LANTERNS TO PERFORM THEIR ASSIGNED DUTIES.
WHY ARE THEY SO DAMNED IMPORTANT ALL OF A SUDDEN?
DID YOU NEVER WONDER WHY, OF ALL THE PLANETS IN THIS GALAXY, ONLY YOURS HAS PRODUCED SEVEN GREEN LANTERNS IN THE SPAN OF A SINGLE HUMAN LIFETIME?
OR WHY WE CHOSE OA AS OUR HOME? OR WHY MOGO IS A SENTIENT WORLD?
YOU'RE YING...THEY'RE ONNECTED?
THEY ARE *MORE* THAN CONNECTED. THEY ARE VITAL.
EVERY UNIVERSE HAS SEVEN CRUX WORLDS, PLANETS WHERE WONDERS HAPPEN TO SPUR GROWTH AND EVOLUTION AND PRESERVE THE LIFE OF THAT COSMOS.

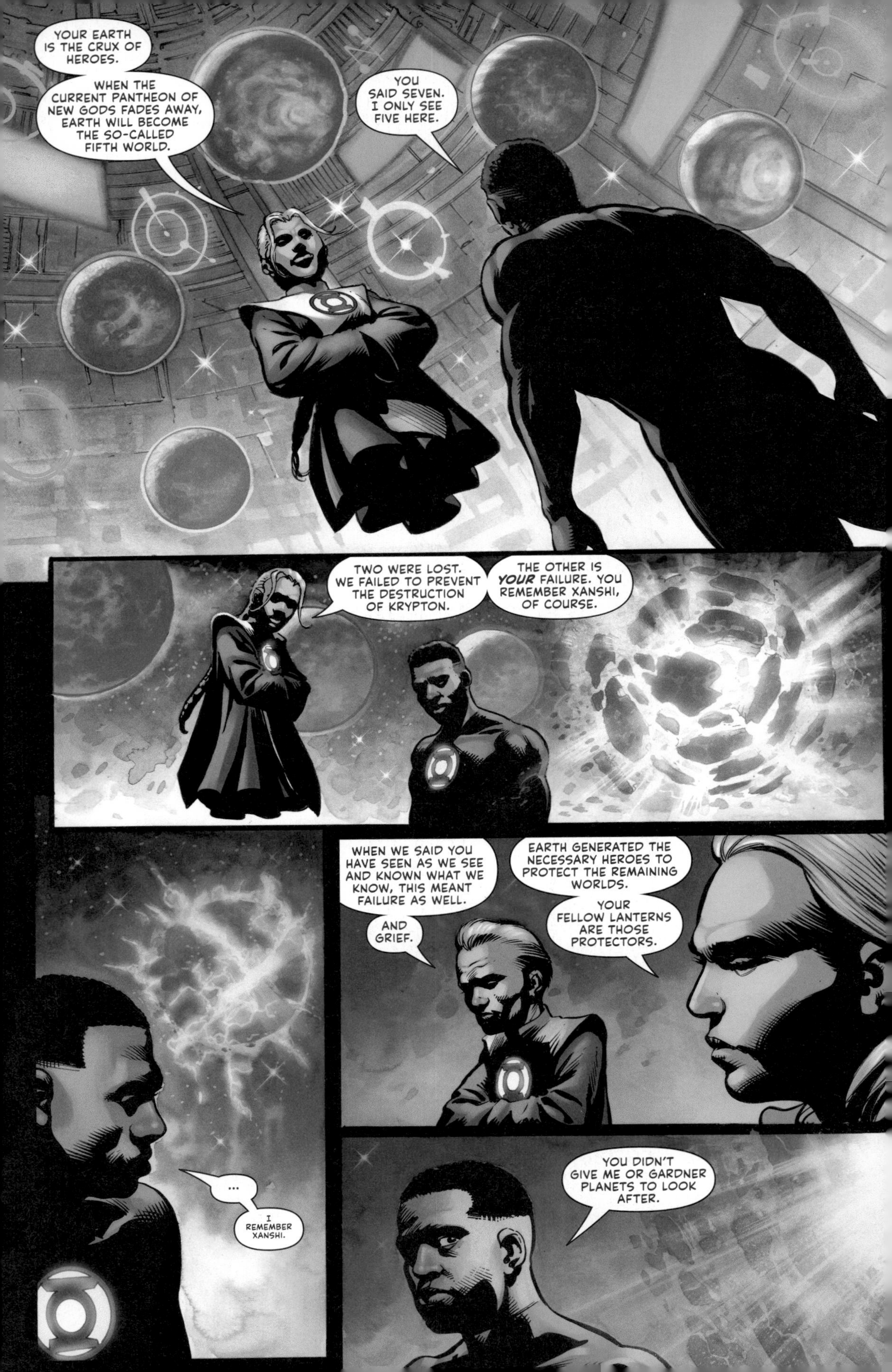
YOUR EARTH IS THE CRUX OF HEROES.
WHEN THE CURRENT PANTHEON OF NEW GODS FADES AWAY, EARTH WILL BECOME THE SO-CALLED FIFTH WORLD.
YOU SAID SEVEN. I ONLY SEE FIVE HERE.
TWO WERE LOST. WE FAILED TO PREVENT THE DESTRUCTION OF KRYPTON.
THE OTHER IS *YOUR* FAILURE. YOU REMEMBER XANSHI, OF COURSE.
...
I REMEMBER XANSHI.
WHEN WE SAID YOU HAVE SEEN AS WE SEE AND KNOWN WHAT WE KNOW, THIS MEANT FAILURE AS WELL.
AND GRIEF.
EARTH GENERATED THE NECESSARY HEROES TO PROTECT THE REMAINING WORLDS.
YOUR FELLOW LANTERNS ARE THOSE PROTECTORS.
YOU DIDN'T GIVE ME OR GARDNER PLANETS TO LOOK AFTER.

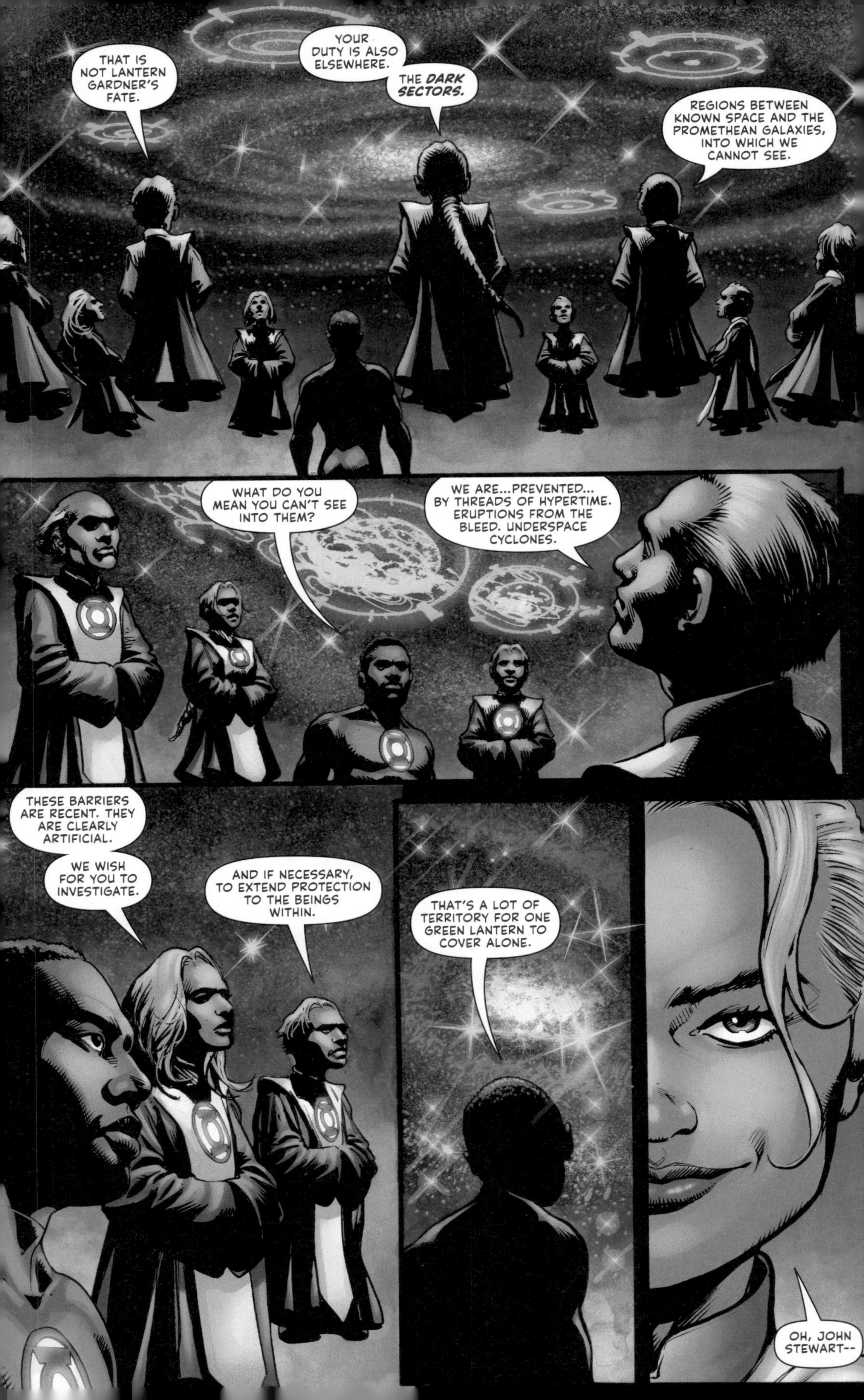
THAT IS NOT LANTERN GARDNER'S FATE.
YOUR DUTY IS ALSO ELSEWHERE.
THE *DARK SECTORS.*
REGIONS BETWEEN KNOWN SPACE AND THE PROMETHEAN GALAXIES, INTO WHICH WE CANNOT SEE.
WHAT DO YOU MEAN YOU CAN'T SEE INTO THEM?
WE ARE...PREVENTED... BY THREADS OF HYPERTIME. ERUPTIONS FROM THE BLEED. UNDERSPACE CYCLONES.
THESE BARRIERS ARE RECENT. THEY ARE CLEARLY ARTIFICIAL.
WE WISH FOR YOU TO INVESTIGATE.
AND IF NECESSARY, TO EXTEND PROTECTION TO THE BEINGS WITHIN.
THAT'S A LOT OF TERRITORY FOR ONE GREEN LANTERN TO COVER ALONE.
OH, JOHN STEWART--

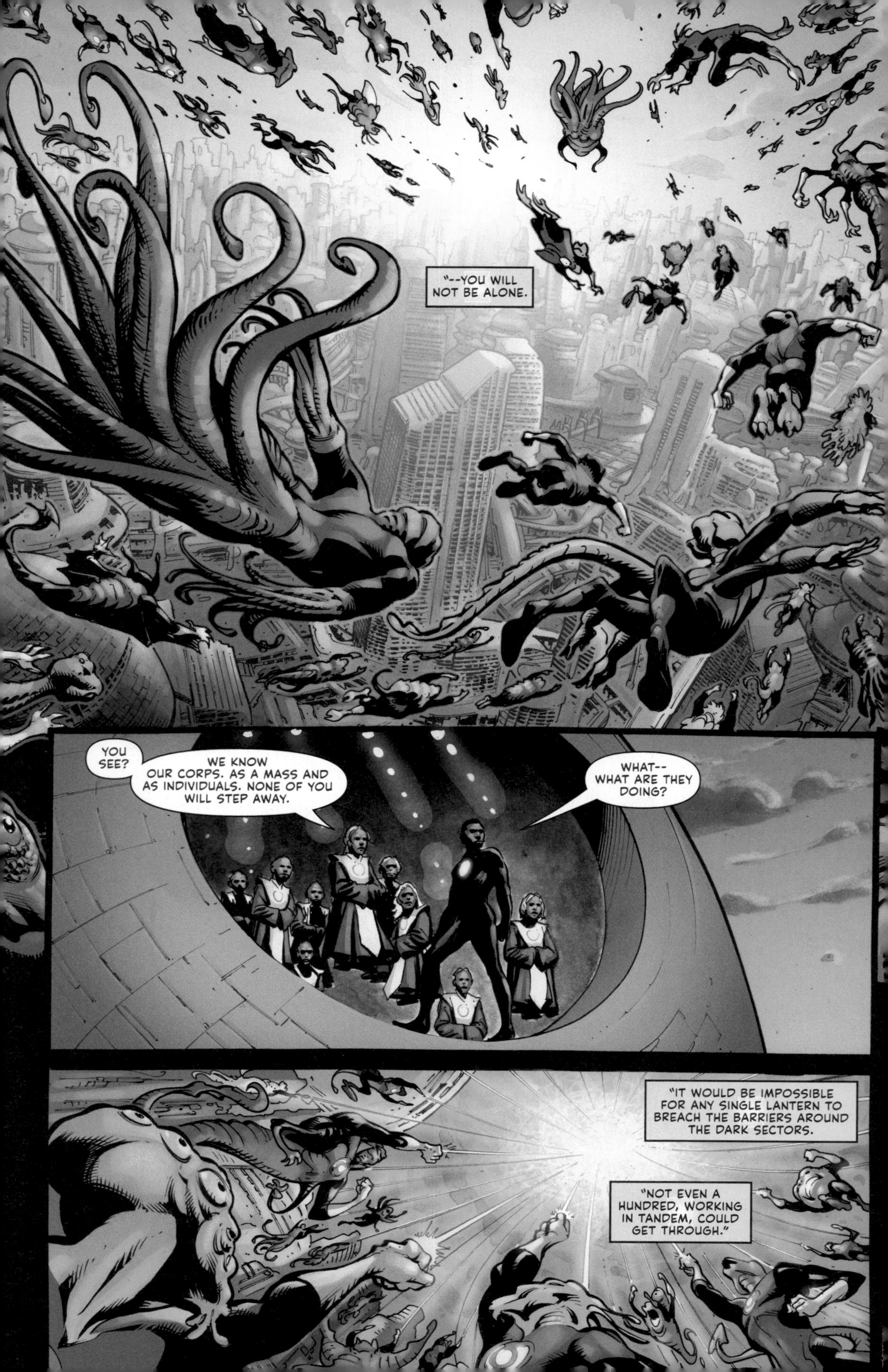
"--YOU WILL NOT BE ALONE.
YOU SEE?
WE KNOW OUR CORPS. AS A MASS AND AS INDIVIDUALS. NONE OF YOU WILL STEP AWAY.
WHAT-- WHAT ARE THEY DOING?
"IT WOULD BE IMPOSSIBLE FOR ANY SINGLE LANTERN TO BREACH THE BARRIERS AROUND THE DARK SECTORS.
"NOT EVEN A HUNDRED, WORKING IN TANDEM, COULD GET THROUGH."

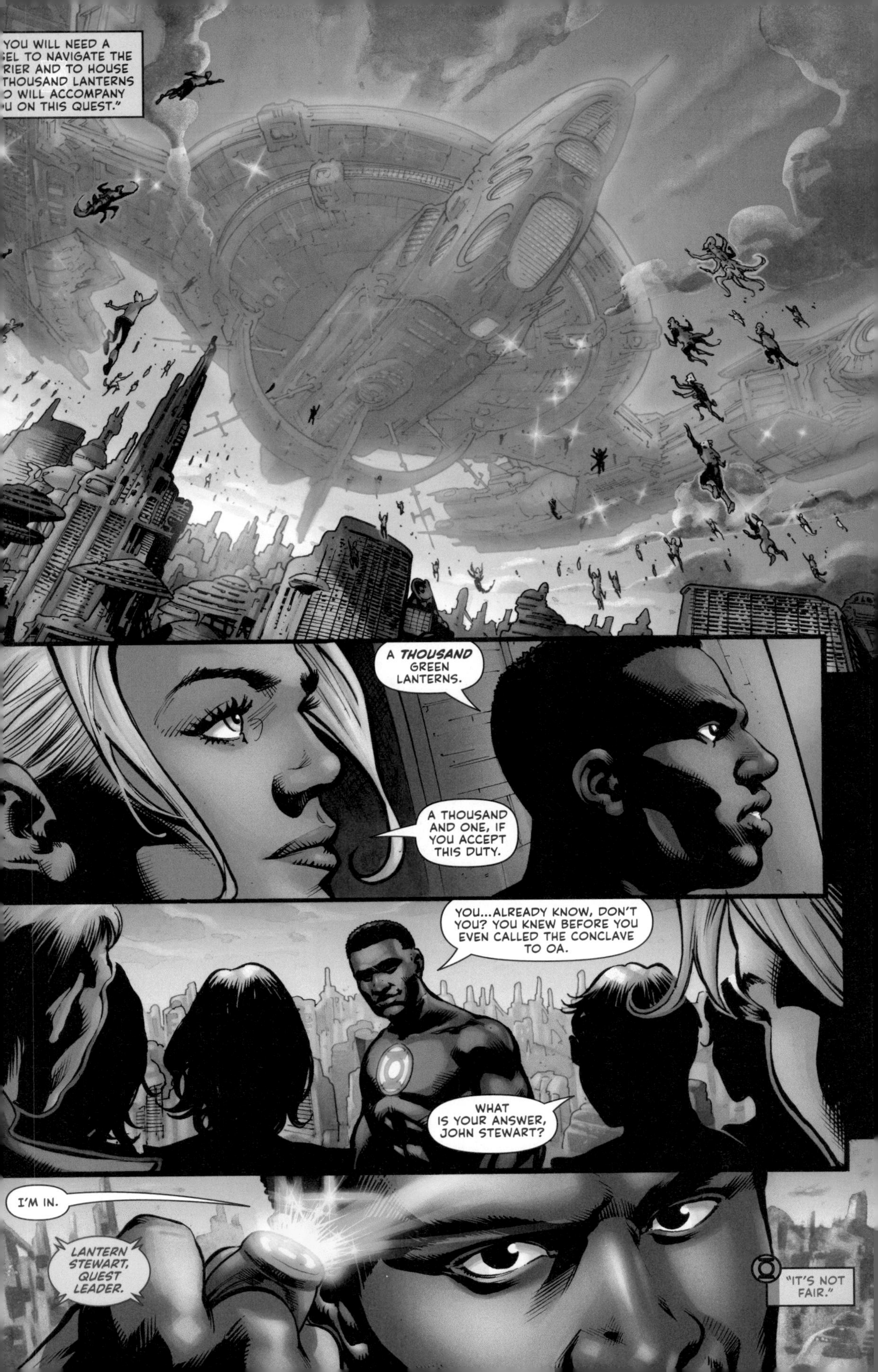
YOU WILL NEED A
SEL TO NAVIGATE THE
RIER AND TO HOUSE
THOUSAND LANTERNS
O WILL ACCOMPANY
U ON THIS QUEST."
A THOUSAND GREEN LANTERNS.
A THOUSAND AND ONE, IF YOU ACCEPT THIS DUTY.
YOU...ALREADY KNOW, DON'T YOU? YOU KNEW BEFORE YOU EVEN CALLED THE CONCLAVE TO OA.
WHAT IS YOUR ANSWER, JOHN STEWART?
I'M IN.
LANTERN STEWART, QUEST LEADER.
"IT'S NOT FAIR."

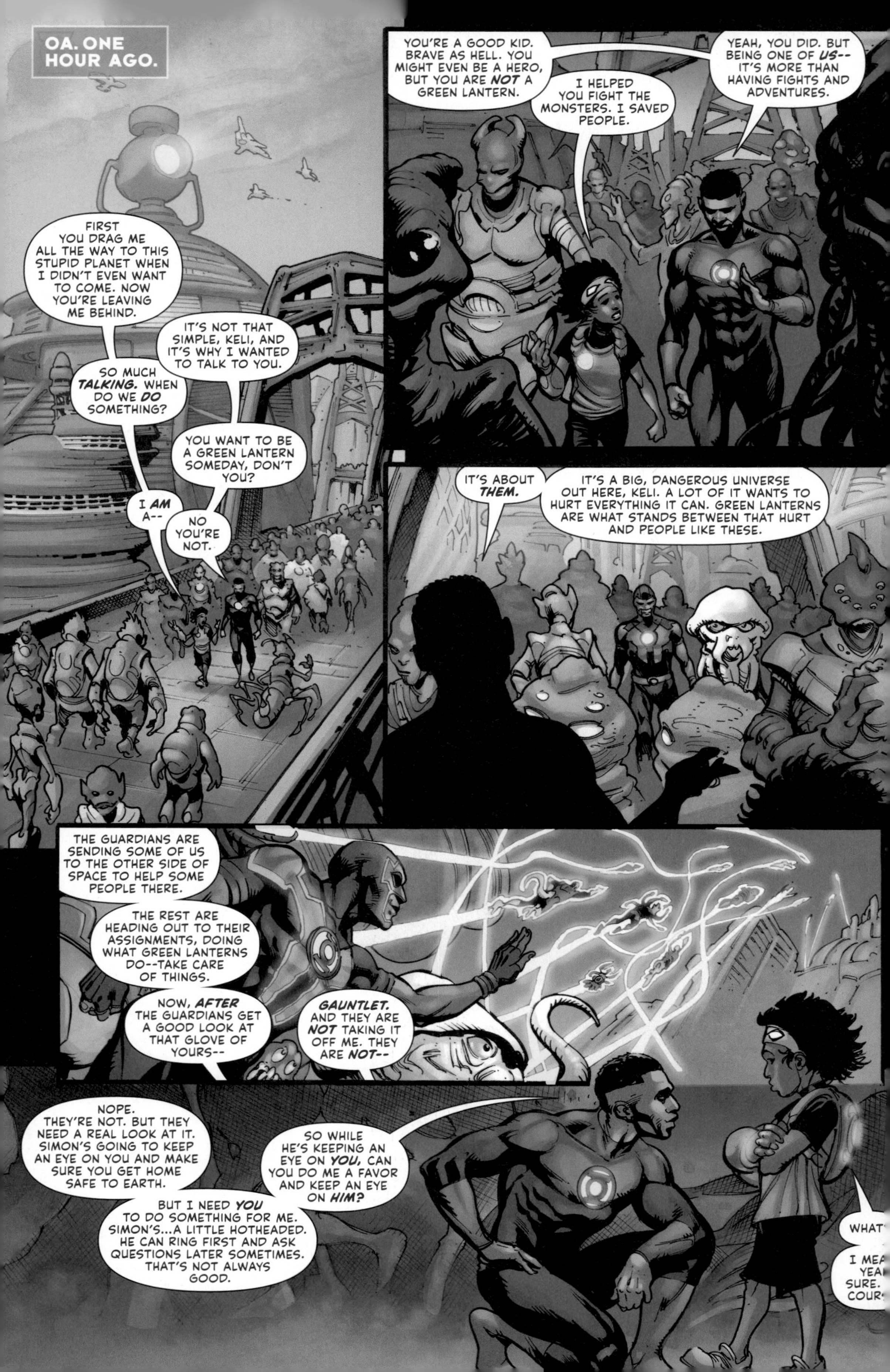
OA. ONE HOUR AGO.
FIRST YOU DRAG ME ALL THE WAY TO THIS STUPID PLANET WHEN I DIDN'T EVEN WANT TO COME. NOW YOU'RE LEAVING ME BEHIND.
IT'S NOT THAT SIMPLE, KELI, AND IT'S WHY I WANTED TO TALK TO YOU.
SO MUCH *TALKING.* WHEN DO WE *DO* SOMETHING?
YOU WANT TO BE A GREEN LANTERN SOMEDAY, DON'T YOU?
I *AM* A--
NO YOU'RE NOT.
YOU'RE A GOOD KID. BRAVE AS HELL. YOU MIGHT EVEN BE A HERO, BUT YOU ARE *NOT* A GREEN LANTERN.
I HELPED YOU FIGHT THE MONSTERS. I SAVED PEOPLE.
YEAH, YOU DID. BUT BEING ONE OF *US--* IT'S MORE THAN HAVING FIGHTS AND ADVENTURES.
IT'S ABOUT *THEM.*
IT'S A BIG, DANGEROUS UNIVERSE OUT HERE, KELI. A LOT OF IT WANTS TO HURT EVERYTHING IT CAN. GREEN LANTERNS ARE WHAT STANDS BETWEEN THAT HURT AND PEOPLE LIKE THESE.
THE GUARDIANS ARE SENDING SOME OF US TO THE OTHER SIDE OF SPACE TO HELP SOME PEOPLE THERE.
THE REST ARE HEADING OUT TO THEIR ASSIGNMENTS, DOING WHAT GREEN LANTERNS DO--TAKE CARE OF THINGS.
NOW, *AFTER* THE GUARDIANS GET A GOOD LOOK AT THAT GLOVE OF YOURS--
GAUNTLET. AND THEY ARE *NOT* TAKING IT OFF ME. THEY ARE *NOT--*
NOPE. THEY'RE NOT. BUT THEY NEED A REAL LOOK AT IT. SIMON'S GOING TO KEEP AN EYE ON YOU AND MAKE SURE YOU GET HOME SAFE TO EARTH.
BUT I NEED *YOU* TO DO SOMETHING FOR ME. SIMON'S...A LITTLE HOTHEADED. HE CAN RING FIRST AND ASK QUESTIONS LATER SOMETIMES. THAT'S NOT ALWAYS GOOD.
SO WHILE HE'S KEEPING AN EYE ON *YOU,* CAN YOU DO ME A FAVOR AND KEEP AN EYE ON *HIM?*

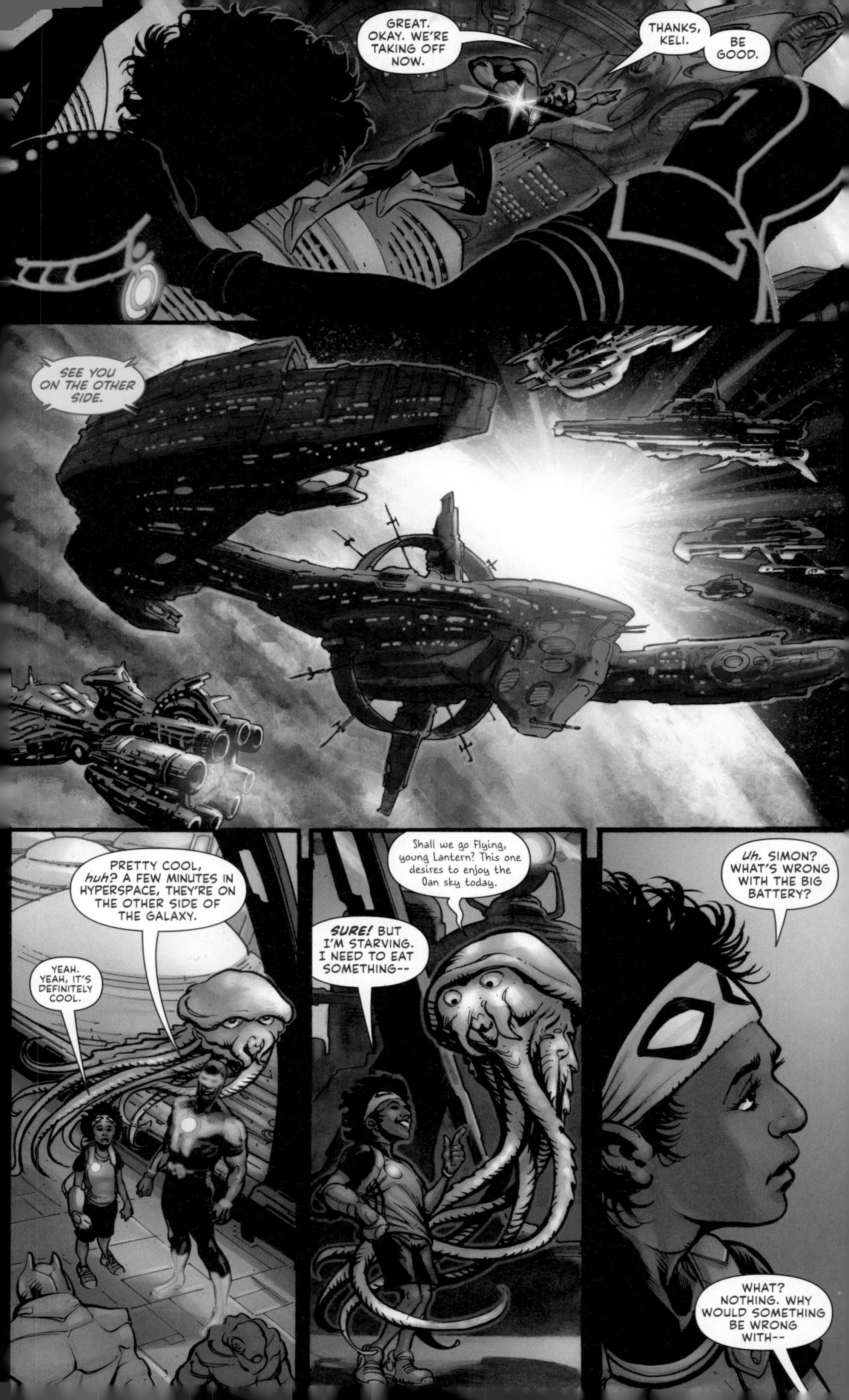

GREAT. OKAY. WE'RE TAKING OFF NOW.
THANKS, KELI.
BE GOOD.
SEE YOU ON THE OTHER SIDE.
PRETTY COOL, *huh?* A FEW MINUTES IN HYPERSPACE, THEY'RE ON THE OTHER SIDE OF THE GALAXY.
YEAH. YEAH, IT'S DEFINITELY COOL.
Shall we go flying, young Lantern? This one desires to enjoy the Oan sky today.
SURE! BUT I'M STARVING. I NEED TO EAT SOMETHING--
Uh. SIMON? WHAT'S WRONG WITH THE BIG BATTERY?
WHAT? NOTHING. WHY WOULD SOMETHING BE WRONG WITH--

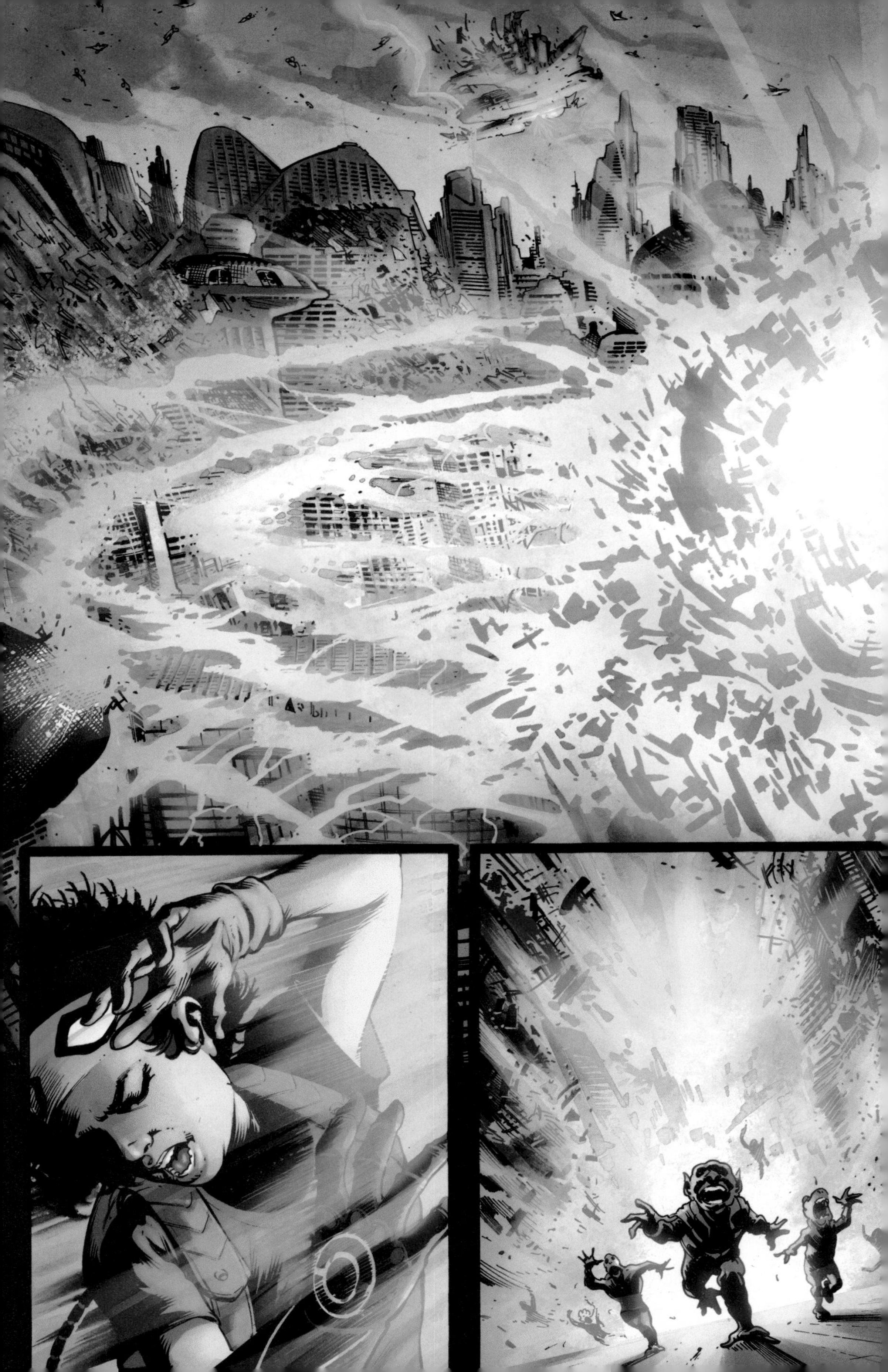

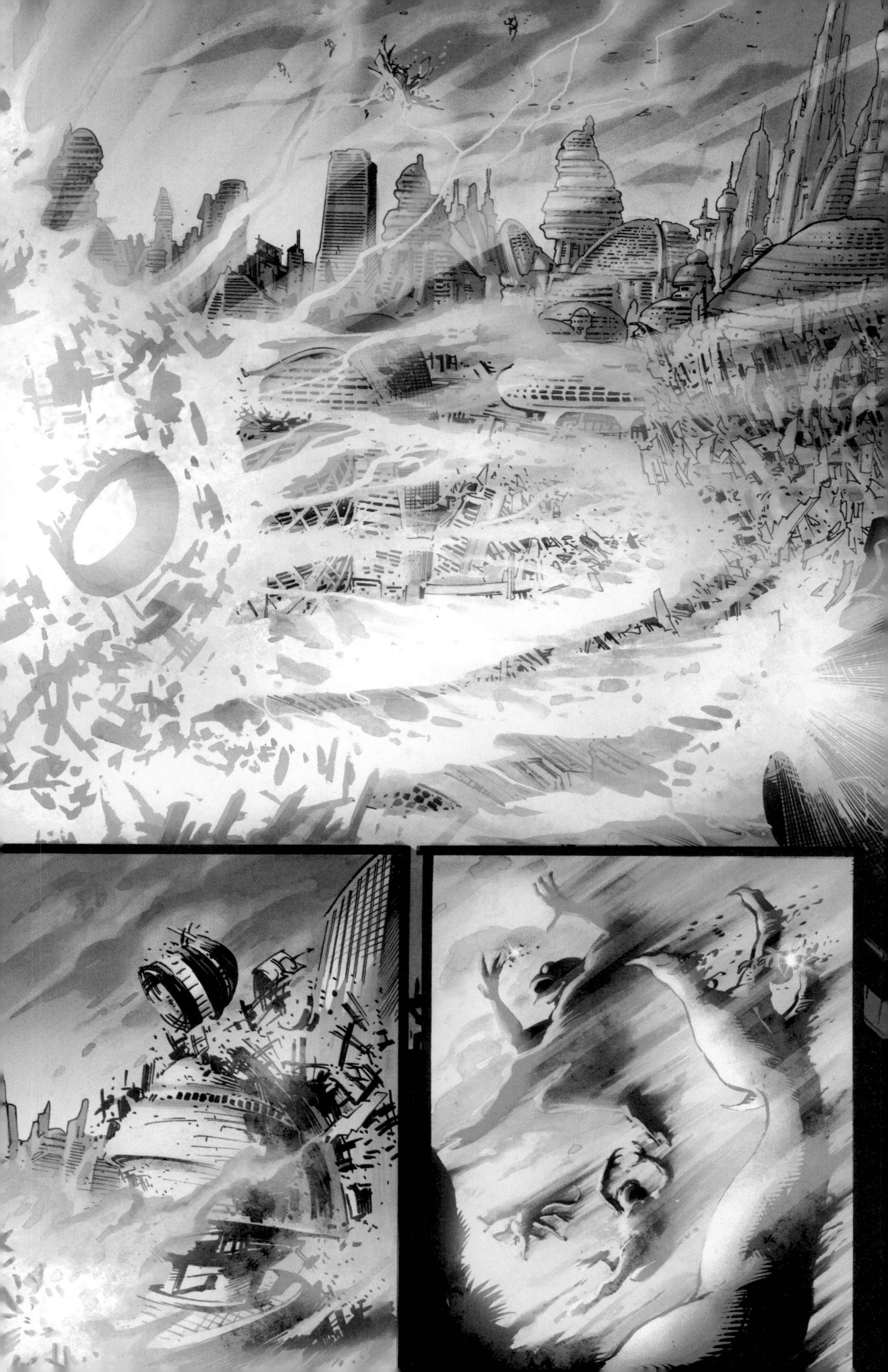

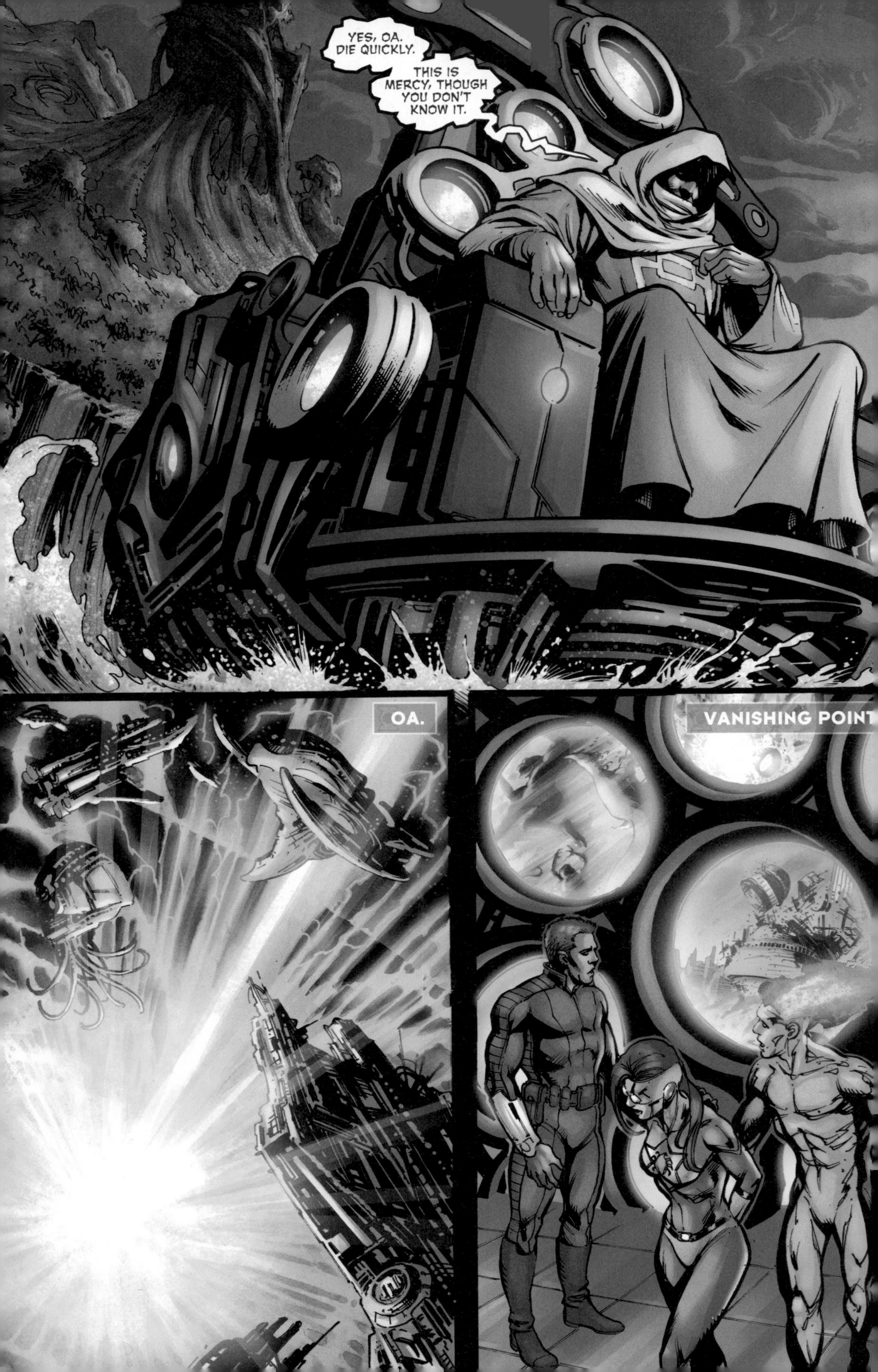
YES, OA. DIE QUICKLY.
THIS IS MERCY, THOUGH YOU DON'T KNOW IT.
OA.
VANISHING POINT

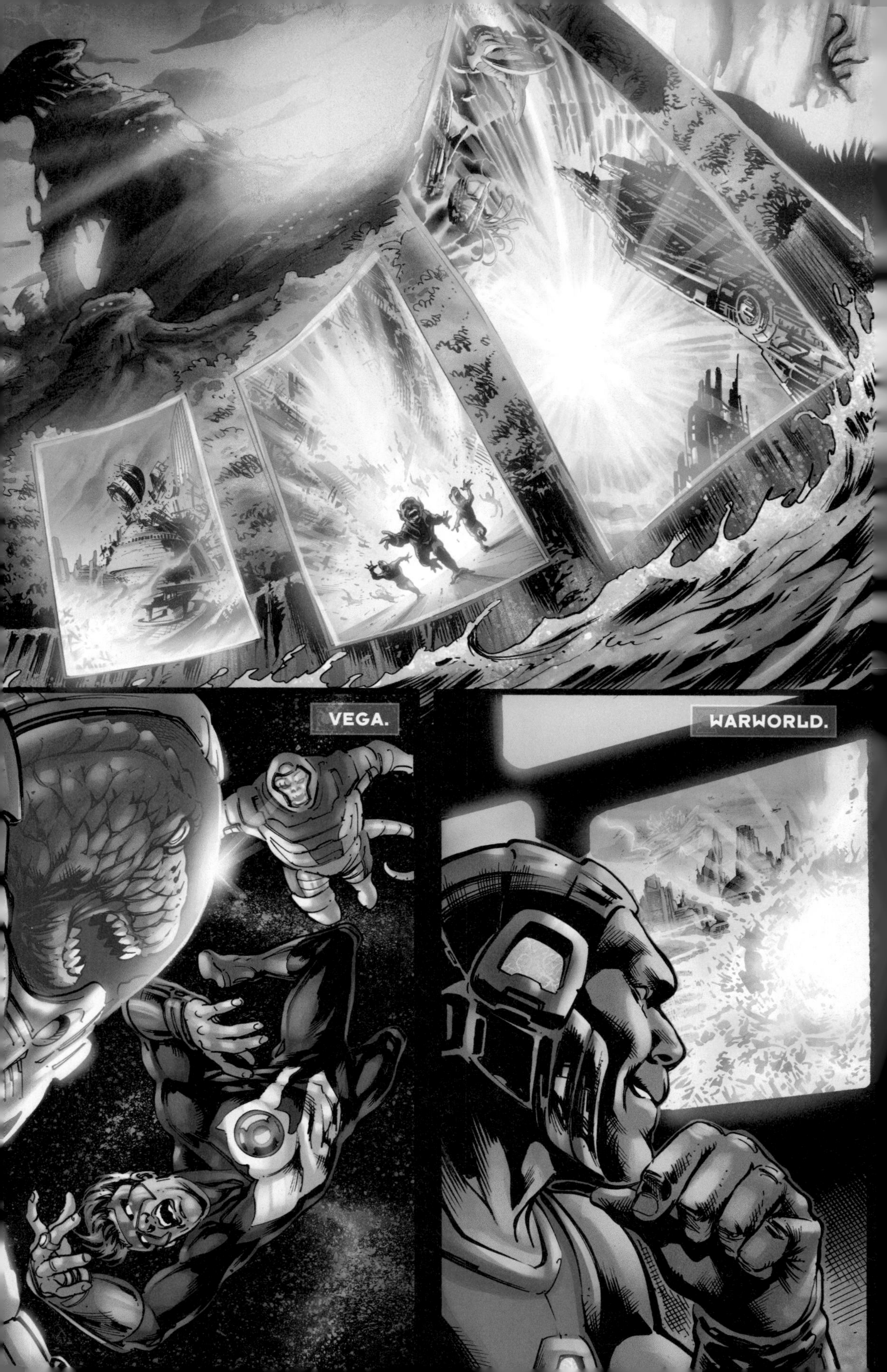
VEGA.
WARWORLD.

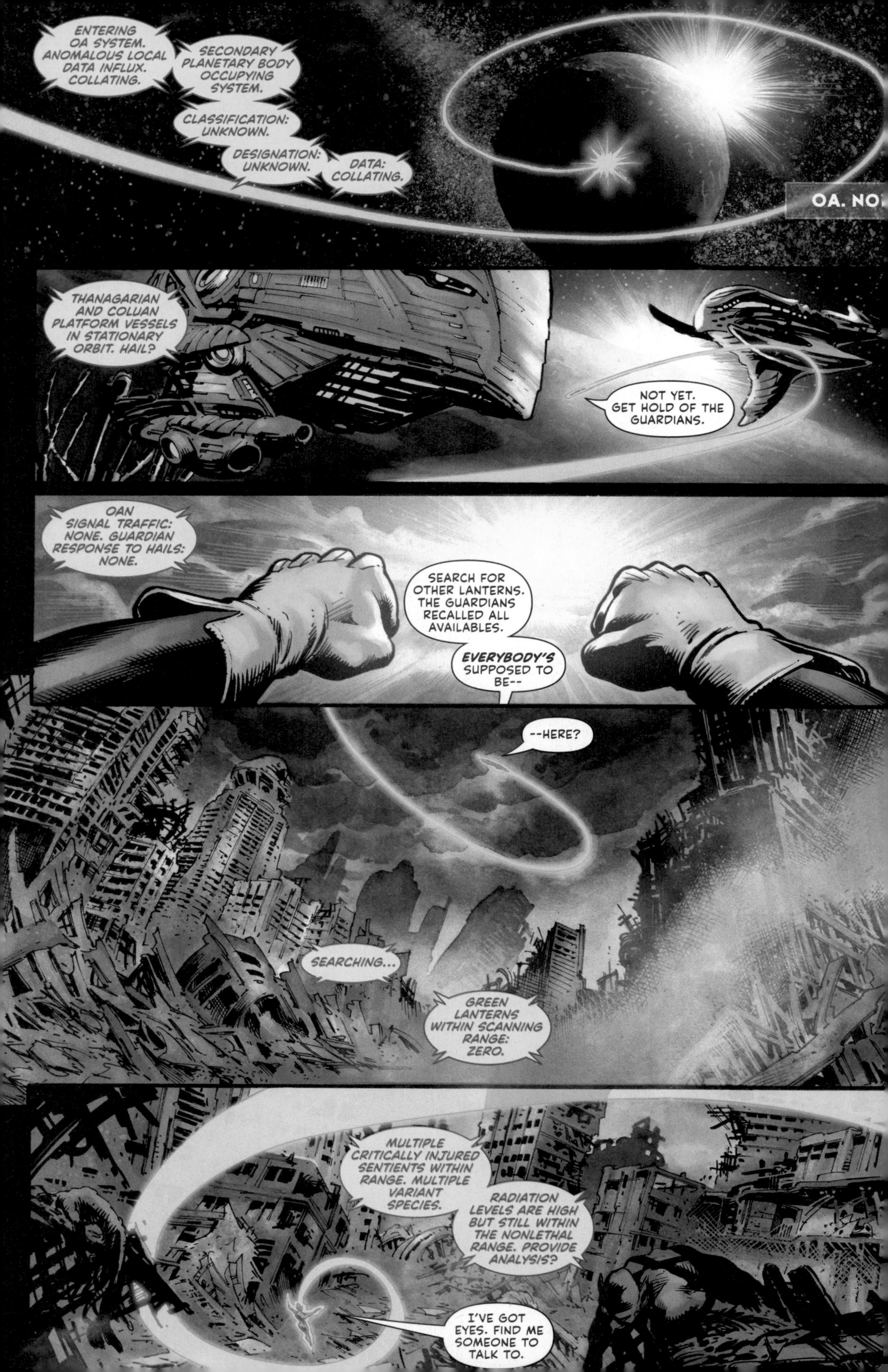
ENTERING OA SYSTEM. ANOMALOUS LOCAL DATA INFLUX. COLLATING.
SECONDARY PLANETARY BODY OCCUPYING SYSTEM.
CLASSIFICATION: UNKNOWN.
DESIGNATION: UNKNOWN.
DATA: COLLATING.
OA. NO
THANAGARIAN AND COLUAN PLATFORM VESSELS IN STATIONARY ORBIT. HAIL?
NOT YET. GET HOLD OF THE GUARDIANS.
OAN SIGNAL TRAFFIC: NONE. GUARDIAN RESPONSE TO HAILS: NONE.
SEARCH FOR OTHER LANTERNS. THE GUARDIANS RECALLED ALL AVAILABLES.
EVERYBODY'S SUPPOSED TO BE--
--HERE?
SEARCHING...
GREEN LANTERNS WITHIN SCANNING RANGE: ZERO.
MULTIPLE CRITICALLY INJURED SENTIENTS WITHIN RANGE. MULTIPLE VARIANT SPECIES.
RADIATION LEVELS ARE HIGH BUT STILL WITHIN THE NONLETHAL RANGE. PROVIDE ANALYSIS?
I'VE GOT EYES. FIND ME SOMEONE TO TALK TO.

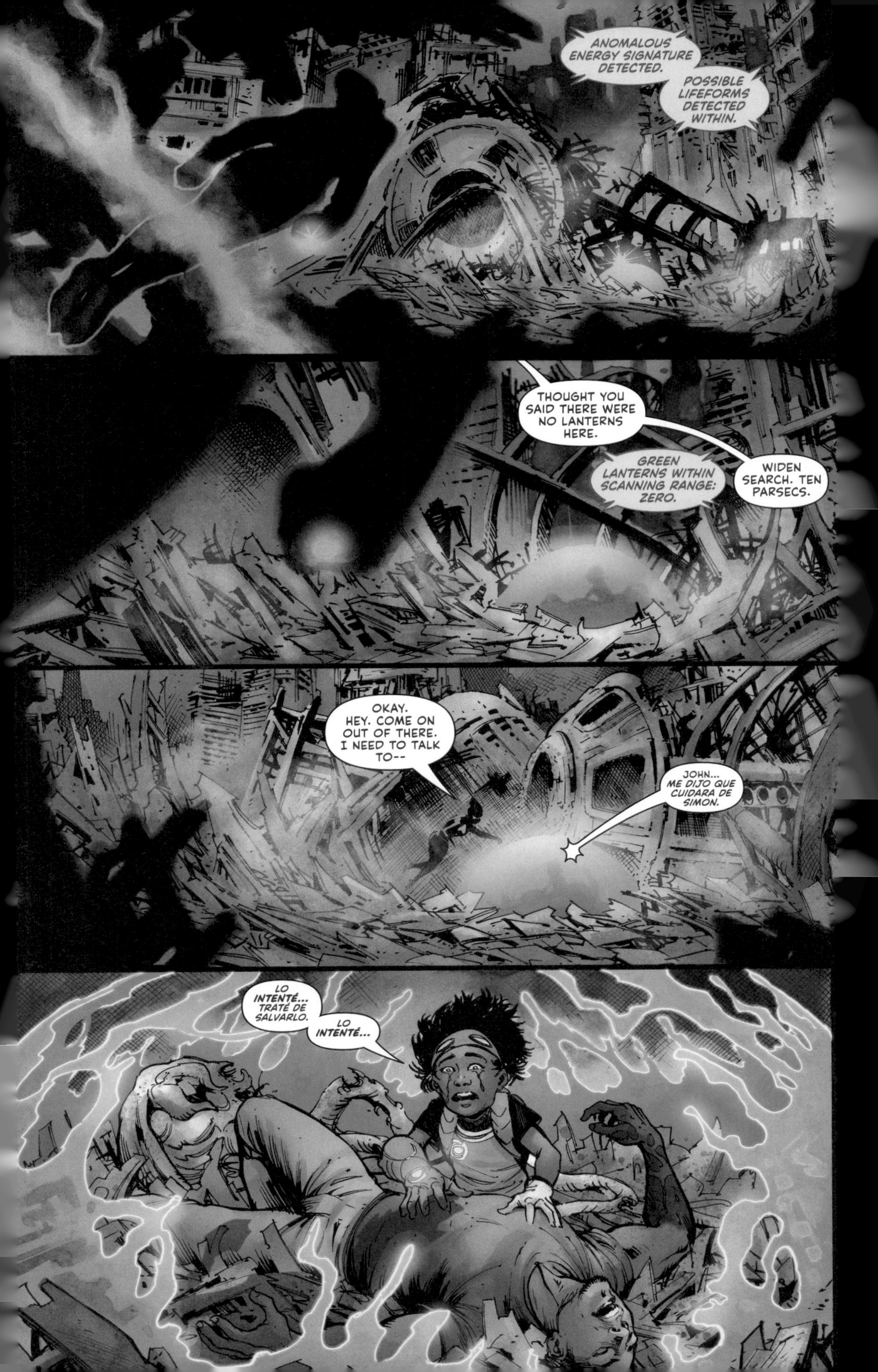

ANOMALOUS ENERGY SIGNATURE DETECTED.
POSSIBLE LIFEFORMS DETECTED WITHIN.
THOUGHT YOU SAID THERE WERE NO LANTERNS HERE.
GREEN LANTERNS WITHIN SCANNING RANGE: ZERO.
WIDEN SEARCH. TEN PARSECS.
OKAY. HEY. COME ON OUT OF THERE. I NEED TO TALK TO--
JOHN... ME DIJO QUE CUIDARA DE SIMON.
LO INTENTÉ... TRATÉ DE SALVARLO.
LO INTENTÉ...

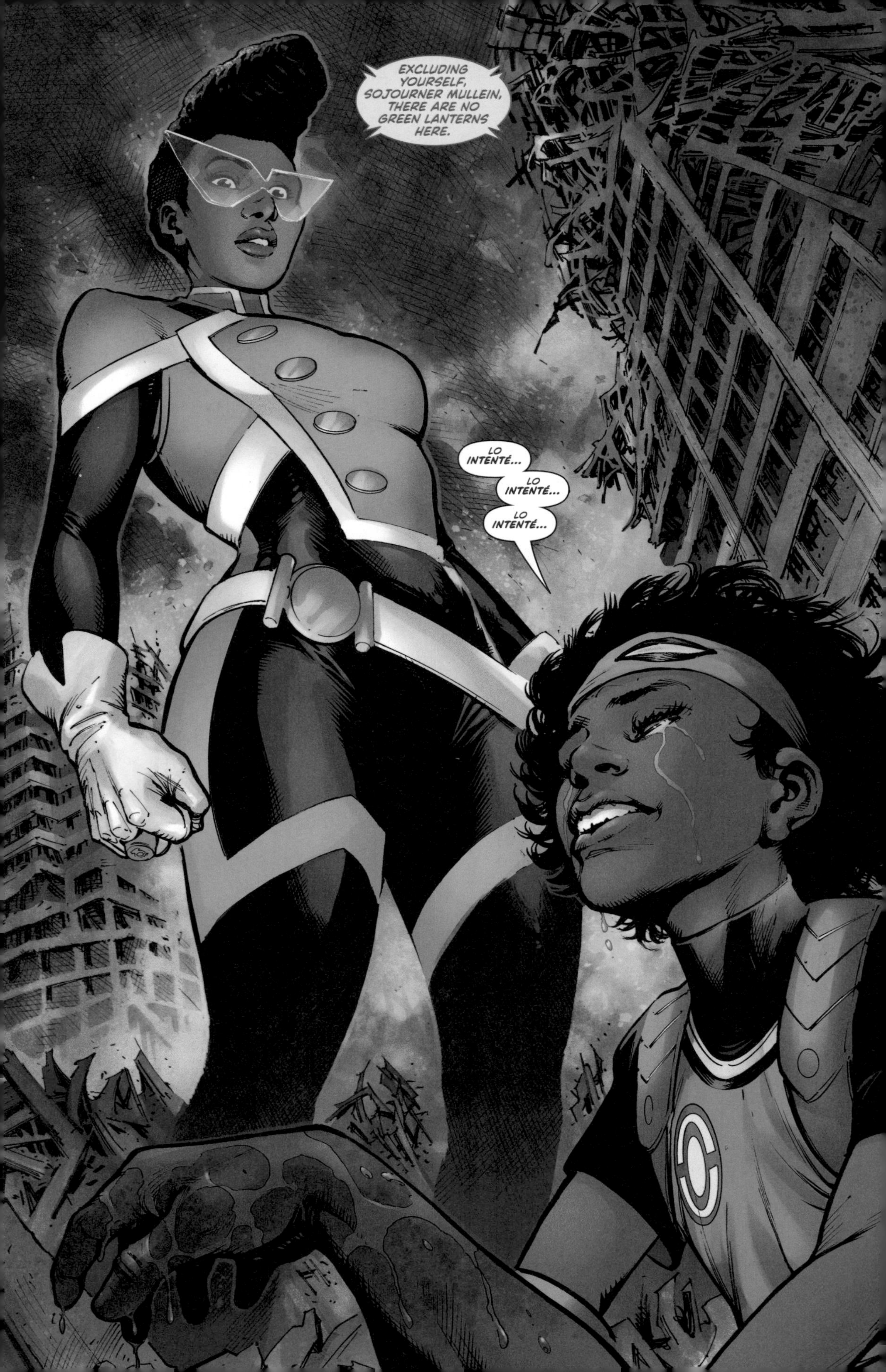
EXCLUDING YOURSELF, SOJOURNER MULLEIN, THERE ARE NO GREEN LANTERNS HERE.
LO INTENTÉ...
LO INTENTÉ...
LO INTENTÉ...

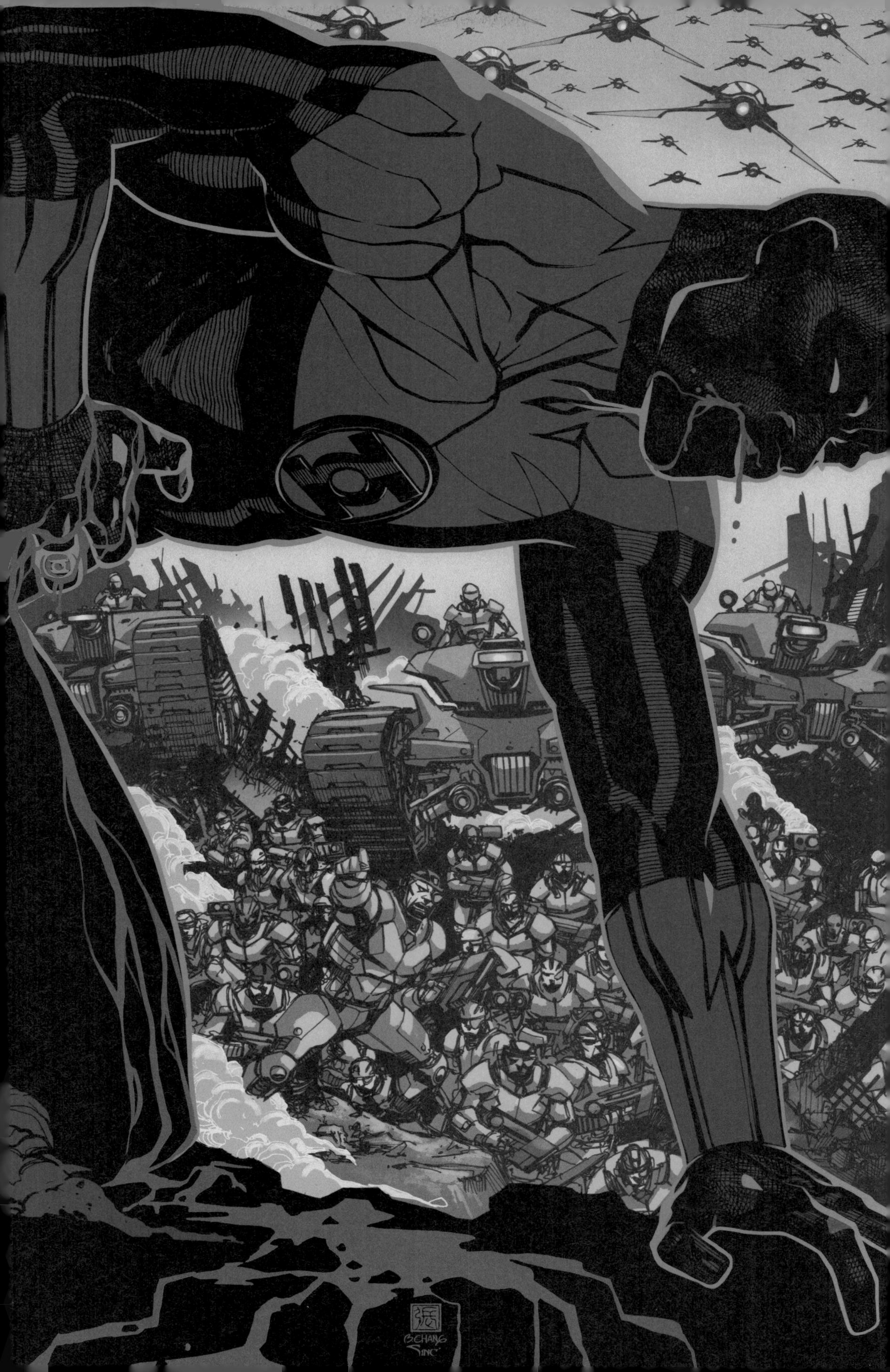
B.CHANG
SINC

Green Lantern #3 main cover art
by Bernard Chang and Alex Sinclair

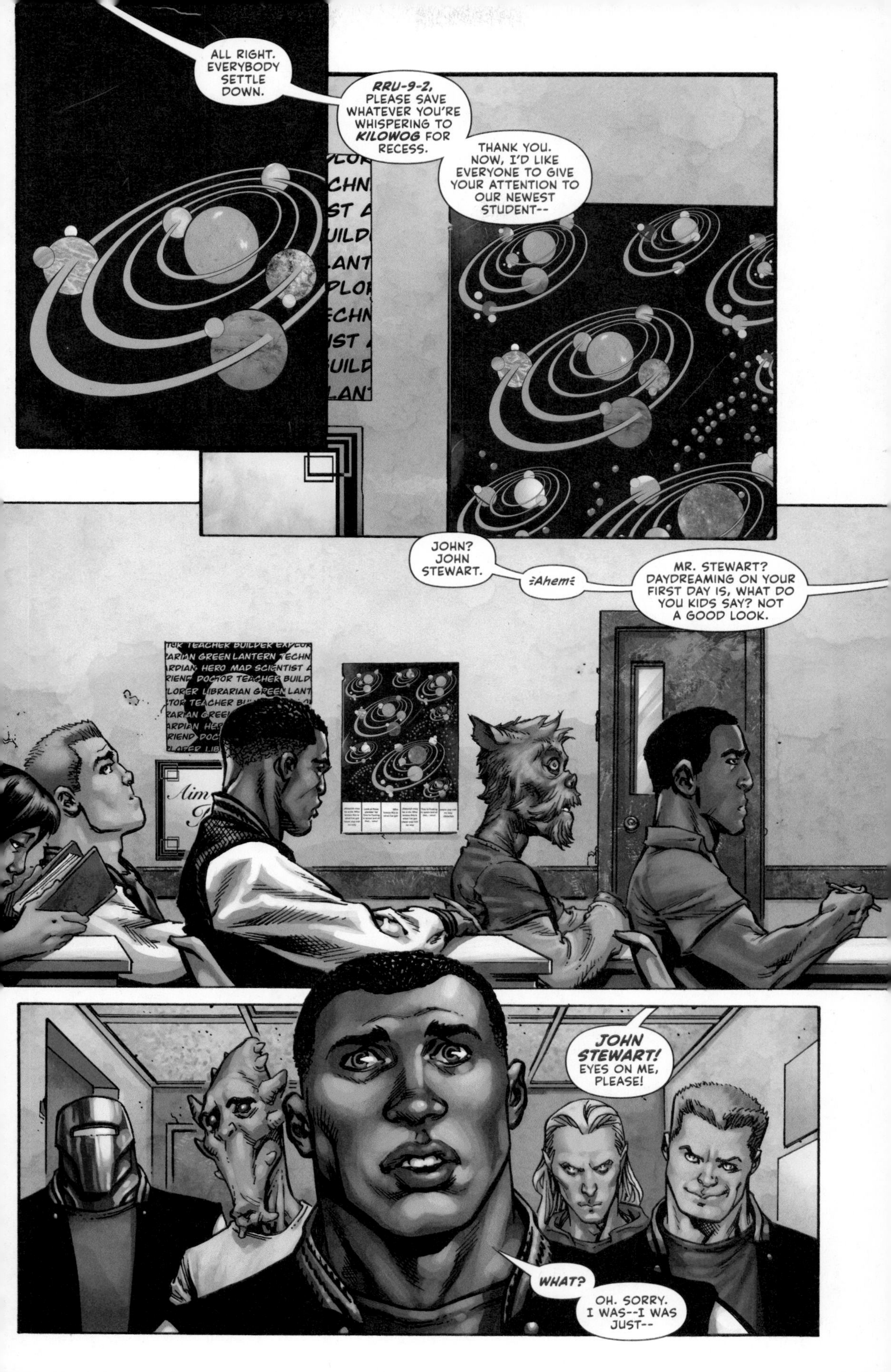
ALL RIGHT. EVERYBODY SETTLE DOWN.
RRU-9-2, PLEASE SAVE WHATEVER YOU'RE WHISPERING TO KILOWOG FOR RECESS.
THANK YOU. NOW, I'D LIKE EVERYONE TO GIVE YOUR ATTENTION TO OUR NEWEST STUDENT--
JOHN? JOHN STEWART.
Ahem
MR. STEWART? DAYDREAMING ON YOUR FIRST DAY IS, WHAT DO YOU KIDS SAY? NOT A GOOD LOOK.
JOHN STEWART! EYES ON ME, PLEASE!
WHAT?
OH. SORRY. I WAS--I WAS JUST--

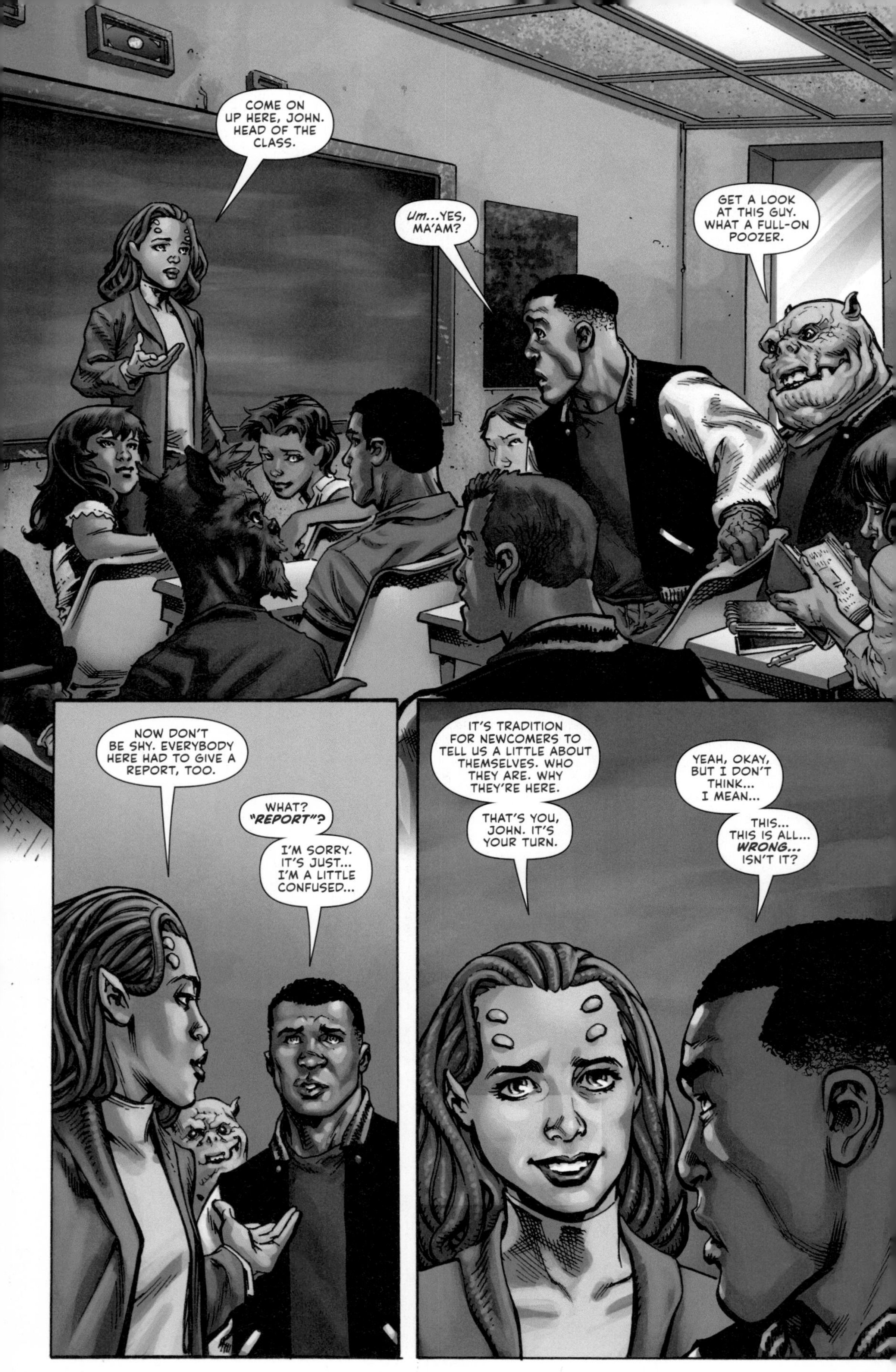
COME ON UP HERE, JOHN. HEAD OF THE CLASS.
*UM...*YES, MA'AM?
GET A LOOK AT THIS GUY. WHAT A FULL-ON POOZER.
NOW DON'T BE SHY. EVERYBODY HERE HAD TO GIVE A REPORT, TOO.
WHAT? ***"REPORT"***?
I'M SORRY. IT'S JUST... I'M A LITTLE CONFUSED...
IT'S TRADITION FOR NEWCOMERS TO TELL US A LITTLE ABOUT THEMSELVES. WHO THEY ARE. WHY THEY'RE HERE.
THAT'S YOU, JOHN. IT'S YOUR TURN.
YEAH, OKAY, BUT I DON'T THINK... I MEAN...
THIS... THIS IS ALL... ***WRONG...*** ISN'T IT?

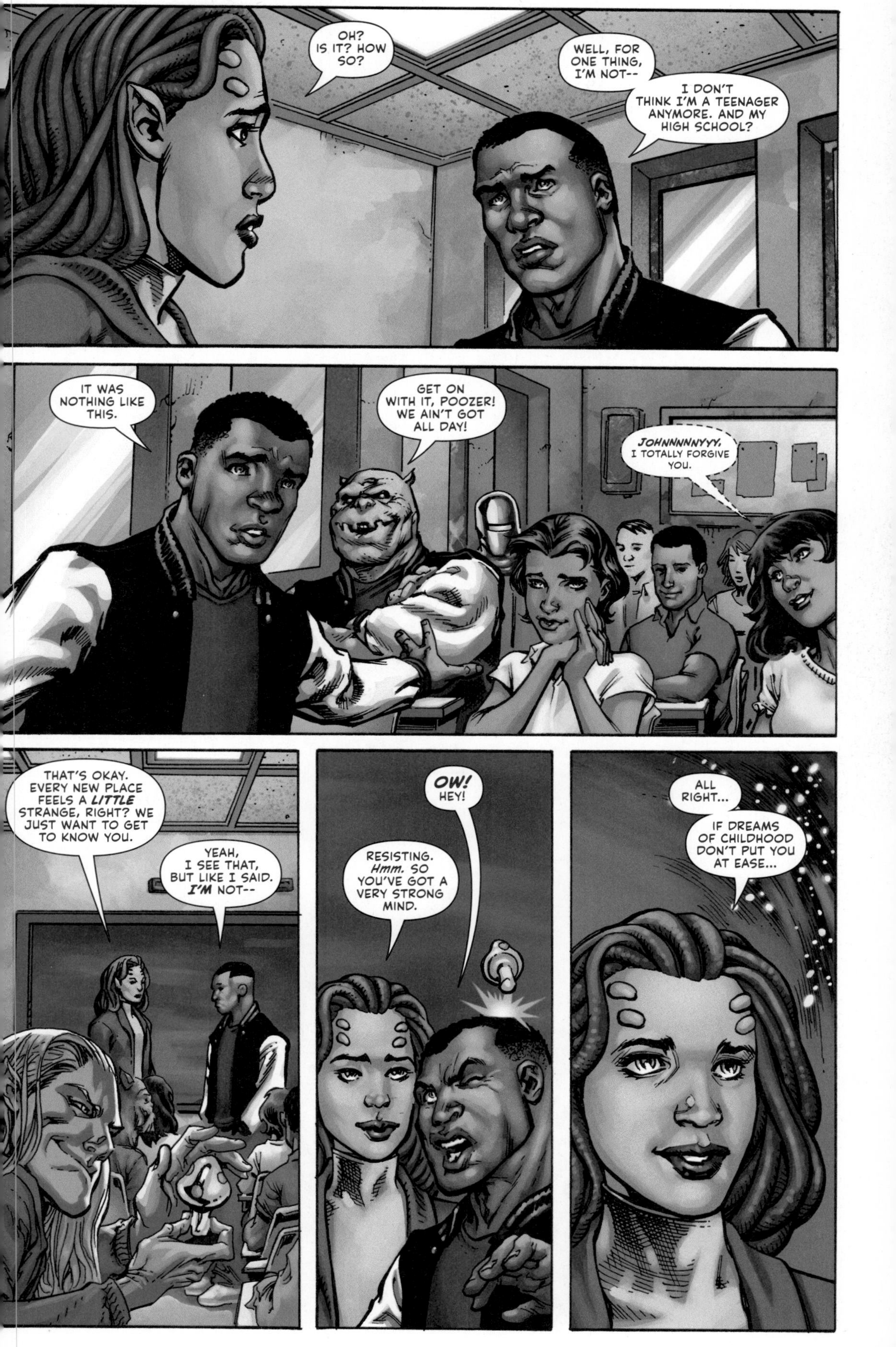

OH? IS IT? HOW SO?
WELL, FOR ONE THING, I'M NOT--
I DON'T THINK I'M A TEENAGER ANYMORE. AND MY HIGH SCHOOL?
IT WAS NOTHING LIKE THIS.
GET ON WITH IT, POOZER! WE AIN'T GOT ALL DAY!
JOHNNNNNYYY, I TOTALLY FORGIVE YOU.
THAT'S OKAY. EVERY NEW PLACE FEELS A *LITTLE* STRANGE, RIGHT? WE JUST WANT TO GET TO KNOW YOU.
YEAH, I SEE THAT, BUT LIKE I SAID. *I'M* NOT--
OW! HEY!
RESISTING. *Hmm.* SO YOU'VE GOT A VERY STRONG MIND.
ALL RIGHT...
IF DREAMS OF CHILDHOOD DON'T PUT YOU AT EASE...

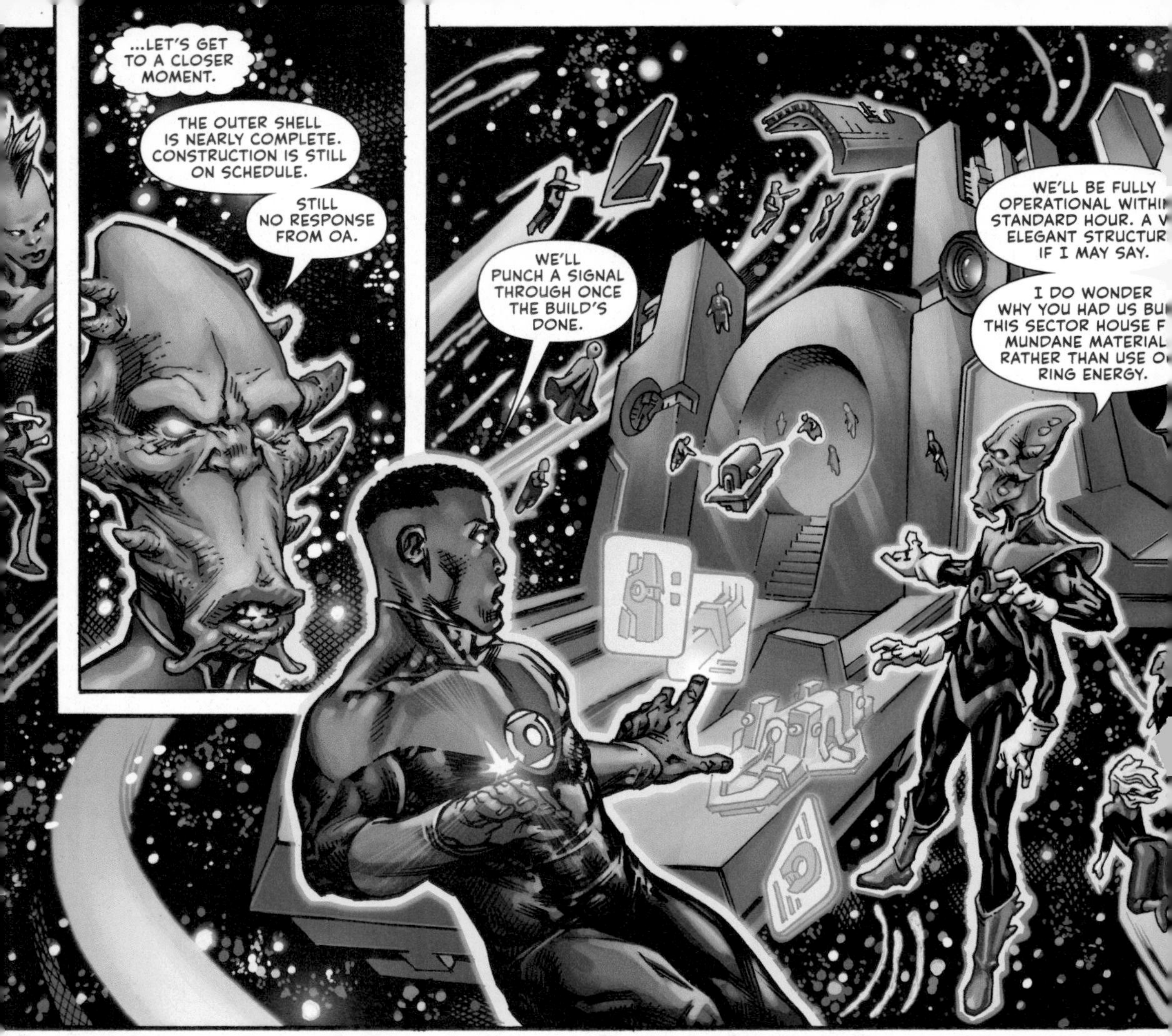
...LET'S GET TO A CLOSER MOMENT.
THE OUTER SHELL IS NEARLY COMPLETE. CONSTRUCTION IS STILL ON SCHEDULE.
STILL NO RESPONSE FROM OA.
WE'LL PUNCH A SIGNAL THROUGH ONCE THE BUILD'S DONE.
WE'LL BE FULLY OPERATIONAL WITHI STANDARD HOUR. A V ELEGANT STRUCTUR IF I MAY SAY.
I DO WONDER WHY YOU HAD US BU THIS SECTOR HOUSE F MUNDANE MATERIAL RATHER THAN USE O RING ENERGY.

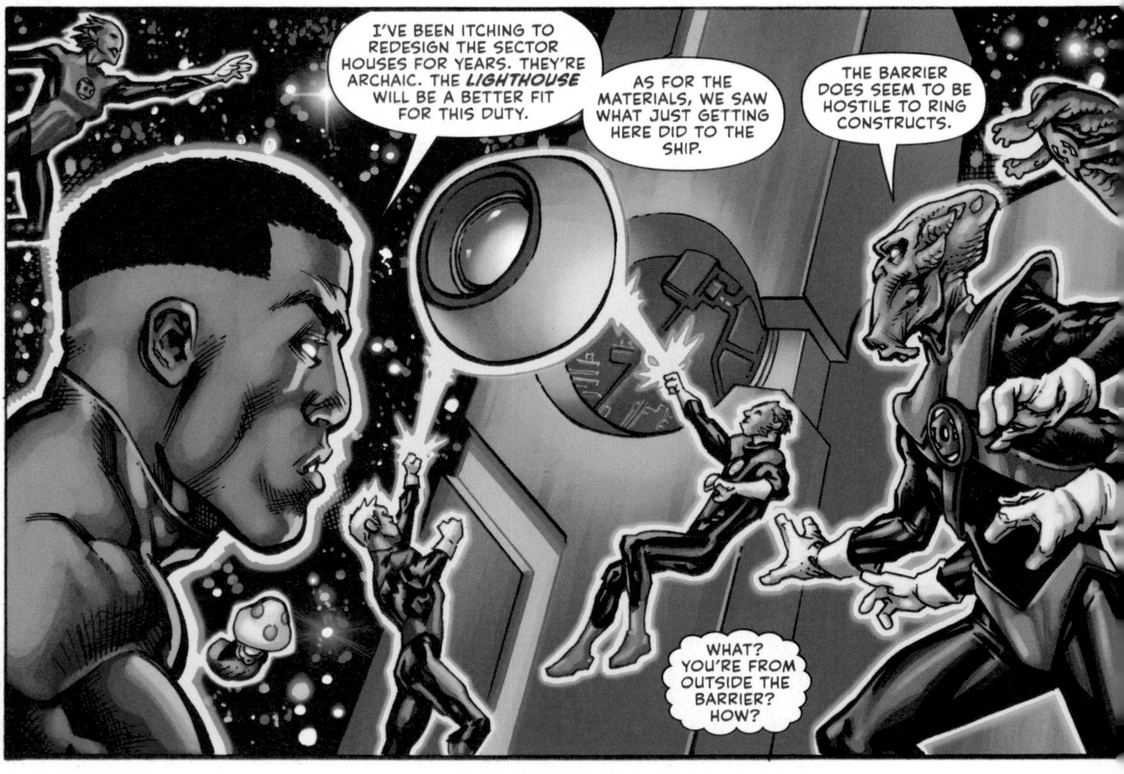
I'VE BEEN ITCHING TO REDESIGN THE SECTOR HOUSES FOR YEARS. THEY'RE ARCHAIC. THE ***LIGHTHOUSE*** WILL BE A BETTER FIT FOR THIS DUTY.
AS FOR THE MATERIALS, WE SAW WHAT JUST GETTING HERE DID TO THE SHIP.
THE BARRIER DOES SEEM TO BE HOSTILE TO RING CONSTRUCTS.
WHAT? YOU'RE FROM OUTSIDE THE BARRIER? HOW?

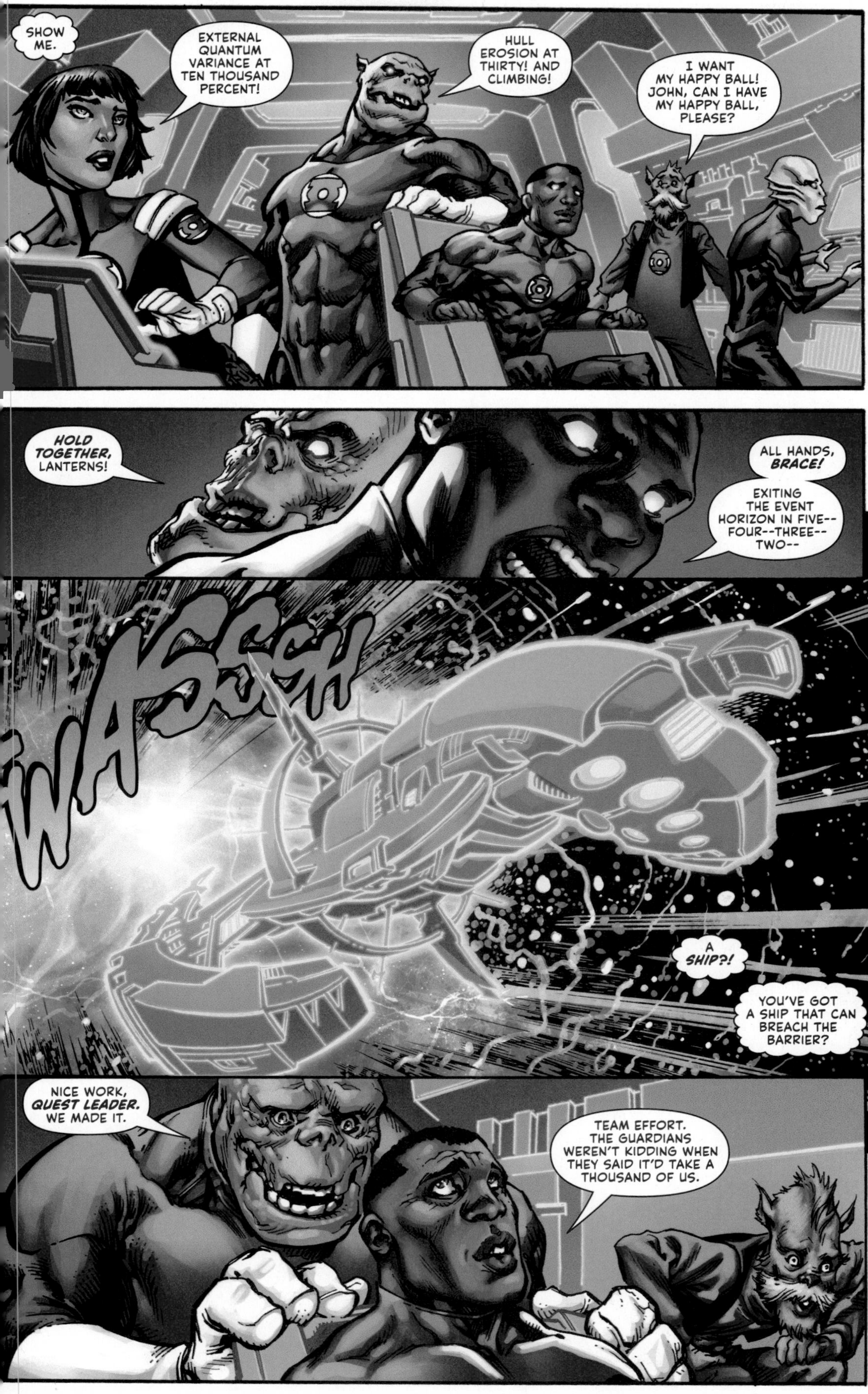
SHOW ME.
EXTERNAL QUANTUM VARIANCE AT TEN THOUSAND PERCENT!
HULL EROSION AT THIRTY! AND CLIMBING!
I WANT MY HAPPY BALL! JOHN, CAN I HAVE MY HAPPY BALL, PLEASE?
HOLD TOGETHER, LANTERNS!
ALL HANDS, BRACE!
EXITING THE EVENT HORIZON IN FIVE-- FOUR--THREE-- TWO--
WASSSH
A SHIP?!
YOU'VE GOT A SHIP THAT CAN BREACH THE BARRIER?
NICE WORK, QUEST LEADER. WE MADE IT.
TEAM EFFORT. THE GUARDIANS WEREN'T KIDDING WHEN THEY SAID IT'D TAKE A THOUSAND OF US.

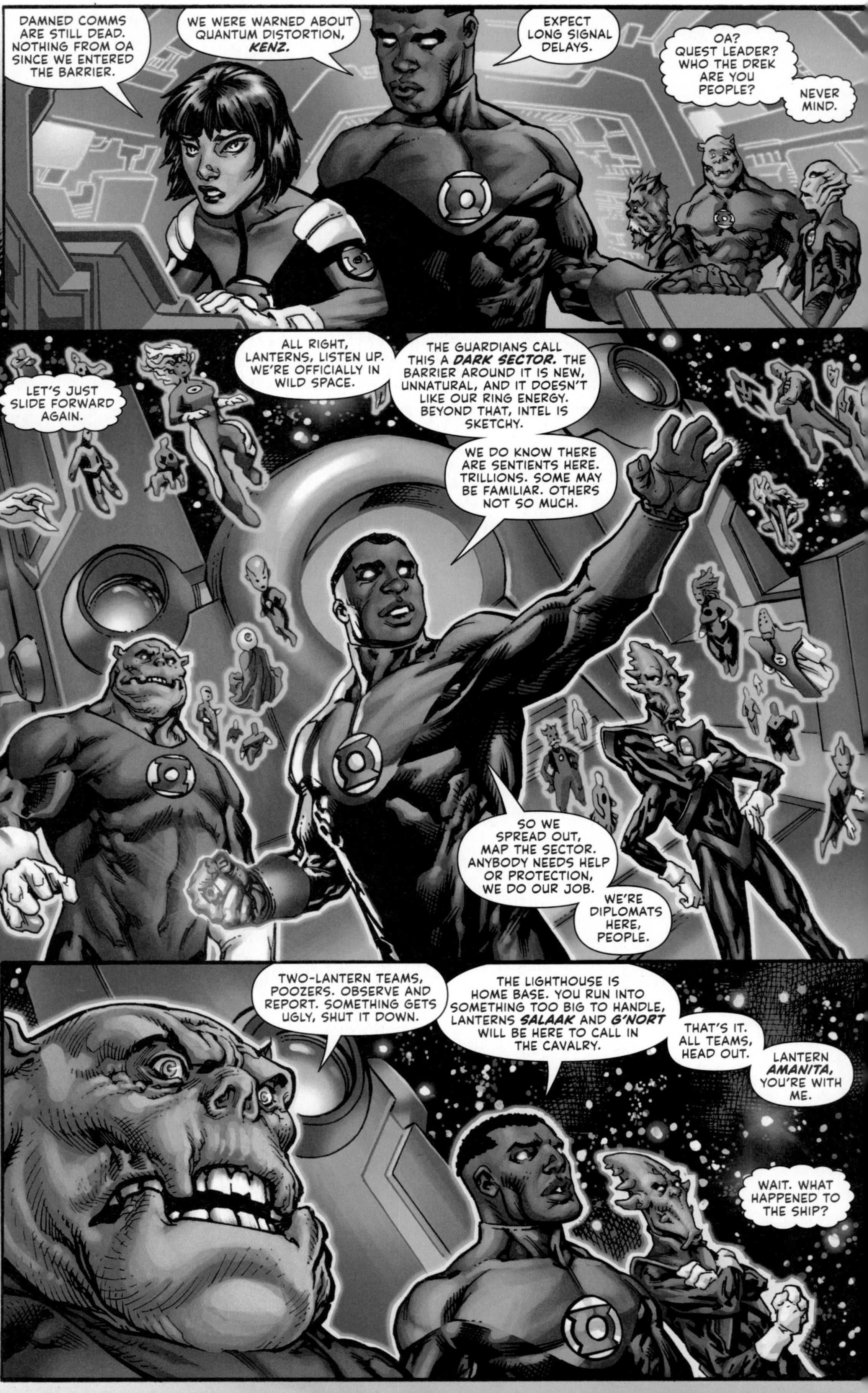
DAMNED COMMS ARE STILL DEAD. NOTHING FROM OA SINCE WE ENTERED THE BARRIER.
WE WERE WARNED ABOUT QUANTUM DISTORTION, KENZ.
EXPECT LONG SIGNAL DELAYS.
OA? QUEST LEADER? WHO THE DREK ARE YOU PEOPLE?
NEVER MIND.
LET'S JUST SLIDE FORWARD AGAIN.
ALL RIGHT, LANTERNS, LISTEN UP. WE'RE OFFICIALLY IN WILD SPACE.
THE GUARDIANS CALL THIS A DARK SECTOR. THE BARRIER AROUND IT IS NEW, UNNATURAL, AND IT DOESN'T LIKE OUR RING ENERGY. BEYOND THAT, INTEL IS SKETCHY.
WE DO KNOW THERE ARE SENTIENTS HERE. TRILLIONS. SOME MAY BE FAMILIAR. OTHERS NOT SO MUCH.
SO WE SPREAD OUT, MAP THE SECTOR. ANYBODY NEEDS HELP OR PROTECTION, WE DO OUR JOB.
WE'RE DIPLOMATS HERE, PEOPLE.
TWO-LANTERN TEAMS, POOZERS. OBSERVE AND REPORT. SOMETHING GETS UGLY, SHUT IT DOWN.
THE LIGHTHOUSE IS HOME BASE. YOU RUN INTO SOMETHING TOO BIG TO HANDLE, LANTERNS SALAAK AND G'NORT WILL BE HERE TO CALL IN THE CAVALRY.
THAT'S IT. ALL TEAMS, HEAD OUT.
LANTERN AMANITA, YOU'RE WITH ME.
WAIT. WHAT HAPPENED TO THE SHIP?

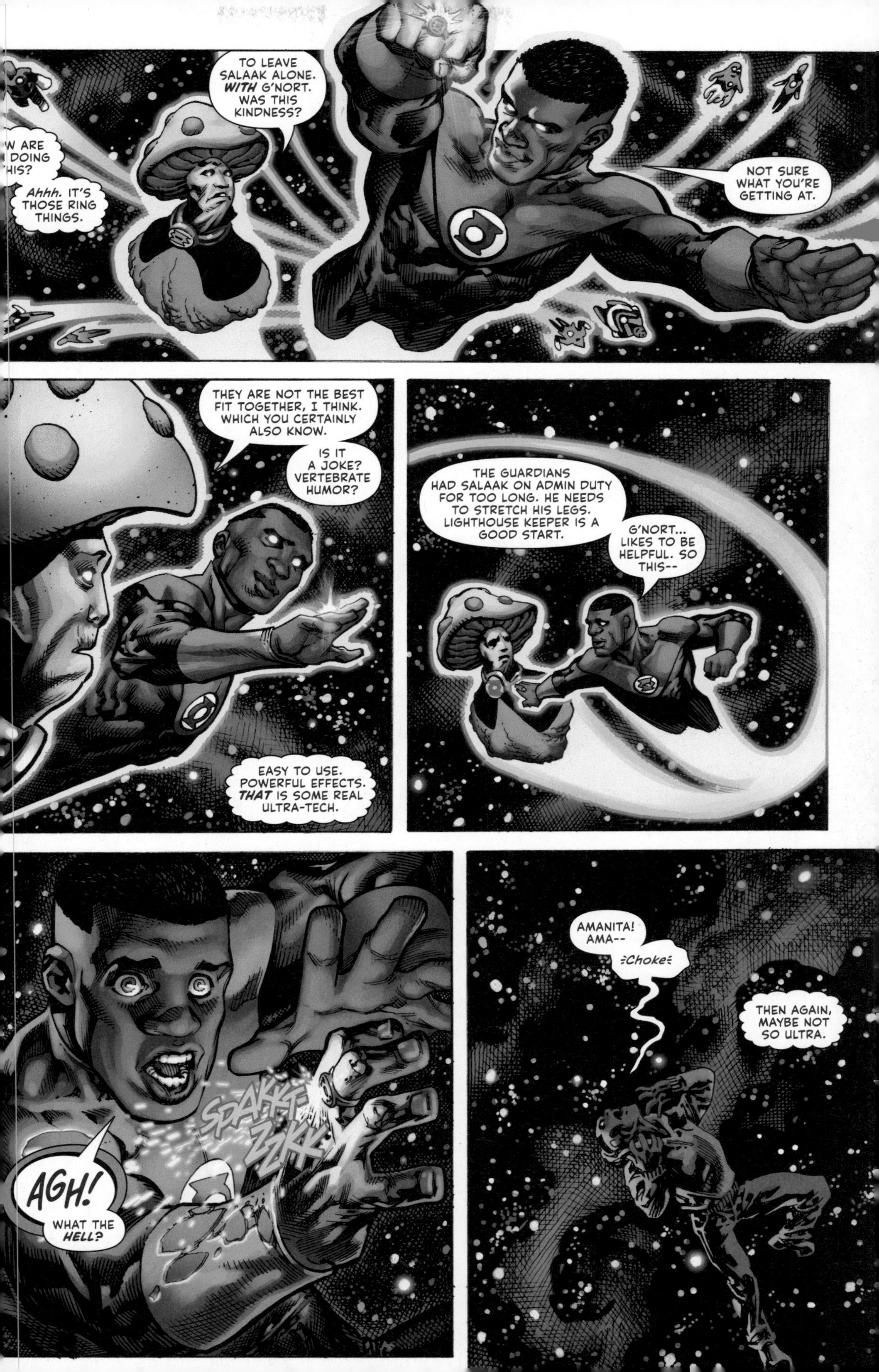

TO LEAVE SALAAK ALONE. *WITH* G'NORT. WAS THIS KINDNESS?
W ARE DOING HIS?
Ahhh. IT'S THOSE RING THINGS.
NOT SURE WHAT YOU'RE GETTING AT.
THEY ARE NOT THE BEST FIT TOGETHER, I THINK. WHICH YOU CERTAINLY ALSO KNOW.
IS IT A JOKE? VERTEBRATE HUMOR?
EASY TO USE. POWERFUL EFFECTS. *THAT* IS SOME REAL ULTRA-TECH.
THE GUARDIANS HAD SALAAK ON ADMIN DUTY FOR TOO LONG. HE NEEDS TO STRETCH HIS LEGS. LIGHTHOUSE KEEPER IS A GOOD START.
G'NORT... LIKES TO BE HELPFUL. SO THIS--
SPAKKT
ZZKK
AGH!
WHAT THE *HELL?*
AMANITA! AMA--
Choke
THEN AGAIN, MAYBE NOT SO ULTRA.

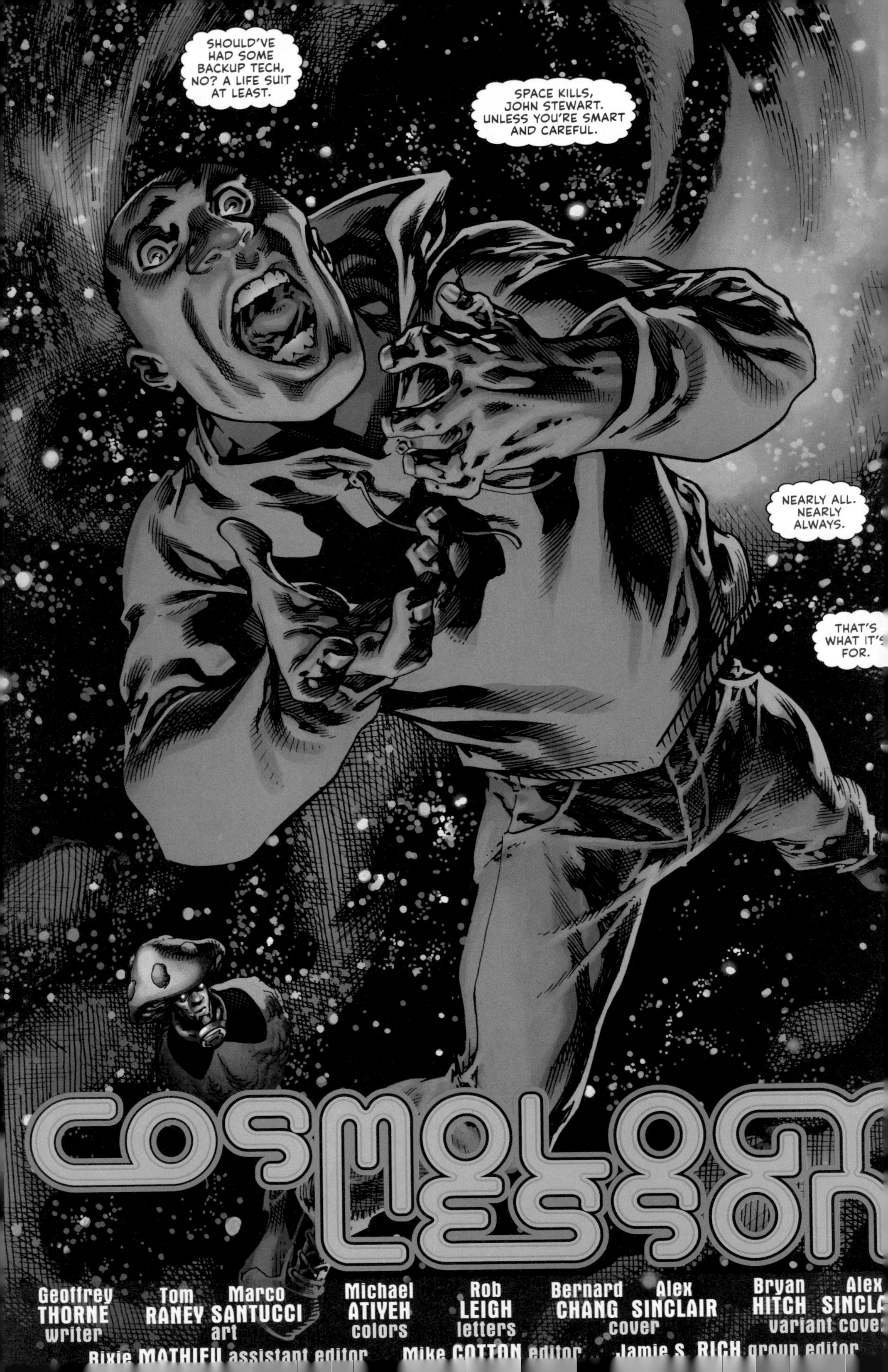

SHOULD'VE HAD SOME BACKUP TECH, NO? A LIFE SUIT AT LEAST.
SPACE KILLS, JOHN STEWART. UNLESS YOU'RE SMART AND CAREFUL.
NEARLY ALL. NEARLY ALWAYS.
THAT'S WHAT IT'S FOR.
COSMOLOGY LESSON
Geoffrey THORNE writer
Tom RANEY Marco SANTUCCI art
Michael ATIYEH colors
Rob LEIGH letters
Bernard CHANG Alex SINCLAIR cover
Bryan HITCH Alex SINCLA variant cove
Bixie MATHIEU assistant editor Mike COTTON editor Jamie S. RICH group editor

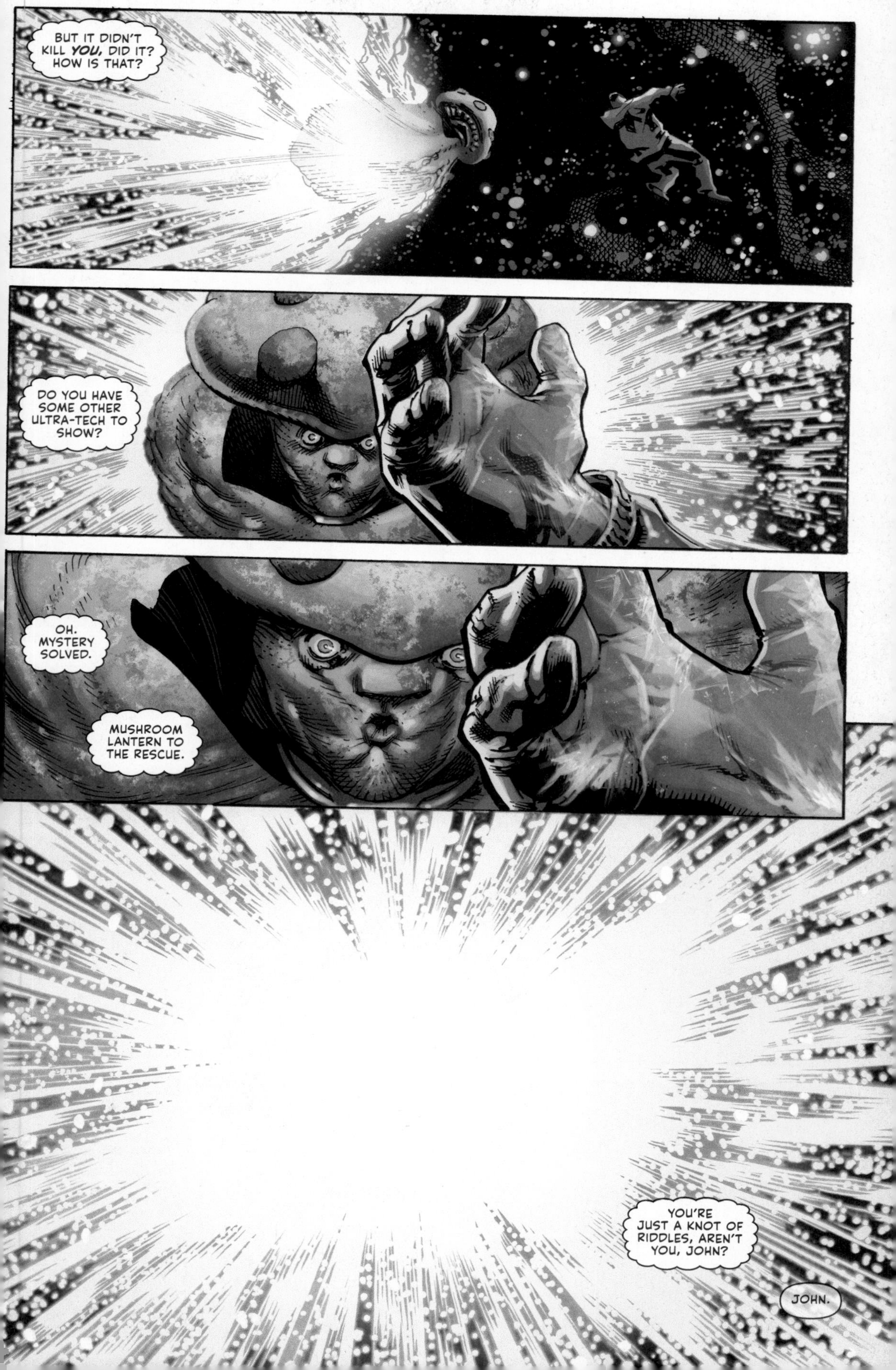
BUT IT DIDN'T KILL *YOU,* DID IT? HOW IS THAT?
DO YOU HAVE SOME OTHER ULTRA-TECH TO SHOW?
OH. MYSTERY SOLVED.
MUSHROOM LANTERN TO THE RESCUE.
YOU'RE JUST A KNOT OF RIDDLES, AREN'T YOU, JOHN?
JOHN.

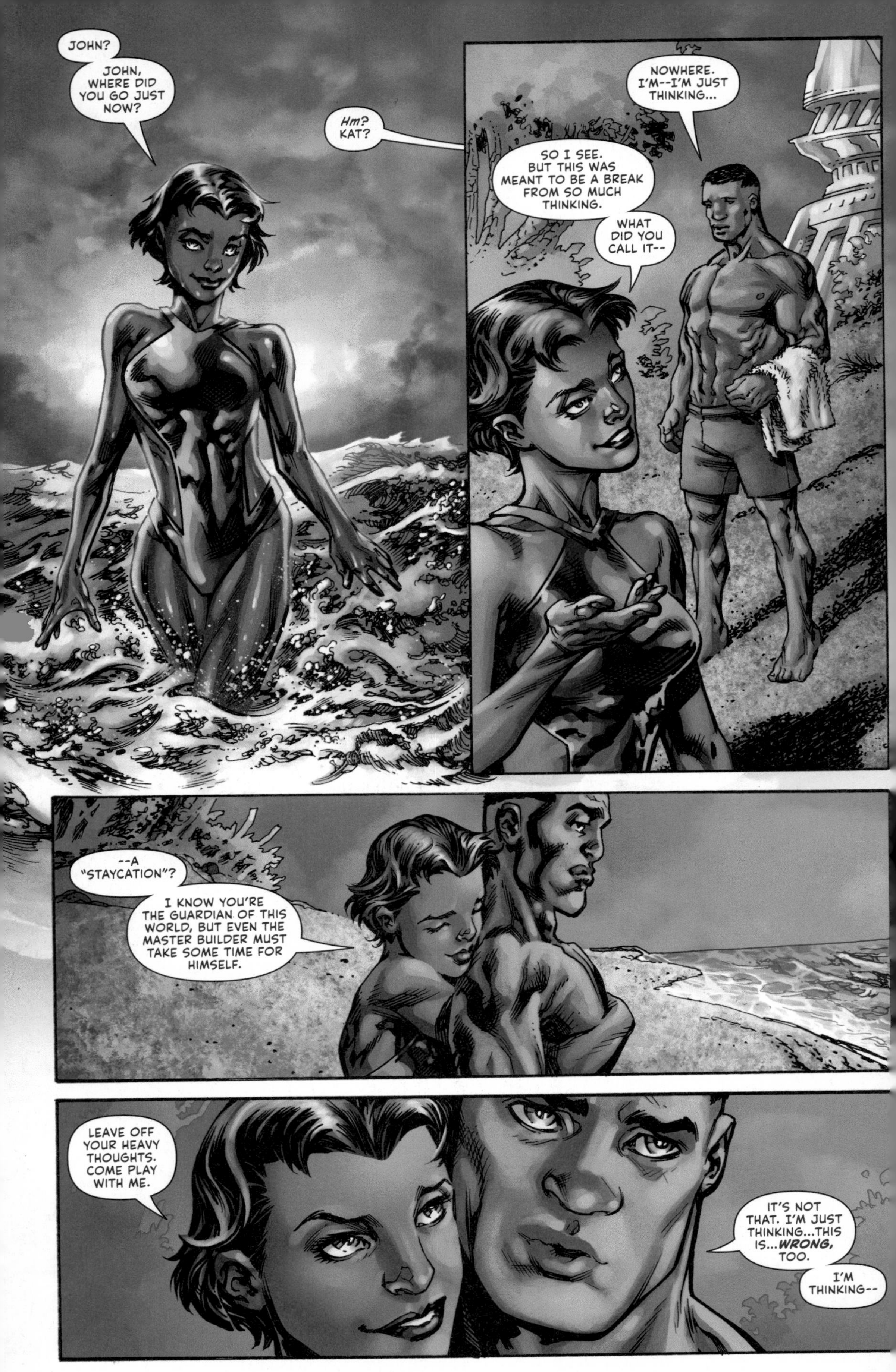
JOHN?
JOHN, WHERE DID YOU GO JUST NOW?
Hm? KAT?
NOWHERE. I'M--I'M JUST THINKING...
SO I SEE. BUT THIS WAS MEANT TO BE A BREAK FROM SO MUCH THINKING.
WHAT DID YOU CALL IT--
--A "STAYCATION"?
I KNOW YOU'RE THE GUARDIAN OF THIS WORLD, BUT EVEN THE MASTER BUILDER MUST TAKE SOME TIME FOR HIMSELF.
LEAVE OFF YOUR HEAVY THOUGHTS. COME PLAY WITH ME.
IT'S NOT THAT. I'M JUST THINKING...THIS IS...WRONG, TOO.
I'M THINKING--

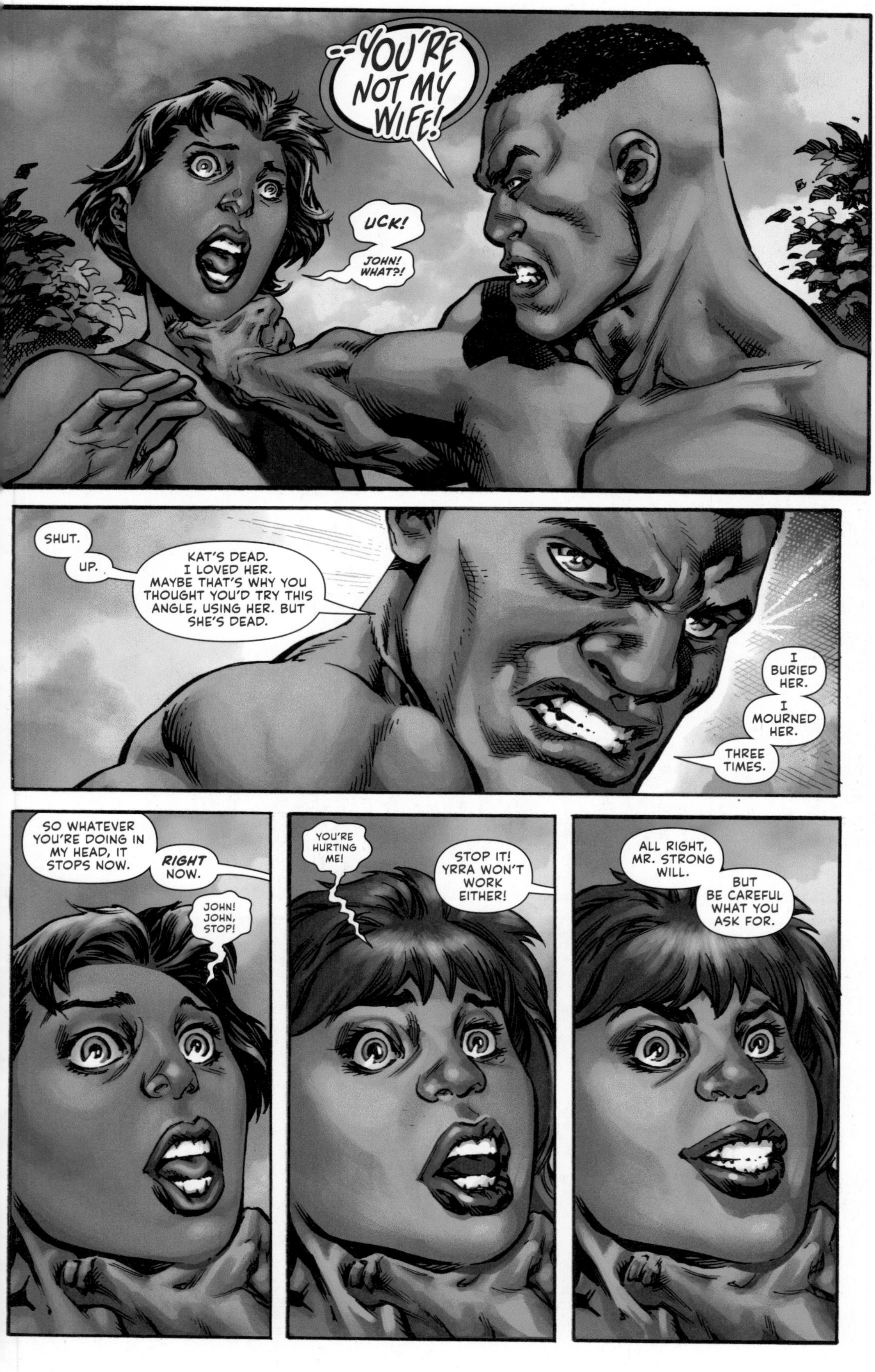

--YOU'RE NOT MY WIFE!
UCK!
JOHN! WHAT?!
SHUT.
UP.
KAT'S DEAD. I LOVED HER. MAYBE THAT'S WHY YOU THOUGHT YOU'D TRY THIS ANGLE, USING HER. BUT SHE'S DEAD.
I BURIED HER.
I MOURNED HER.
THREE TIMES.
SO WHATEVER YOU'RE DOING IN MY HEAD, IT STOPS NOW.
RIGHT NOW.
JOHN! JOHN, STOP!
YOU'RE HURTING ME!
STOP IT! YRRA WON'T WORK EITHER!
ALL RIGHT, MR. STRONG WILL.
BUT BE CAREFUL WHAT YOU ASK FOR.

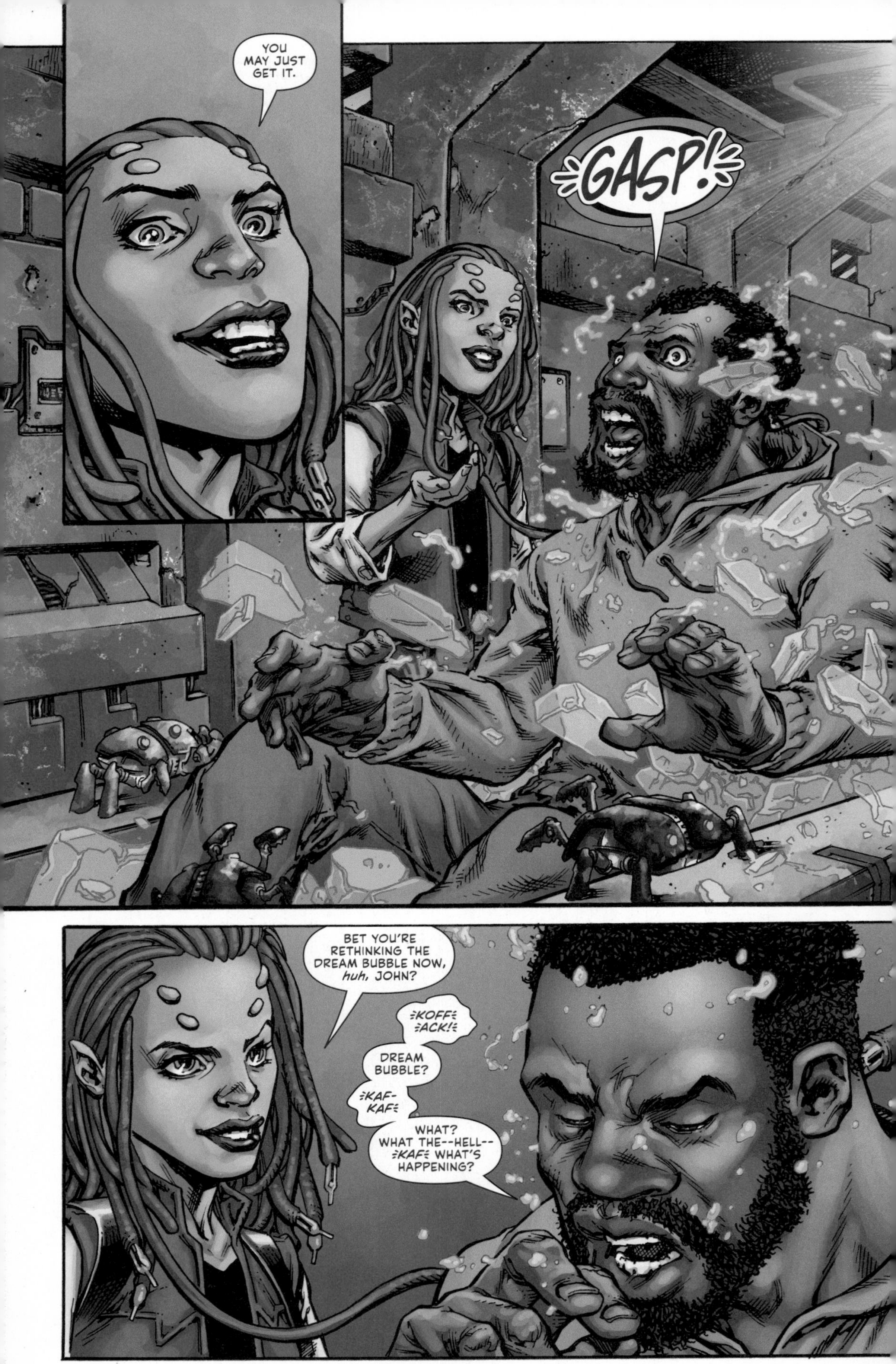
YOU MAY JUST GET IT.
GASP!
BET YOU'RE RETHINKING THE DREAM BUBBLE NOW, *huh*, JOHN?
KOFF ACK!
DREAM BUBBLE?
KAF-KAF
WHAT? WHAT THE--HELL-- KAF WHAT'S HAPPENING?

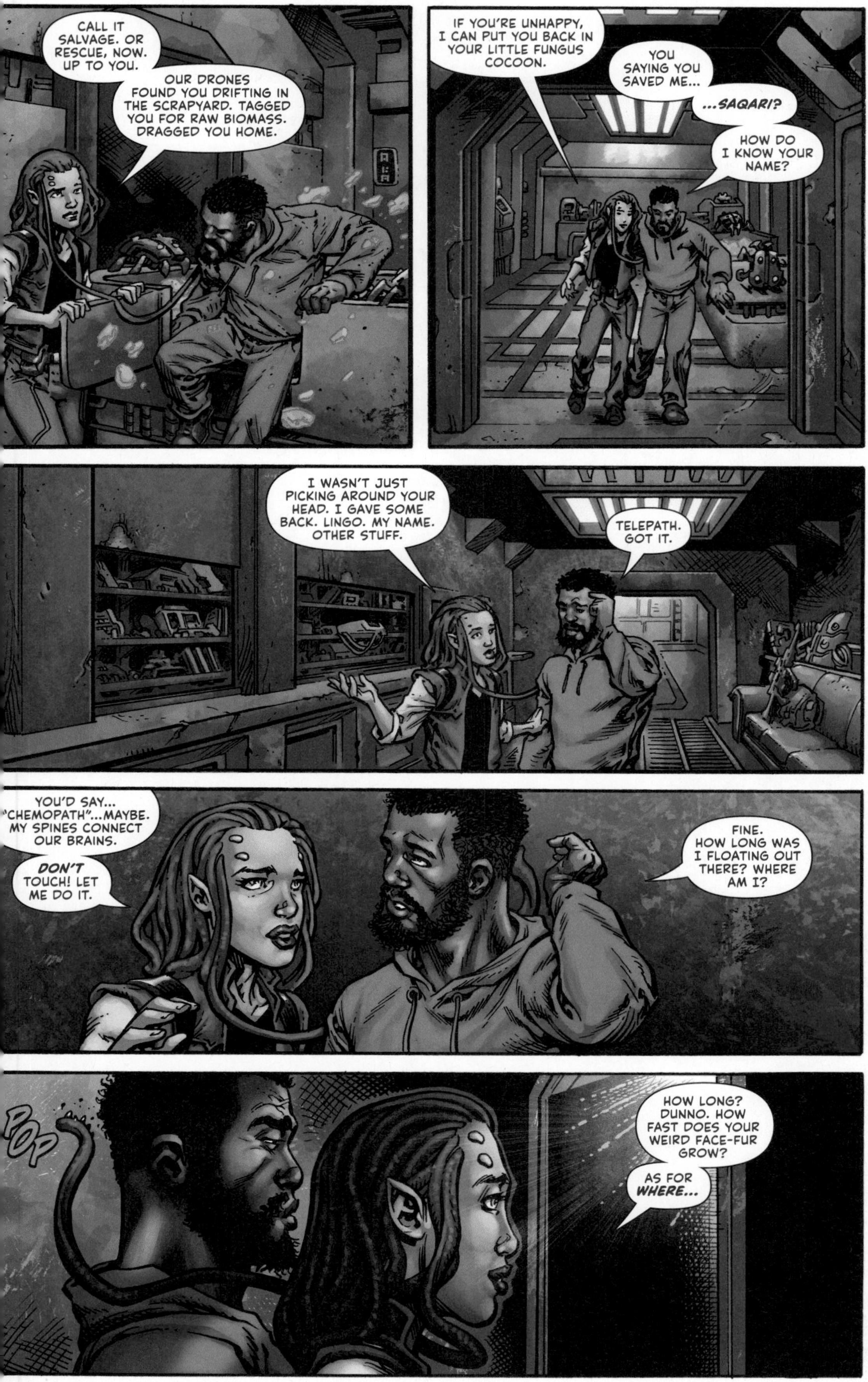

CALL IT SALVAGE. OR RESCUE, NOW. UP TO YOU.
OUR DRONES FOUND YOU DRIFTING IN THE SCRAPYARD. TAGGED YOU FOR RAW BIOMASS. DRAGGED YOU HOME.
IF YOU'RE UNHAPPY, I CAN PUT YOU BACK IN YOUR LITTLE FUNGUS COCOON.
YOU SAYING YOU SAVED ME...
...SAQARI?
HOW DO I KNOW YOUR NAME?
I WASN'T JUST PICKING AROUND YOUR HEAD. I GAVE SOME BACK. LINGO. MY NAME. OTHER STUFF.
TELEPATH. GOT IT.
YOU'D SAY... "CHEMOPATH"...MAYBE. MY SPINES CONNECT OUR BRAINS.
DON'T TOUCH! LET ME DO IT.
FINE. HOW LONG WAS I FLOATING OUT THERE? WHERE AM I?
POP
HOW LONG? DUNNO. HOW FAST DOES YOUR WEIRD FACE-FUR GROW?
AS FOR WHERE...

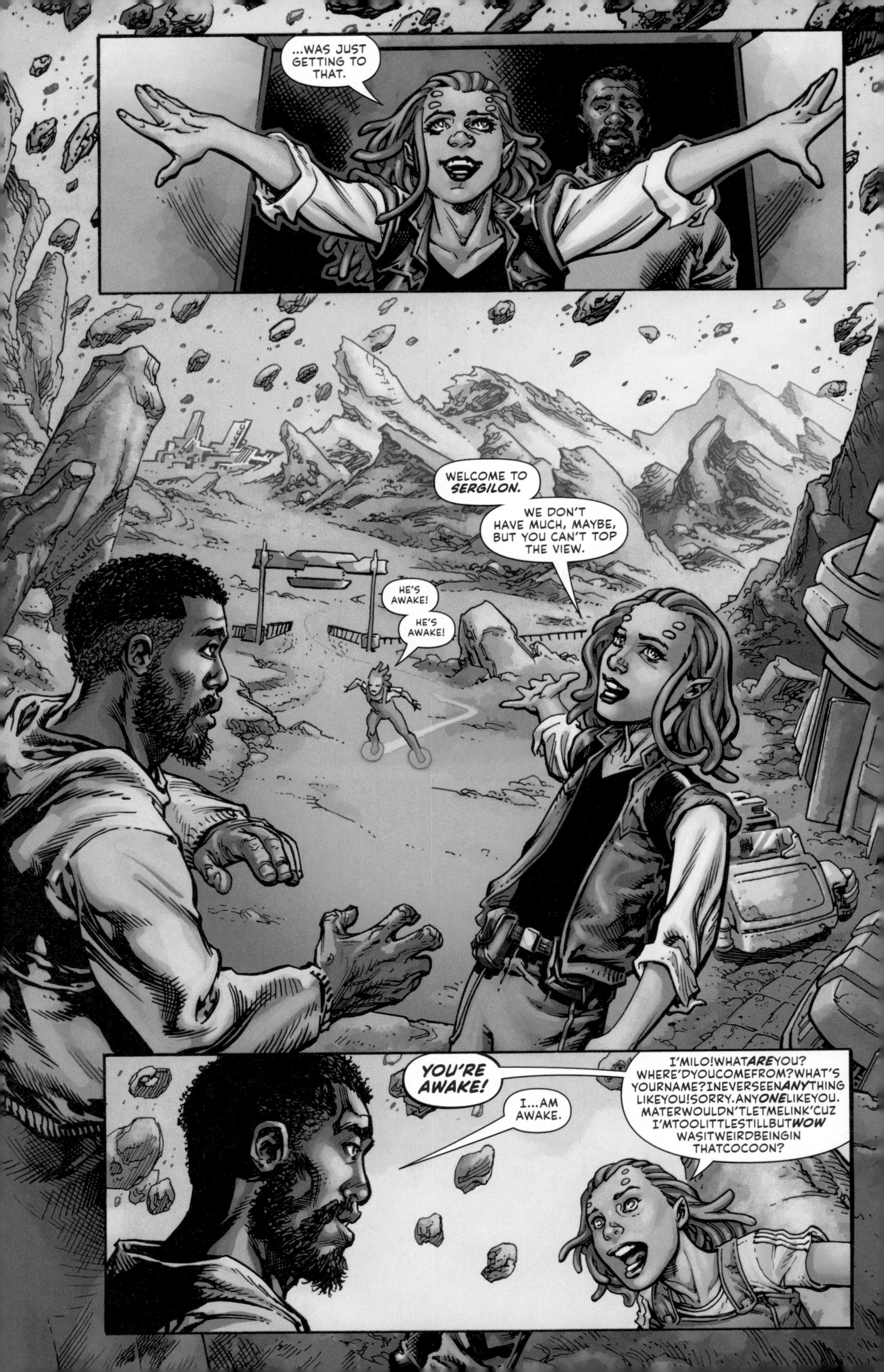
...WAS JUST GETTING TO THAT.
WELCOME TO SERGILON.
WE DON'T HAVE MUCH, MAYBE, BUT YOU CAN'T TOP THE VIEW.
HE'S AWAKE!
HE'S AWAKE!
YOU'RE AWAKE!
I'MILO!WHATAREYOU? WHERE'DYOUCOMEFROM?WHAT'S YOURNAME?INEVERSEENANYTHING LIKEYOU!SORRY.ANYONELIKEYOU. MATERWOULDN'TLETMELINK'CUZ I'MTOOLITTLESTILLBUTWOW WASITWEIRDBEINGIN THATCOCOON?
I...AM AWAKE.

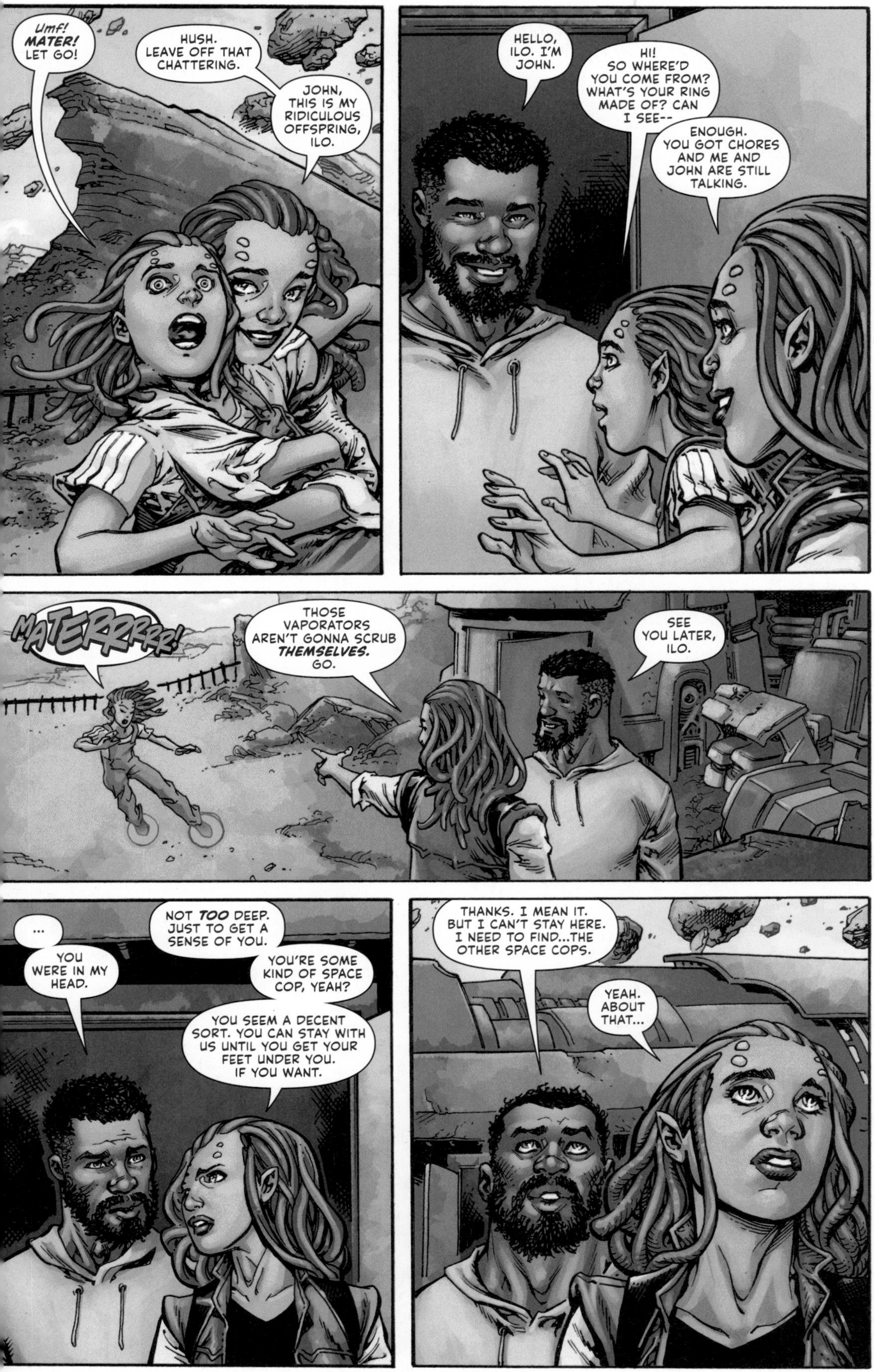
Umf! ***MATER!*** LET GO!
HUSH. LEAVE OFF THAT CHATTERING.
JOHN, THIS IS MY RIDICULOUS OFFSPRING, ILO.
HELLO, ILO. I'M JOHN.
HI! SO WHERE'D YOU COME FROM? WHAT'S YOUR RING MADE OF? CAN I SEE--
ENOUGH. YOU GOT CHORES AND ME AND JOHN ARE STILL TALKING.
MATERRRRR!
THOSE VAPORATORS AREN'T GONNA SCRUB ***THEMSELVES.*** GO.
SEE YOU LATER, ILO.
...
YOU WERE IN MY HEAD.
NOT ***TOO*** DEEP. JUST TO GET A SENSE OF YOU.
YOU'RE SOME KIND OF SPACE COP, YEAH?
YOU SEEM A DECENT SORT. YOU CAN STAY WITH US UNTIL YOU GET YOUR FEET UNDER YOU. IF YOU WANT.
THANKS. I MEAN IT. BUT I CAN'T STAY HERE. I NEED TO FIND...THE OTHER SPACE COPS.
YEAH. ABOUT THAT...

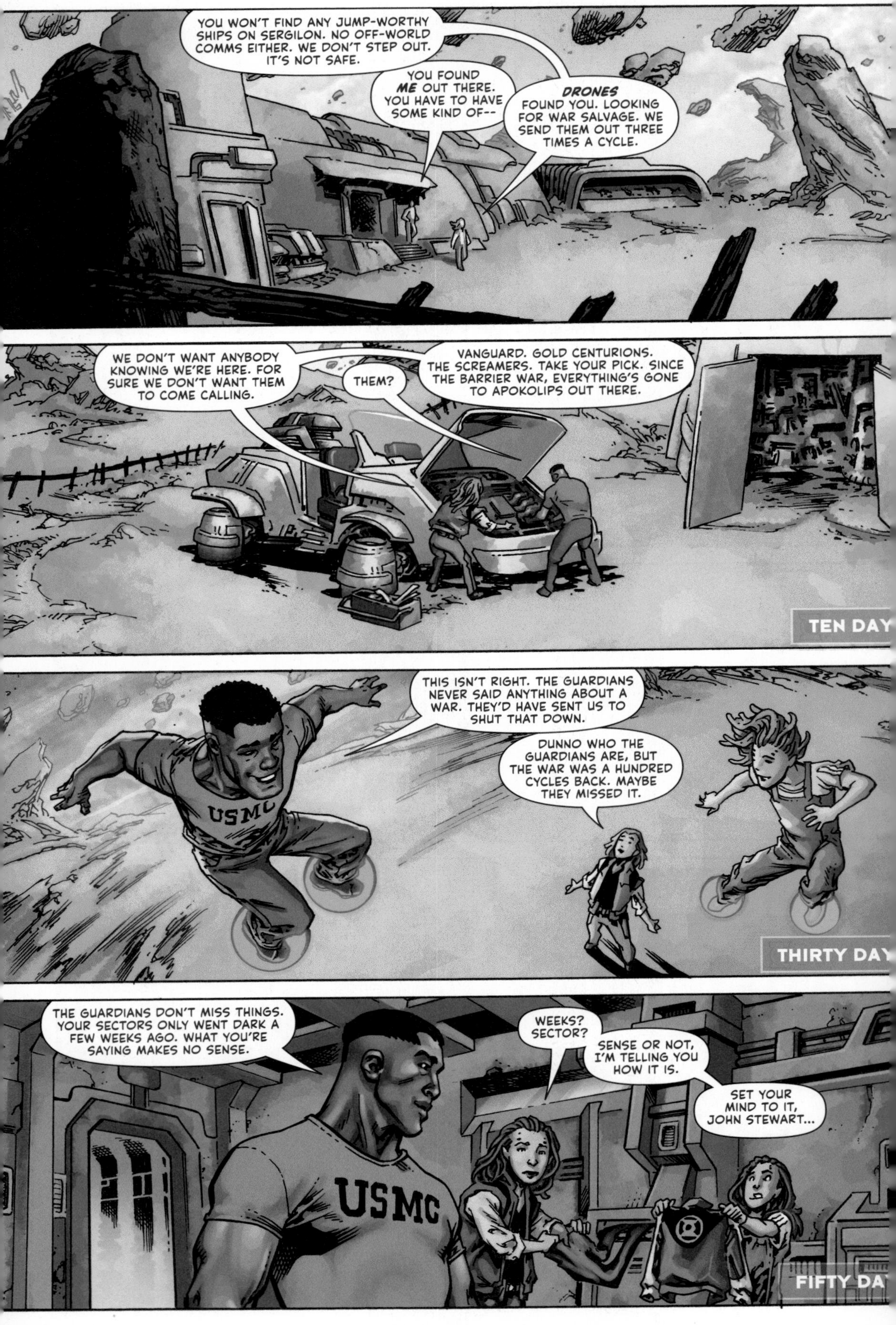

YOU WON'T FIND ANY JUMP-WORTHY SHIPS ON SERGILON. NO OFF-WORLD COMMS EITHER. WE DON'T STEP OUT. IT'S NOT SAFE.
YOU FOUND *ME* OUT THERE. YOU HAVE TO HAVE SOME KIND OF--
DRONES FOUND YOU. LOOKING FOR WAR SALVAGE. WE SEND THEM OUT THREE TIMES A CYCLE.
WE DON'T WANT ANYBODY KNOWING WE'RE HERE. FOR SURE WE DON'T WANT THEM TO COME CALLING.
THEM?
VANGUARD. GOLD CENTURIONS. THE SCREAMERS. TAKE YOUR PICK. SINCE THE BARRIER WAR, EVERYTHING'S GONE TO APOKOLIPS OUT THERE.
TEN DAY
THIS ISN'T RIGHT. THE GUARDIANS NEVER SAID ANYTHING ABOUT A WAR. THEY'D HAVE SENT US TO SHUT THAT DOWN.
DUNNO WHO THE GUARDIANS ARE, BUT THE WAR WAS A HUNDRED CYCLES BACK. MAYBE THEY MISSED IT.
USMC
THIRTY DAY
THE GUARDIANS DON'T MISS THINGS. YOUR SECTORS ONLY WENT DARK A FEW WEEKS AGO. WHAT YOU'RE SAYING MAKES NO SENSE.
WEEKS? SECTOR?
SENSE OR NOT, I'M TELLING YOU HOW IT IS.
SET YOUR MIND TO IT, JOHN STEWART...
USMC
FIFTY DAY

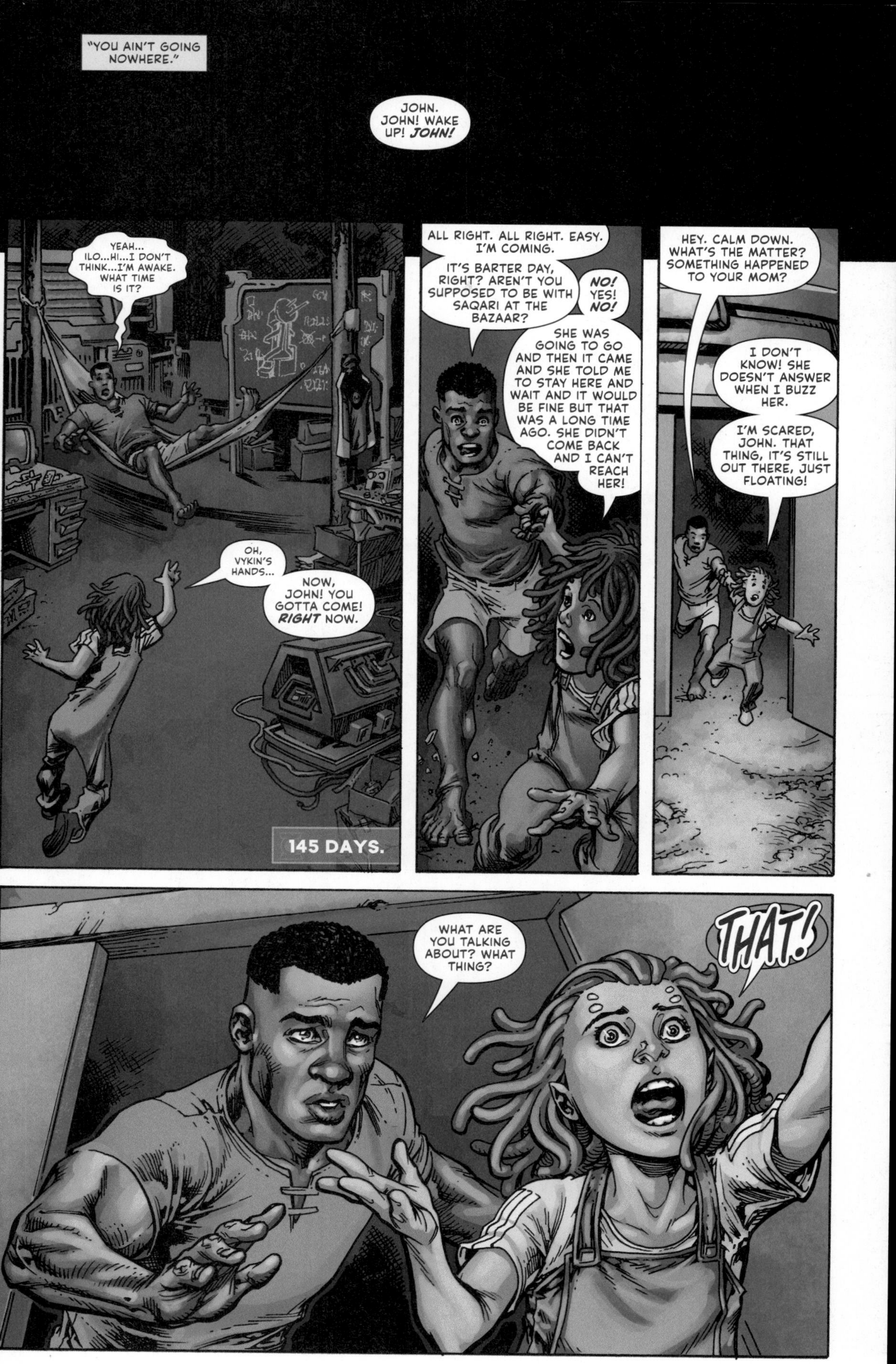
"YOU AIN'T GOING NOWHERE."
JOHN. JOHN! WAKE UP! *JOHN!*
YEAH... ILO...HI...I DON'T THINK...I'M AWAKE. WHAT TIME IS IT?
OH, VYKIN'S HANDS...
NOW, JOHN! YOU GOTTA COME! *RIGHT* NOW.
145 DAYS.
ALL RIGHT. ALL RIGHT. EASY. I'M COMING.
IT'S BARTER DAY, RIGHT? AREN'T YOU SUPPOSED TO BE WITH SAQARI AT THE BAZAAR?
NO! YES! *NO!*
SHE WAS GOING TO GO AND THEN IT CAME AND SHE TOLD ME TO STAY HERE AND WAIT AND IT WOULD BE FINE BUT THAT WAS A LONG TIME AGO. SHE DIDN'T COME BACK AND I CAN'T REACH HER!
HEY. CALM DOWN. WHAT'S THE MATTER? SOMETHING HAPPENED TO YOUR MOM?
I DON'T KNOW! SHE DOESN'T ANSWER WHEN I BUZZ HER.
I'M SCARED, JOHN. THAT THING, IT'S STILL OUT THERE, JUST FLOATING!
WHAT ARE YOU TALKING ABOUT? WHAT THING?
THAT!

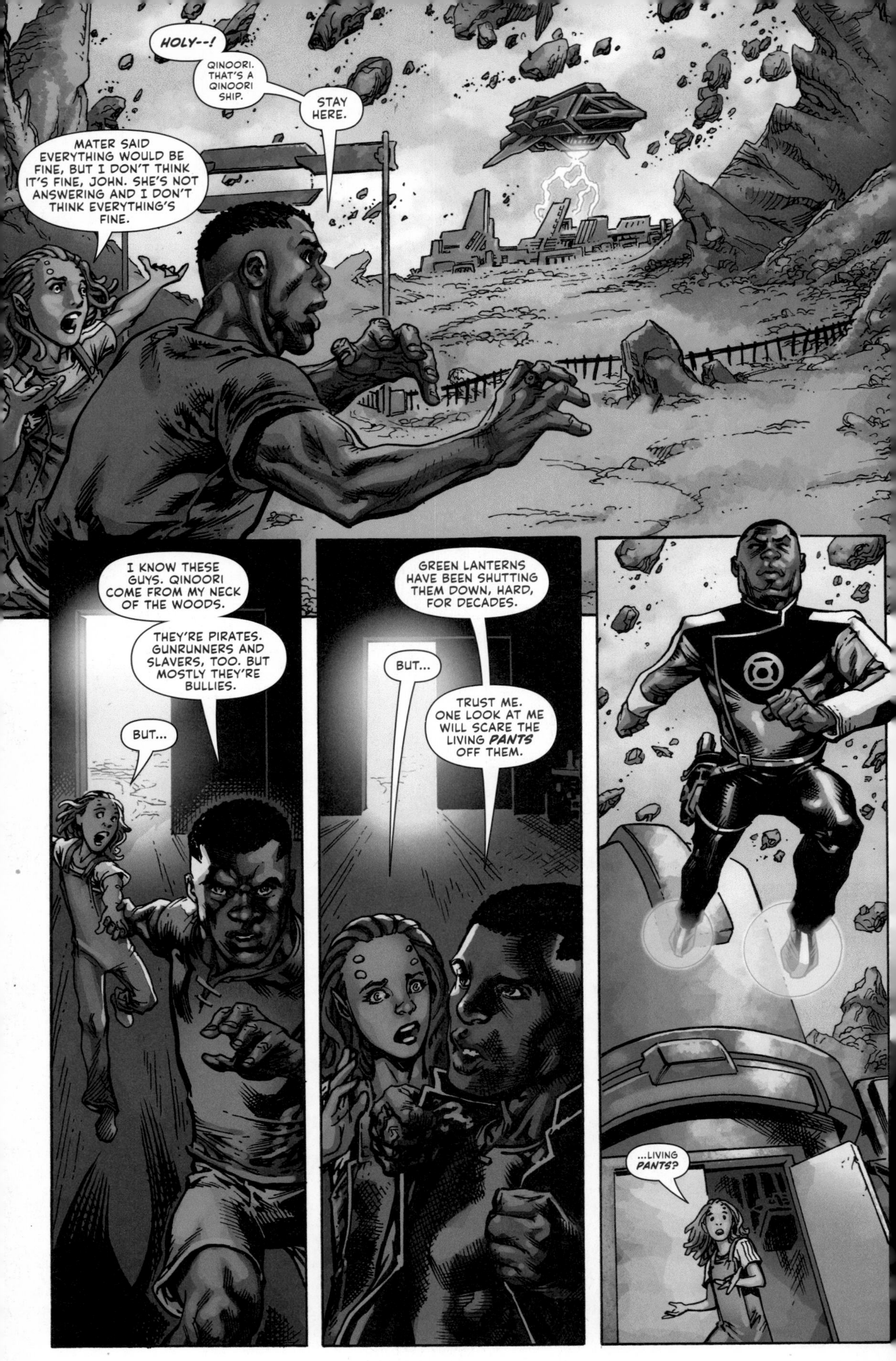
HOLY--!
QINOORI. THAT'S A QINOORI SHIP.
STAY HERE.
MATER SAID EVERYTHING WOULD BE FINE, BUT I DON'T THINK IT'S FINE, JOHN. SHE'S NOT ANSWERING AND I DON'T THINK EVERYTHING'S FINE.
I KNOW THESE GUYS. QINOORI COME FROM MY NECK OF THE WOODS.
THEY'RE PIRATES. GUNRUNNERS AND SLAVERS, TOO. BUT MOSTLY THEY'RE BULLIES.
BUT...
GREEN LANTERNS HAVE BEEN SHUTTING THEM DOWN, HARD, FOR DECADES.
BUT...
TRUST ME. ONE LOOK AT ME WILL SCARE THE LIVING PANTS OFF THEM.
...LIVING PANTS?

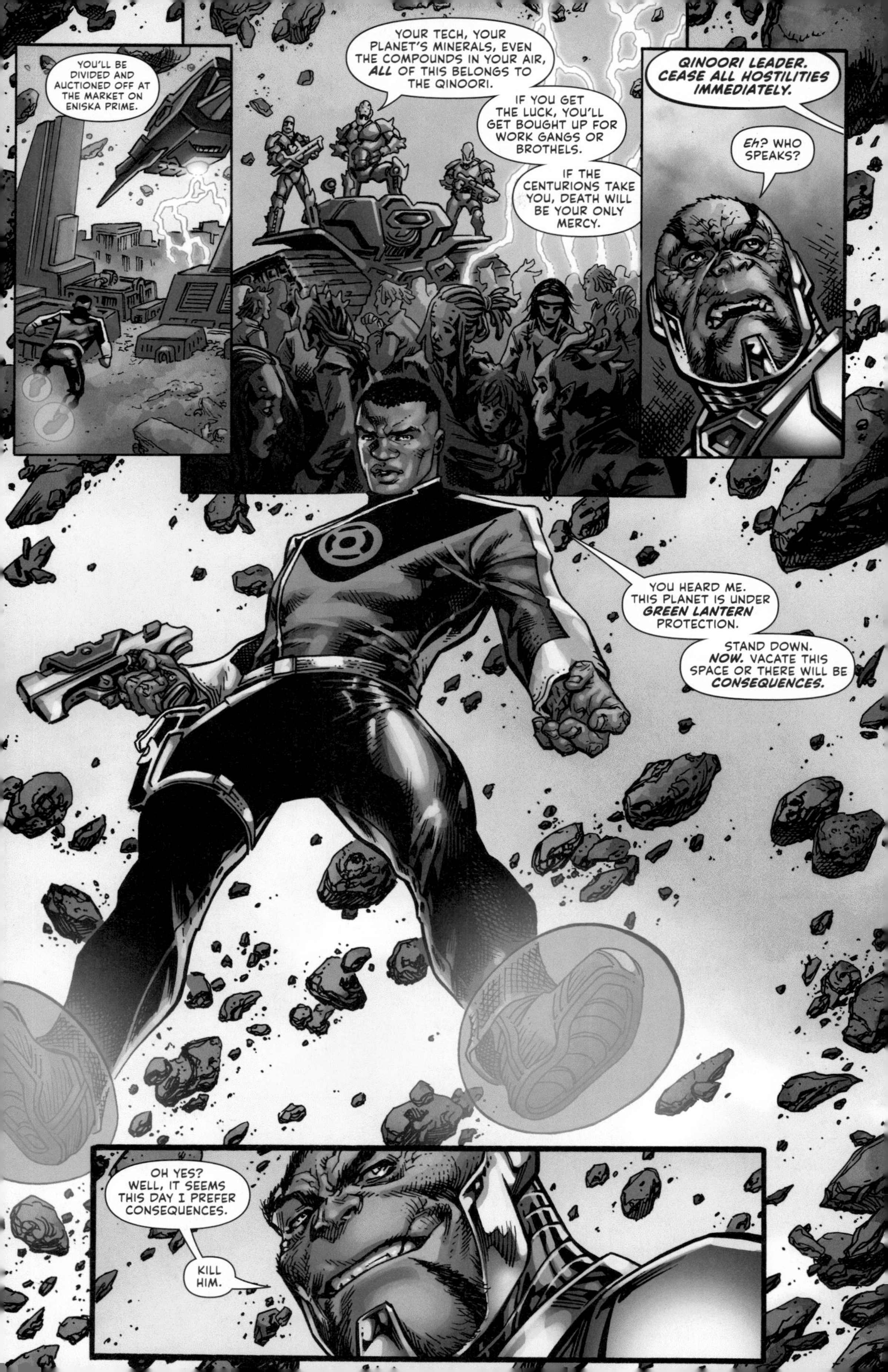
YOU'LL BE DIVIDED AND AUCTIONED OFF AT THE MARKET ON ENISKA PRIME.
YOUR TECH, YOUR PLANET'S MINERALS, EVEN THE COMPOUNDS IN YOUR AIR, ALL OF THIS BELONGS TO THE QINOORI.
IF YOU GET THE LUCK, YOU'LL GET BOUGHT UP FOR WORK GANGS OR BROTHELS.
IF THE CENTURIONS TAKE YOU, DEATH WILL BE YOUR ONLY MERCY.
QINOORI LEADER. CEASE ALL HOSTILITIES IMMEDIATELY.
Eh? WHO SPEAKS?
YOU HEARD ME. THIS PLANET IS UNDER GREEN LANTERN PROTECTION.
STAND DOWN. NOW. VACATE THIS SPACE OR THERE WILL BE CONSEQUENCES.
OH YES? WELL, IT SEEMS THIS DAY I PREFER CONSEQUENCES.
KILL HIM.

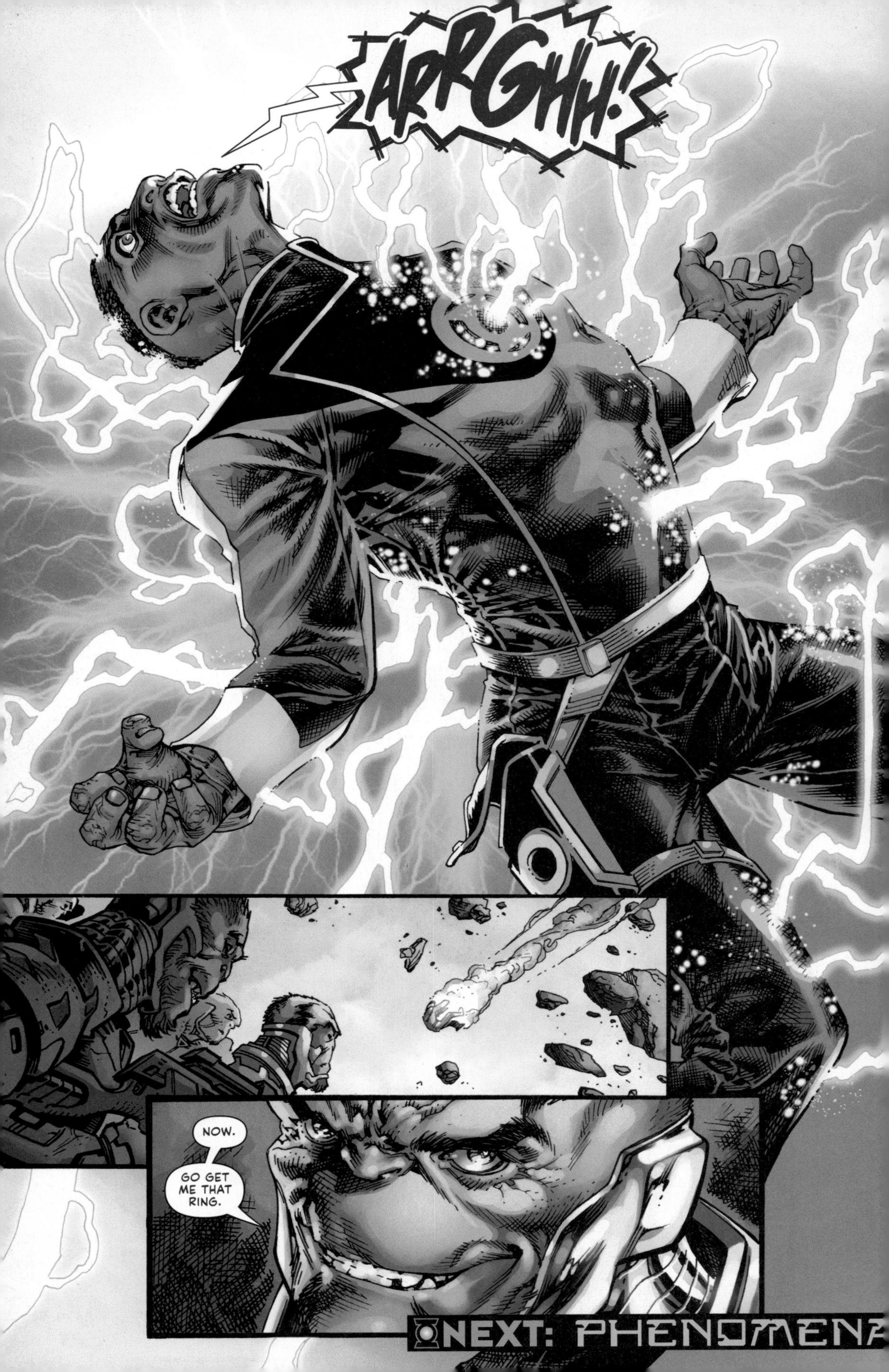
ARRGHH!
NOW.
GO GET ME THAT RING.
NEXT: PHENOMENA

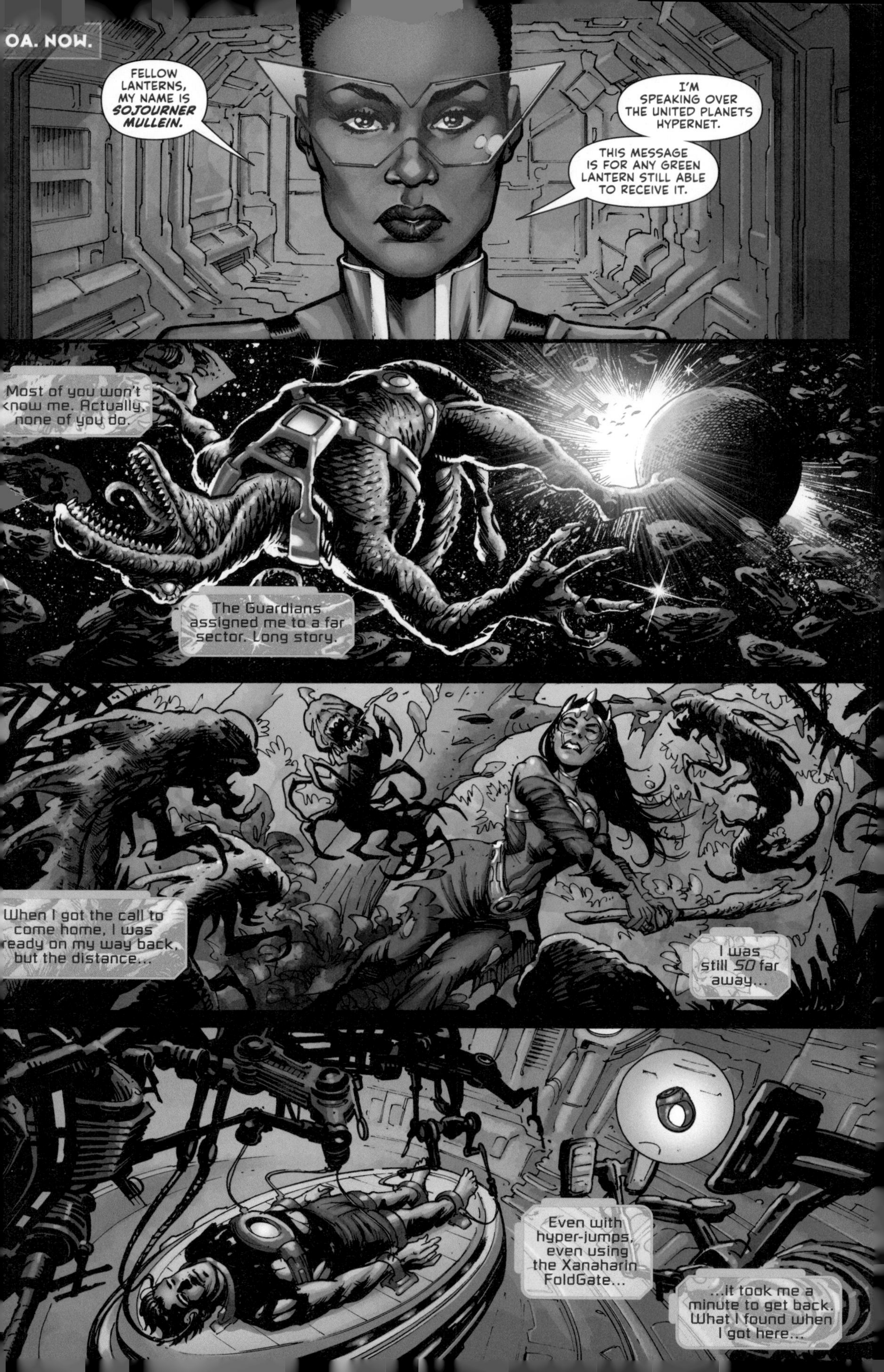
OA. NOW.
FELLOW LANTERNS, MY NAME IS SOJOURNER MULLEIN.
I'M SPEAKING OVER THE UNITED PLANETS HYPERNET.
THIS MESSAGE IS FOR ANY GREEN LANTERN STILL ABLE TO RECEIVE IT.
Most of you won't know me. Actually, none of you do.
The Guardians assigned me to a far sector. Long story.
When I got the call to come home, I was ready on my way back, but the distance...
I was still SO far away...
Even with hyper-jumps, even using the Xanaharin FoldGate...
...it took me a minute to get back. What I found when I got here...

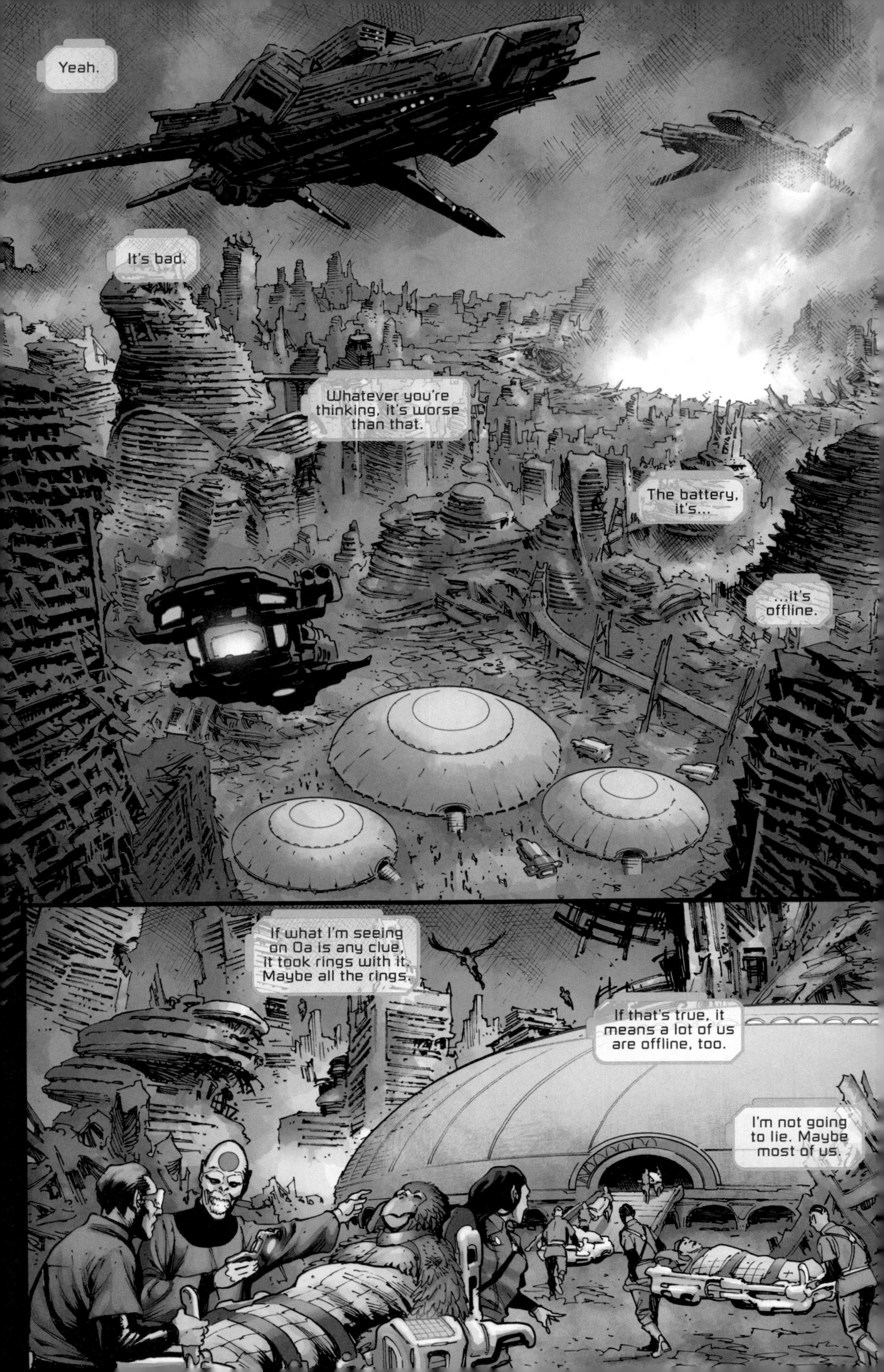
Yeah.
It's bad.
Whatever you're thinking, it's worse than that.
The battery, it's...
...it's offline.
If what I'm seeing on Oa is any clue, it took rings with it. Maybe all the rings.
If that's true, it means a lot of us are offline, too.
I'm not going to lie. Maybe most of us.

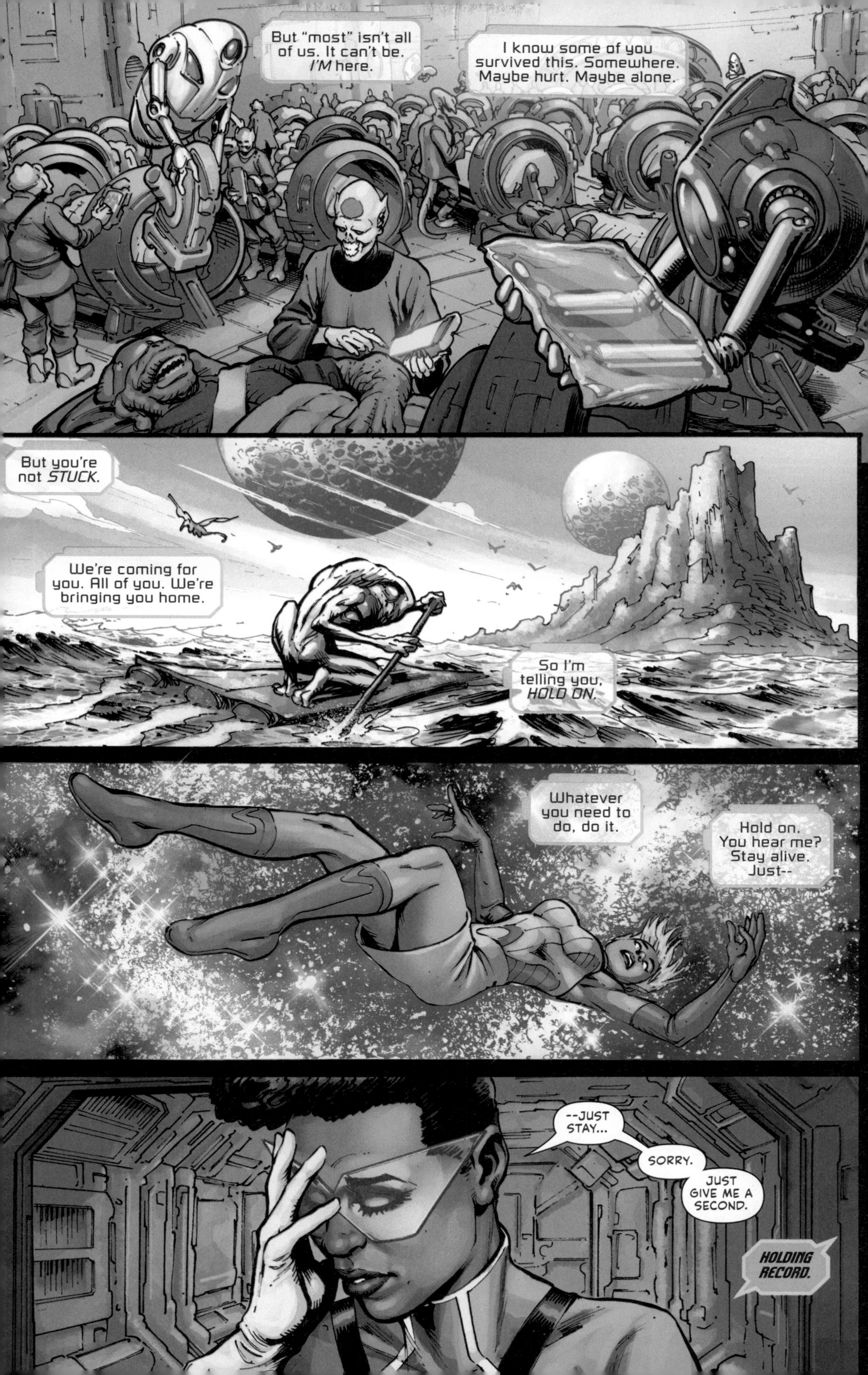

But "most" isn't all of us. It can't be. *I'M* here.
I know some of you survived this. Somewhere. Maybe hurt. Maybe alone.
But you're not *STUCK*.
We're coming for you. All of you. We're bringing you home.
So I'm telling you, *HOLD ON*.
Whatever you need to do, do it.
Hold on. You hear me? Stay alive. Just--
--JUST STAY...
SORRY.
JUST GIVE ME A SECOND.
HOLDING RECORD.

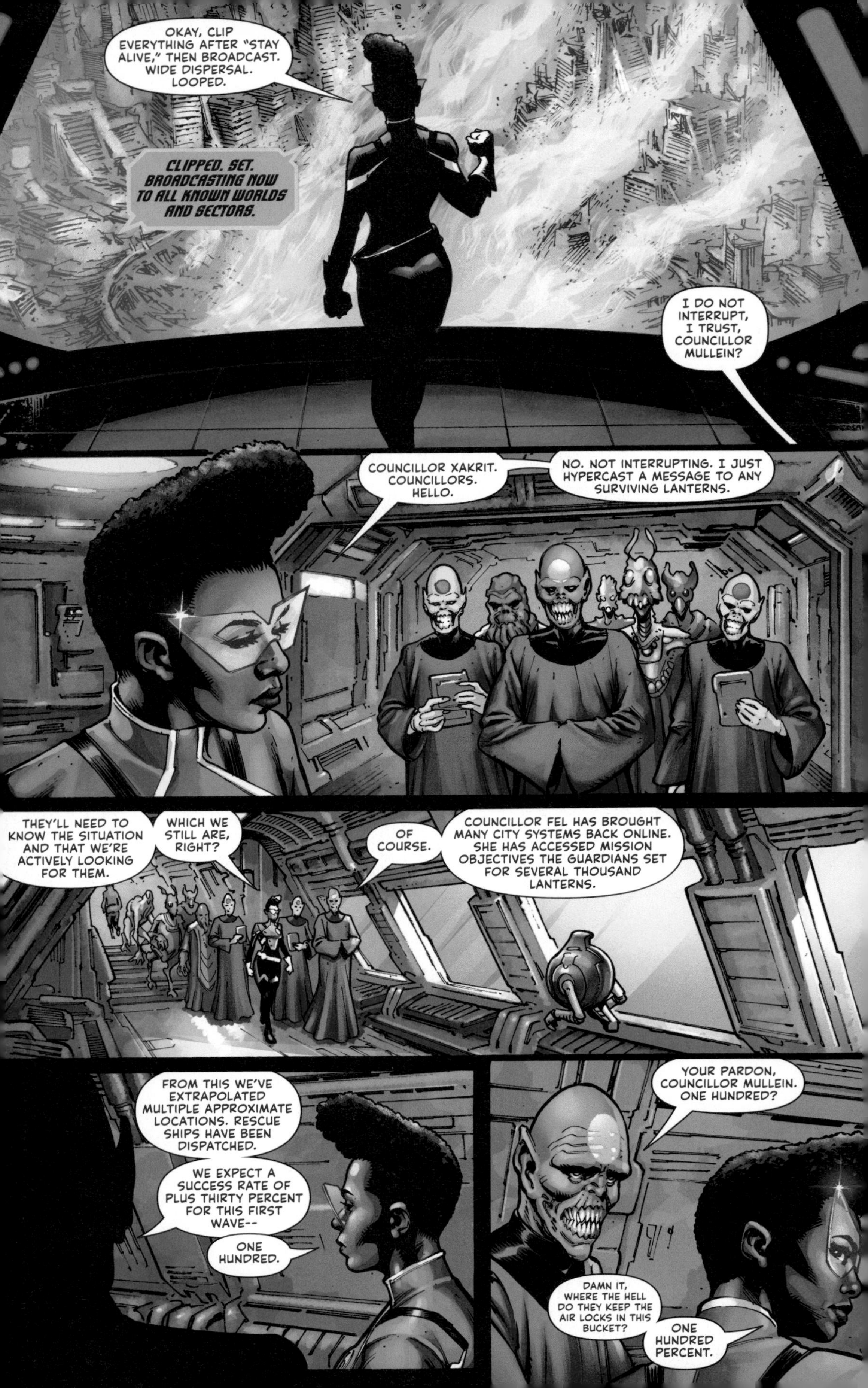
OKAY, CLIP EVERYTHING AFTER "STAY ALIVE," THEN BROADCAST. WIDE DISPERSAL. LOOPED.
CLIPPED. SET. BROADCASTING NOW TO ALL KNOWN WORLDS AND SECTORS.
I DO NOT INTERRUPT, I TRUST, COUNCILLOR MULLEIN?
COUNCILLOR XAKRIT. COUNCILLORS. HELLO.
NO. NOT INTERRUPTING. I JUST HYPERCAST A MESSAGE TO ANY SURVIVING LANTERNS.
THEY'LL NEED TO KNOW THE SITUATION AND THAT WE'RE ACTIVELY LOOKING FOR THEM.
WHICH WE STILL ARE, RIGHT?
OF COURSE.
COUNCILLOR FEL HAS BROUGHT MANY CITY SYSTEMS BACK ONLINE. SHE HAS ACCESSED MISSION OBJECTIVES THE GUARDIANS SET FOR SEVERAL THOUSAND LANTERNS.
FROM THIS WE'VE EXTRAPOLATED MULTIPLE APPROXIMATE LOCATIONS. RESCUE SHIPS HAVE BEEN DISPATCHED.
WE EXPECT A SUCCESS RATE OF PLUS THIRTY PERCENT FOR THIS FIRST WAVE--
ONE HUNDRED.
YOUR PARDON, COUNCILLOR MULLEIN. ONE HUNDRED?
DAMN IT, WHERE THE HELL DO THEY KEEP THE AIR LOCKS IN THIS BUCKET?
ONE HUNDRED PERCENT.

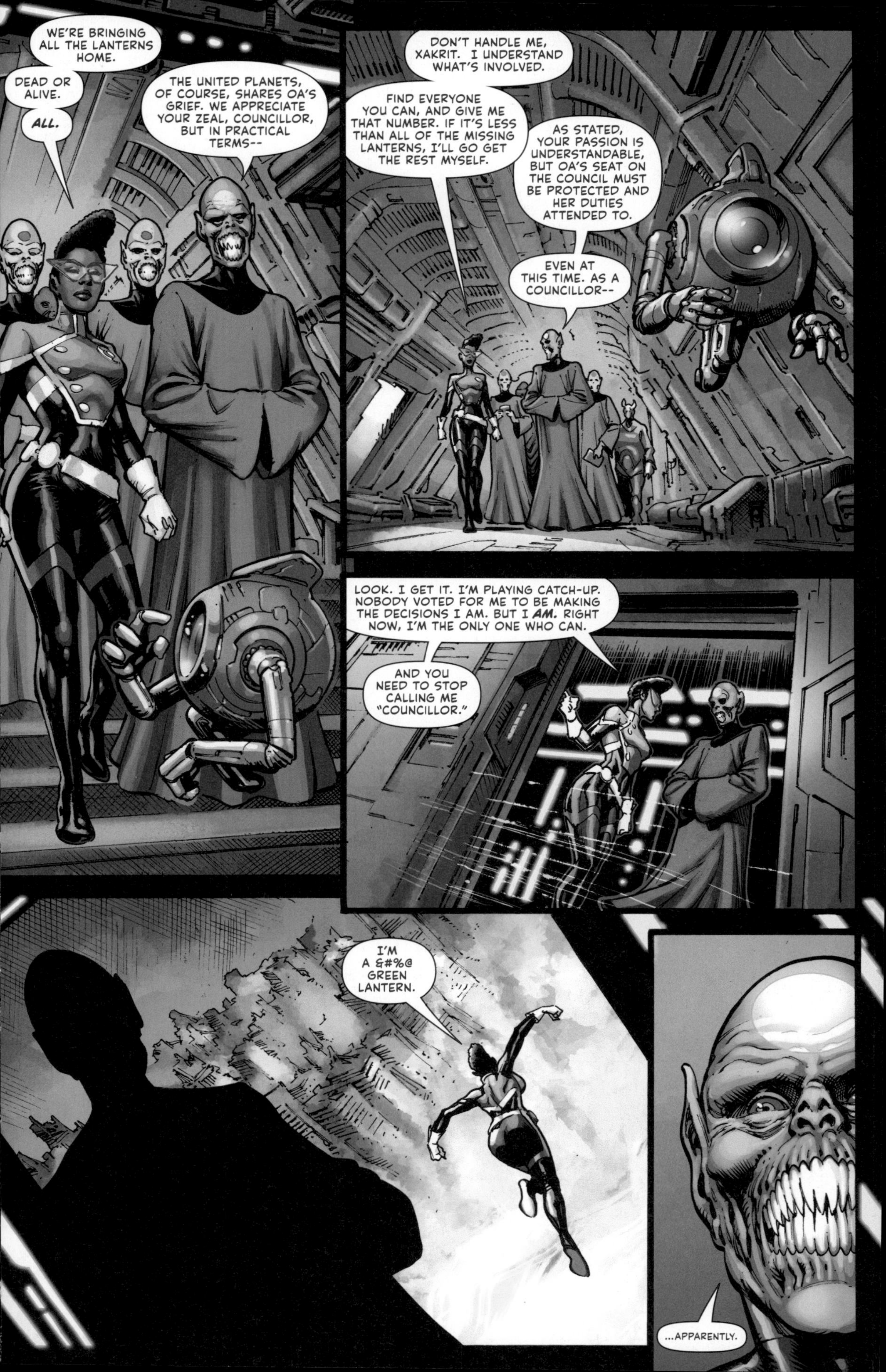
WE'RE BRINGING ALL THE LANTERNS HOME.
DEAD OR ALIVE.
ALL.
THE UNITED PLANETS, OF COURSE, SHARES OA'S GRIEF. WE APPRECIATE YOUR ZEAL, COUNCILLOR, BUT IN PRACTICAL TERMS--
DON'T HANDLE ME, XAKRIT. I UNDERSTAND WHAT'S INVOLVED.
FIND EVERYONE YOU CAN, AND GIVE ME THAT NUMBER. IF IT'S LESS THAN ALL OF THE MISSING LANTERNS, I'LL GO GET THE REST MYSELF.
AS STATED, YOUR PASSION IS UNDERSTANDABLE, BUT OA'S SEAT ON THE COUNCIL MUST BE PROTECTED AND HER DUTIES ATTENDED TO.
EVEN AT THIS TIME. AS A COUNCILLOR--
LOOK. I GET IT. I'M PLAYING CATCH-UP. NOBODY VOTED FOR ME TO BE MAKING THE DECISIONS I AM. BUT I *AM.* RIGHT NOW, I'M THE ONLY ONE WHO CAN.
AND YOU NEED TO STOP CALLING ME "COUNCILLOR."
I'M A &#%@ GREEN LANTERN.
...APPARENTLY.

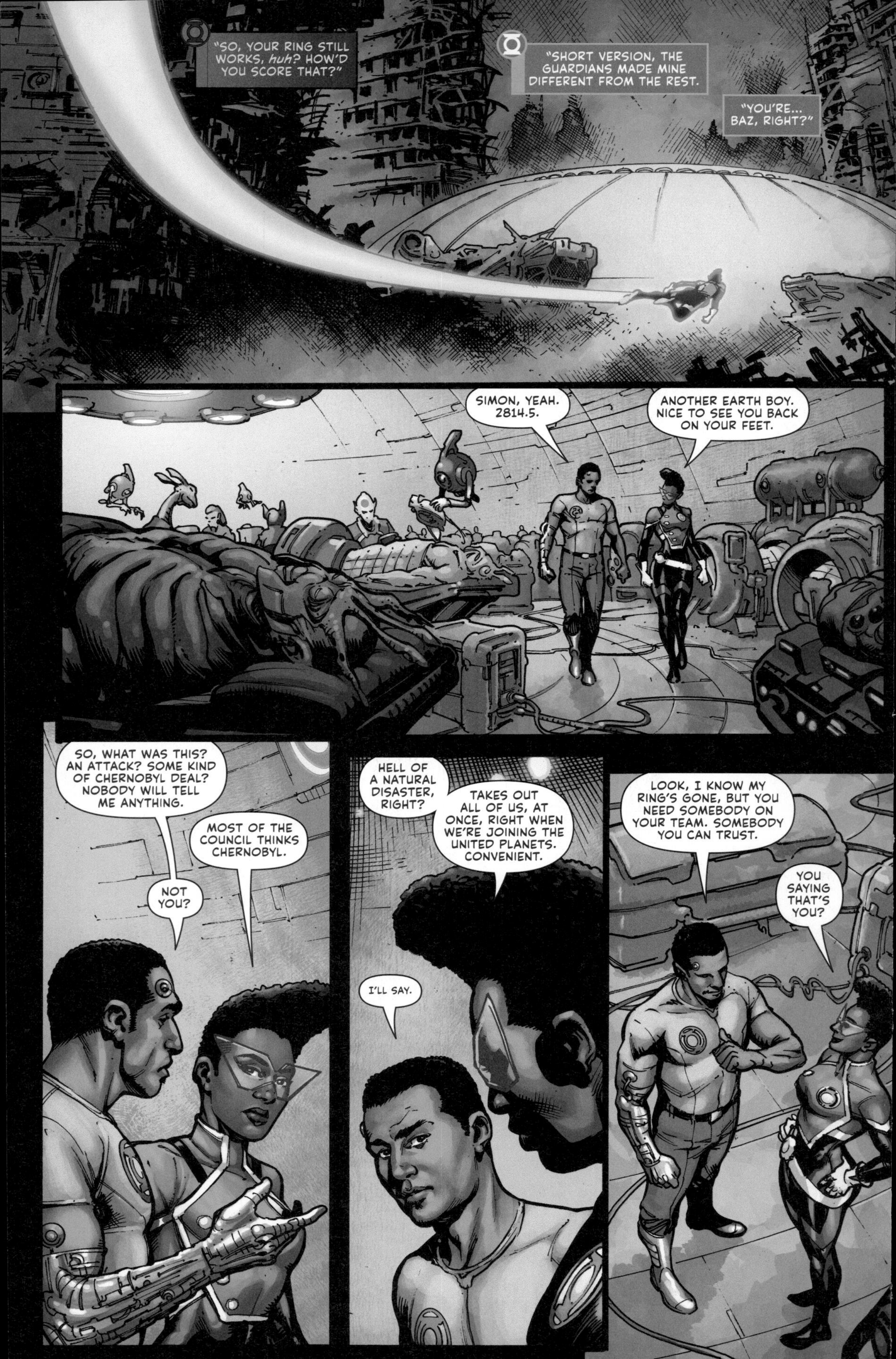
"SO, YOUR RING STILL WORKS, *huh*? HOW'D YOU SCORE THAT?"
"SHORT VERSION, THE GUARDIANS MADE MINE DIFFERENT FROM THE REST.
"YOU'RE... BAZ, RIGHT?"
SIMON, YEAH. 2814.5.
ANOTHER EARTH BOY. NICE TO SEE YOU BACK ON YOUR FEET.
SO, WHAT WAS THIS? AN ATTACK? SOME KIND OF CHERNOBYL DEAL? NOBODY WILL TELL ME ANYTHING.
MOST OF THE COUNCIL THINKS CHERNOBYL.
NOT YOU?
HELL OF A NATURAL DISASTER, RIGHT?
TAKES OUT ALL OF US, AT ONCE, RIGHT WHEN WE'RE JOINING THE UNITED PLANETS. CONVENIENT.
I'LL SAY.
LOOK, I KNOW MY RING'S GONE, BUT YOU NEED SOMEBODY ON YOUR TEAM. SOMEBODY YOU CAN TRUST.
YOU SAYING THAT'S YOU?

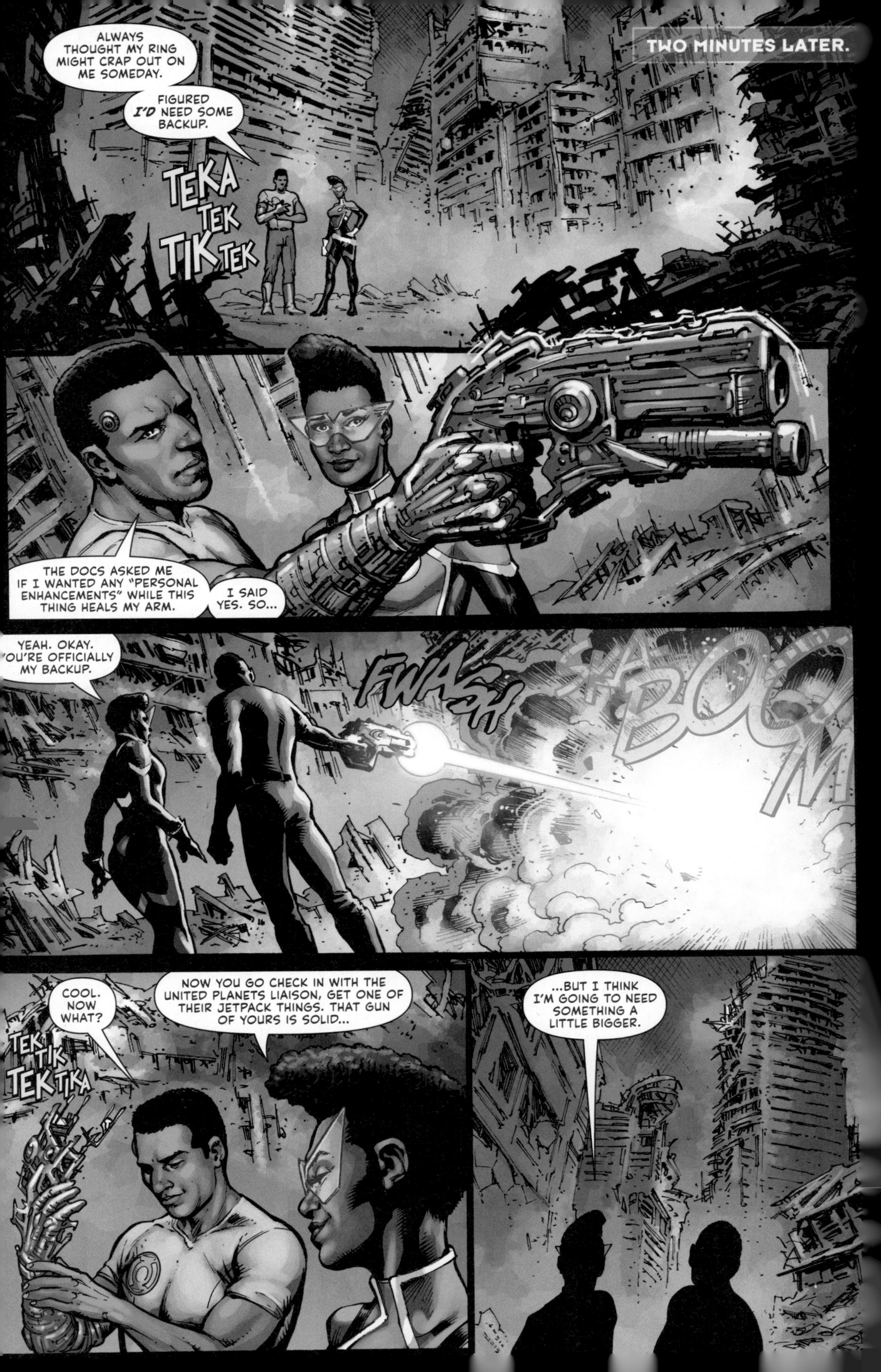
TWO MINUTES LATER.
ALWAYS THOUGHT MY RING MIGHT CRAP OUT ON ME SOMEDAY.
FIGURED I'D NEED SOME BACKUP.
TEKA TEK TIK TEK
THE DOCS ASKED ME IF I WANTED ANY "PERSONAL ENHANCEMENTS" WHILE THIS THING HEALS MY ARM.
I SAID YES. SO...
YEAH. OKAY. YOU'RE OFFICIALLY MY BACKUP.
FWASH
COOL. NOW WHAT?
TEK TIK TEK TIKA
NOW YOU GO CHECK IN WITH THE UNITED PLANETS LIAISON, GET ONE OF THEIR JETPACK THINGS. THAT GUN OF YOURS IS SOLID...
...BUT I THINK I'M GOING TO NEED SOMETHING A LITTLE BIGGER.

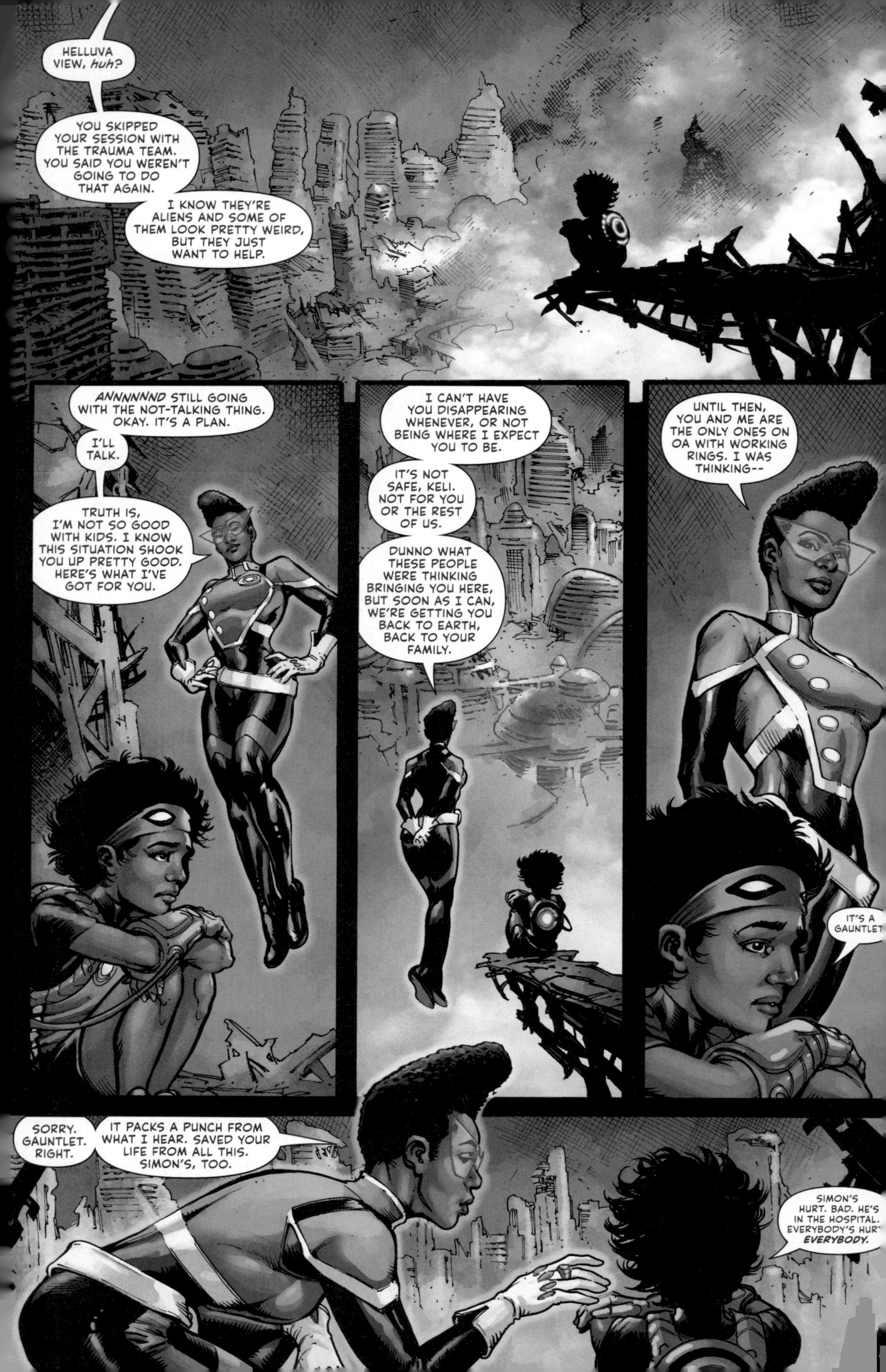
HELLUVA VIEW, *huh?*
YOU SKIPPED YOUR SESSION WITH THE TRAUMA TEAM. YOU SAID YOU WEREN'T GOING TO DO THAT AGAIN.
I KNOW THEY'RE ALIENS AND SOME OF THEM LOOK PRETTY WEIRD, BUT THEY JUST WANT TO HELP.
ANNNNNND STILL GOING WITH THE NOT-TALKING THING. OKAY. IT'S A PLAN.
I'LL TALK.
TRUTH IS, I'M NOT SO GOOD WITH KIDS. I KNOW THIS SITUATION SHOOK YOU UP PRETTY GOOD. HERE'S WHAT I'VE GOT FOR YOU.
I CAN'T HAVE YOU DISAPPEARING WHENEVER, OR NOT BEING WHERE I EXPECT YOU TO BE.
IT'S NOT SAFE, KELI. NOT FOR YOU OR THE REST OF US.
DUNNO WHAT THESE PEOPLE WERE THINKING BRINGING YOU HERE, BUT SOON AS I CAN, WE'RE GETTING YOU BACK TO EARTH, BACK TO YOUR FAMILY.
UNTIL THEN, YOU AND ME ARE THE ONLY ONES ON OA WITH WORKING RINGS. I WAS THINKING--
IT'S A GAUNTLET
SORRY. GAUNTLET. RIGHT.
IT PACKS A PUNCH FROM WHAT I HEAR. SAVED YOUR LIFE FROM ALL THIS. SIMON'S, TOO.
SIMON'S HURT. BAD. HE'S IN THE HOSPITAL. EVERYBODY'S HURT *EVERYBODY.*

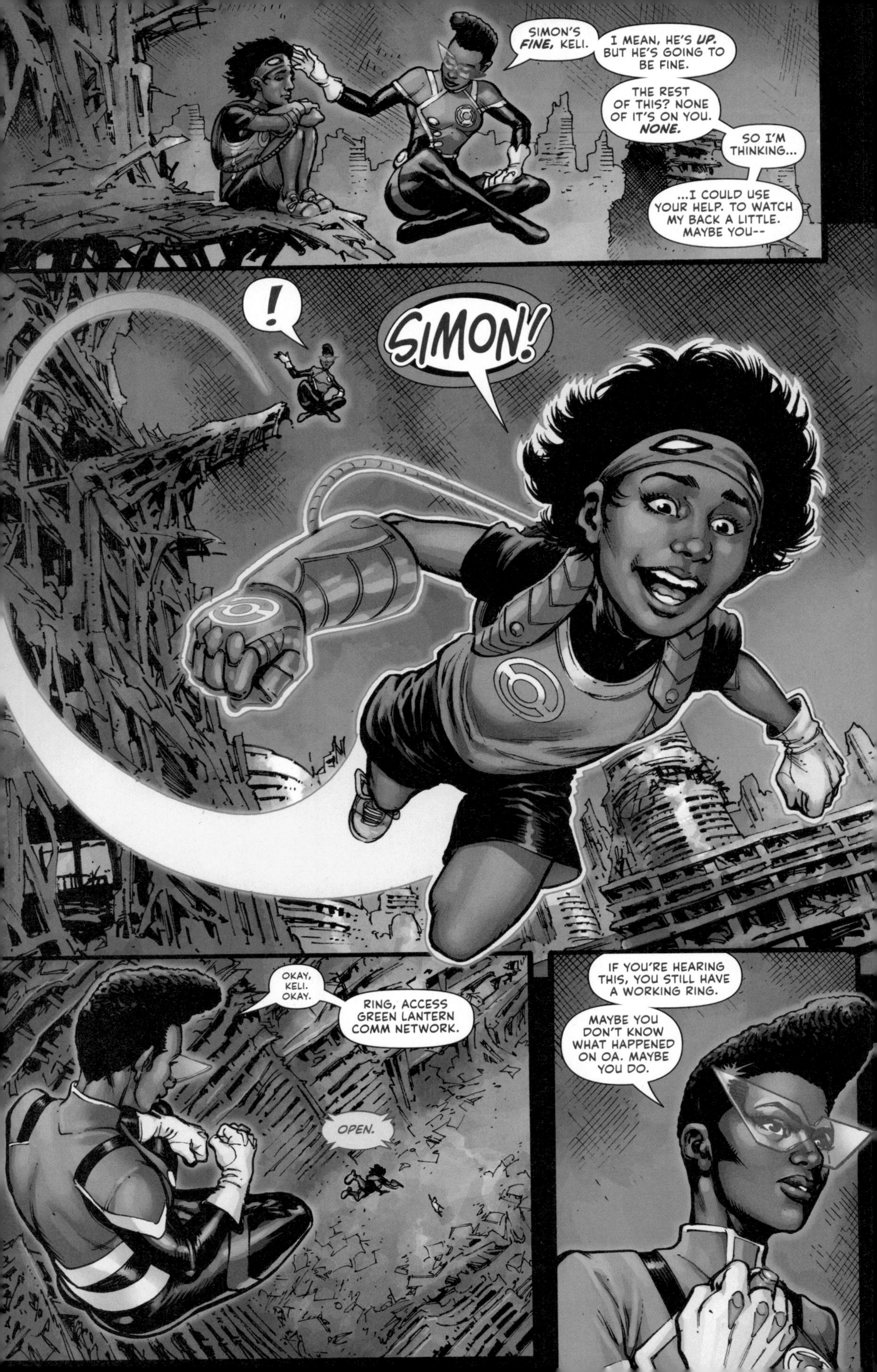
SIMON'S *FINE,* KELI.
I MEAN, HE'S *UP.* BUT HE'S GOING TO BE FINE.
THE REST OF THIS? NONE OF IT'S ON YOU. *NONE.*
SO I'M THINKING...
...I COULD USE YOUR HELP. TO WATCH MY BACK A LITTLE. MAYBE YOU--
!
SIMON!
OKAY, KELI. OKAY.
RING, ACCESS GREEN LANTERN COMM NETWORK.
OPEN.
IF YOU'RE HEARING THIS, YOU STILL HAVE A WORKING RING.
MAYBE YOU DON'T KNOW WHAT HAPPENED ON OA. MAYBE YOU DO.

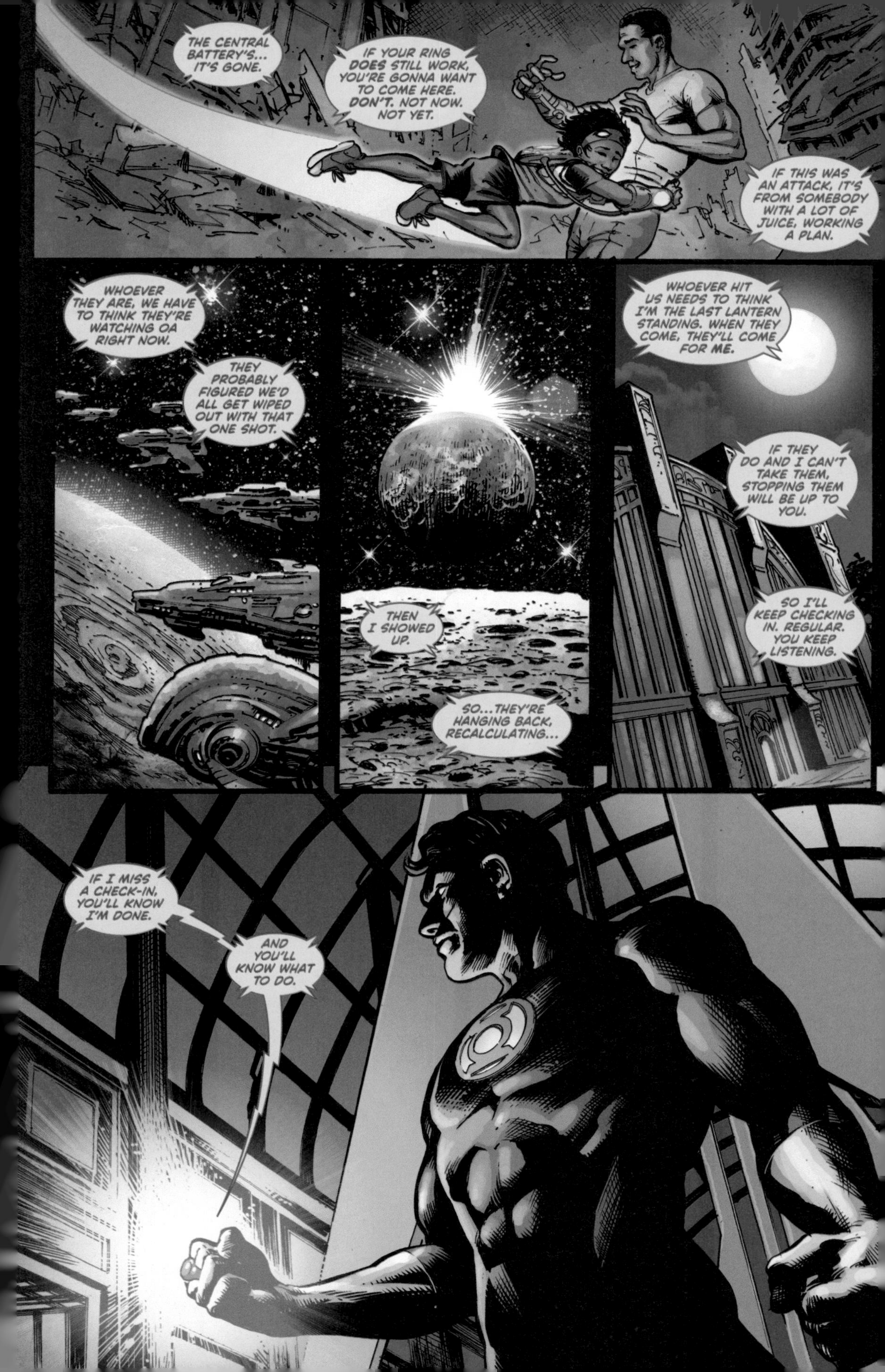
THE CENTRAL BATTERY'S... IT'S GONE.
IF YOUR RING DOES STILL WORK, YOU'RE GONNA WANT TO COME HERE. DON'T. NOT NOW. NOT YET.
IF THIS WAS AN ATTACK, IT'S FROM SOMEBODY WITH A LOT OF JUICE, WORKING A PLAN.
WHOEVER THEY ARE, WE HAVE TO THINK THEY'RE WATCHING OA RIGHT NOW.
THEY PROBABLY FIGURED WE'D ALL GET WIPED OUT WITH THAT ONE SHOT.
THEN I SHOWED UP.
SO...THEY'RE HANGING BACK, RECALCULATING...
WHOEVER HIT US NEEDS TO THINK I'M THE LAST LANTERN STANDING. WHEN THEY COME, THEY'LL COME FOR ME.
IF THEY DO AND I CAN'T TAKE THEM, STOPPING THEM WILL BE UP TO YOU.
SO I'LL KEEP CHECKING IN. REGULAR. YOU KEEP LISTENING.
IF I MISS A CHECK-IN, YOU'LL KNOW I'M DONE.
AND YOU'LL KNOW WHAT TO DO.

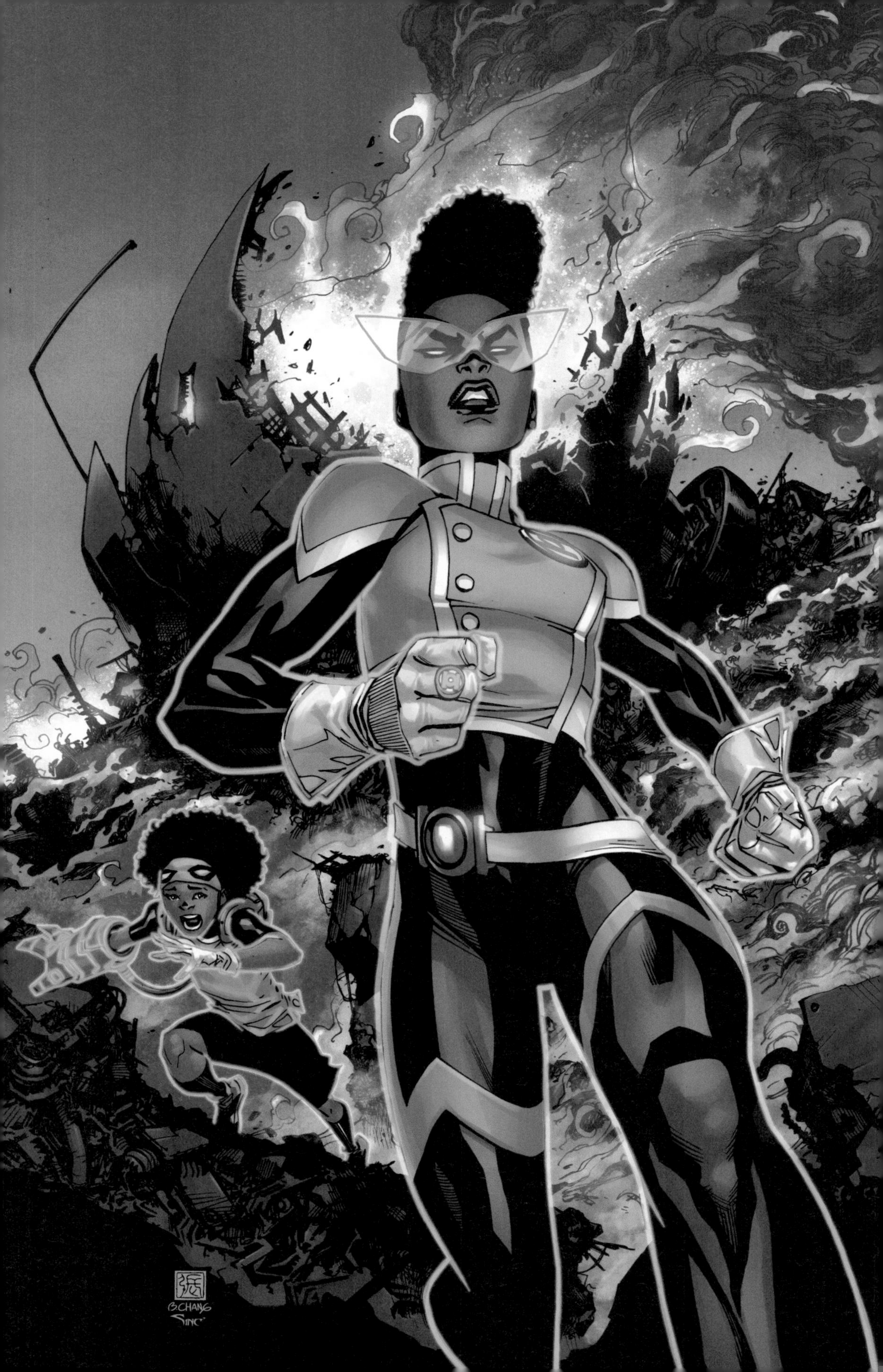
B.CHANG
SINC

Green Lantern #4 main cover art
by Bernard Chang and Alex Sinclair

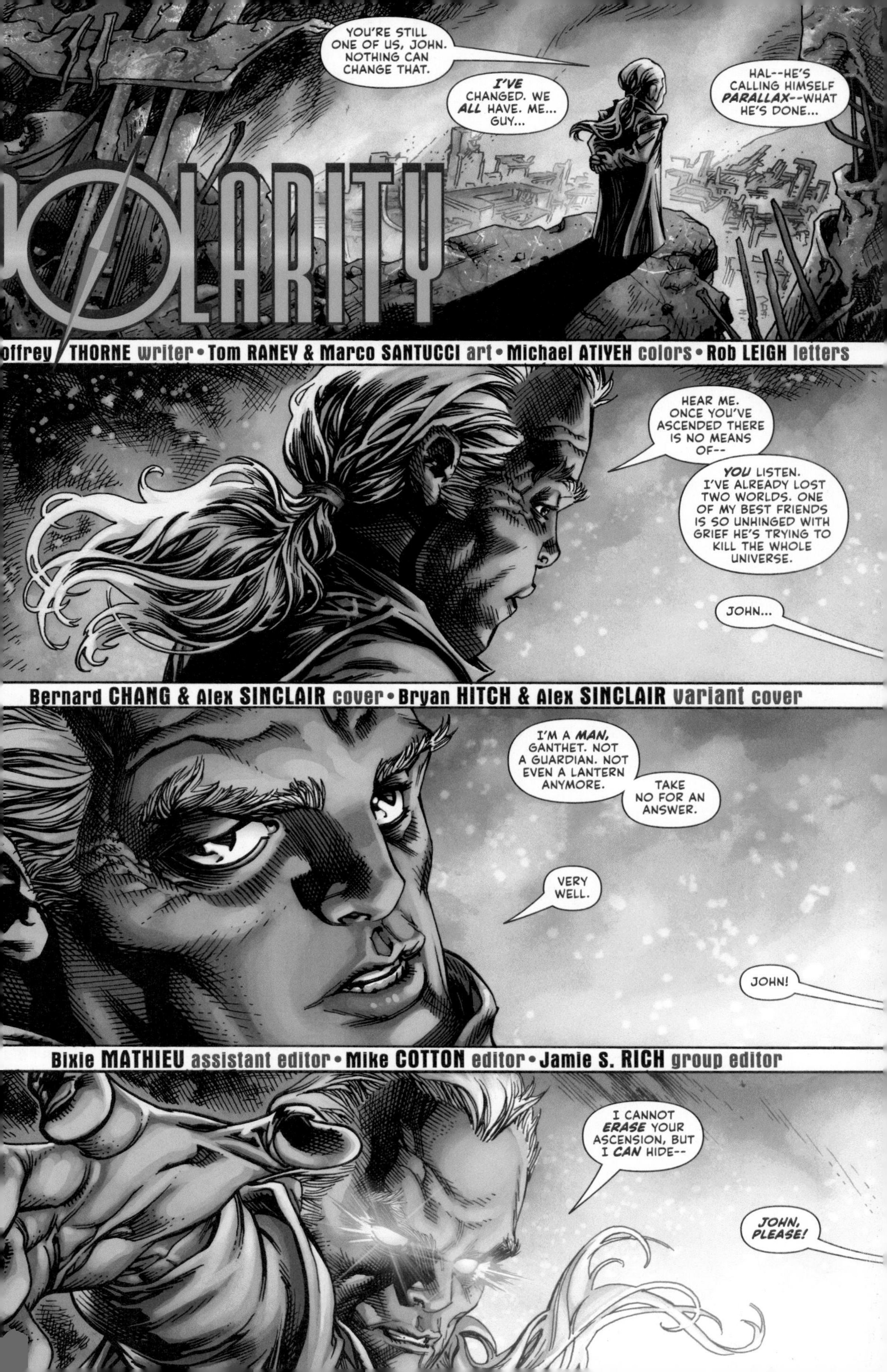
YOU'RE STILL ONE OF US, JOHN. NOTHING CAN CHANGE THAT.
I'VE CHANGED. WE ALL HAVE. ME... GUY...
HAL--HE'S CALLING HIMSELF PARALLAX--WHAT HE'S DONE...
POLARITY
offrey THORNE writer • Tom RANEY & Marco SANTUCCI art • Michael ATIYEH colors • Rob LEIGH letters
HEAR ME. ONCE YOU'VE ASCENDED THERE IS NO MEANS OF--
YOU LISTEN. I'VE ALREADY LOST TWO WORLDS. ONE OF MY BEST FRIENDS IS SO UNHINGED WITH GRIEF HE'S TRYING TO KILL THE WHOLE UNIVERSE.
JOHN...
Bernard CHANG & Alex SINCLAIR cover • Bryan HITCH & Alex SINCLAIR variant cover
I'M A MAN, GANTHET. NOT A GUARDIAN. NOT EVEN A LANTERN ANYMORE.
TAKE NO FOR AN ANSWER.
VERY WELL.
JOHN!
Bixie MATHIEU assistant editor • Mike COTTON editor • Jamie S. RICH group editor
I CANNOT ERASE YOUR ASCENSION, BUT I CAN HIDE--
JOHN, PLEASE!

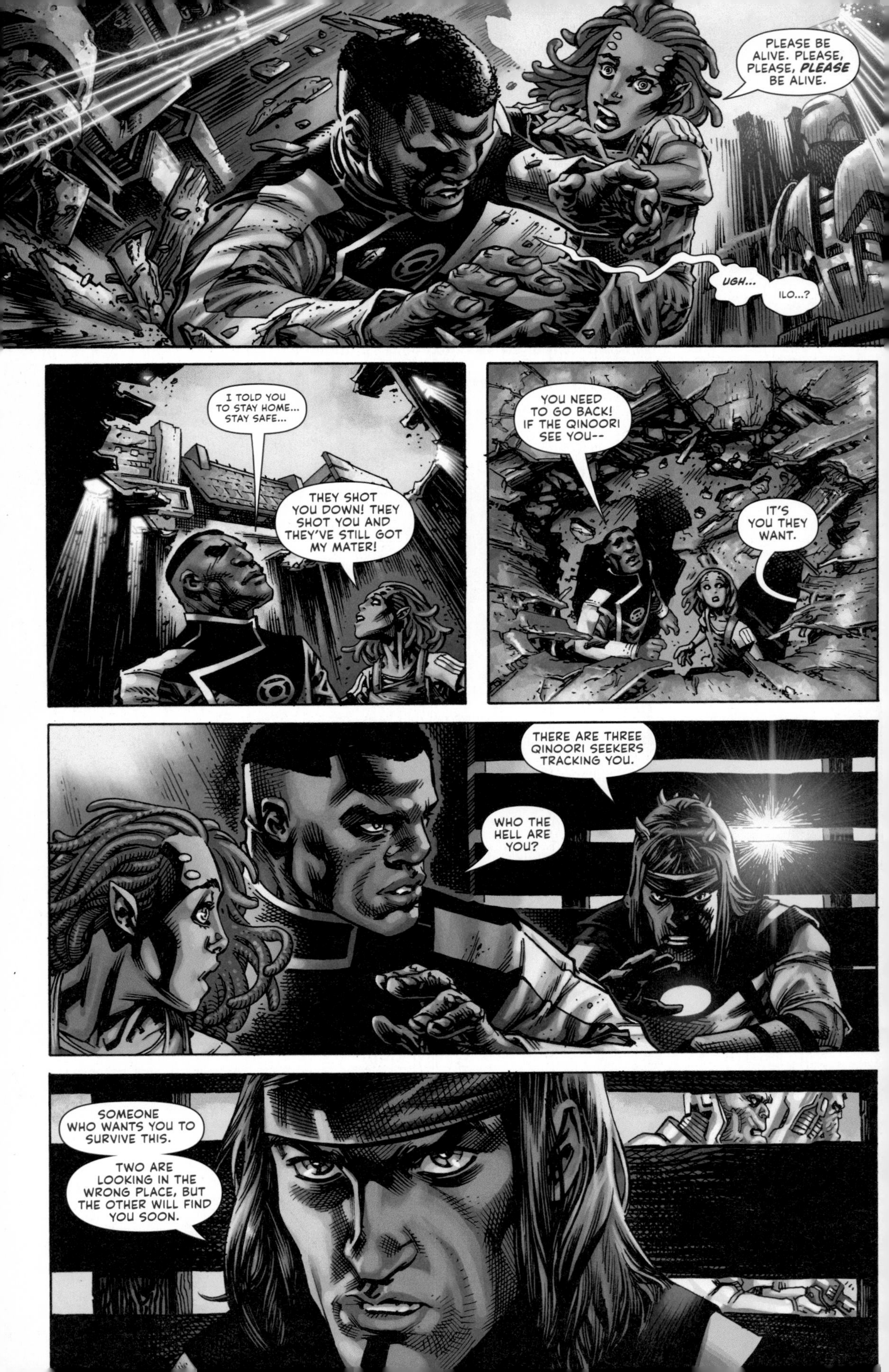
PLEASE BE ALIVE. PLEASE, PLEASE, *PLEASE* BE ALIVE.
UGH...
ILO...?
I TOLD YOU TO STAY HOME... STAY SAFE...
THEY SHOT YOU DOWN! THEY SHOT YOU AND THEY'VE STILL GOT MY MATER!
YOU NEED TO GO BACK! IF THE QINOORI SEE YOU--
IT'S YOU THEY WANT.
THERE ARE THREE QINOORI SEEKERS TRACKING YOU.
WHO THE HELL ARE YOU?
SOMEONE WHO WANTS YOU TO SURVIVE THIS.
TWO ARE LOOKING IN THE WRONG PLACE, BUT THE OTHER WILL FIND YOU SOON.

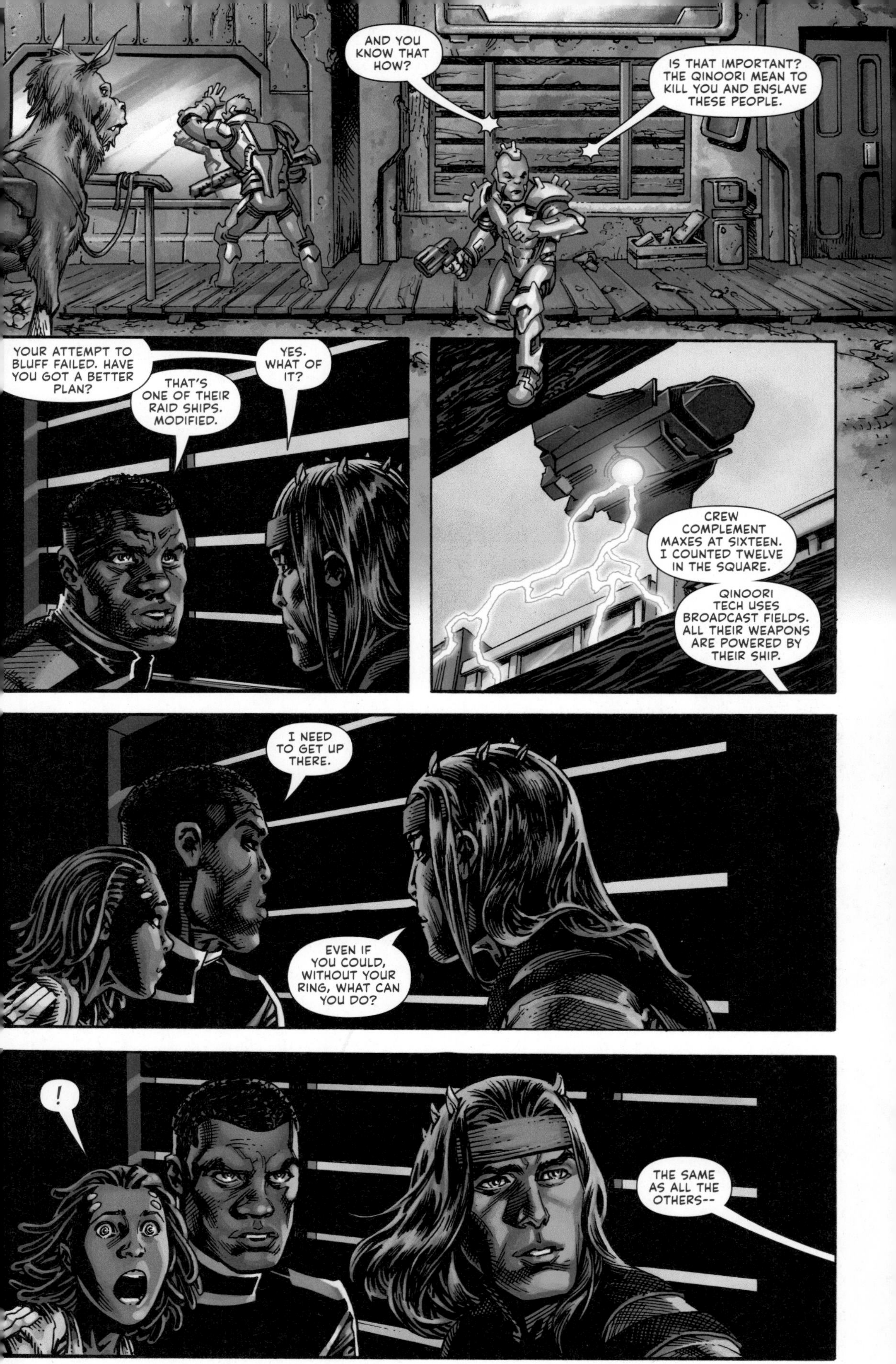
AND YOU KNOW THAT HOW?
IS THAT IMPORTANT? THE QINOORI MEAN TO KILL YOU AND ENSLAVE THESE PEOPLE.
YOUR ATTEMPT TO BLUFF FAILED. HAVE YOU GOT A BETTER PLAN?
THAT'S ONE OF THEIR RAID SHIPS. MODIFIED.
YES. WHAT OF IT?
CREW COMPLEMENT MAXES AT SIXTEEN. I COUNTED TWELVE IN THE SQUARE.
QINOORI TECH USES BROADCAST FIELDS. ALL THEIR WEAPONS ARE POWERED BY THEIR SHIP.
I NEED TO GET UP THERE.
EVEN IF YOU COULD, WITHOUT YOUR RING, WHAT CAN YOU DO?
!
THE SAME AS ALL THE OTHERS--

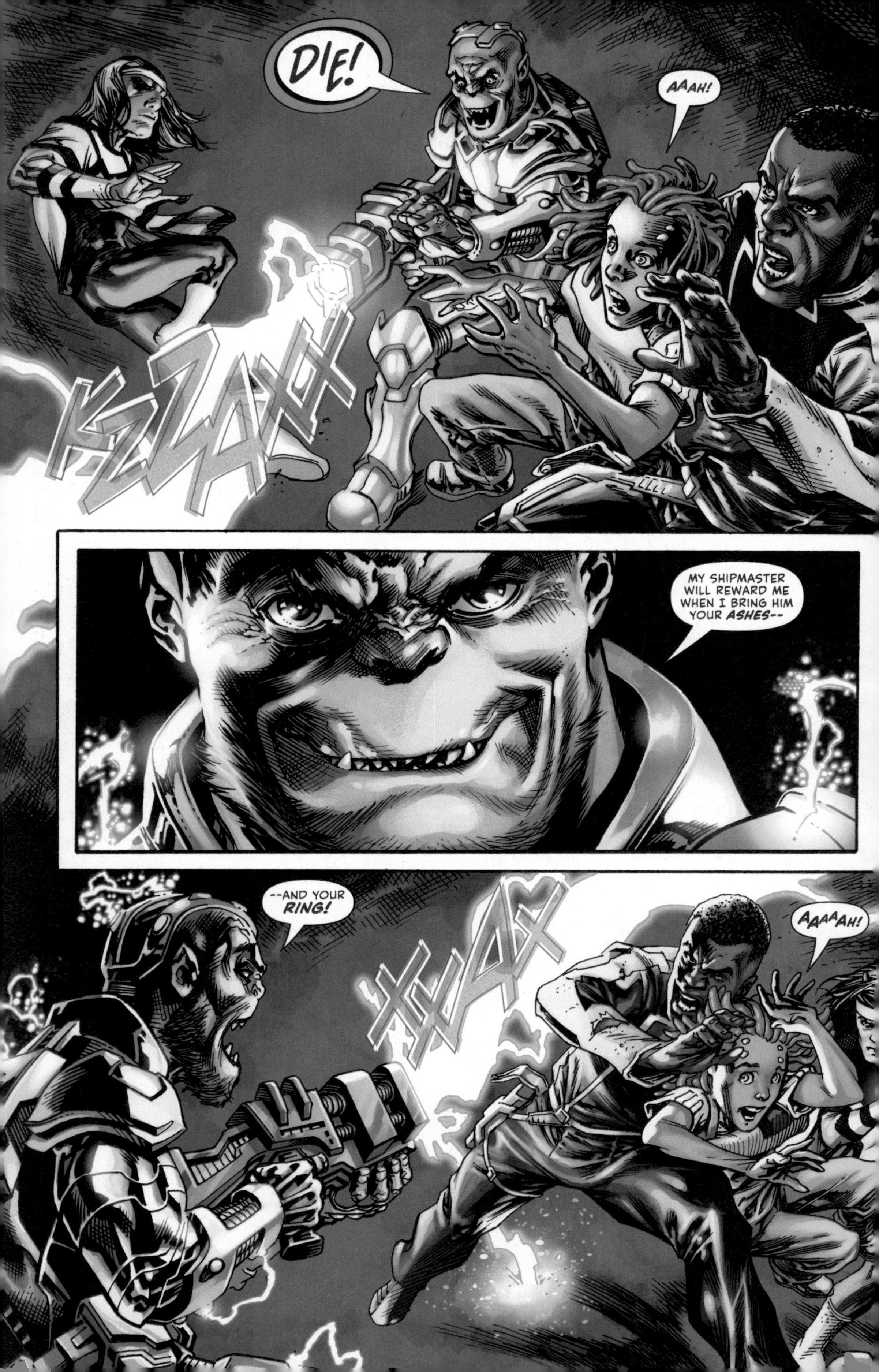

DIE!
AAAH!
KZZAX
MY SHIPMASTER WILL REWARD ME WHEN I BRING HIM YOUR ASHES--
--AND YOUR RING!
XXZAX
AAAAAH!

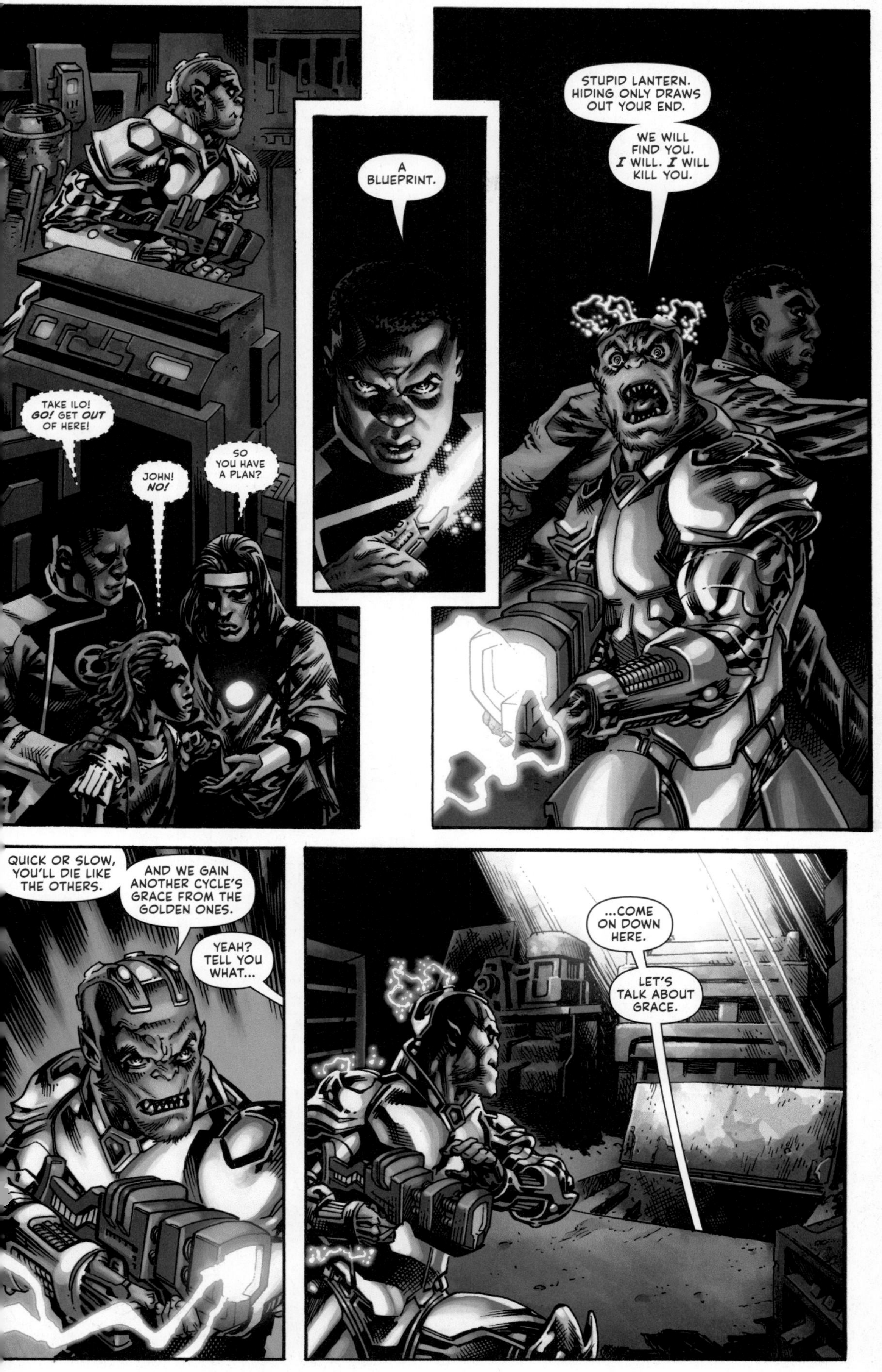
TAKE ILO! GO! GET OUT OF HERE!
JOHN! NO!
SO YOU HAVE A PLAN?
A BLUEPRINT.
STUPID LANTERN. HIDING ONLY DRAWS OUT YOUR END.
WE WILL FIND YOU. I WILL. I WILL KILL YOU.
QUICK OR SLOW, YOU'LL DIE LIKE THE OTHERS.
AND WE GAIN ANOTHER CYCLE'S GRACE FROM THE GOLDEN ONES.
YEAH? TELL YOU WHAT...
...COME ON DOWN HERE.
LET'S TALK ABOUT GRACE.

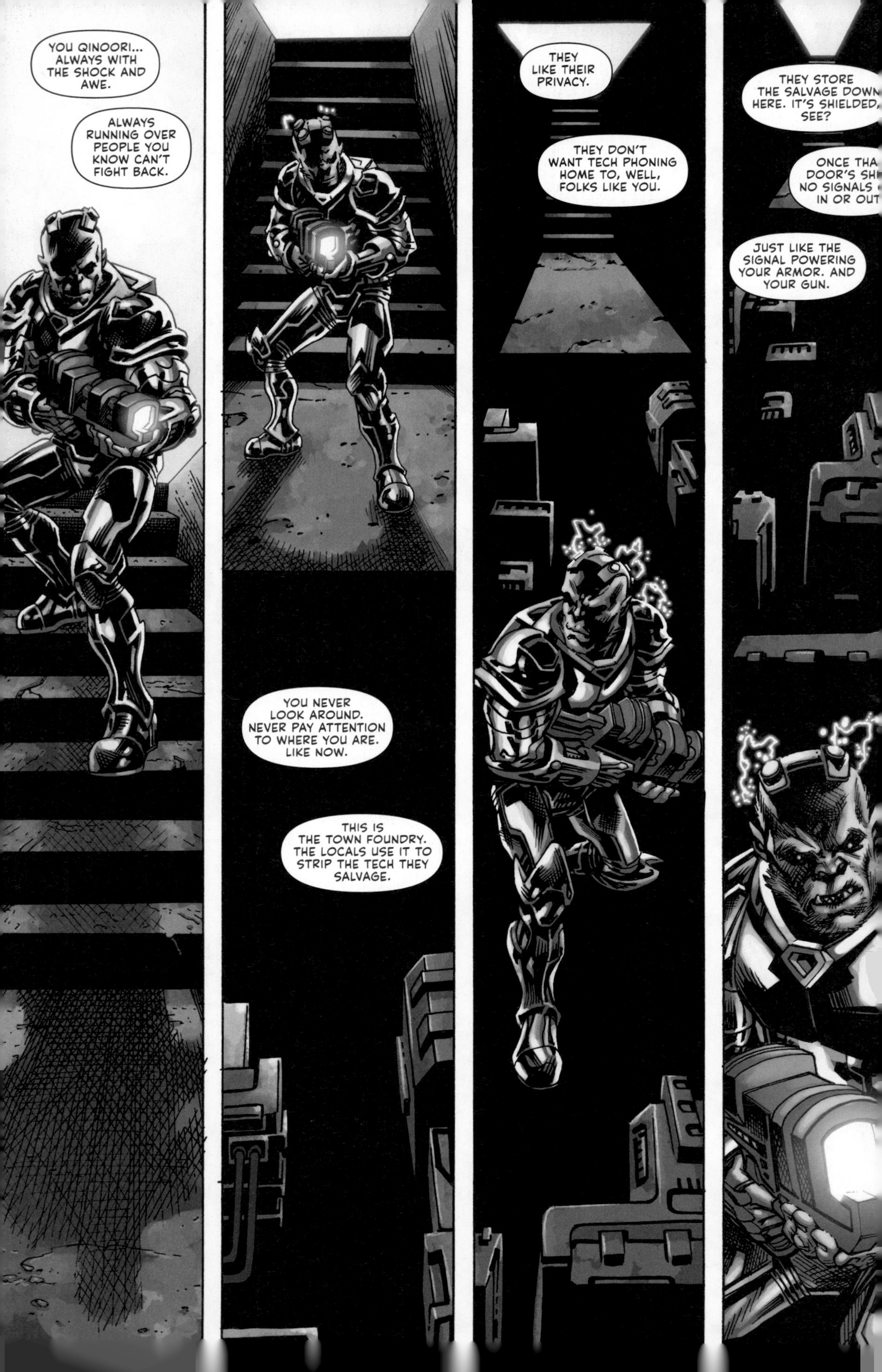
YOU QINOORI... ALWAYS WITH THE SHOCK AND AWE.
ALWAYS RUNNING OVER PEOPLE YOU KNOW CAN'T FIGHT BACK.
YOU NEVER LOOK AROUND. NEVER PAY ATTENTION TO WHERE YOU ARE. LIKE NOW.
THIS IS THE TOWN FOUNDRY. THE LOCALS USE IT TO STRIP THE TECH THEY SALVAGE.
THEY LIKE THEIR PRIVACY.
THEY DON'T WANT TECH PHONING HOME TO, WELL, FOLKS LIKE YOU.
THEY STORE THE SALVAGE DOWN HERE. IT'S SHIELDED, SEE?
JUST LIKE THE SIGNAL POWERING YOUR ARMOR. AND YOUR GUN.

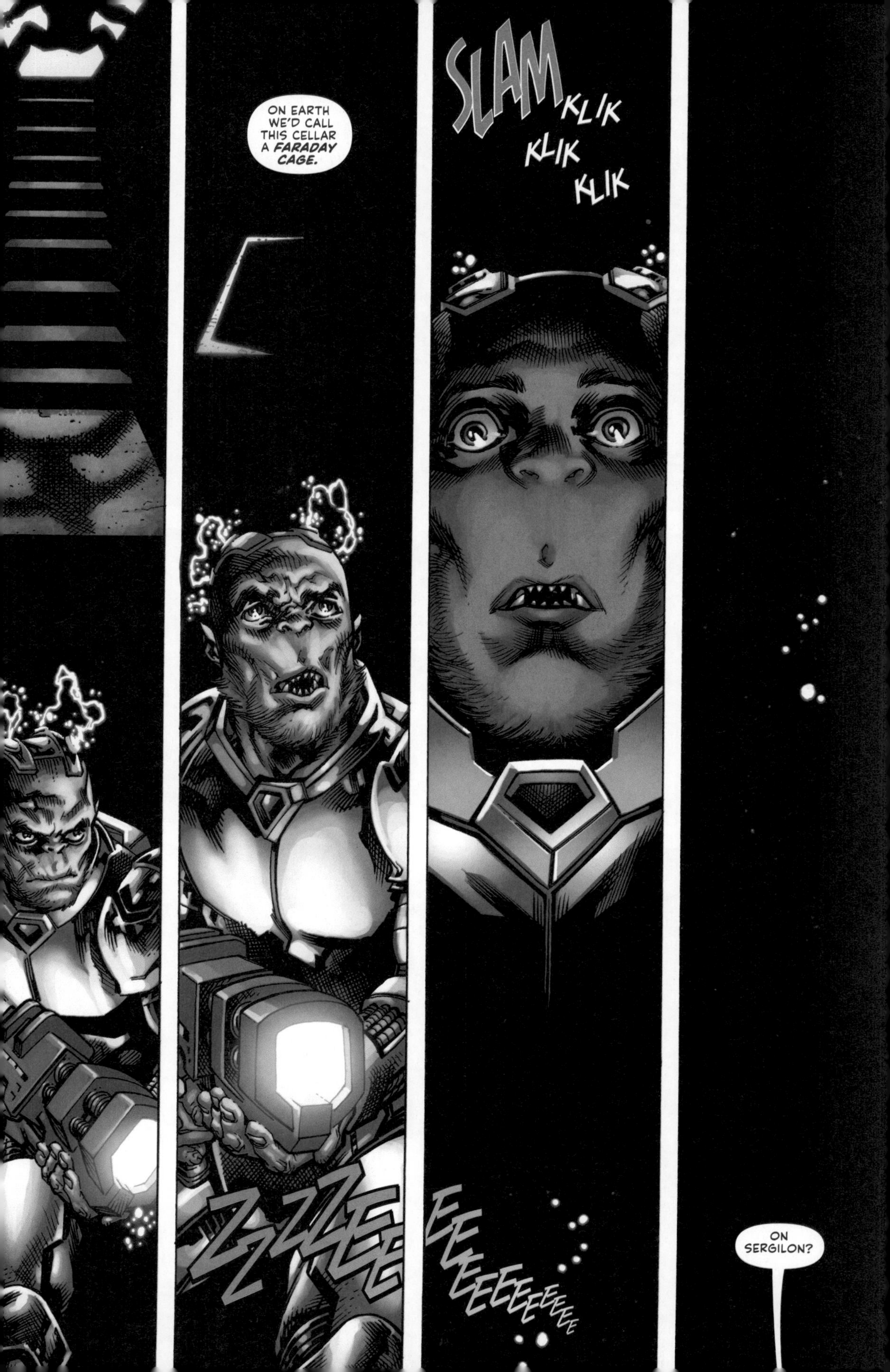
ON EARTH WE'D CALL THIS CELLAR A *FARADAY CAGE.*
SLAM
KLIK
KLIK
KLIK
ZZZZEEEEEEEEEEEEEEEE
ON SERGILON?

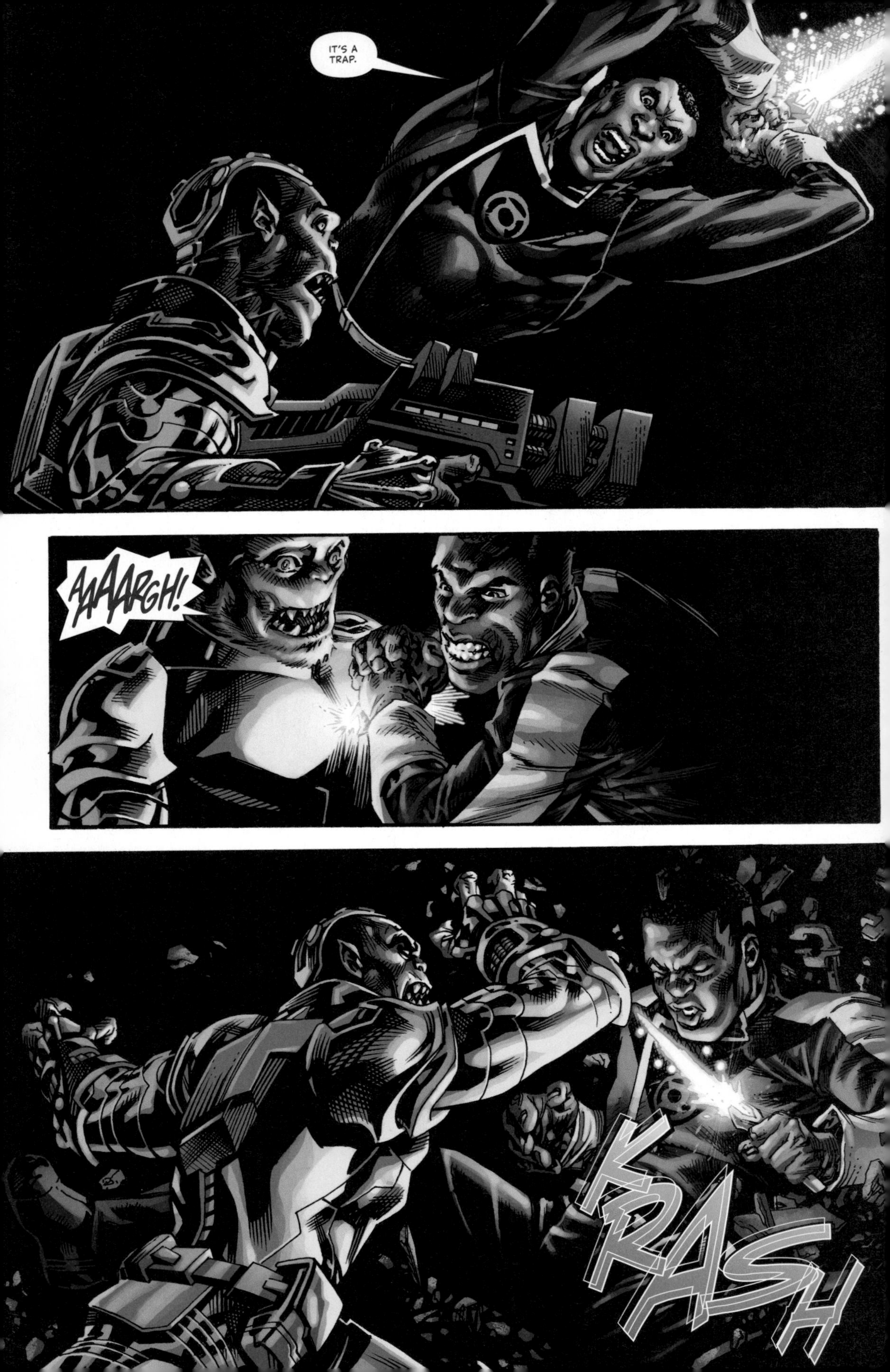
IT'S A TRAP.
AAAARGH!
KRASH

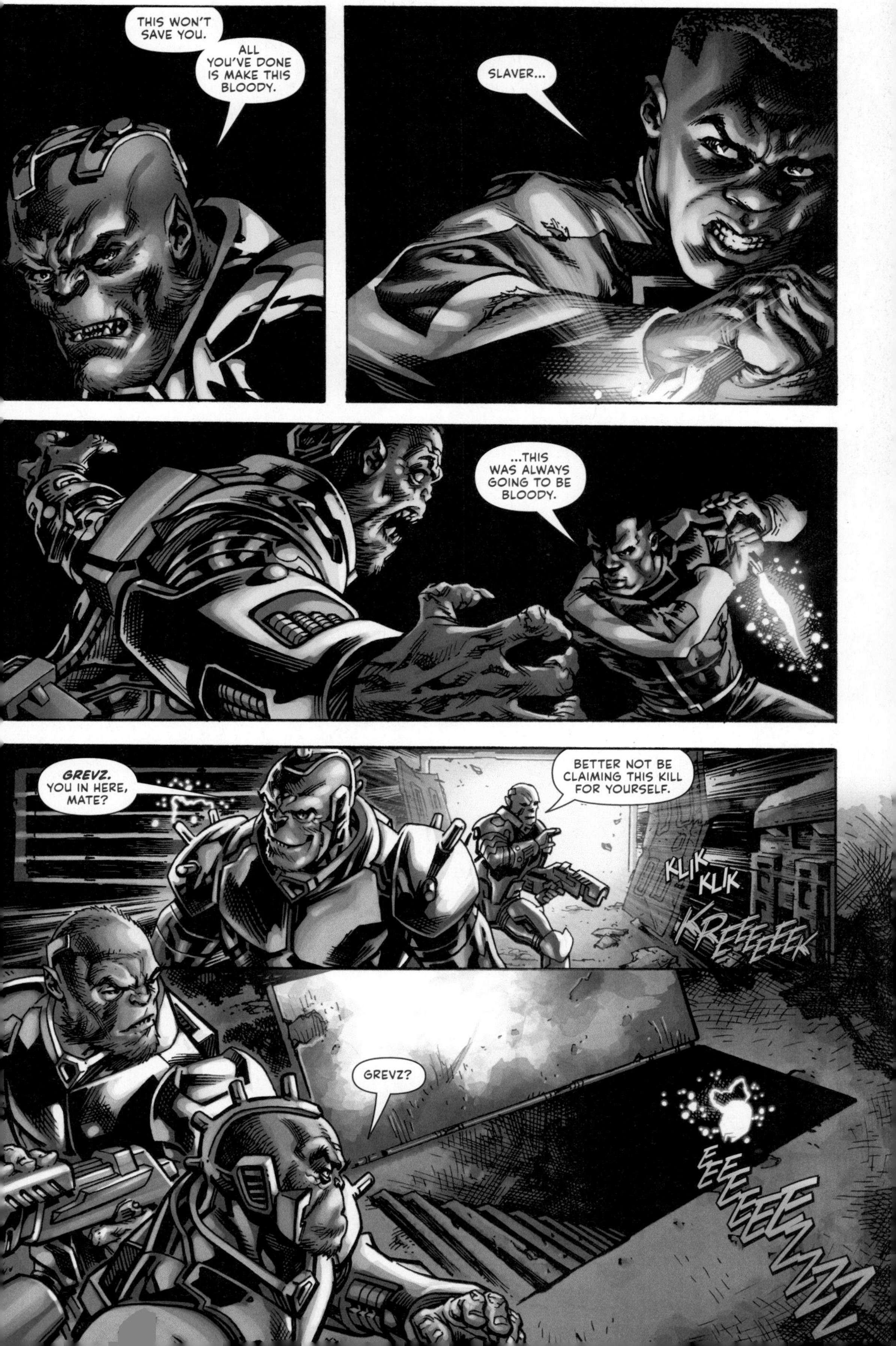
THIS WON'T SAVE YOU.
ALL YOU'VE DONE IS MAKE THIS BLOODY.
SLAVER...
...THIS WAS ALWAYS GOING TO BE BLOODY.
GREVZ. YOU IN HERE, MATE?
BETTER NOT BE CLAIMING THIS KILL FOR YOURSELF.
KLIK KLIK
KREEEEEEK
GREVZ?
EEEEEEZZZZ

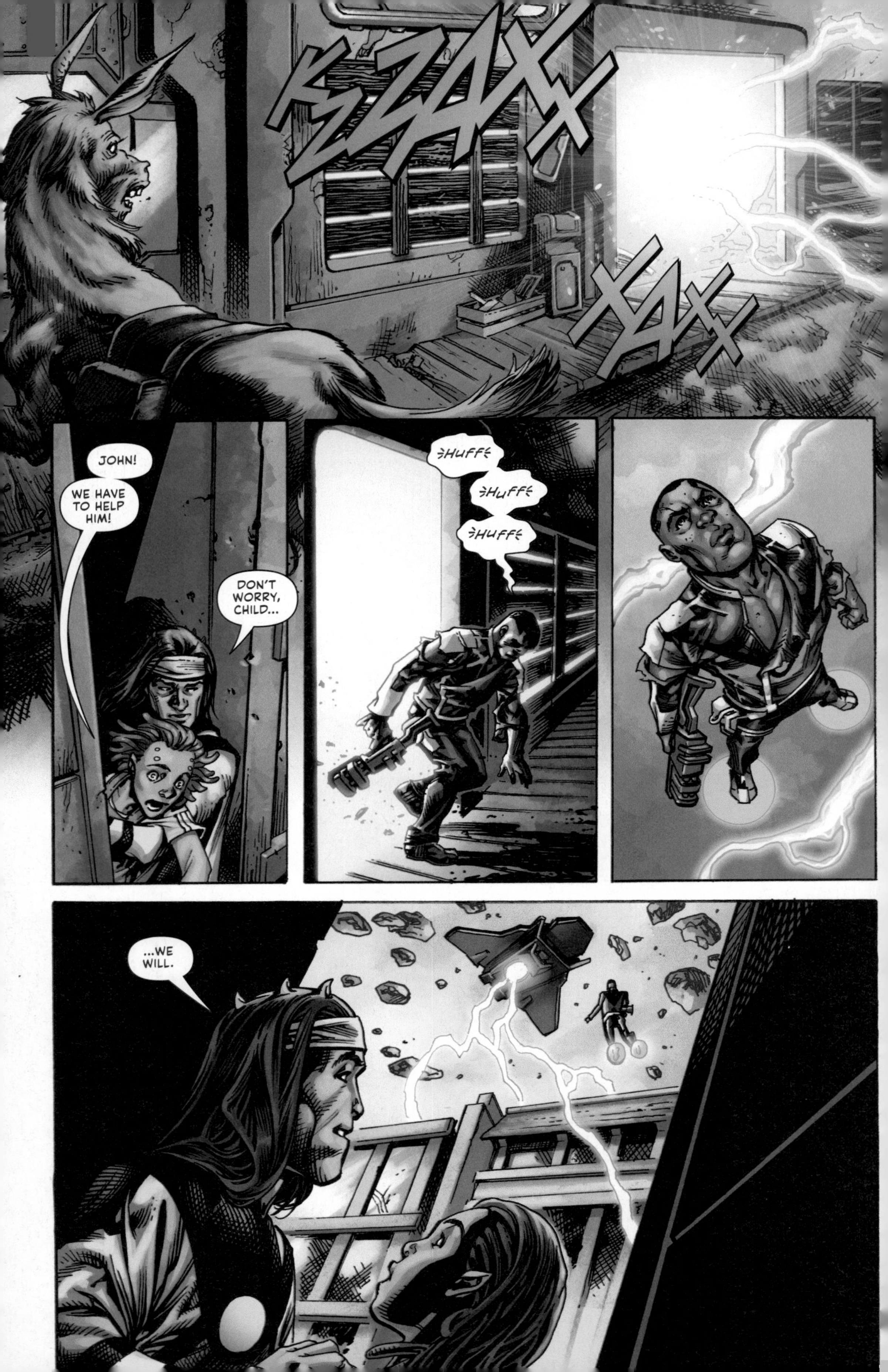
KZZAXX
XZAXX
JOHN!
WE HAVE TO HELP HIM!
DON'T WORRY, CHILD...
HUFF
HUFF
HUFF
...WE WILL.

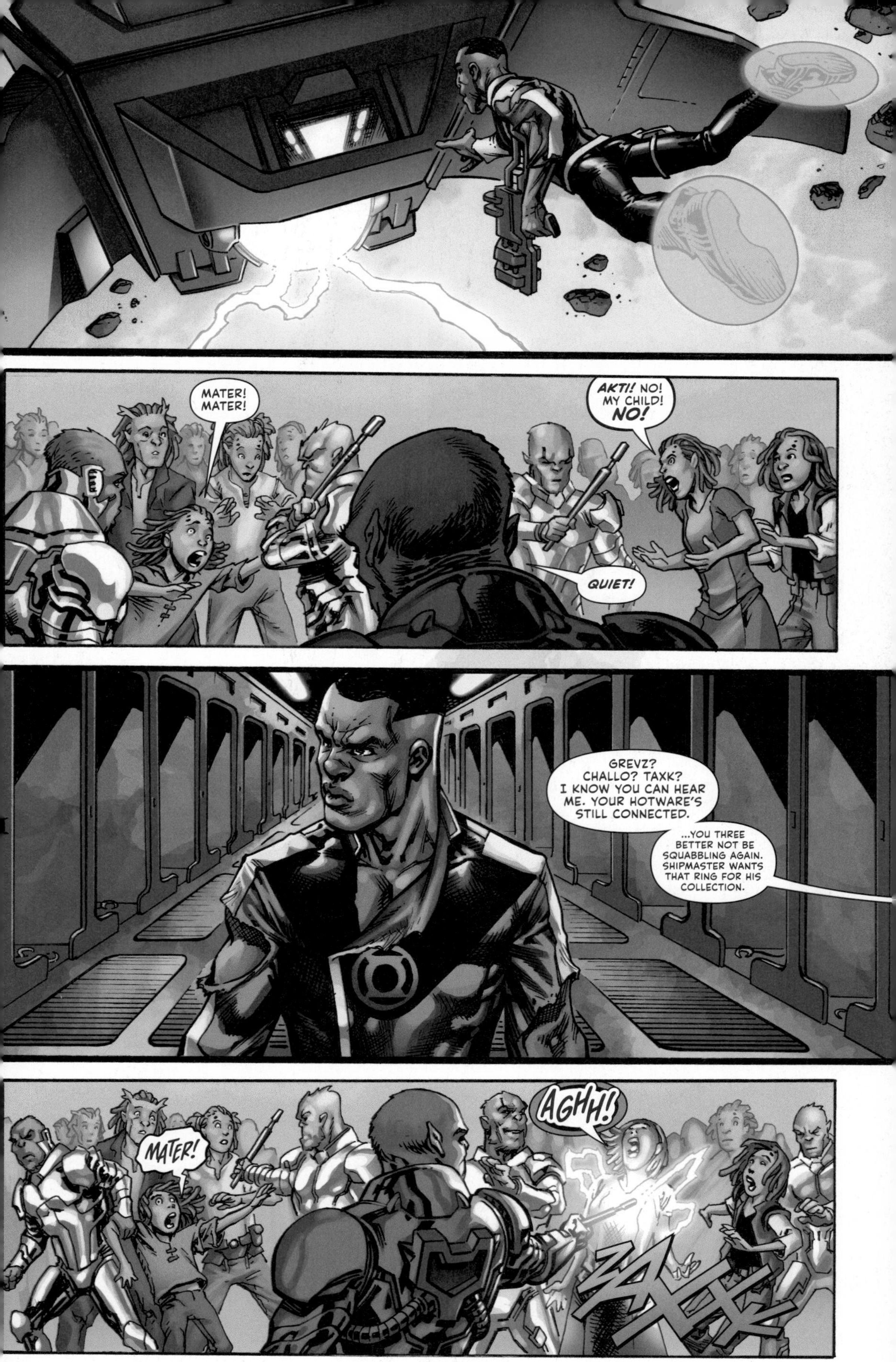
MATER! MATER!
AKTI! NO! MY CHILD! NO!
QUIET!
GREVZ? CHALLO? TAXK? I KNOW YOU CAN HEAR ME. YOUR HOTWARE'S STILL CONNECTED.
...YOU THREE BETTER NOT BE SQUABBLING AGAIN. SHIPMASTER WANTS THAT RING FOR HIS COLLECTION.
MATER!
AGHH!
ZAXX

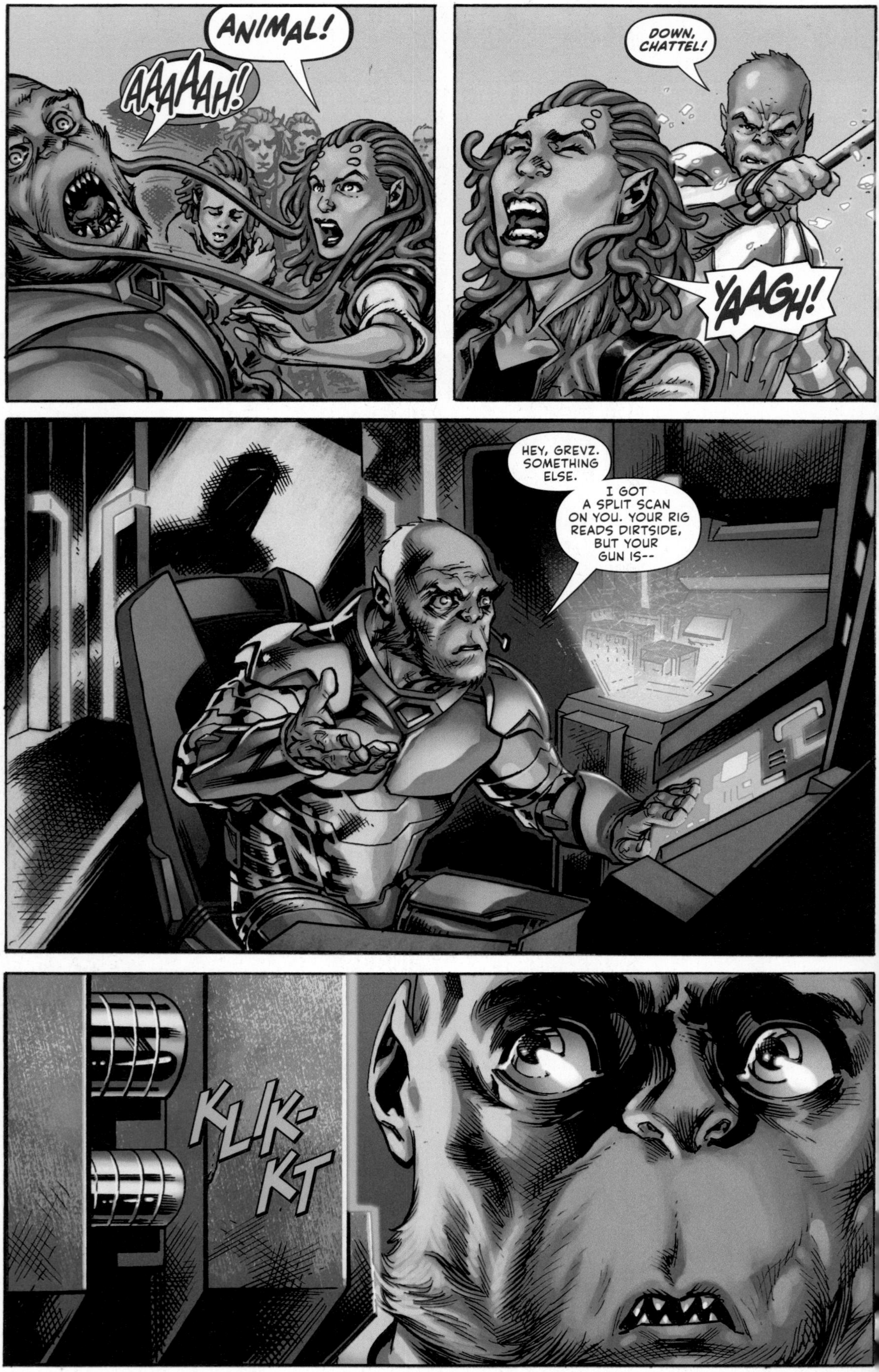
ANIMAL!
AAAAAH!
DOWN, CHATTEL!
YAAGH!
HEY, GREVZ. SOMETHING ELSE.
I GOT A SPLIT SCAN ON YOU. YOUR RIG READS DIRTSIDE, BUT YOUR GUN IS--
KLIK-KT

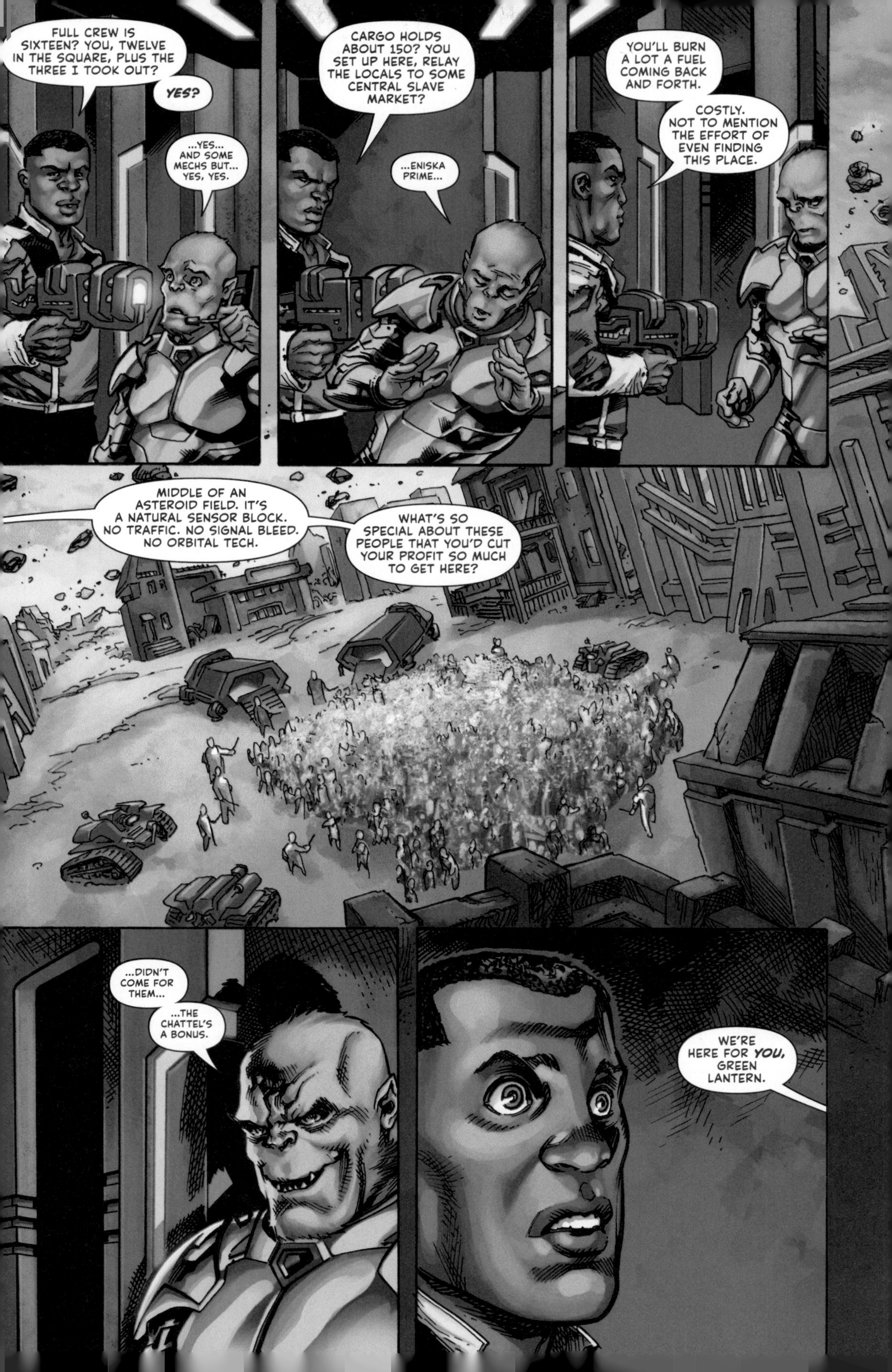
FULL CREW IS SIXTEEN? YOU, TWELVE IN THE SQUARE, PLUS THE THREE I TOOK OUT?
YES?
...YES... AND SOME MECHS BUT... YES, YES.
CARGO HOLDS ABOUT 150? YOU SET UP HERE, RELAY THE LOCALS TO SOME CENTRAL SLAVE MARKET?
...ENISKA PRIME...
YOU'LL BURN A LOT A FUEL COMING BACK AND FORTH.
COSTLY. NOT TO MENTION THE EFFORT OF EVEN FINDING THIS PLACE.
MIDDLE OF AN ASTEROID FIELD. IT'S A NATURAL SENSOR BLOCK. NO TRAFFIC. NO SIGNAL BLEED. NO ORBITAL TECH.
WHAT'S SO SPECIAL ABOUT THESE PEOPLE THAT YOU'D CUT YOUR PROFIT SO MUCH TO GET HERE?
...DIDN'T COME FOR THEM...
...THE CHATTEL'S A BONUS.
WE'RE HERE FOR *YOU,* GREEN LANTERN.

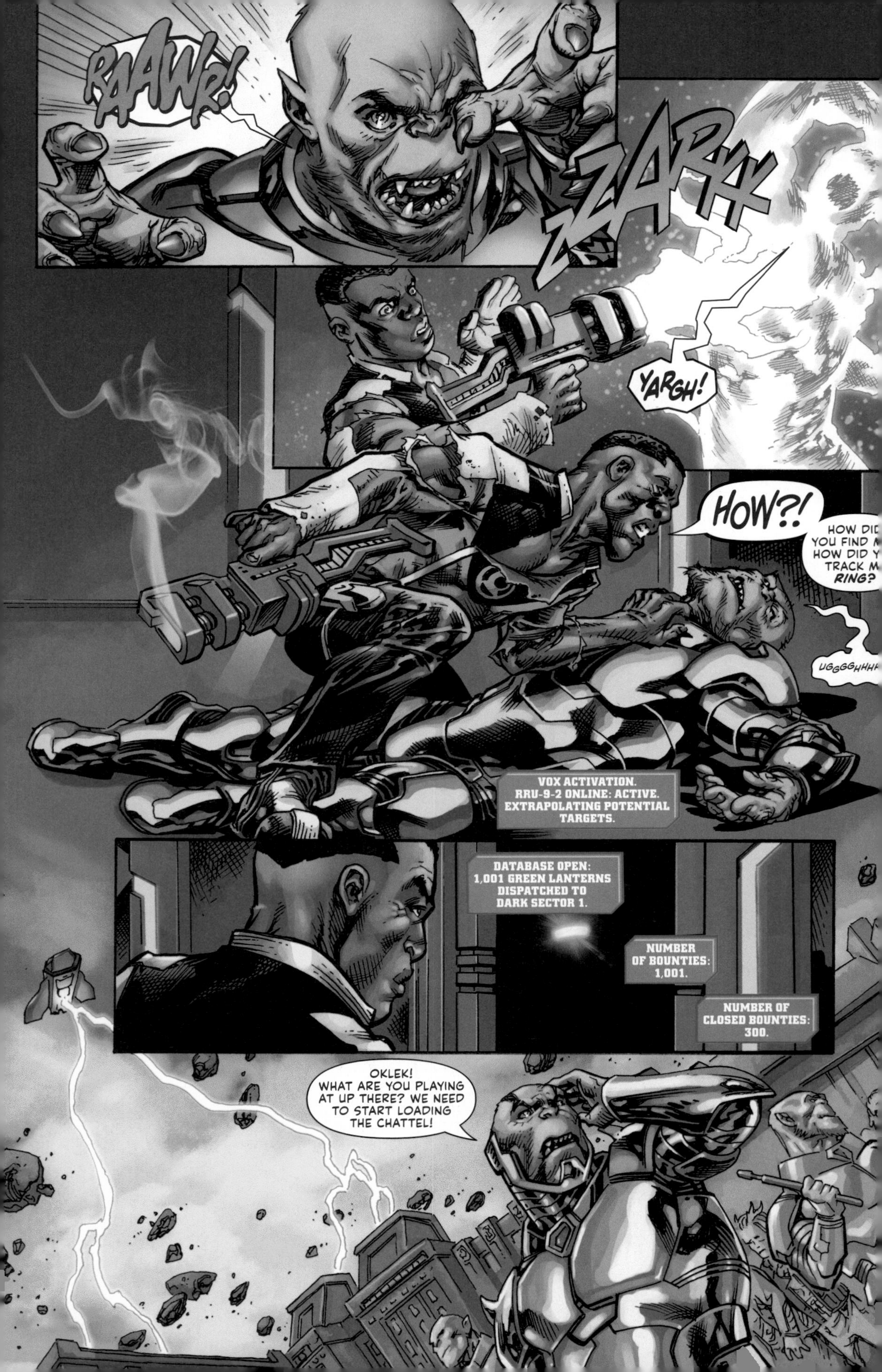

RAAWR!
ZZARKK
YARGH!
HOW?!
HOW DID
YOU FIND M
HOW DID Y
TRACK M
RING?
UGGGGHHH
VOX ACTIVATION.
RRU-9-2 ONLINE: ACTIVE.
EXTRAPOLATING POTENTIAL
TARGETS.
DATABASE OPEN:
1,001 GREEN LANTERNS
DISPATCHED TO
DARK SECTOR 1.
NUMBER
OF BOUNTIES:
1,001.
NUMBER OF
CLOSED BOUNTIES:
300.
OKLEK!
WHAT ARE YOU PLAYING
AT UP THERE? WE NEED
TO START LOADING
THE CHATTEL!

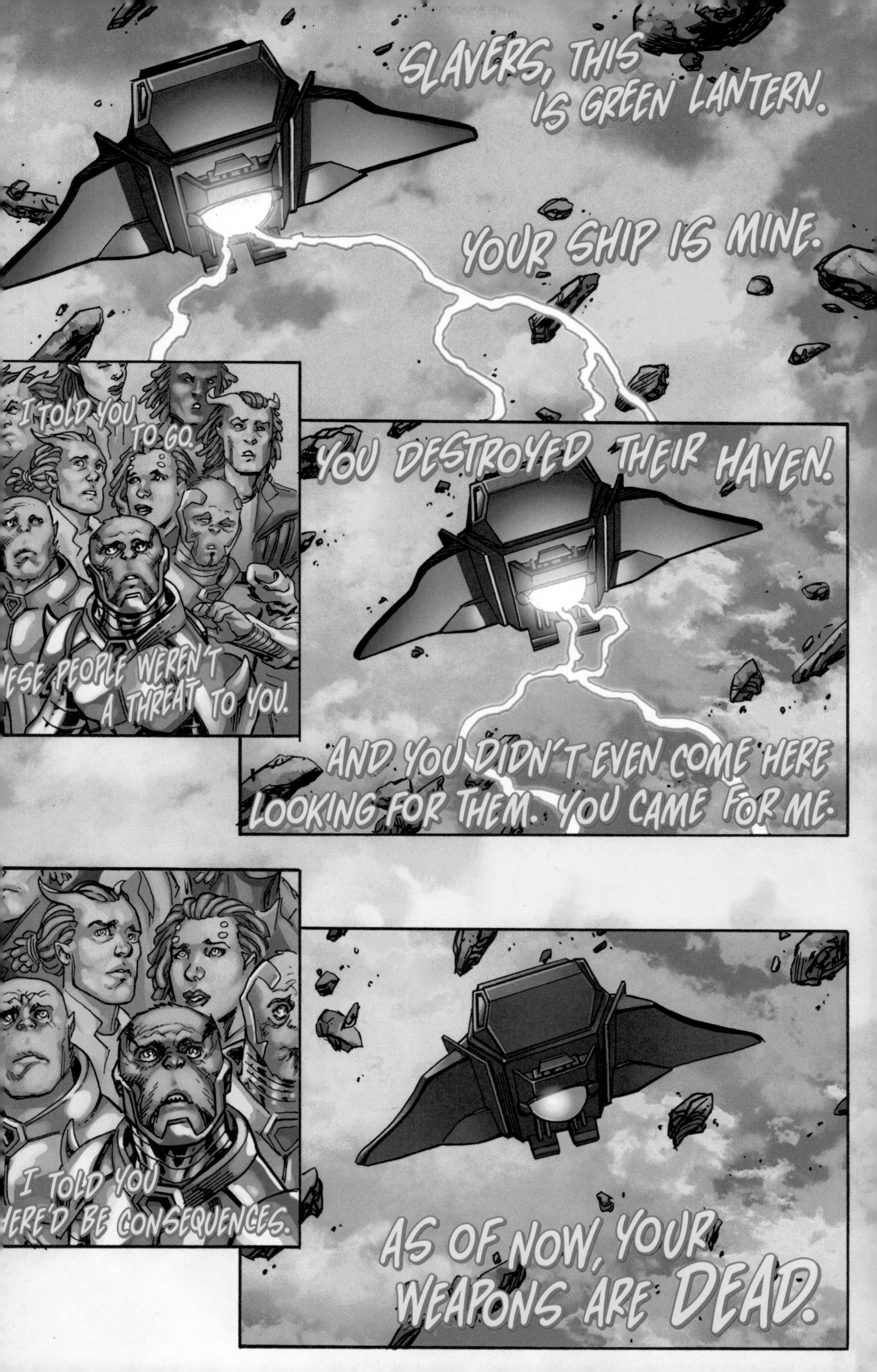
SLAVERS, THIS IS GREEN LANTERN.
YOUR SHIP IS MINE.
I TOLD YOU TO GO.
YOU DESTROYED THEIR HAVEN.
ESE PEOPLE WEREN'T A THREAT TO YOU.
AND YOU DIDN'T EVEN COME HERE LOOKING FOR THEM. YOU CAME FOR ME.
I TOLD YOU HERE'D BE CONSEQUENCES.
AS OF NOW, YOUR WEAPONS ARE DEAD.

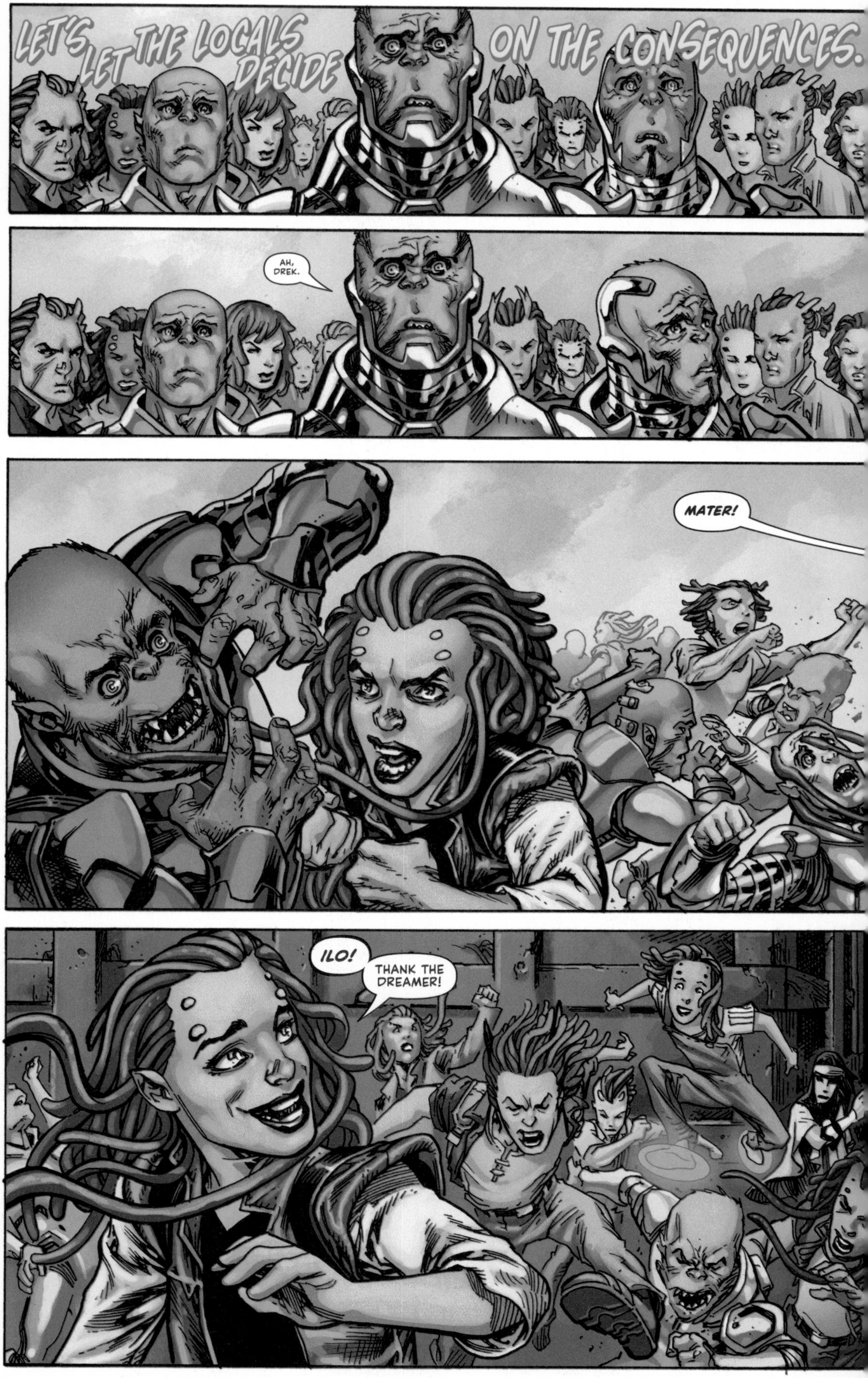
LET'S LET THE LOCALS DECIDE
ON THE CONSEQUENCES.
AH, DREK.
MATER!
ILO!
THANK THE DREAMER!

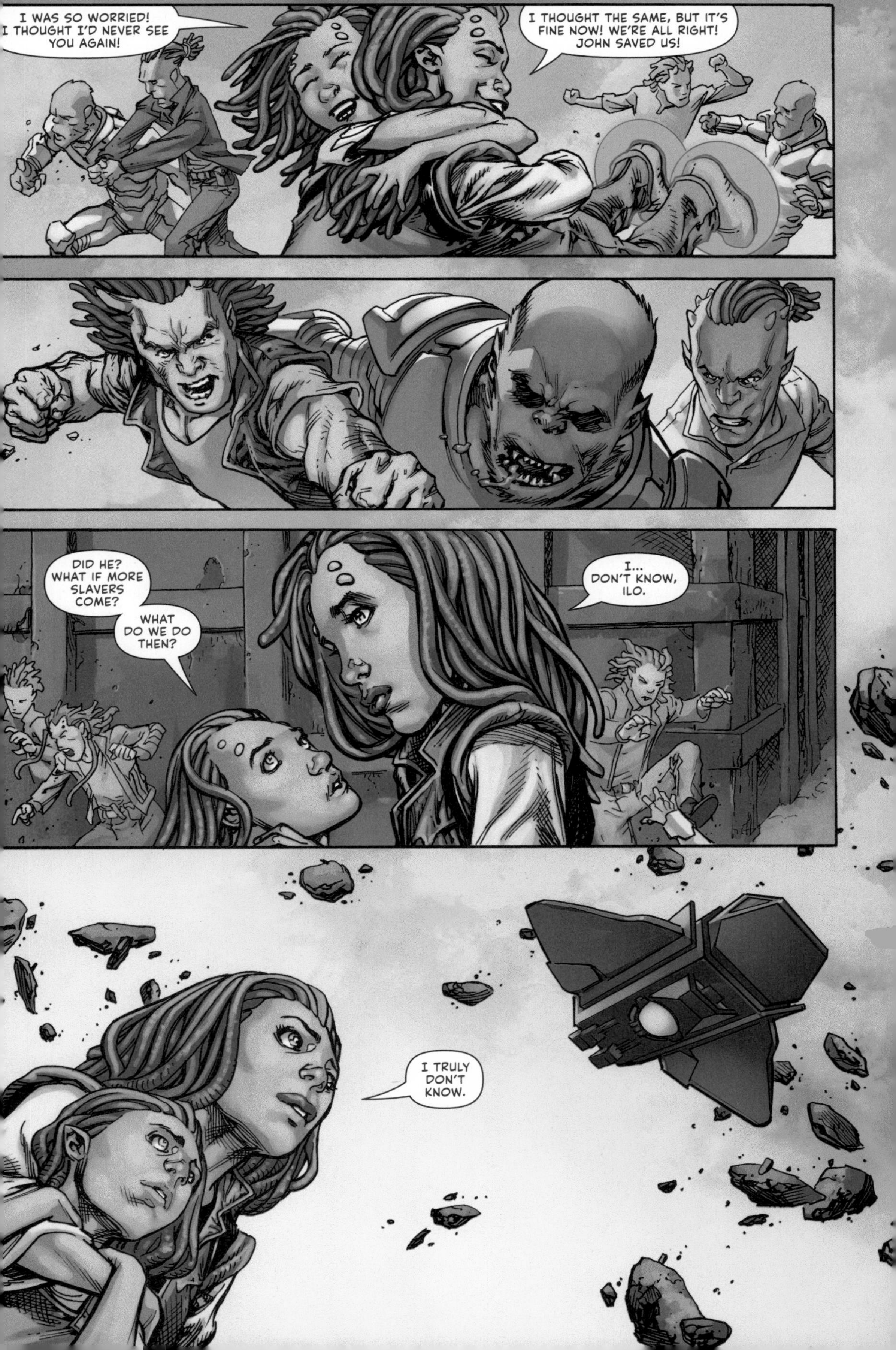
I WAS SO WORRIED! I THOUGHT I'D NEVER SEE YOU AGAIN!
I THOUGHT THE SAME, BUT IT'S FINE NOW! WE'RE ALL RIGHT! JOHN SAVED US!
DID HE? WHAT IF MORE SLAVERS COME?
WHAT DO WE DO THEN?
I... DON'T KNOW, ILO.
I TRULY DON'T KNOW.

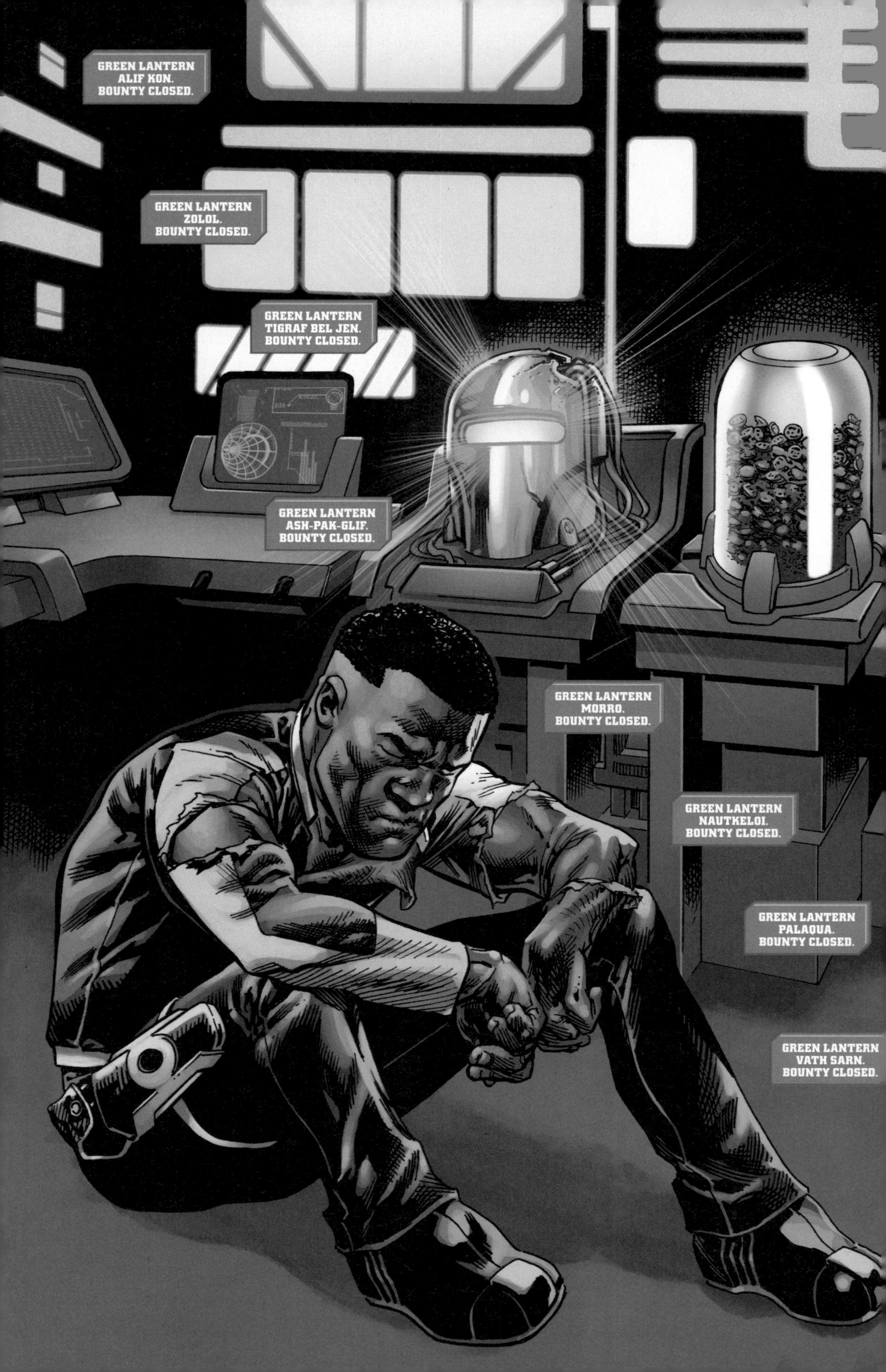
GREEN LANTERN ALIF KON. BOUNTY CLOSED.
GREEN LANTERN ZOLOL. BOUNTY CLOSED.
GREEN LANTERN TIGRAF BEL JEN. BOUNTY CLOSED.
GREEN LANTERN ASH-PAK-GLIF. BOUNTY CLOSED.
GREEN LANTERN MORRO. BOUNTY CLOSED.
GREEN LANTERN NAUTKELOI. BOUNTY CLOSED.
GREEN LANTERN PALAQUA. BOUNTY CLOSED.
GREEN LANTERN VATH SARN. BOUNTY CLOSED.

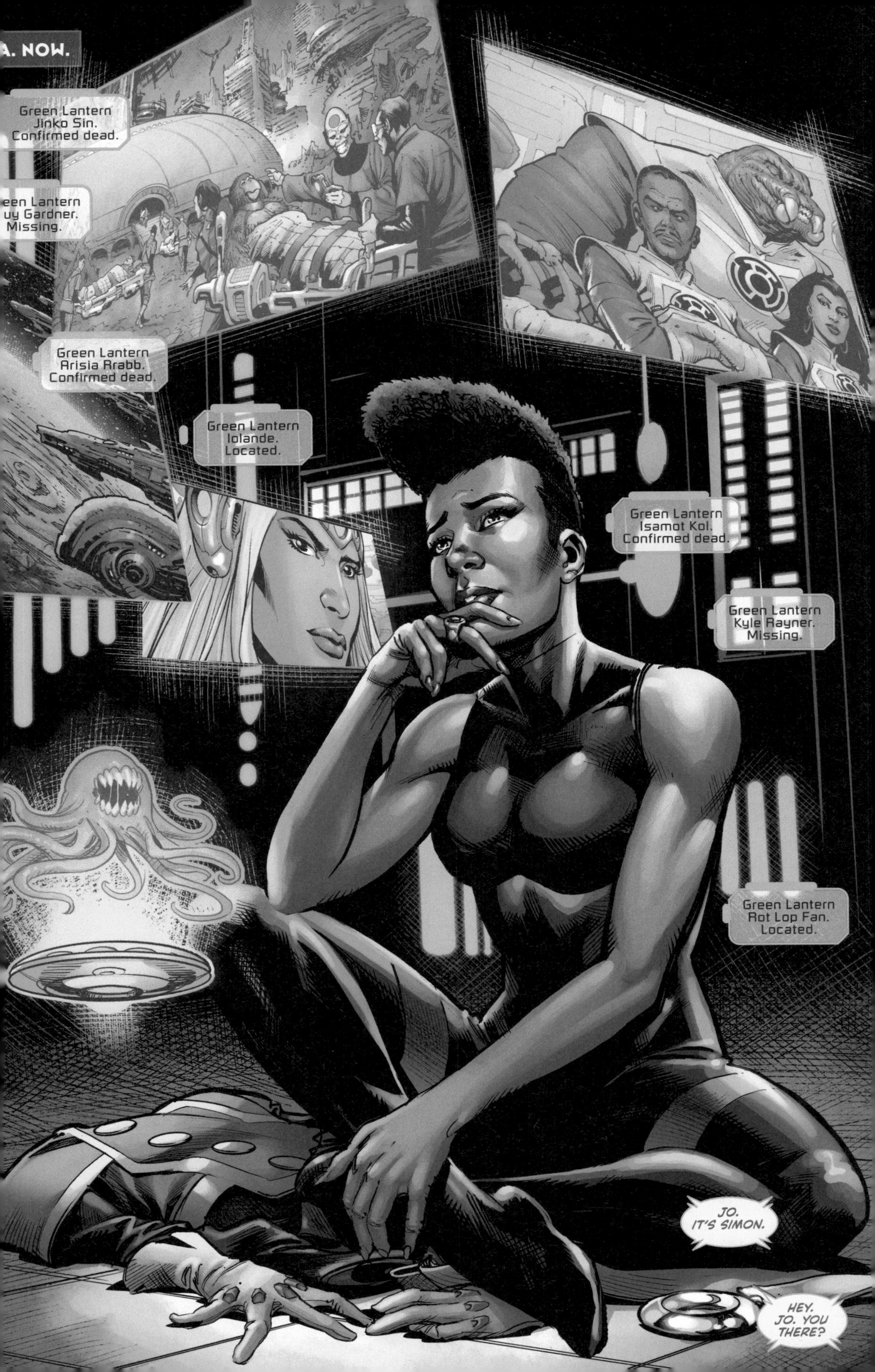
A. NOW.
Green Lantern Jinko Sin. Confirmed dead.
een Lantern uy Gardner. Missing.
Green Lantern Arisia Rrabb. Confirmed dead.
Green Lantern Iolande. Located.
Green Lantern Isamot Kol. Confirmed dead.
Green Lantern Kyle Rayner. Missing.
Green Lantern Rot Lop Fan. Located.
JO. IT'S SIMON.
HEY. JO. YOU THERE?

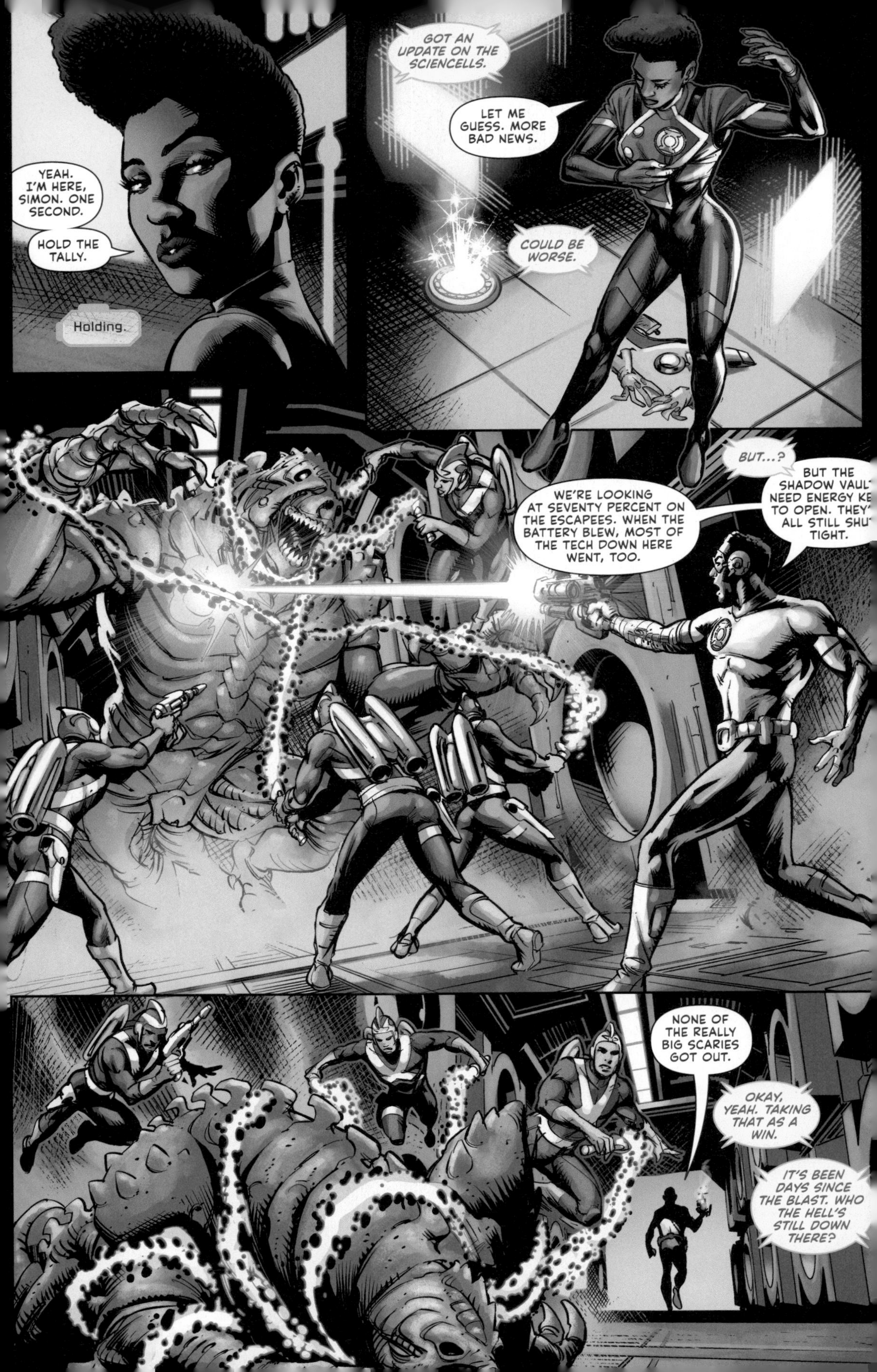
YEAH. I'M HERE, SIMON. ONE SECOND.
HOLD THE TALLY.
Holding.
GOT AN UPDATE ON THE SCIENCELLS.
LET ME GUESS. MORE BAD NEWS.
COULD BE WORSE.
WE'RE LOOKING AT SEVENTY PERCENT ON THE ESCAPEES. WHEN THE BATTERY BLEW, MOST OF THE TECH DOWN HERE WENT, TOO.
BUT...?
BUT THE SHADOW VAUL
NEED ENERGY KE
TO OPEN. THEY'
ALL STILL SHU
TIGHT.
NONE OF THE REALLY BIG SCARIES GOT OUT.
OKAY, YEAH. TAKING THAT AS A WIN.
IT'S BEEN DAYS SINCE THE BLAST. WHO THE HELL'S STILL DOWN THERE?

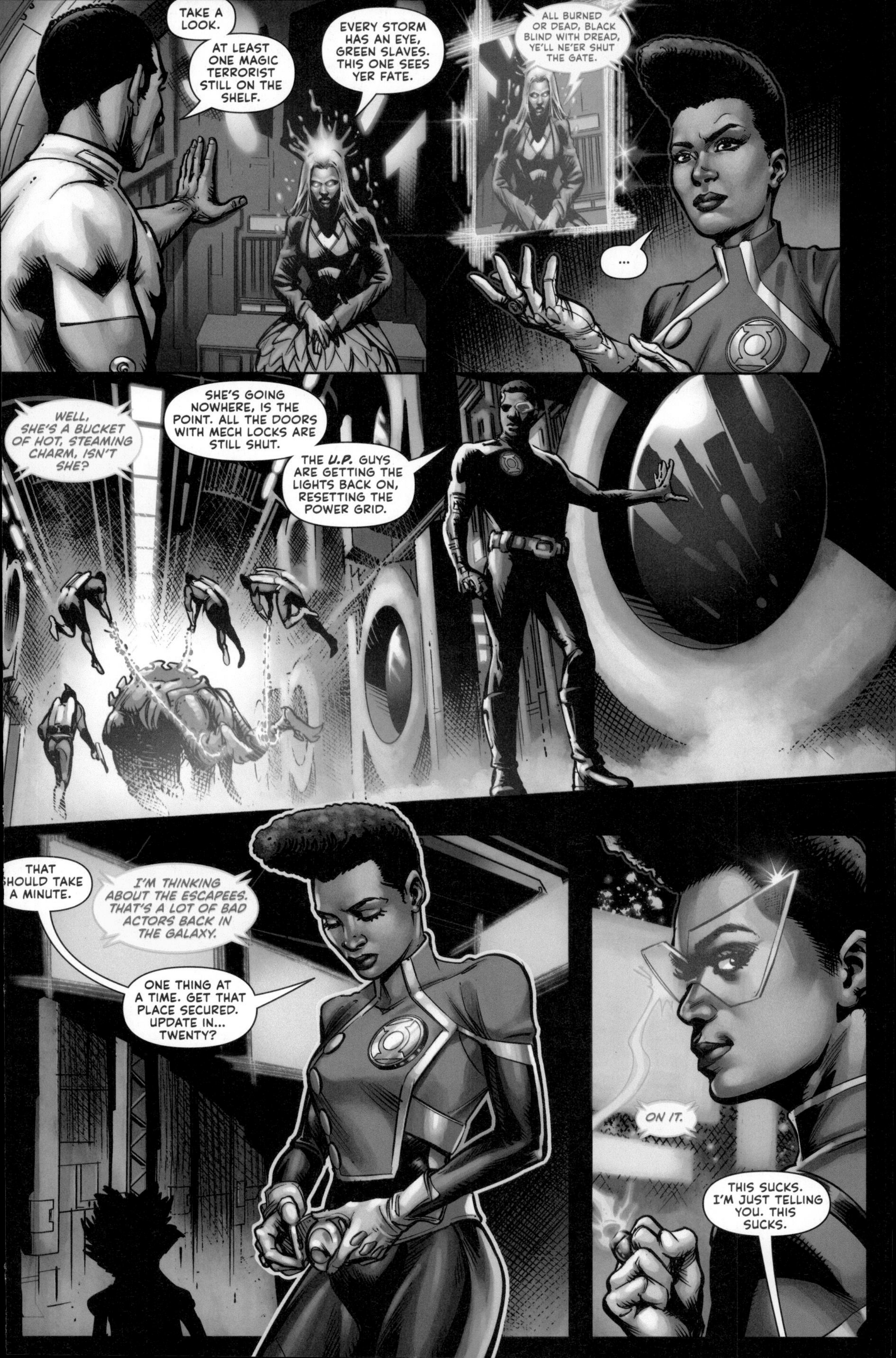
TAKE A LOOK.
AT LEAST ONE MAGIC TERRORIST STILL ON THE SHELF.
EVERY STORM HAS AN EYE, GREEN SLAVES. THIS ONE SEES YER FATE.
ALL BURNED OR DEAD, BLACK BLIND WITH DREAD, YE'LL NE'ER SHUT THE GATE.
...
WELL, SHE'S A BUCKET OF HOT, STEAMING CHARM, ISN'T SHE?
SHE'S GOING NOWHERE, IS THE POINT. ALL THE DOORS WITH MECH LOCKS ARE STILL SHUT.
THE U.P. GUYS ARE GETTING THE LIGHTS BACK ON, RESETTING THE POWER GRID.
THAT SHOULD TAKE A MINUTE.
I'M THINKING ABOUT THE ESCAPEES. THAT'S A LOT OF BAD ACTORS BACK IN THE GALAXY.
ONE THING AT A TIME. GET THAT PLACE SECURED. UPDATE IN... TWENTY?
ON IT.
THIS SUCKS. I'M JUST TELLING YOU. THIS SUCKS.

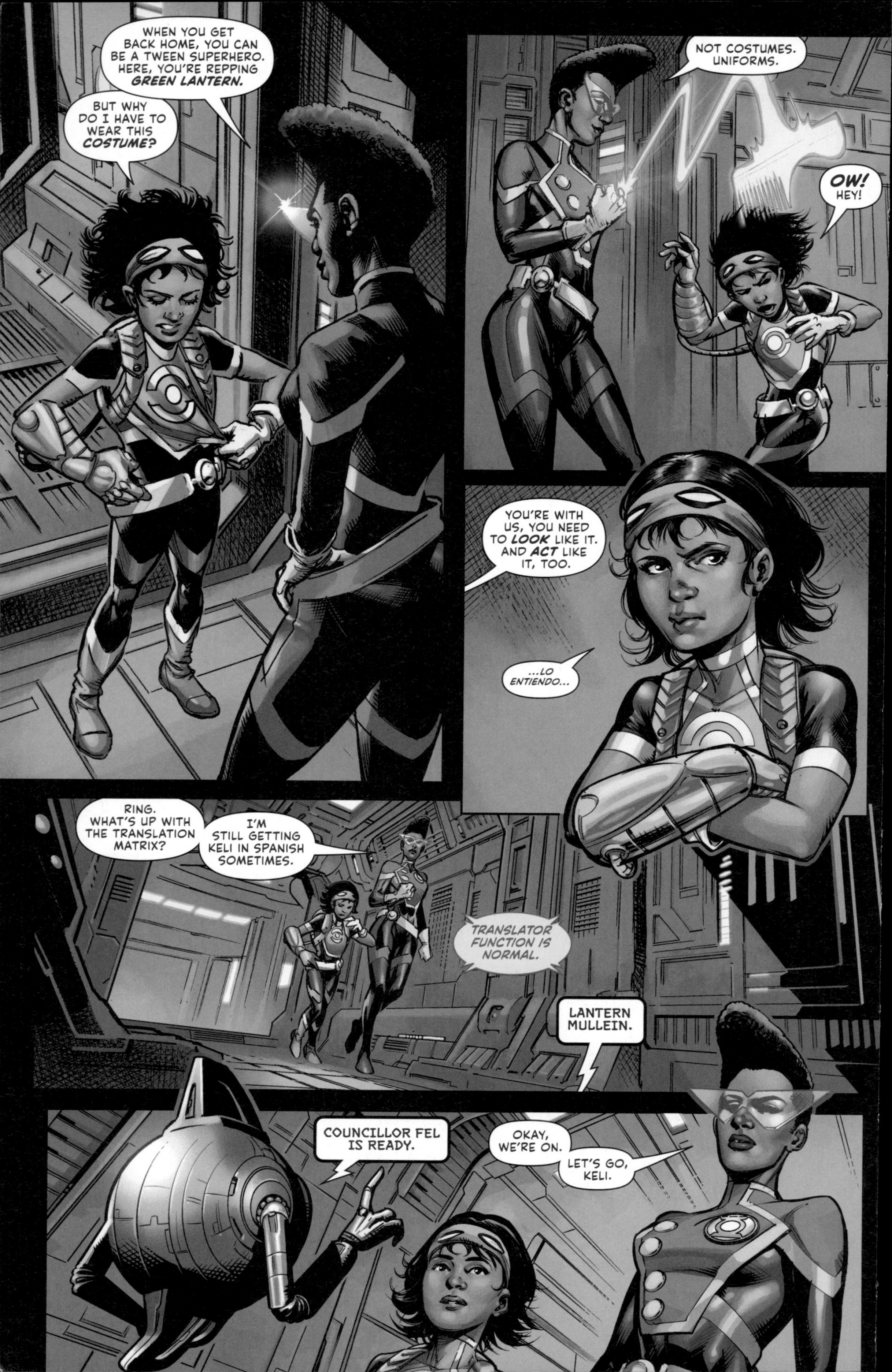

WHEN YOU GET BACK HOME, YOU CAN BE A TWEEN SUPERHERO. HERE, YOU'RE REPPING GREEN LANTERN.
BUT WHY DO I HAVE TO WEAR THIS COSTUME?
NOT COSTUMES. UNIFORMS.
OW! HEY!
YOU'RE WITH US, YOU NEED TO LOOK LIKE IT. AND ACT LIKE IT, TOO.
...LO ENTIENDO...
RING. WHAT'S UP WITH THE TRANSLATION MATRIX?
I'M STILL GETTING KELI IN SPANISH SOMETIMES.
TRANSLATOR FUNCTION IS NORMAL.
LANTERN MULLEIN.
COUNCILLOR FEL IS READY.
OKAY, WE'RE ON.
LET'S GO, KELI.

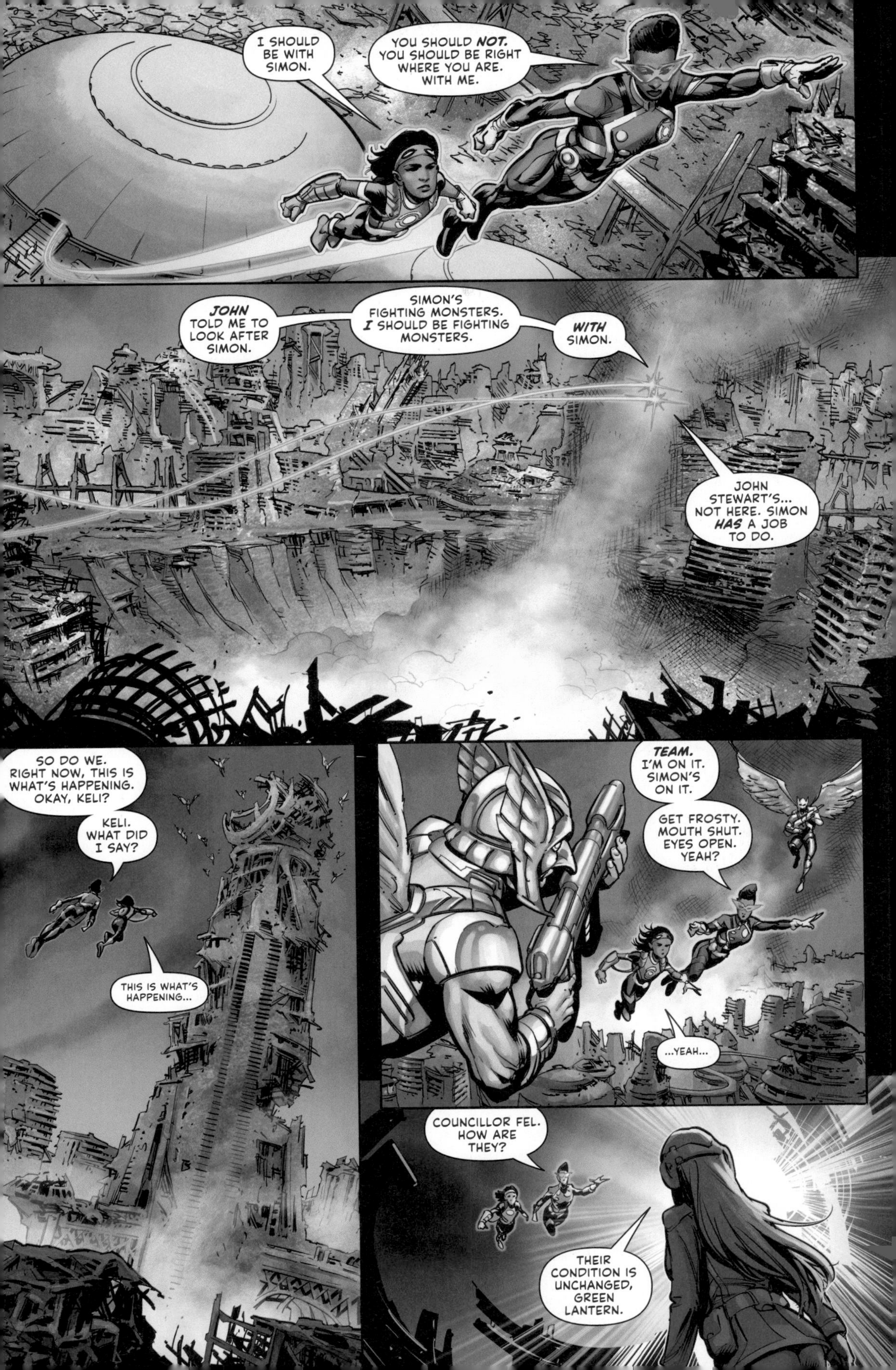

I SHOULD BE WITH SIMON.
YOU SHOULD ***NOT.*** YOU SHOULD BE RIGHT WHERE YOU ARE. WITH ME.
JOHN TOLD ME TO LOOK AFTER SIMON.
SIMON'S FIGHTING MONSTERS. ***I*** SHOULD BE FIGHTING MONSTERS.
WITH SIMON.
JOHN STEWART'S... NOT HERE. SIMON ***HAS*** A JOB TO DO.
SO DO WE. RIGHT NOW, THIS IS WHAT'S HAPPENING. OKAY, KELI?
KELI. WHAT DID I SAY?
THIS IS WHAT'S HAPPENING...
TEAM. I'M ON IT. SIMON'S ON IT.
GET FROSTY. MOUTH SHUT. EYES OPEN. YEAH?
...YEAH...
COUNCILLOR FEL. HOW ARE THEY?
THEIR CONDITION IS UNCHANGED, GREEN LANTERN.

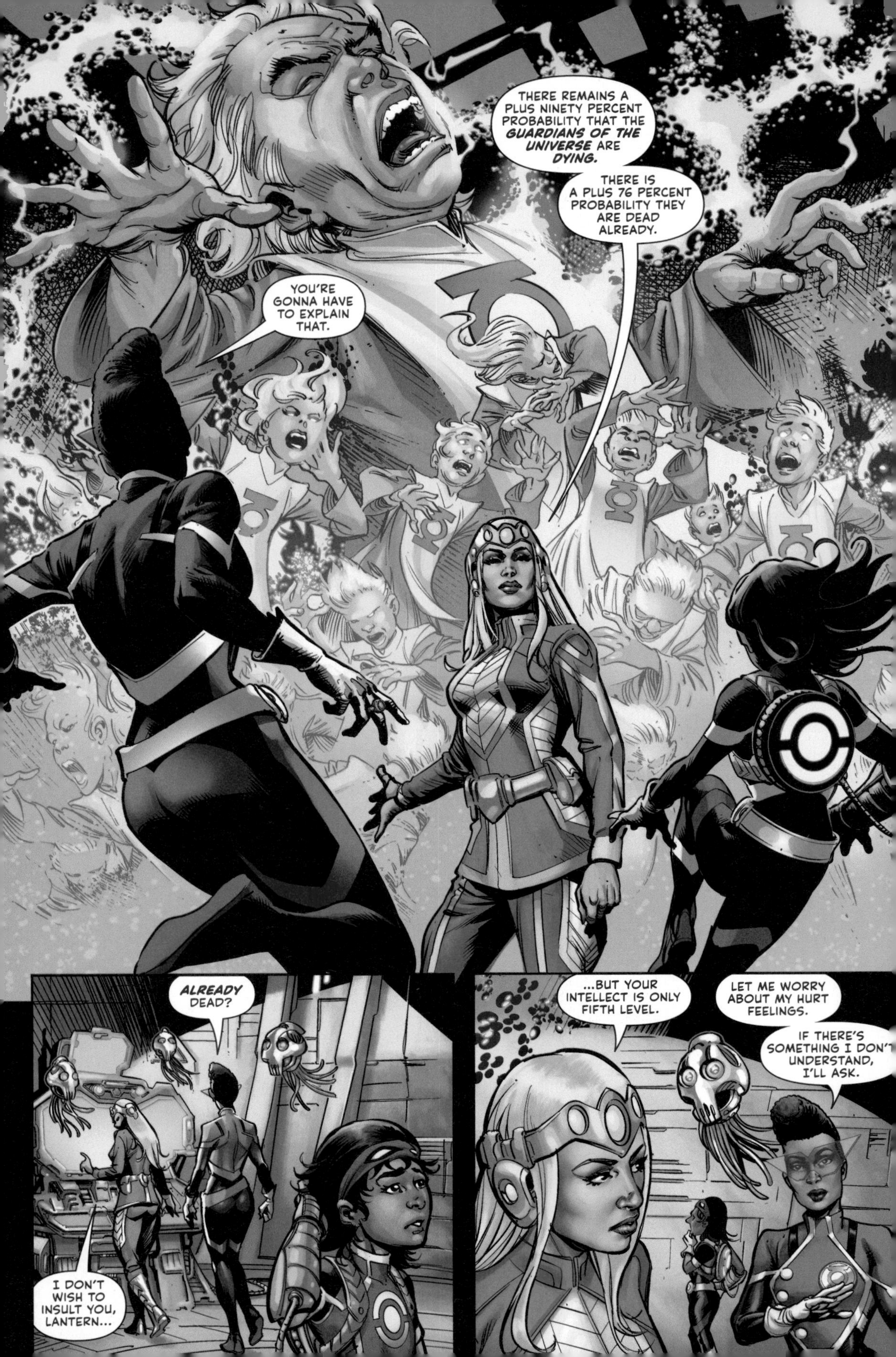
THERE REMAINS A PLUS NINETY PERCENT PROBABILITY THAT THE ***GUARDIANS OF THE UNIVERSE*** ARE ***DYING.***
THERE IS A PLUS 76 PERCENT PROBABILITY THEY ARE DEAD ALREADY.
YOU'RE GONNA HAVE TO EXPLAIN THAT.
ALREADY DEAD?
I DON'T WISH TO INSULT YOU, LANTERN...
...BUT YOUR INTELLECT IS ONLY FIFTH LEVEL.
LET ME WORRY ABOUT MY HURT FEELINGS.
IF THERE'S SOMETHING I DON'T UNDERSTAND, I'LL ASK.

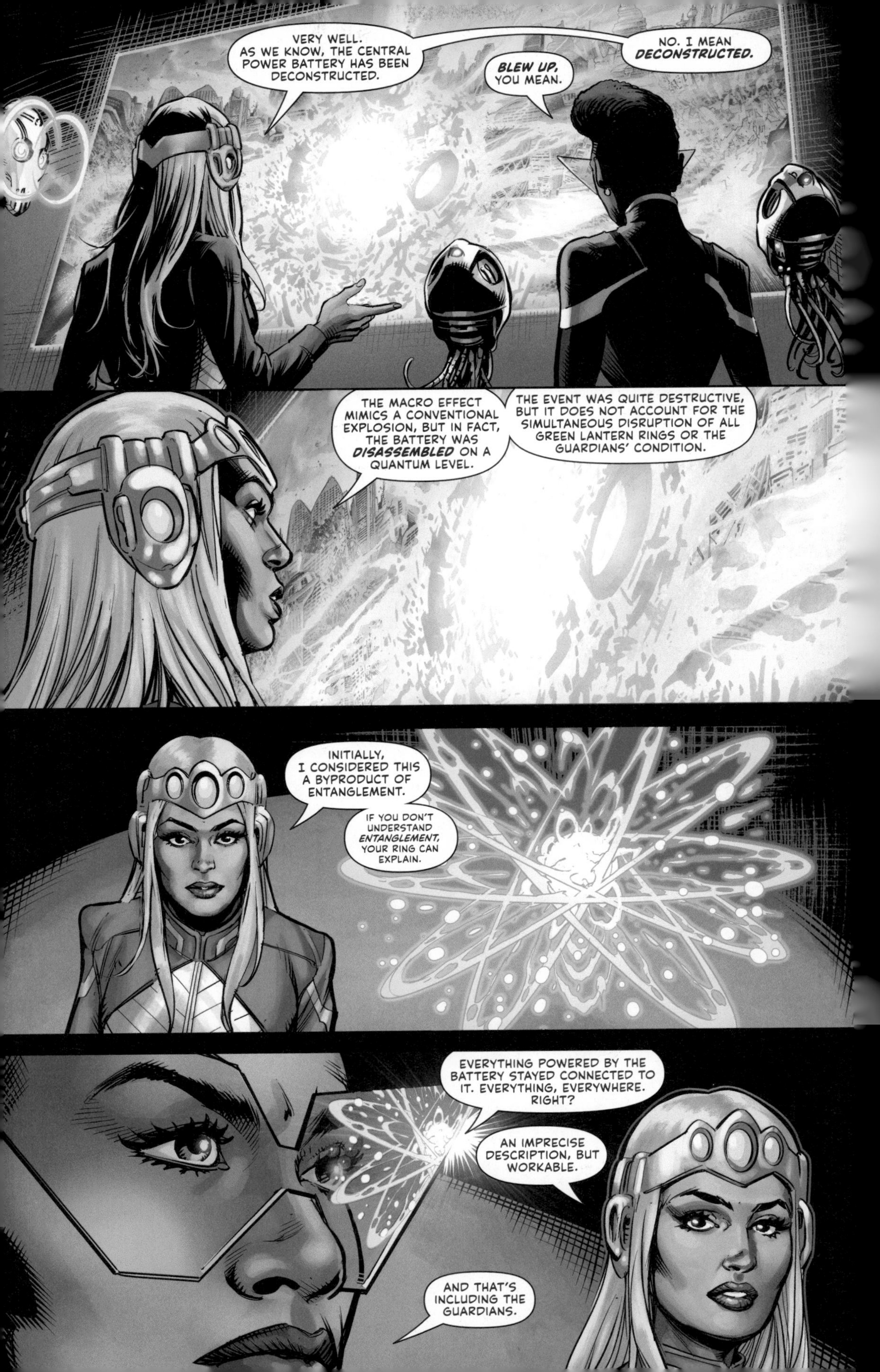
VERY WELL. AS WE KNOW, THE CENTRAL POWER BATTERY HAS BEEN DECONSTRUCTED.
BLEW UP, YOU MEAN.
NO. I MEAN DECONSTRUCTED.
THE MACRO EFFECT MIMICS A CONVENTIONAL EXPLOSION, BUT IN FACT, THE BATTERY WAS DISASSEMBLED ON A QUANTUM LEVEL.
THE EVENT WAS QUITE DESTRUCTIVE, BUT IT DOES NOT ACCOUNT FOR THE SIMULTANEOUS DISRUPTION OF ALL GREEN LANTERN RINGS OR THE GUARDIANS' CONDITION.
INITIALLY, I CONSIDERED THIS A BYPRODUCT OF ENTANGLEMENT.
IF YOU DON'T UNDERSTAND ENTANGLEMENT, YOUR RING CAN EXPLAIN.
EVERYTHING POWERED BY THE BATTERY STAYED CONNECTED TO IT. EVERYTHING, EVERYWHERE. RIGHT?
AN IMPRECISE DESCRIPTION, BUT WORKABLE.
AND THAT'S INCLUDING THE GUARDIANS.

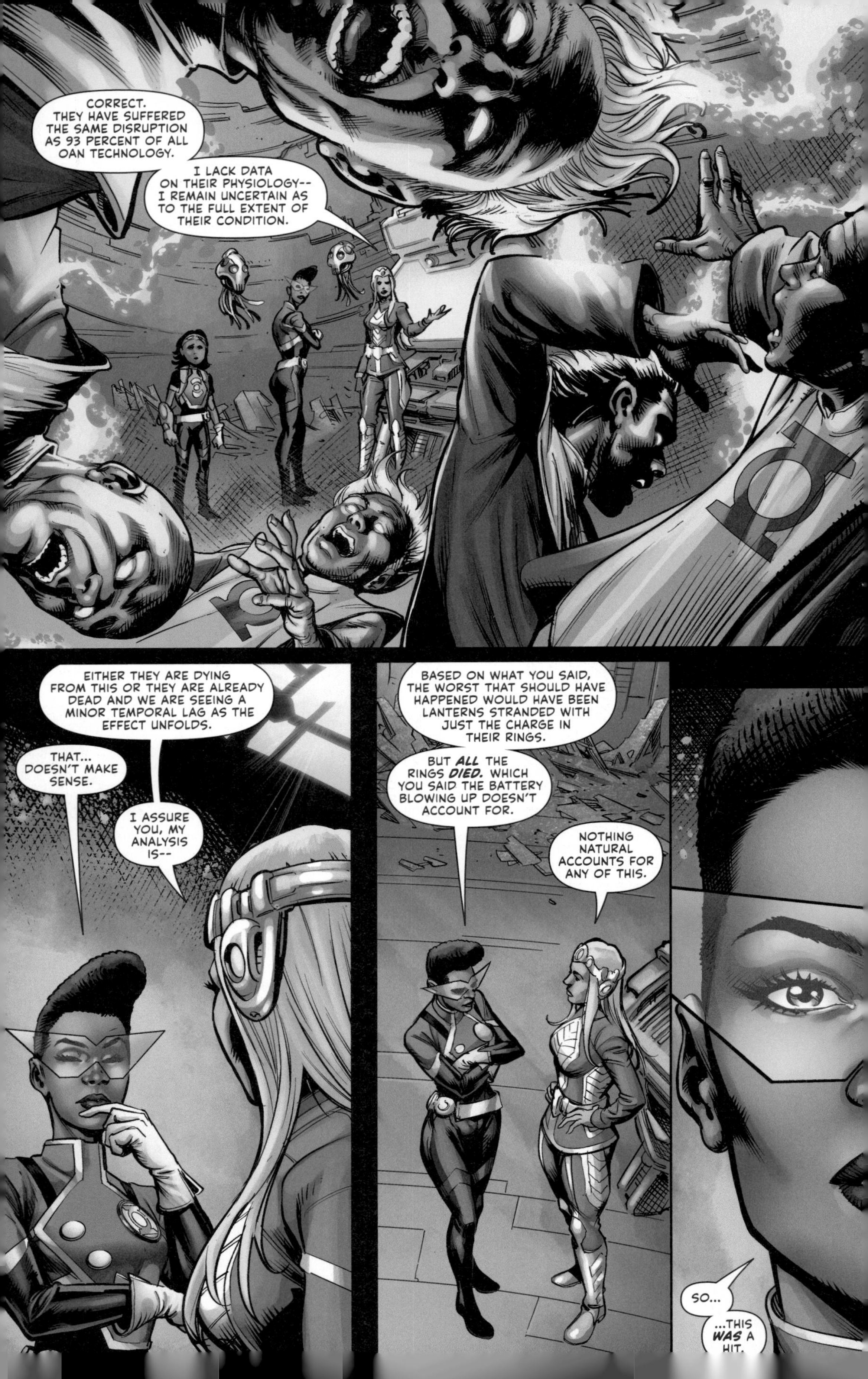
CORRECT. THEY HAVE SUFFERED THE SAME DISRUPTION AS 93 PERCENT OF ALL OAN TECHNOLOGY.
I LACK DATA ON THEIR PHYSIOLOGY-- I REMAIN UNCERTAIN AS TO THE FULL EXTENT OF THEIR CONDITION.
EITHER THEY ARE DYING FROM THIS OR THEY ARE ALREADY DEAD AND WE ARE SEEING A MINOR TEMPORAL LAG AS THE EFFECT UNFOLDS.
THAT... DOESN'T MAKE SENSE.
I ASSURE YOU, MY ANALYSIS IS--
BASED ON WHAT YOU SAID, THE WORST THAT SHOULD HAVE HAPPENED WOULD HAVE BEEN LANTERNS STRANDED WITH JUST THE CHARGE IN THEIR RINGS.
BUT ALL THE RINGS DIED. WHICH YOU SAID THE BATTERY BLOWING UP DOESN'T ACCOUNT FOR.
NOTHING NATURAL ACCOUNTS FOR ANY OF THIS.
SO...
...THIS WAS A HIT.

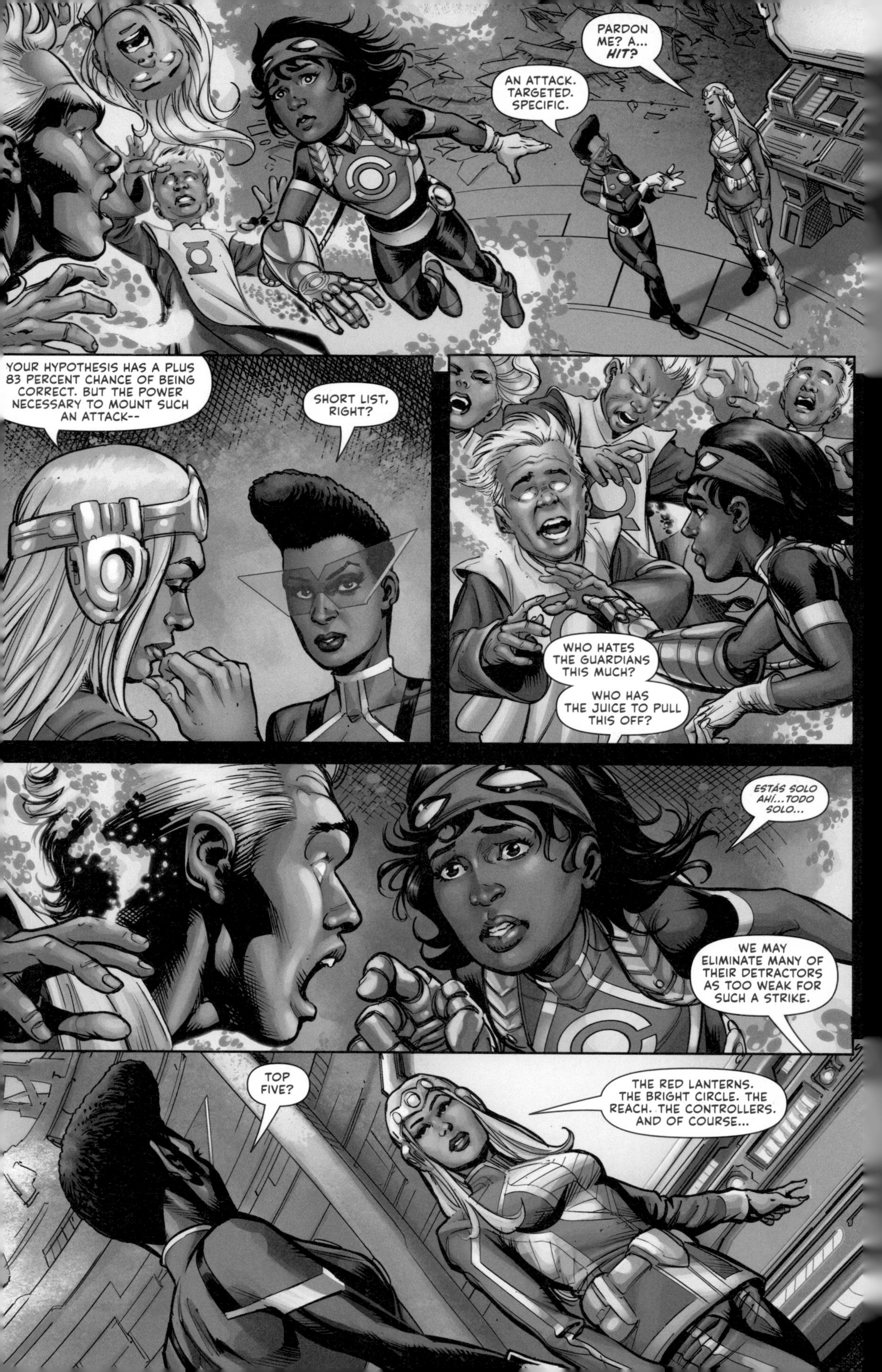
PARDON ME? A... *HIT?*
AN ATTACK. TARGETED. SPECIFIC.
YOUR HYPOTHESIS HAS A PLUS 83 PERCENT CHANCE OF BEING CORRECT. BUT THE POWER NECESSARY TO MOUNT SUCH AN ATTACK--
SHORT LIST, RIGHT?
WHO HATES THE GUARDIANS THIS MUCH?
WHO HAS THE JUICE TO PULL THIS OFF?
ESTÁS SOLO AHÍ...TODO SOLO...
WE MAY ELIMINATE MANY OF THEIR DETRACTORS AS TOO WEAK FOR SUCH A STRIKE.
TOP FIVE?
THE RED LANTERNS. THE BRIGHT CIRCLE. THE REACH. THE CONTROLLERS. AND OF COURSE...

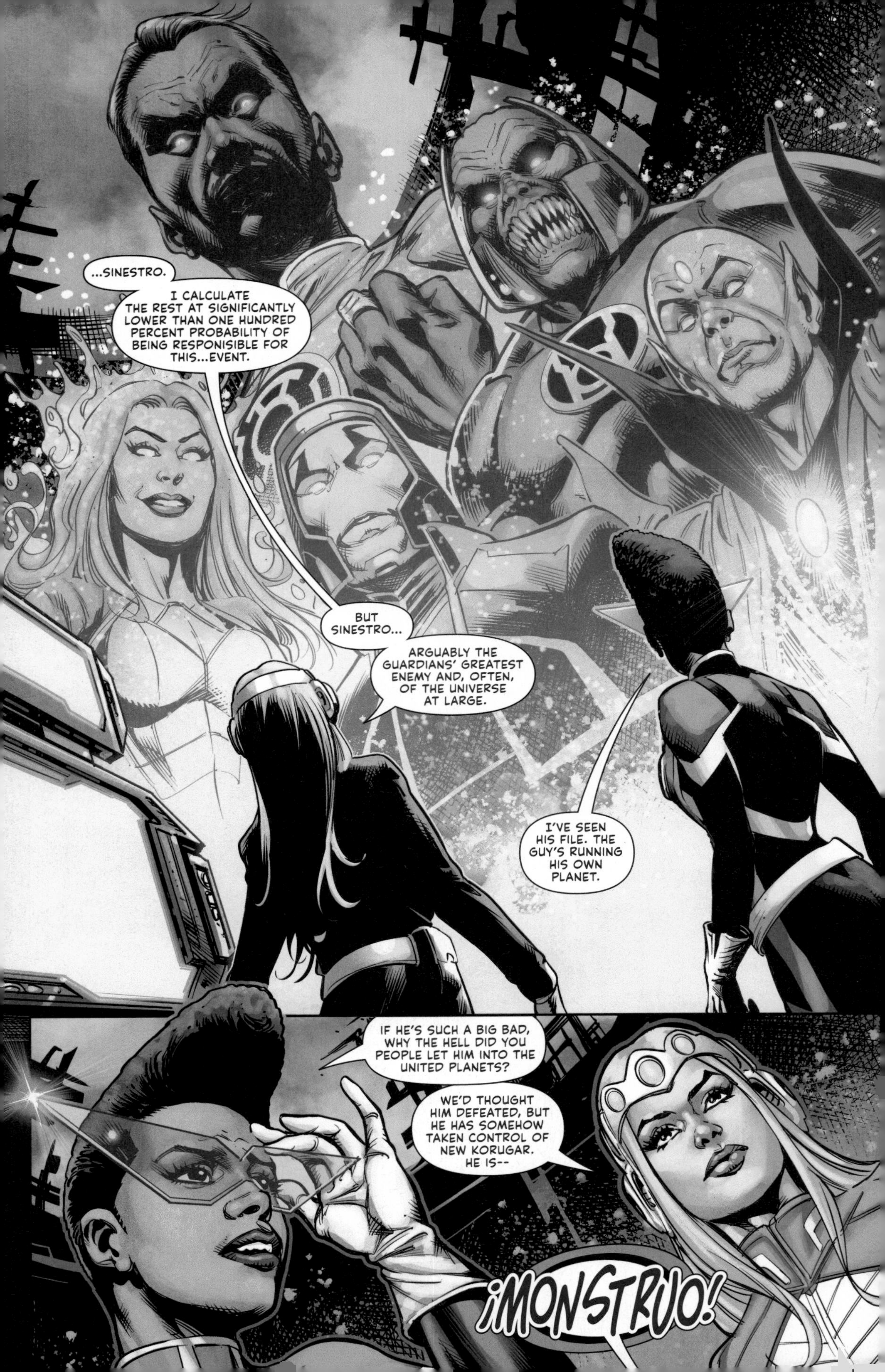
...SINESTRO.
I CALCULATE THE REST AT SIGNIFICANTLY LOWER THAN ONE HUNDRED PERCENT PROBABILITY OF BEING RESPONISIBLE FOR THIS...EVENT.
BUT SINESTRO...
ARGUABLY THE GUARDIANS' GREATEST ENEMY AND, OFTEN, OF THE UNIVERSE AT LARGE.
I'VE SEEN HIS FILE. THE GUY'S RUNNING HIS OWN PLANET.
IF HE'S SUCH A BIG BAD, WHY THE HELL DID YOU PEOPLE LET HIM INTO THE UNITED PLANETS?
WE'D THOUGHT HIM DEFEATED, BUT HE HAS SOMEHOW TAKEN CONTROL OF NEW KORUGAR. HE IS--
¡MONSTRUO!

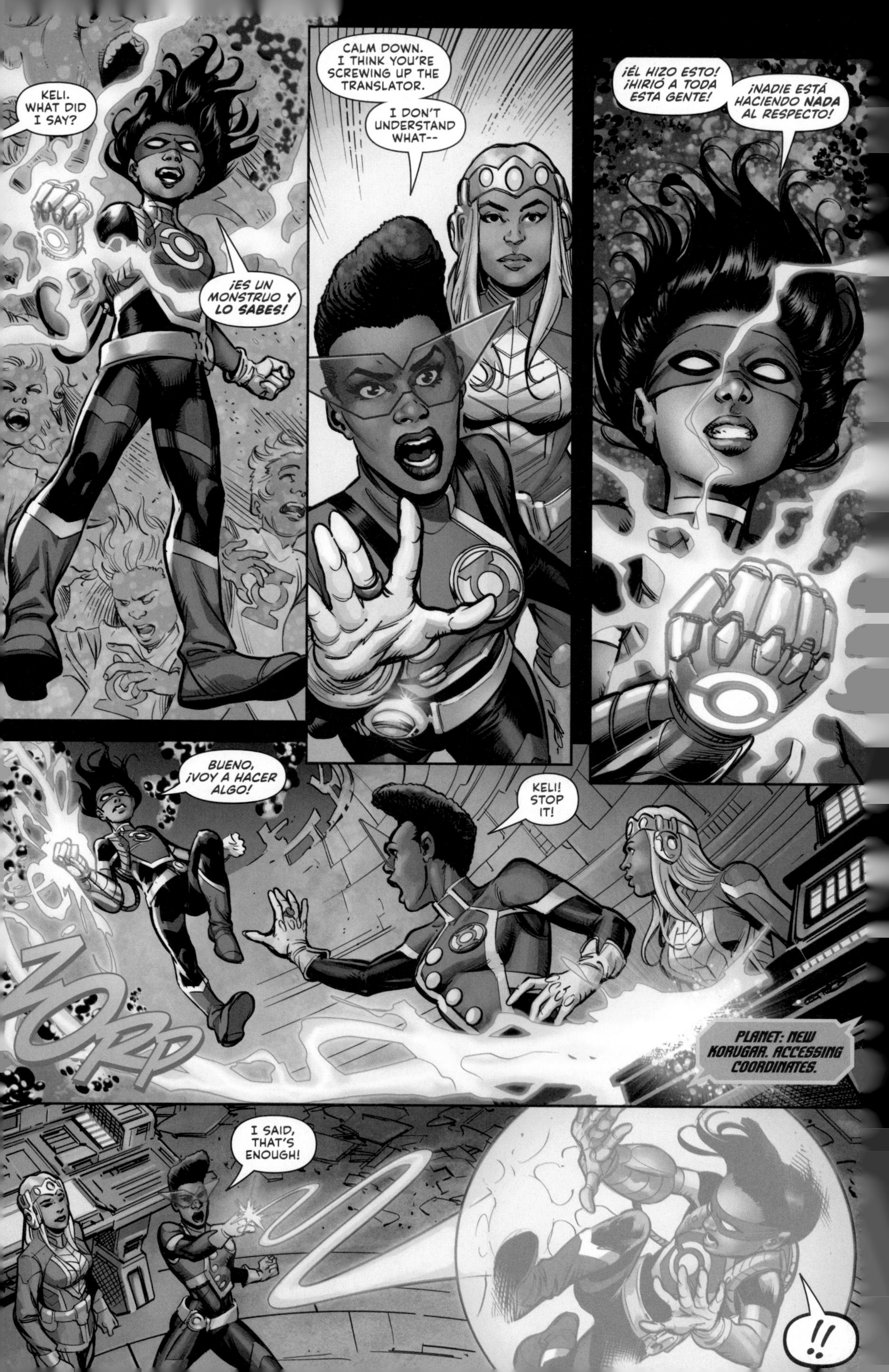
KELI. WHAT DID I SAY?
¡ES UN MONSTRUO Y LO SABES!
CALM DOWN. I THINK YOU'RE SCREWING UP THE TRANSLATOR.
I DON'T UNDERSTAND WHAT--
¡ÉL HIZO ESTO! ¡HIRIÓ A TODA ESTA GENTE!
¡NADIE ESTÁ HACIENDO NADA AL RESPECTO!
BUENO, ¡VOY A HACER ALGO!
KELI! STOP IT!
VORP
PLANET: NEW KORUGAR. ACCESSING COORDINATES.
I SAID, THAT'S ENOUGH!
!!

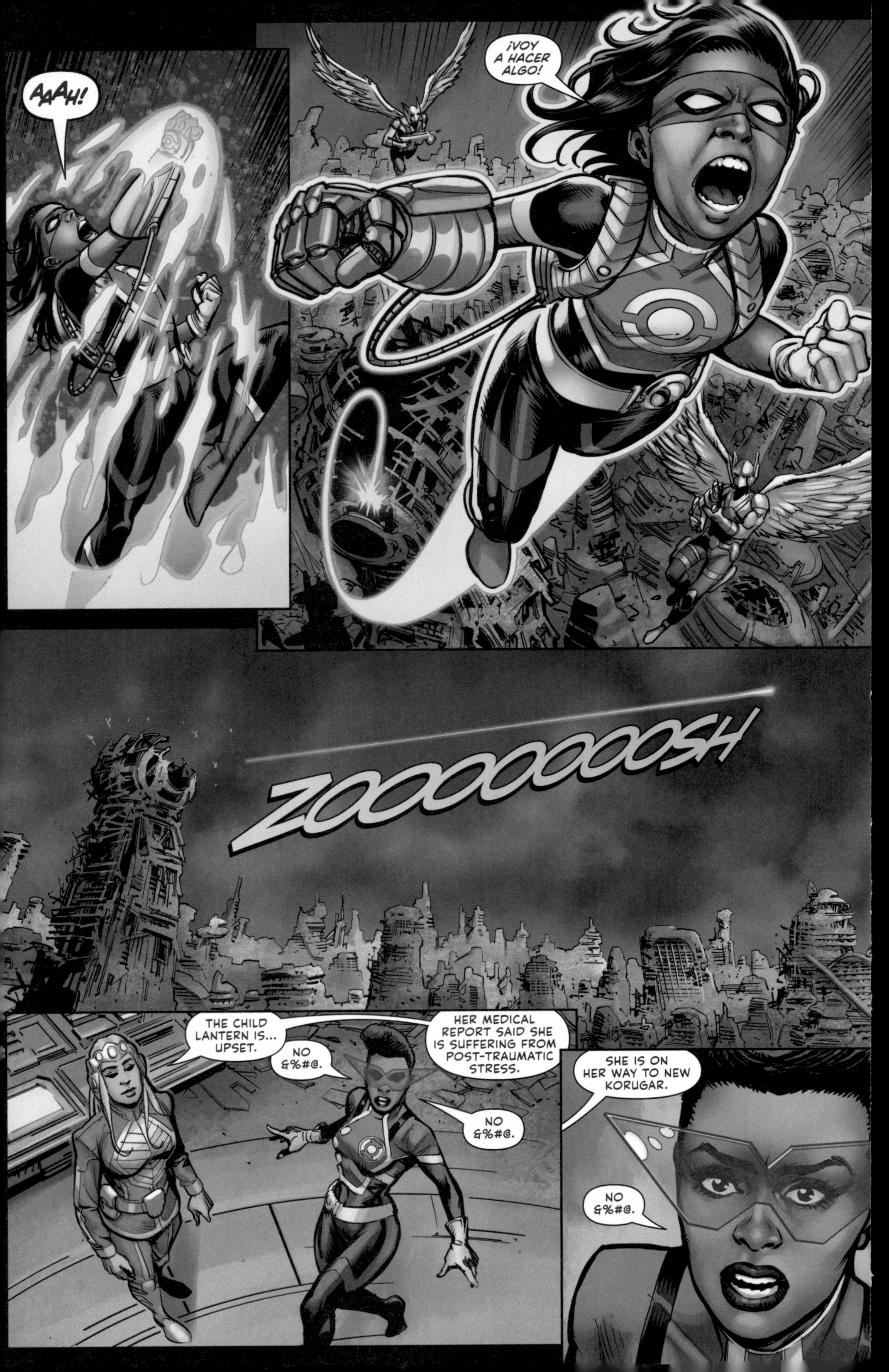
AAAH!
¡VOY A HACER ALGO!
ZOOOOOOOOSH
THE CHILD LANTERN IS... UPSET.
NO &%#@.
HER MEDICAL REPORT SAID SHE IS SUFFERING FROM POST-TRAUMATIC STRESS.
NO &%#@.
SHE IS ON HER WAY TO NEW KORUGAR.
NO &%#@.

VARIANT
COVER
GALLERY

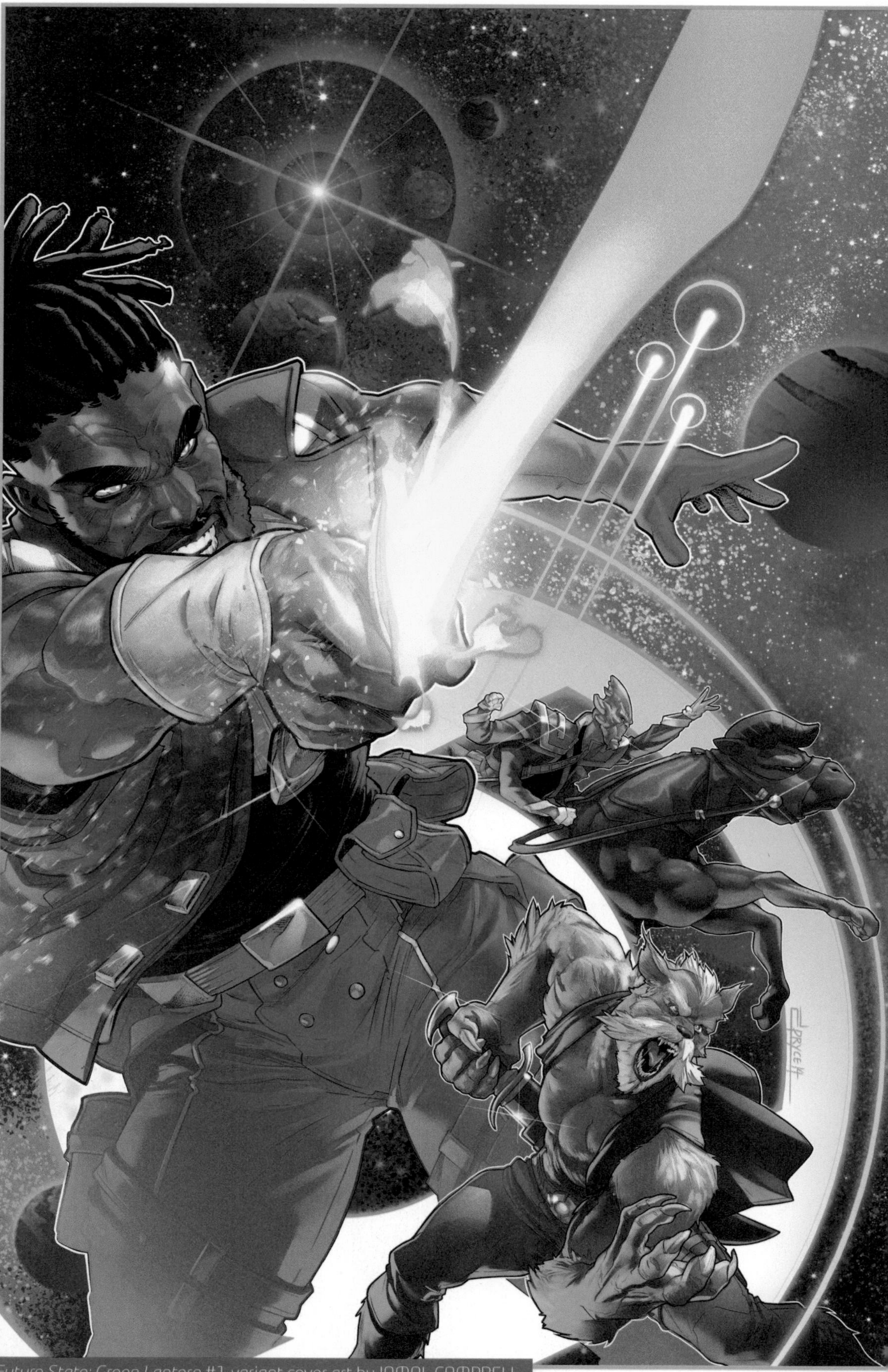

Future State: Green Lantern #1 variant cover art by JAMAL CAMPBELL

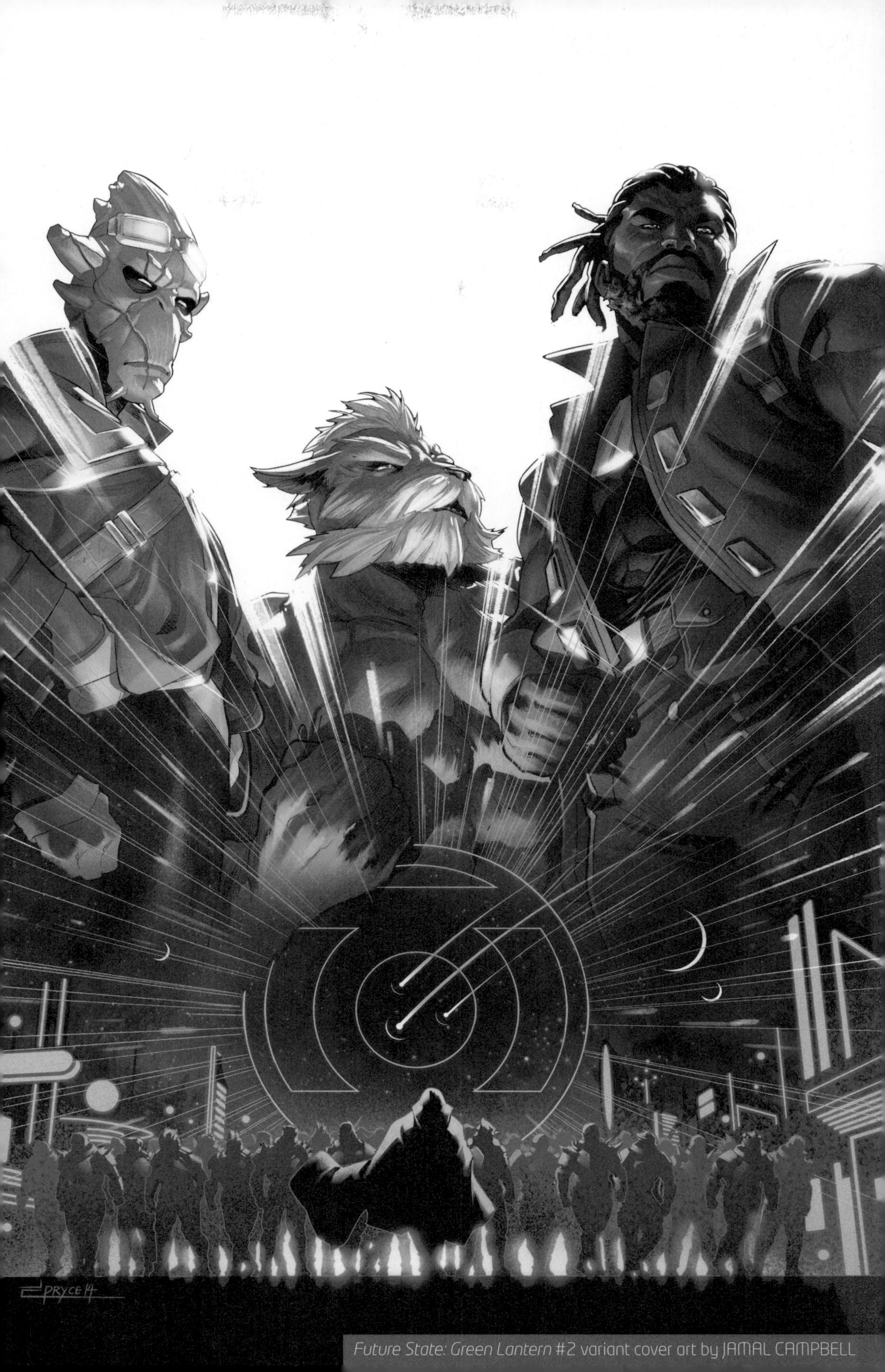
PRYCE 14

Future State: Green Lantern #2 variant cover art by JAMAL CAMPBELL

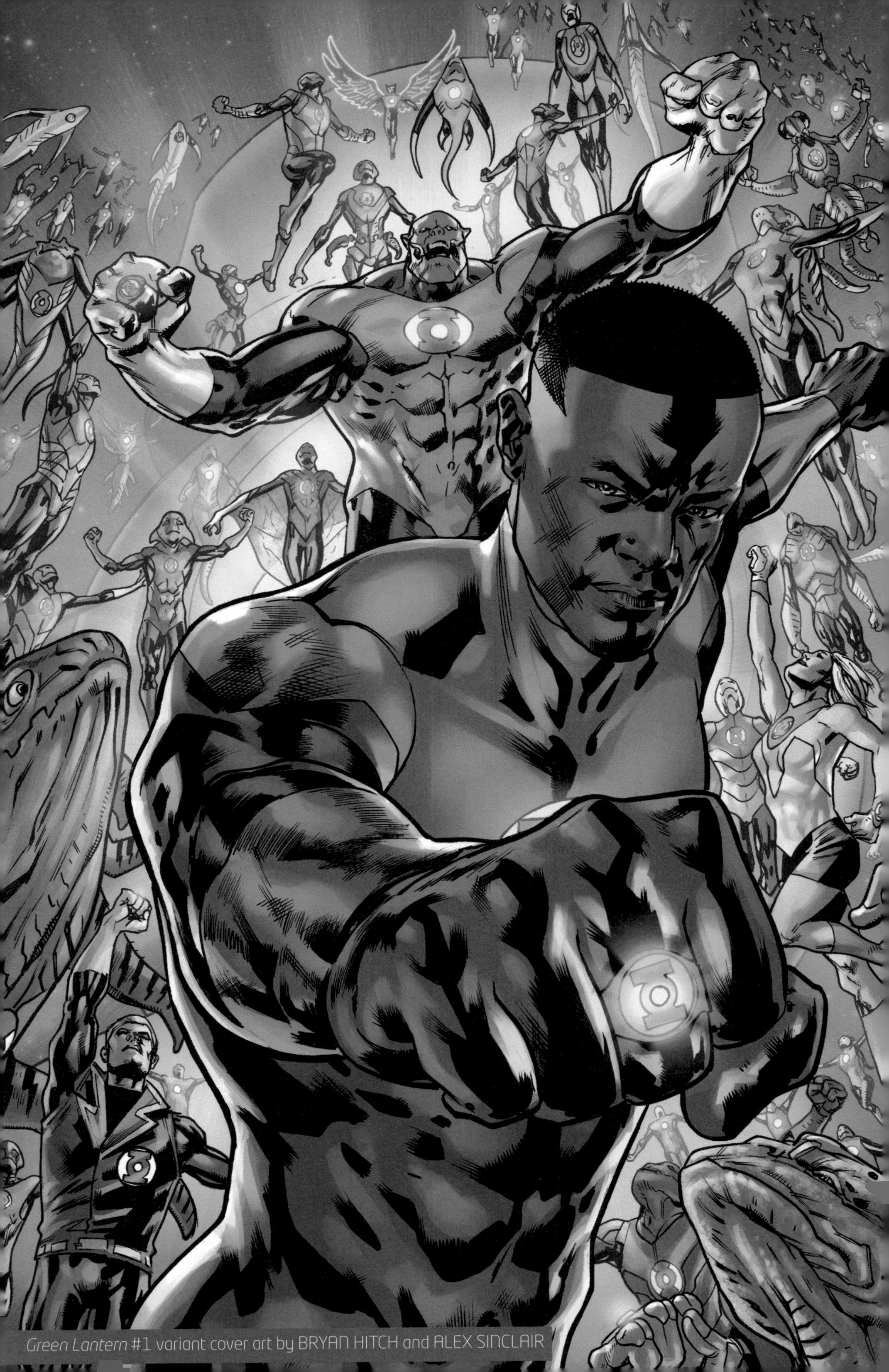

Green Lantern #1 variant cover art by BRYAN HITCH and ALEX SINCLAIR

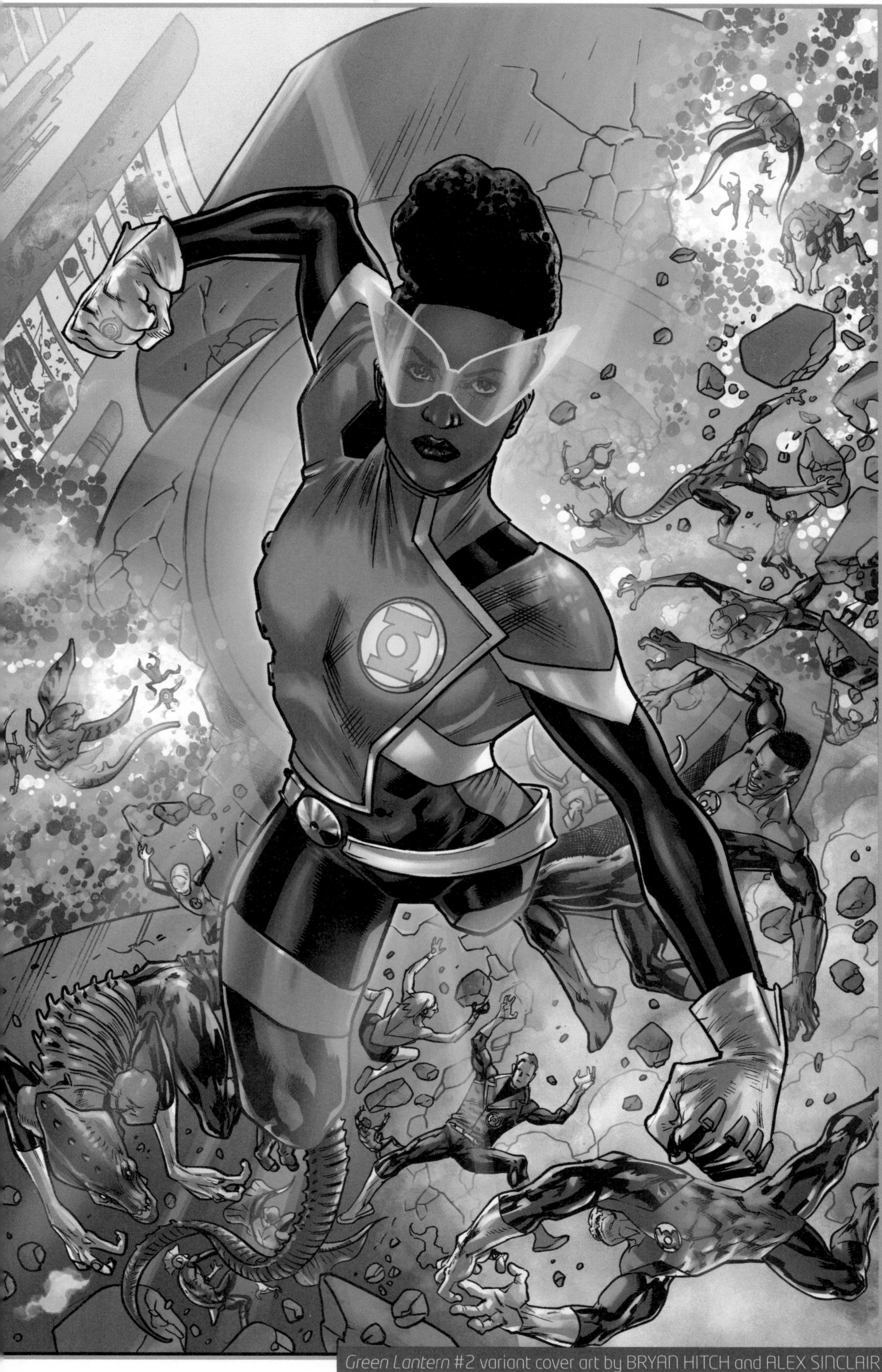

Green Lantern #2 variant cover art by BRYAN HITCH and ALEX SINCLAIR

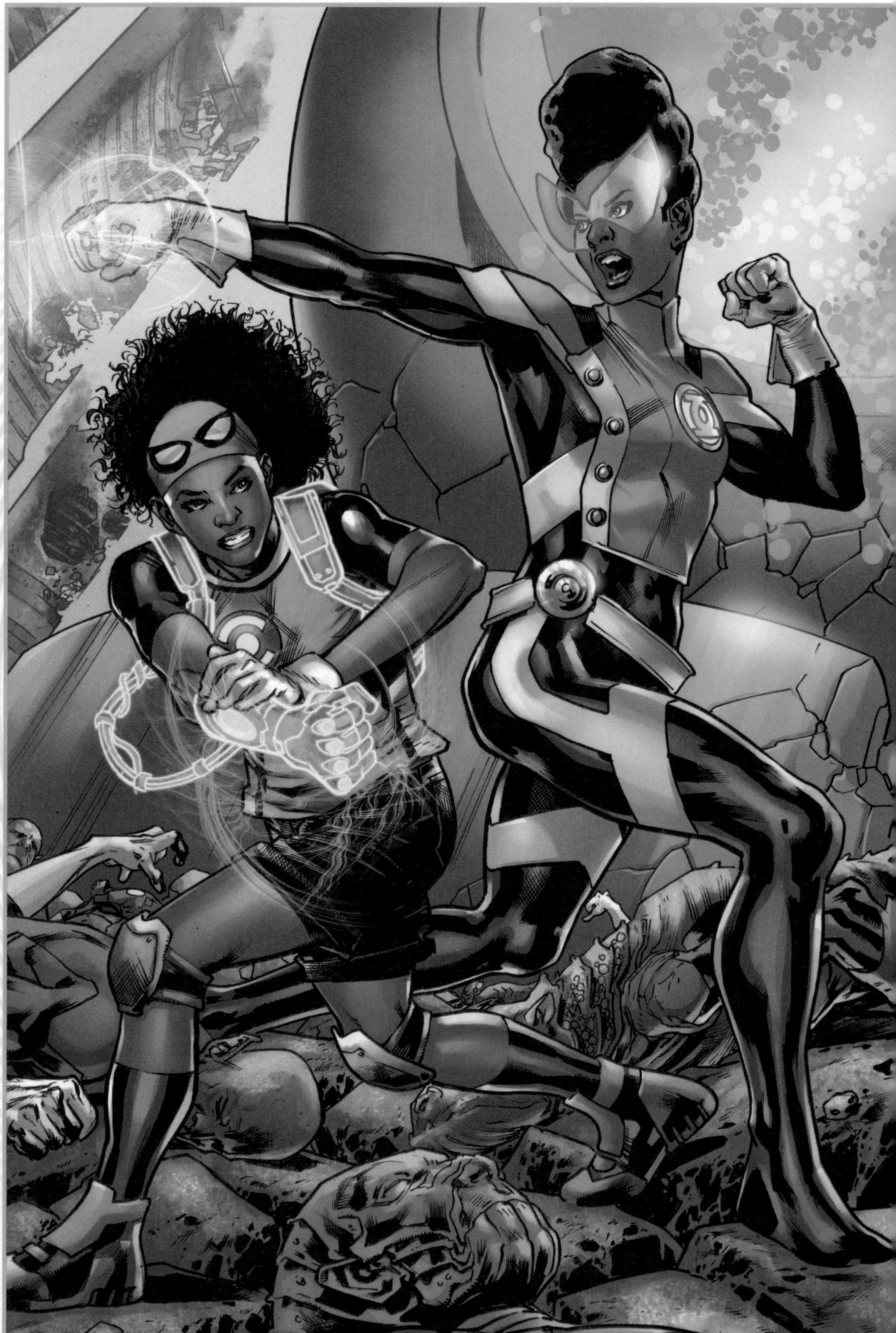

Green Lantern #3 variant cover art by BRYAN HITCH and ALEX SINCLAIR

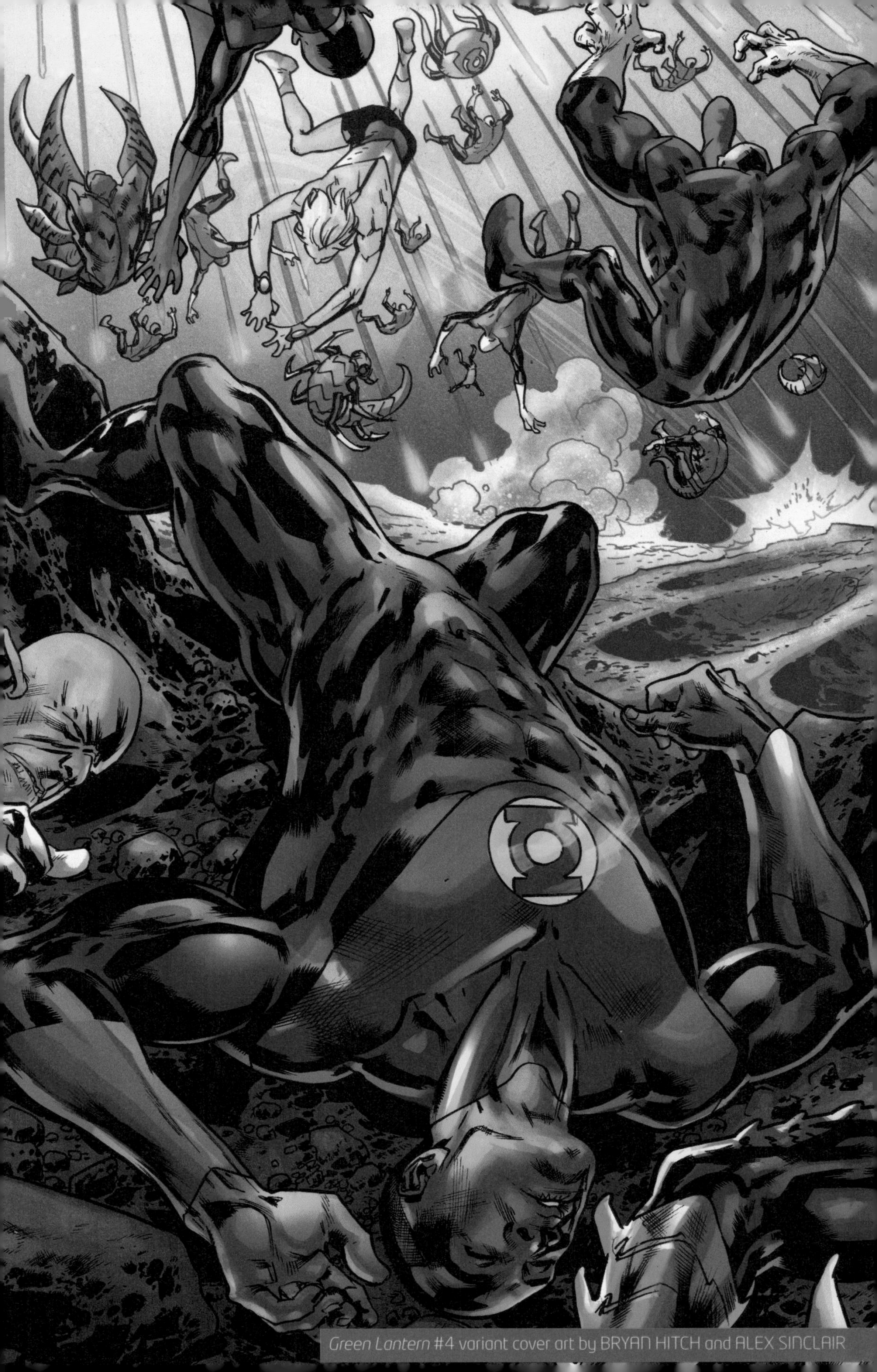

Green Lantern #4 variant cover art by BRYAN HITCH and ALEX SINCLAIR

DC UNIVERSE REBIRTH

GREEN LANTERNS

VOL. 1: RAGE PLANET

SAM HUMPHRIES
with ETHAN VAN SCIVER

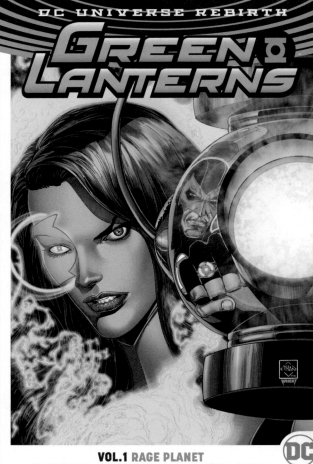

DC UNIVERSE REBIRTH

GREEN LANTERNS

VOL.1 RAGE PLANET
SAM HUMPHRIES * ROBSON ROCHA * ETHAN VAN SCIVER * ED BENES

DC UNIVERSE REBIRTH

HAL JORDAN AND THE GREEN LANTERN CORPS

VOL.1 SINESTRO'S LAW
ROBERT VENDITTI * RAFA SANDOVAL * ETHAN VAN SCIVER

HAL JORDAN AND THE GREEN LANTERN CORPS VOL. 1: SINESTRO'S LAW

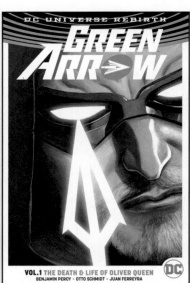

DC UNIVERSE REBIRTH

GREEN ARROW

VOL.1 THE DEATH & LIFE OF OLIVER QUEEN
BENJAMIN PERCY * OTTO SCHMIDT * JUAN FERREYRA

GREEN ARROW VOL. 1: THE DEATH & LIFE OF OLIVER QUEEN

DC UNIVERSE REBIRTH

BATGIRL AND THE BIRDS OF PREY

VOL.1 WHO IS ORACLE?
JULIE BENSON * SHAWNA BENSON * CLAIRE ROE

BATGIRL AND THE BIRDS OF PREY VOL. 1: WHO IS ORACLE?

Get more DC graphic novels wherever comics and books are sold!

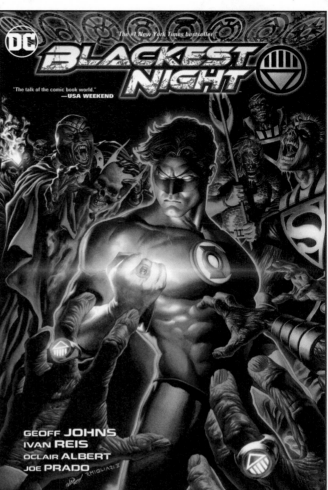

BLACKEST NIGHT

GEOFF JOHNS
with IVAN REIS

**BLACKEST NIGHT:
GREEN LANTERN**

**BLACKEST NIGHT:
GREEN LANTERN CORPS**

READ THE ENTIRE EPIC!

BLACKEST NIGHT

BLACKEST NIGHT:
GREEN LANTERN

BLACKEST NIGHT:
GREEN LANTERN CORPS

BLACKEST NIGHT:
BLACK LANTERN CORPS VOL. 1

BLACKEST NIGHT:
BLACK LANTERN CORPS VOL. 2

BLACKEST NIGHT:
RISE OF THE BLACK LANTERNS

BLACKEST NIGHT:
TALES OF THE CORPS

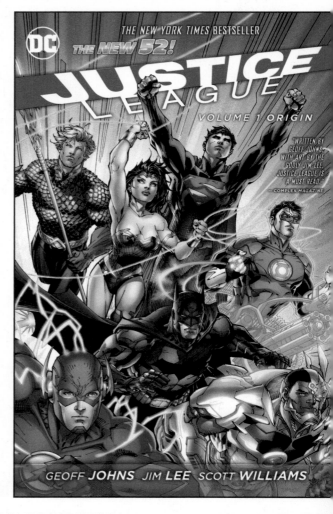

JUSTICE LEAGUE

VOL. 1: ORIGIN
GEOFF JOHNS and JIM LEE

**JUSTICE LEAGUE
VOL. 2: THE VILLAIN'S JOURNEY**

**JUSTICE LEAGUE
VOL. 3: THRONE OF ATLANTIS**

READ THE ENTIRE EPIC

JUSTICE LEAGUE VOL.
THE GR

JUSTICE LEAGUE VOL.
FOREVER HERO

JUSTICE LEAGUE VOL.
INJUSTICE LEAGU

JUSTICE LEAGUE VOL.
DARKSEID WAR PAR

JUSTICE LEAGUE VOL.
DARKSEID WAR PART